SOURCEBOOK OF ARCHITECTURAL ORNAMENT

Designers, Craftsmen, Manufacturers & Distributors of Custom & Ready-made Exterior Ornament

BRENT C. BROLIN
JEAN RICHARDS

VNR VAN NOSTRAND REINHOLD COMPANY
NEW YORK CINCINNATI TORONTO LONDON MELBOURNE

To Hans

Library of Congress Catalog Card Number 81-16093
ISBN 0-442-26331-7

Printed in the United States of America
Designed by Ginger Legato

Published by Van Nostrand Reinhold Company Inc.
135 West 50th Street
New York, NY 10020

Van Nostrand Reinhold Publishing
1410 Birchmount Road
Scarborough, Ontario M1P 2E7, Canada

Van Nostrand Reinhold Australia Pty. Ltd.
17 Queen Street
Mitcham, Victoria 3132 Australia

Van Nostrand Reinhold Company Limited
Molly Millars Lane
Wokingham, Berkshire, England
16 15 14 13 12 11 10 9 8 7 6 5 4 3 2 1

Library of Congress Cataloging in Publication Data
Brolin, Brent C.
Sourcebook of architectural ornament.

Includes index.
1. Decoration and ornament, Architectural—Handbooks, manuals, etc. 2. Architecture, Modern—20th Century—Handbooks, manuals, etc. I. Richards, Jean. II. Title.
NA3485.B76 729 81-16093
ISBN 0-442-26331-7 AACR2

The information contained herein was compiled from questionnaires sent to over 5,000 sources. Every effort was made to ensure its accuracy. However, neither the authors nor the publisher warrant that the data herein are complete and accurate.

If you would like to be listed in a possible future edition, or if you know a company or individual who would like to be listed, please send the name, address, and category to:

Sourcebook of Architectural Ornament
c/o Van Nostrand Reinhold Company
135 West 50th Street
New York, NY 10020

Acknowledgments

We wish to thank all those who are listed in this *Sourcebook*—artisans, artists, manufacturers, and distributors of architectural ornament. Their prompt responses and helpful attention made the sometimes burdensome task of compiling this information much more enjoyable.

Our thanks also to Michael Curtis, whose diligence provided us with the list of some 5,000 names, addresses, and telephone numbers from which we worked, and the others whose organizational skills were helpful along the way: John Zeisel, J. B. Waters and Christiane McKenna.

For help with questionnaires, we thank Ilse Zeisel and Clem Labine. We recommend Clem Labine's *Old-House Journal,* which lists makers of interior and exterior architectural ornament for houses built before 1914.

Ellen Berkeley, Peter Millard, Richard Newman, Angus Macdonald and Carol Strober are all to be thanked for their kind advice about the organization of the categories in the *Sourcebook*.

Contents

Foreword

Since time immemorial the natural impulse has been to enrich life by delighting the eye through design. The first page of the Bible speaks of the tree God made to grow out of the ground—"to be pleasant to the eye." The design of the Tabernacle that Moses received from God abounded in cherubim and bells of gold, pomegranates of blue and purple, and candlesticks with knobs and flowers "for Glory and for Beauty."

On Assyrian clay tablets the great king Nebuhadnezar proclaimed his magnificent feats: "For the admiration of the people I built sumptuous decorations of my palaces. Its cornices I adorned with bricks glazed in lovely colors of lapis lazuli . . . the entrance of the chapel with yellow tiles . . . the pavement of the shrine I made of bricks cast in silver color . . . around the base of the palace I placed large carved slabs of limestone and made them worthy of admiration . . . ."

Ornament attracted the admiration of people until, in the beginning of this century, aesthetic reformers rejected such embellishment as uncultured, primitive, and childish. By 1908 the famous Austrian architect and writer Adolph Loos had been preaching for a decade that there was no place for ornament in modern architecture. At his rhetorical height, he declared ornament to be a crime. "Without ornament," he said, "the streets of the cities will shine like white walls, like Zion the heavenly metropolis."

At its most elegant, Loos' vision did come true. The white walls of the heavenly metropolis of modern architecture and design are exquisite. Stepping from the hodgepodge of decorative arts into a modern display at the 1925 Paris exhibition, I felt as if I had come into a cleansed, elevated atmosphere of peace, into a new world of beauty of a higher order where you should talk in hushed tones and behave with propriety. A Breuer interior of a few years later seemed equally unreal. Everything defied gravity—furniture was attached to the walls; the lighting cast no shadows. It was unearthly loveliness.

But modern buildings have their own ornament. Loos' most famous building, opposite the royal Palace in Vienna, was covered with elegant, green marble slabs. The Seagram Building has costly bronze veins. And the famous Mies van der Rohe chair, which I coveted when it first appeared, relied for its beauty on the luxury of the best highly polished spring steel and the softest, finest leather.

Without these splendid materials, modern design could be forbidding, almost terrifying. The poor materials and shabbily built geometry of the huge Ukrainian office building called the Gosprom was a depressing sight. When I came upon it for the first time, in 1933, it was clear to me that luxurious materials were the ornament of modernism. It was the elegant materials that created visual and tactile enchantment—without them simplicity meant only deprivation.

Modernism is the first style in the geneology of Western styles that does not permit eclecticism. All former styles happily dipped into the reservoir of ornamental elements of the past—using different intonations, emphases, and deformations of lines and weights—incorporating those for which they felt an affinity.

Having been taught the duty of expressing their times, the modern designer might try to invent "today's" ornament. Unfortunately, ornament cannot grow from such earnest intentions. Conscious search does not yield the one quality all ornament must have: it must look as if it belongs.

Loos sensed this after having preached against ornament for twenty-six years. In 1924 he made a dramatic turnabout that, because of the momentum of modernism, received little attention. Loos explained that it was only *modern* ornament that provoked his ire:

> the ornament which is created today has no connection with us . . . it does not lend itself to development . . . [it] has no parents, no descendants, no past and no future. . . . *I have never meant what the puritans carried ad absurdum,* [*namely*] *to eliminate ornament systematically and consistently.*

In the same paper, he even suggested teaching classical ornament in schools because, like grammar, it disciplines us and, in spite of ethnographic and language differences, it brings order into our lives by creating a community of forms and aesthetic concepts.

When today's architects and designers seek visual variety they realize that their education has been limited to a form vocabulary of relatively few words—a vocabulary composed mainly of geometric and structural elements. This language has passed through several dialects, but it has not changed since it came into fashion toward the end of the last century. From the cafe on top of the new Pompidou Center, in Paris, you can look through airy steel trusses to see a nearby working crane framing the distant Eiffel tower, built nearly a century before. All three—Pompidou Center, crane, and Eiffel Tower—have the same structural vocabulary.

Another concept that shapes our attitude toward ornament stems from the Industrial Revolution. The division of labor, praised as a great contribution of the industrial age, also bequeathed the misconception that design was divided into two parts: the technical form, produced for use, and the embellishment, to enhance that "necessary" form. Because modernists esteemed naked structural technical forms and rejected ornament we came to think of these elements as having different ranks: the former essential, the latter something one might choose to add or not, as one chooses a necktie or hat, or flowers on the table. We have forgotten that in other times skeleton and flesh were conceived and perceived as one, and if any aspect had priority it was beauty.

When we glide past the dreamlike palazzos of the Grand Canal, how can we believe these lovely creatures were first thought of as naked? Can one think of the Escorial as a box, with its graceful towers and filigree metal ornaments stuck on later? Was the Capitol in Washington first flat-roofed; and was the Cupola, found to be pleasing, added for beauty?

Many architects who would like their drawing boards to sprout fresh visual delights—because "modernism is dead"—find themselves frustrated and their boards barren. The present yearning for richer visual forms is often referred to as a *return* to old ways, a derogative term for today's architect who seeks to *take* a step forward, to be post-modern. But the word "post-modern" is itself negative, and negative programs always inhibit creativity rather than produce an atmosphere in which ideas can soar.

The people in this book are professionals. Many have spent their careers continuing the unbroken, ornamental tradition of crafts that goes back as far as man. Today they are probably the only group of artists with the courage to admit that the aim of their art is to delight the eye. Their exquisite metalwork, amusing gargoyles, stained glass, carved brick walls, rich textiles, and other work justify the growing public attention given to these fields.

At a time of hesitant and searching transition, this book may contribute to the development of a freer world of lines and shapes. The people listed in its pages not only execute their own designs and the designs of others; many will also collaborate in the creation of designs. They offer not only their skill and their art, but also their attitude, a familiarity with ornament, ease in playful, creative experimentation, and an uninhibited acceptance of styles to which they feel an affinity. Architects may find them valuable companions in the design process.

The men and women presented here are, as the Bible says, "filled with ability and intelligence, knowledge and craftsmanship to devise artistic designs . . . for work in every craft." They should again work together with architects to fuse beauty and usefulness in the art in which we live.

Eva Zeisel
New York City

Preface

This book was written because of an experience I had while researching an earlier book—*Architecture in Context: Fitting New Buildings with Old* (Van Nostrand Reinhold, 1980). That book examined the problem of fitting new buildings into existing architectural settings. I spent two years traveling to, looking at, and photographing several hundred buildings. During this time, it became evident that the buildings that fit into their surroundings most gracefully were those that used ornament, either contemporary or traditional, to establish the relationship. Although some buildings followed the presently accepted rules for "fitting in"—maintaining the scale, continuing the cornice line, using similar colors—they often looked naked and out of place because they lacked ornament. Still other buildings, which disregarded these supposedly essential guidelines, did "fit in" because the placement and scale of their ornament gave them a visual texture sympathetic to that of the neighboring buildings.

This book grew out of a conviction that, in addition to reintroducing an element of beauty and richness that architecture has been lacking for too long, ornament can help us capture the sense of visual continuity—of harmony-with-variety—that was commonplace in townscapes before modernism banished ornament.

Introduction

A few years ago a well-known architect was commissioned to design a new façade next to a gracefully ornamented older building. He was discouraged because he knew that without ornament his design would never sit comfortably next to its older neighbor. "Unfortunately, there's just no one around anymore who can do that kind of work," he told us. A week later we spoke to an artisan who works in plaster and fiber glass, and who said the opposite: "I must have been born in the wrong century. No one needs my services."

For decades architects have explained the nakedness of their buildings by saying the skilled workers to produce architectural ornament no longer existed. We hope this book will refute that idea, and be a matchmaker for the architect and the artist, artisan, and manufacturer of ornament. If there are fewer makers of ornament today than in the 1920s, that is understandable; the architectural profession has spurned them for nearly three generations. Yet craftsmen and manufacturers who can make ornament have been with us all along. It only took the recent shift in architectural fashion to permit them to become contributing members of the design community once again. The stone carvers that this architect's façade desperately needed were, and are, available. Within two years of his sad lament a building faced with cut and carved stone was under construction within blocks of his wan façade.

It is true that many old-time craftsmen have died, retired, or gone out of business, but others are still working in studios and small factories—and training the next generation. Some members of the counterculture of the 1960s have become skilled professionals in ironwork, stained glass, ceramics, and other fields that produce architectural ornament. Other groups

Swan-neck pediment and doorway, 1980; eighteenth-century-style joinery by Maurer and Shepard, Glastonbury, CT. See listing under Wood. (Photo courtesy of Maurer and Shepard)

of ornamenters are waiting to be discovered in the most improbable places: many decorative painters who can ornament buildings are painting trucks; some of the stone carvers our architect needed are carving cemetery monuments in stone yards, and so on. Preservation societies and museums that do restoration work are also possible sources of skilled craftsmen for a variety of ornamental work. Then there are the large manufacturers who have been providing readymade ornamental elements all along. Many of them will also do custom work. Finally, there are the closet ornamentalists—architects and designers who have been enchanted by ornament for years, but so guilt-ridden because of modernist dogma that they have been afraid to explore its possibilities.

Method

The *Sourcebook of Architectural Ornament* offers architects and designers direct access to people who can produce exterior ornament in twenty categories. The names of the ornamenters listed were culled, in part, from the telephone directories of nearly forty major cities in the United States. These cities were chosen on the basis of the number of architects living in or near them. This list was supplemented by responses from queries placed in professional trade and craft journals and from the membership lists of professional societies. We sent questionnaires to our combined list of ornamenters asking for specific information about the services they offer, the materials and techniques they use, and their ability to offer design assistance.

In an effort to include as wide a variety of styles as possible, we did not limit our listings to those whose work satisfied our particular idea of "beauty." Nor have we consciously endorsed any one style, as there is no guarantee that our taste would match that of the architects and designers who will be using this book. We have only tried to show where to find the skills, materials, and techniques architects need to carry out an ornamented design. Where an ornamenter works in only one style we have mentioned it. We have not attempted to verify quality of work; it would have been impossible to evaluate each of the hundreds of listings. To be listed in this book individuals or companies had only to indicate that they provide professional services to architects and designers. It is our feeling that, by and large, the refinement and sophistication of ornament that can be produced by those who are listed is limited not by the maker's capabilities, but by the designer's imagination.

The Relationship Between Artist, Artisan, and Architect

Most of us have been conditioned to distinguish between "artists" and "artisans," but in fact this separation is rather recent; the *Shorter Oxford English Dictionary on Historical Principles* places it around 1850. The research we did for this book showed that the line between artist and artisan—or designer and fabricator—is not always clear. Some "artists" we contacted design but do not fabricate; others fabricate their own designs; and a few will fabricate the work of fellow artists. Some "craftsmen" fabricate their own designs as well as those of others. Among both artists and artisans are those who will do their own designs only, those who will develop or refine an

Concrete block, a relatively unsophisticated material in terms of ornamental potential, becomes a refined and articulate means of decoration in skillful hands. Robert T. Wolfe Apartments, New Haven, CT; Charles W. Moore, Associates, Architects, 1972.

A traditional precursor of Charles Moore's elegant concrete block ornament is found in this machine-cut, stone façade on Union Square in New York City.

architect's sketch or idea, those who will fabricate from a measured drawing only, and those who will supply readymade ornamental elements. All of these are represented in our book.

Some architects prefer to design the ornament themselves and have the ornamenter execute it; others may be pleased by the ornamenter's design; a third group will enjoy watching a design evolve while working with an artisan or artist. We feel that each of these relationships is valid, and we do not advocate one over another. We have, however, indicated when the ornamenter is flexible in this respect.

There is a lot of discussion today about when an artist whose work will be part of a building should be brought into the design process. Conventional wisdom seems to feel that the artist must be involved from the instant the architect begins conceptualizing the project. This view gained currency in the latter part of the nineteenth century and came about, at least in part, in response to the division of labor that had been imposed by industrialization and had separated the artist from the execution of his work. Yet, while many fine buildings that incorporate art have been designed as integrated units, the artist should not feel he has to "make do" when he is asked to work on a finished building. The Sistine Chapel was not designed with Michelangelo's frescoes in mind; he designed his paintings to fit the space.

Some artists will be uncomfortable at having their "art" thought of as architectural "ornament." We feel that whether a work of art is decorative or not depends largely on its location and our expectations, rather than its quality. When we see a statue in a museum, we think of it as "art;" the fact that it may also "ornament" the room in which it stands is secondary. If the same statue is placed in a niche in the side of a building, it retains the qualities that make it art; but it also embellishes, and we think of it as ornamenting the architecture.

If the variety of crafts that can enhance architecture is to be fully utilized, architects and ornamenters may find it beneficial to share some creative decisions, as they often did in the past. We have a friend who, like most other architects of our generation, learned to make working drawings that were complete to the last nail. So he was somewhat in awe, a few years ago, when he got a glimpse of the teamwork that had existed between architect and ornamenter. While looking at the working drawings for the Carnegie Mansion in New York (built in 1901), he came upon a reflected plan of one of the carved ceilings. This drawing only indicated the general elements of the ceiling. When it came to details of rosettes and moldings the architect had given loose sketches, alongside which he had penciled an instruction to the carver: "Capture this feeling."

There is no reason why the architect and ornamenter cannot profit, once again, from the rich potential of such a flexible relationship.

Defining Architectural Ornament

Adolph Loos, the famous Austrian architect, established a famous link between ornament and crime; this link still haunts us. Many architects we spoke to treated the word "ornament" like a hot potato: "*I* don't design with ornament!" Others hedged: "It depends on what you mean by ornament." And in our conversations with architects we found the only definition of ornament we could all agree on was "something fancy."

Had we been able to pursue the definition of ornament a little further we would probably have found some agreement on a few other attributes:

> Ornament almost always embellishes something.
> Ornament is usually intentional—although accidental ornament, such as reflective glass, is often consciously exploited after it has been discovered.

Beyond these rudimentary parameters lies relatively unexplored territory for contemporary architects, as the past three generations of professionals have simply not given much thought to the word "ornament." Nevertheless, one attitude

A detail showing one bay of the Palazzo dei Conservatori, The Capitol, Rome. All three façades on the Capitoline Hill were reconstructed from 1564 to 1568 by Michelangelo. Contrary to the nineteenth- and twentieth-century view that artistic originality demands that the artist invent everything himself, Michelangelo was original within the relatively restricted confines of the classical architectural vocabulary, creating unique elements such as the broken, arched pediment with an inserted shell.

Perhaps for the first time in the history of art, nineteenth-century architects and art reformers evolved nonvisual rules—rules of conscience—that were intended to control the use of ornament. Their influence remains strong today. According to such righteous reformers as A. W. Pugin, ornament should be restricted to the structure of a building. The post and bracket ornament of this carpenter Gothic New England house would have been considered "appropriate," structure-related ornament.

The idea that linked acceptable ornament to structure appealed even to modernists. One of the main thrusts of modernism has been the "expression," or emphasis, of the structure—often to the point of making it a decorative element itself, as in Pompidou Center, Paris.

turns up with some regularity. It originated, surprisingly enough, in the early nineteenth century, and holds that "appropriate" ornament is ornament that is integrally related to a building's structure. But the relationship between structure and ornament is often ambiguous; there are at least four possibilities:

1. The ornament can be limited mainly to the structure of a building. (Example: the pinnacle on a Gothic flying buttress.)
2. The structure itself can become an ornament. (Example: the exterior, diagonal bracing of the Hancock Tower in Chicago.)
3. "Fake" structural elements, having nothing to do with the real structure, can be used ornamentally. (Examples: painted columns on a Bavarian house with bearing wall construction; the I-beam mullions applied to nonstructural spandrels in modern office buildings.)
4. The ornament can have nothing to do with either actual or "fake" structure. (Examples: Many types of murals and mosaics; the garlands and plaques favored by the late Renaissance.)

Given the residual "functional" bias of modernism, the present idea of structure-related ornament would seem to favor the first of these alternatives. We feel, however, that the structure-related definition of ornament is unnecessarily restrictive, and suggest that all four categories are acceptable.

In a discussion of this sort the idea of "honesty of materials" (using a material in a way that expresses its "nature") almost always comes up. This is a complex matter. What is the "honest" appearance, or "nature," of fiber glass? This material can take any shape, match any color, and imitate any surface texture with remarkably fine detail. And what is an "honest" concrete surface? It, too, can take any shape the form takes, and be colored—or painted—in any hue. Or the "honest" shape of iron, which can look rigid or as supple as windblown grass?

We feel that the "nature" of a material is an arbitrary quality, usually decided upon to satisfy the designer's taste. (Stone

Structure as ornament. Hancock Tower, Chicago. Skidmore, Owings & Merrill, Architects.

Structure-related ornament is seldom considered superfluous, yet it often is. Eiffel's famous tower was considered the epitome of rational design when it was built for the Paris Exposition of 1889. Yet it, too, has its "unessential" ornament. Early photos of the half-completed structure show it standing firmly—but without these graceful, decorative arches with their stylized floral motifs.

is a heavy, hard material, but Baroque masons often made it look like pulled taffy.) The modernists took the concept of honesty word for word, from the nineteenth-century Gothic Revivalists. There can hardly be anything absolute in it, given the remarkably different styles that came out of it.

We should be flexible, therefore, on the topic of honesty of materials. From close up, you can enjoy the smooth polish or gorgeous veining of marble, the delicate grain of exotic wood, or the fine detail of terracotta. The farther away a material is, however, the less likely you are to know if it actually is what it seems to be. In short, we feel that all materials, new and old, should be approached from the point of view of expanding, rather than restricting choices; that they should be used in many different ways: traditional and modern, honest and dishonest.

In the blizzard of words enveloping most discussions of ornament, it is easy to lose sight of the fundamentally visual nature of this commodity. Our feeling about most contemporary attitudes toward ornament is that they take too little account of its purely visual aspect.

We have intentionally chosen a broad definition of ornament. It does not fall back on nineteenth- or twentieth-century

One of the most common "ornaments" of modernism is the I-beam mullion. Its only purpose is visual: to cast shadows. As you can see from this view up the façade of the Seagrams Building, it is structurally superfluous.

More structure-related modern ornament: the chromium-steel corners on this Swiss office building secure the glass the way snapshots used to be held in picture albums.

"Dishonesty" of structure carried to a delightful extreme. This façade—in Salzburg, Austria—is absolutely flat. Its elaborate lintels, sills, and attic frieze are all painted.

rationalizations of "morality" for its authority. It relies, instead, on Noah Webster:

> *ornament:* anything serving to adorn; decoration; embellishment.
>
> *decoration:* that which decorates or adorns; an ornament.

Please note that, according to Webster, "decoration" and "ornament" are synonymous, and so will be used interchangeably in this book.

Our definition leaves the final choice of what constitutes "ornament" up to the eye, as we feel that is the proper organ with which to judge visual effects. If the eye feels an element embellishes or beautifies, it "is" decoration.

While we do not feel this is too naive a view of ornament, its simplicity should obviate some of the weighty intellectualizations that have often obscured the visual nature of this subject in the past, and that threaten to do so once again as the popularity of ornament spreads.

Within our definition there are varying degrees of ornamental intensity. Some materials can be used decoratively although their decorative potential may not be immediately evident. Concrete block, glass block, and shingles fall into this category. Used conventionally, shingles are not particularly decorative; they create an overall texture rather than a specific ornament. Cut them and arrange them in patterns—alternating bands of round and diamond-cut shingles—and their decorativeness increases. Add color and they become still more decorative. Ridged concrete block creates a low order decoration when used over a large area, but its decorative quotient increases when it is used in well-defined patterns or as an accent against a plain background.

While we felt that it should be stated, it is not necessary for you to share our definition of ornament to find this book useful. We hope we have provided enough choices to suit anyone's definition.

The standard shingle is not particularly ornamental. Insert a few rows with ornamentally cut ends, however, as in this garage façade in Martha's Vineyard, and you have strong pattern.

Laid in common bond, brick is not thought of as "ornamental." But turn one course at an angle, or lay a course in which every other brick is cantilevered, and you have a strong, simple decoration. Warehouse, West Springfield, Massachusetts.

Some Common Questions About Ornament

Why do most architects get "designers block" when they think about using ornament?

For over half a century traditional, historically-based ornament has been anathema to architects trained in the Spartan ways of modernism. Our anxiety about it even led us to exorcise the word from the professional vocabulary: what used to be called ornamental metals (grilles, railings, and other accessories) are referred to as architectural metals by many people. Even today, some designers get an uneasy feeling when ornament is mentioned in the same breath as contemporary architecture. The main reason for this lingering anxiety is that the idea of ornament remains closely tied to that scariest of all realms of design—history. After all, the most familiar way of cataloging ornament is still according to historical style. To alleviate this nagging sensation we suggest trying, for a moment, to dissociate ornament from its historical moorings; think of it in terms of categories that cut across "style" boundaries as much as possible.

To help us do this, let us try looking at ornament simply in terms of visual effects. First, look at a simple unornamented box. When the corners are emphasized the box looks heavier; it becomes more solid. Other changes in ornamental emphasis make the box look more vertical or more horizontal. It is possible for ornament to soften the silhouette. Make some minor adjustments, and the wall plane can be reinforced or made to disappear.

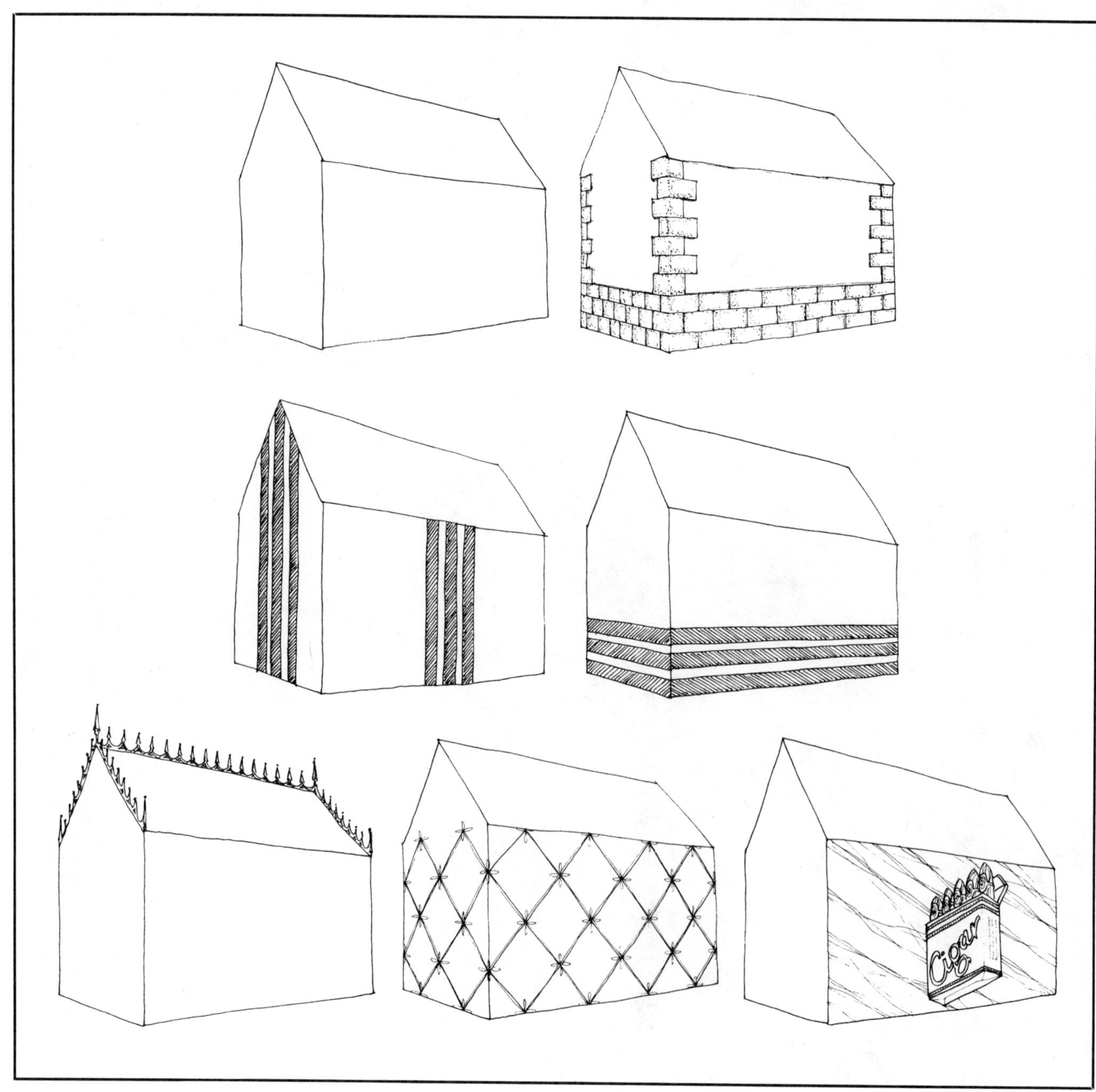

Is ornament an "extra"?

Before modernism, ornament was seldom thought of as separate from architecture. Almost all buildings had some sort of ornament, and it did not occur to either designer or client that one could leave it off. Even a lintel spanning a simple opening was expected to enhance the façade with its own decoration. This unity of architecture and ornament could encompass virtually every part of a building, right down to the decorated inside faces of butt hinges, which could be seen only when a door was opened. In fact, ornament was probably not thought of as an "extra" until our times.

Modernists allegedly never used ornament. Actually, they created their own kind of ornament and, needless to say, it was not thought of as an "extra." Few would deny that fashionable steel pipe railings are minimal forms—although you could argue about how many horizontals are actually needed for stability. But it is equally difficult to deny that they are often used in highly decorative ways; Le Corbusier's Villa Savoie and Richard Meiers' Atheneum are both elegant examples of the decorative use of simple pipe railings.

Ornamental reveals, too, are usually carefully placed so their delicate shadows define the taut, thin-skinned surfaces which some contemporary architects use so skillfully, while the high polish of stainless steel is often used ornamentally to dematerialize a surface.

In the complex architecture of the 1960s and '70s, the building itself was often an ornament. Yale's Art and Architecture Building, by Paul Rudolph, and the more brutal Boston City Hall immediately come to mind.

The idea that "ornament costs more" has also contributed to our feeling that it is an extra. Sometimes ornament is cheap,

To relieve the unbroken roofline, Le Corbusier pulled these columns away from the wall of the Carpenter Arts Center for the Visual Arts, Harvard University.

The cupola is a traditional way to break the line of a harsh silhouette—this one graces Mt. Vernon.

Republic Bank Center, Houston, Texas (project rendering). Johnson/Burgee Architects (1981). The silhouette "feathered" into the sky. (Photo courtesy of Johnson/Burgee Architects)

The simplest and most acceptable way of ornamenting a modern building has been by texture. This differs from the traditional means of ornamenting in that it is not "composed." The façade of a traditionally ornamented building is made up of ornamental subdivisions that, together, made a compositon. It usually consists of a bottom, a middle, and a top, with emphasis at the edges and at the various openings. (See the buildings at the top of the photo.) A modern building (see the center of the photo) generally repeats the same, uniform texture over the entire façade.

Sometimes modern textures are broken up and used in more traditional ways, as in the stamped metal spandrels of 666 Fifth Avenue, New York.

This grandly-scaled ornamental pattern is broken at the central, mechanical floor.

The rich variety of moldings that gave scale and definition to traditional architecture was replaced, in modernist times, by the simple "reveal" which often tries to serve the same purposes. Bronx Developmental Center, Richard Meier & Associates, Architects (1977).

The composite capital is made of fiber glass (suitable for exterior use) and was cast from a plaster model by Saldarini and Pucci. See listing under Plastics.

and sometimes it is expensive. However, you should not assume that ornament is *always* a great expense. Depending on the materials used, the amount of repetition involved, and the amount of handwork, ornament can be less expensive than you would think. Long-term savings must also be considered; ornamental awnings may need replacement every seven or eight years, but they will provide considerable savings in cooling costs during that period. So the question should be: Does the person paying for the ornament feel it is worthwhile?

Modernists have been paying for it all along; they have just been calling it something else. Traditional embellishment was called "ornament;" modernist embellishments were "expressions" of structure, or function, and were further sanctified by the pregnant pronouncement that they reflected the "spirit of the times." The careful substitution of "expression" for decoration or ornament was utterly convincing for decades because we were so infatuated with the idea of utility as beauty, and so frightened of ornament.

In reality, embellishment often can be an added expense—but this is true whether it is the pipe railings on Richard Meiers' Atheneum or the balusters on Michelangelo's St. Peter's. If the person paying for the embellishment considers it worthwhile, then the ornament is not an "extra."

What are some sources of ornament?

It is not enough to argue in favor of ornament merely by saying that it lends grace and beauty to architecture. We can tell from the way modernists evolved their own versions of ornament that they were always aware of this. The problem lies not in getting architects to use ornament, but in enlarging their definition of what constitutes "acceptable" ornament. This is not easy. The vocabulary of ornamental forms in modern architecture is unprecedentedly primitive and pathetically inhibited. You need only compare the modern "reveal" to the rich variety of classical moldings to realize the low ebb at which we find ourselves. If we can begin to dispell our ingrained bias against ornament and look at our world with an unprejudiced eye, we may be able to find a variety of sources that can serve as bases for new ornamental vocabularies.

In addition to totally abstract ornament, nature could once again become a legitimate source of inspiration, although we may still be too closely tied to the last century for that to be a comfortable alternative. Technology, industry, and regional themes can also be fruitful sources; ornament can identify a building with its occupants or with their work; it can reflect personal values as well as attitudes toward the past and one's cultural heritage; or it can make a building "specific" by personalizing it with references to its owner. The Chrysler Building in New York is perhaps the most famous example of this. And we have not begun to touch upon the mine of cultural symbolism.

By drawing on any or all of these sources, we could invest architecture with more subtle, yet more accessible meanings than has been possible with the self-consciously esoteric "form language" of modernism.

The stone ornament on this now-defunct automobile dealership in Chicago came from the technology that made the automobile possible. All these façade decorations are related to the automobile—gears, drive chains, fan belts, pistons, even traffic lights.

Is decoration useless?

Even if we are unrealistic enough to define "useful" in the most practical way, ornament still has its "uses." As suggested above, it can be energy-saving. It can reduce maintenance—the familiar streaks that now disfigure untold square miles of grimy concrete could have been turned to advantage by ornament designed to be enhanced by weathering. Decoration is also helpful in disguising joints that might otherwise require unnecessarily costly workmanship to make presentable.

If we consider a more flexible definition, think how useful an ornamented building is if it evokes, through its decoration, a sense of pride in the community.

The uses of ornament can be even more surprising. We spoke with a New York architect who had recently designed a building faced with ornamentally-cut limestone. He told us that the fund-raising for this building had been relatively easy because the people could see where their money was going. "None of this 'less is more' business," as he put it.

Potential contributors to that building may also have been attracted by what might be termed the "price/appearance ratio;" that limestone wall, complete with decorative cutting, cost less per square foot than the glass curtain wall then under construction a few blocks away. In addition, stone offers better insulation, and that translates into long-term energy savings. And it will also, according to the architect, prove a more reliable defense against the elements over the years than standard curtain wall construction.

Relearning the Art of Ornament

Whatever the complex reasons for ornament's fall from favor in the 1920s, the fact is architects gradually forgot how to create it. If we are to learn to use ornament once again, we must look closely at the ornament of the past and make contact with those people—many of whom are listed in this book—who have never lost these skills.

Perhaps the best way to relearn this art is to create a sympathetic climate in which the wholesome enjoyment of the decorative arts in architecture is possible once again—without the leftover nineteenth- and twentieth-century inhibitions about history, structure-relatedness, honesty, etc. Only when this is possible will ornament be examined in all its facets, without destructive fearfulness and timidity.

The designer who is interested in understanding the nature of ornament will spend hundreds of hours studying—and drawing—traditional and modern ornament. Much of the drawing will have to be done by hand, a time-consuming process but one which is perhaps necessary if one is to get the "feel" of ornament.

This ugly customer, complete with a knife and pistol—the tools of his trade—is one of several thematic grotesques on the Yale Law School. (A grotesque is a gargoyle that does not spew water.)

A more contemporary thematic decoration. Diamonds on a grille ornament this façade in New York's diamond district.

Before modernism, architecture was ornamented whenever and wherever possible. This is a nineteenth-century butt hinge, the decoration of which could only be seen when the door was open. (Courtesy of Spaced Gallery of Architecture, New York, NY)

Modernists tended to obscure the fact that all ornament is an added expense, whether it is the painted marble of Zimmermann's Wies Church (shown here), or the equally decorative, polished marble of Mies van der Rohe's Barcelona Pavillion.

The computer and ornament

Some help in the awesome but pleasurable task of drawing and redrawing ornament may come from an unexpected quarter. Although we are just beginning to understand how they can be used in design, the rise of mini-computers may be an auspicious event for architectural ornament. Computers can show designers hundreds of motifs, and hundreds of variations on each motif, in a fraction of the time it would take to render any one of them in the style to which the Beaux-Arts was once accustomed.

William Grover, of Moore Grover Harper (in Essex, Connecticut), is exploring ways of creating architectural ornament with a program called ORNAMAT. It generates a curve, based on a mathematical equation, which can then be repeated in various combinations to make a decorative element. To get a slightly different curve, Grover inserts a different equation. The proportion of the element can be adjusted by changing its vertical and horizontal dimensions on the screen. Once the architect is satisfied, he prints it out (or photographs it and draws it up) and begins figuring out different ways to put it together: linear patterns that outline planes; panels that define the surface of planes; "jewels," or isolated ornamental elements; or other types of architectural decorations.

At the time of this writing, the firm had not yet incorporated these computer-generated patterns into their designs, but Grover said the first use would most likely be as patterns for painted stencils. Eventually, he sees the two-dimensional patterns being converted into, among other things, three-dimensional inserts for concrete formwork. The small "blocks" of the computer image can be translated into wooden blocks of varying heights which could be used as the mold in a standard vacuum-forming process. The end result would be a bas-relief insert which could be placed in concrete formwork or used as a mold for cast stone or fiber glass.

While there will never be an electronic substitute for the refinements of the human hand, the computer's virtue—providing endless variations on a graphic theme quickly and with relatively little effort—makes it a welcome aid to relearning the art of ornamenting. As the technology becomes more sophisticated, the relationship between computer and designer will become more immediate. Even now, many computer graphic systems permit direct graphic input—drawing on the screen or on an electronic pad—rather than "drawing" a curve indirectly, with intermediate symbols such as mathematical formulas. Each step toward a more direct connection between designer and computer makes this tool more valuable; it becomes both less "visible," in terms of intruding on the design process, and more accessible, because designers do not need specialized knowledge to use it.

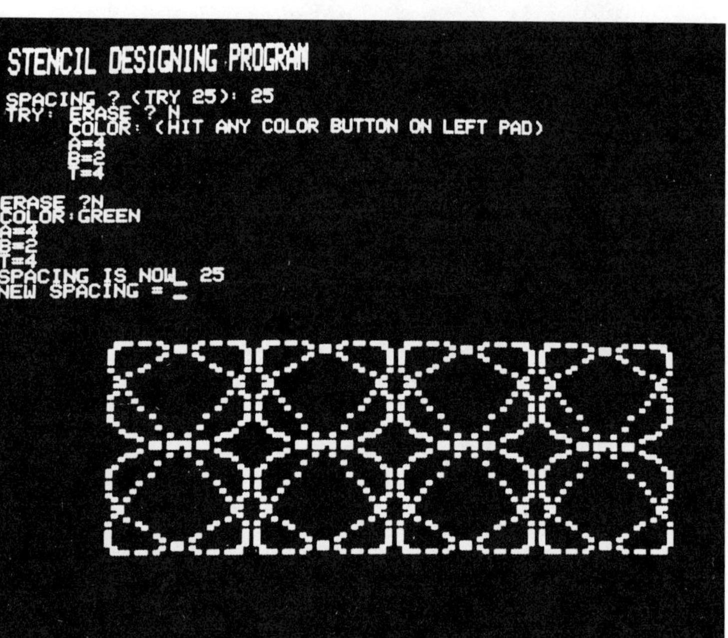

Ornament has always been drawn by hand—until now. Mini-computers promise to take some of the drudgery out of the design of repetitive ornament, while permitting designers to explore endless variations on a theme at the touch of a button. Ornamental studies generated by a program called ORNAMAT, courtesy of Moore Grover Harper, P. C., Essex, CT. (Photo by William H. Grover)

The "Percentage for Art" Programs

Another opportunity for using exterior architectural ornament may be found in the Percentage for Art programs which exist at federal, state, county, and city levels. At the time of this writing, the federal program for the General Services Administration (G.S.A.), for example, stipulated that one-half of one percent of the budget for a federal or federally-funded building may be used for "art," at the discretion of the administration of the G.S.A. Although this money is ostensibly for "art," the G.S.A. is making a genuine effort to include the work of artisans as well. Therefore, artisans and artists who are interested in commissions for such buildings should send labeled 35mm slides in a plastic sheet, along with a résumé, to:

Donald W. Thalacker, Director
Art in Architecture Program
U.S. General Services Administration
Washington, DC 20405
(202) 566-0950

Mr. Thalacker is happy to advise architects, artists, and artisans on any problems or questions that may come up regarding their collaborations: contractual matters, technical advice, installation costs, etc. For an updated look at other federal (as well as state and local) programs, contact the Visual Arts Program of the National Endowment for the Arts.

Visual Arts Program
National Endowment for the Arts
2401 E Street N.W.
Washington, DC 20037
(202) 634-1568

Federal agencies often come to the Visual Arts Program staff for help in choosing artists and craftsmen for federal projects. This division of the N.E.A. has an extensive collection of slides showing the work of artists and craftsmen who have worked in architectural settings. The collection is made available to panels choosing "art" for government percentage-for-art programs. If you would like to submit slides for inclusion in this pool, contact the N.E.A. for details.

The N.E.A. also gives matching grants to nonprofit organizations for art integrated with architecture.

For current information on Percentage for the Arts programs look in your Yellow Pages Directory for "Arts Council," "Arts Commission," or "Arts Programs" under state, city, and county governments, or contact your governor's or mayor's office.

As this is written, about twenty states, forty cities, and five counties in the United States (see the list below) have programs that set aside a percentage of government building budgets for art. Some of these programs are mandatory: a given amount of the budget must be spent on art when a federal, county, or city building is constructed. Other programs leave the decision up to the agencies involved, or to the whims of the political process; in Texas, for example, a separate bill must be introduced into the state legislature for every art appropriation. (One source told us that the Texas legislature has not allotted any money for art under this program since the law was enacted.) Other states, like New Jersey, seem to have evolved a workable relationship between the coordinating state architect, the arts officer, and the project architect who actually designs the building. But as each program works differently you should contact your local state or city arts agency to find out how you can get involved.

States

Alaska
California
Colorado
Connecticut
Florida
Hawaii
Illinois
Iowa
Maine
Massachusetts
Michigan
Nebraska
New Hampshire
New Jersey
New Mexico
New York
Oregon
South Dakota
Texas
Washington
Wisconsin

Counties

Broward County, FL
Dade County, FL
Multnomah County, OR
King County, WA
Tacoma-Pierce County, WA
Pierce County, WA

Cities

Anchorage, AK
Davis, CA
Los Angeles, CA
Palo Alto, CA
Riverside, CA
Sacramento, CA
San Francisco, CA
Santa Barbara, CA
Santa Rosa, CA
Walnut Creek, CA
Boulder, CO
Miami Beach, FL
Atlanta, GA
Honolulu, HI
Boise, ID
Chicago, IL
Baltimore, MD
Rockville, MD
New Orleans, LA
Boston, MA
Cambridge, MA
Grand Rapids, MI
Kansas City, MO
Albuquerque, NM
New York City, NY
Toledo, OH
Tulsa, OK
Eugene, OR
Portland, OR
Philadelphia, PA
Pittsburgh, PA
Wilkes-Barre, PA
Salt Lake City, UT
Bellevue, WA
Edmond, WA
Everett, WA
Mountlake Terrace, WA
Renton, WA
Seattle, WA
Wenatchee, WA
Madison, WI
Milwaukee, WI

For the most up-to-date information on these programs contact:
Public Art Fund, Inc., 25 Central Park West, New York, NY 10023

How to Use the Listings

Information about each listing is given in "text" and "matrix" forms. Text entries include the name, address, telephone number, and a short descirption of the company or individual. The matrix, found at the end of each section, gives a quick, overall picture of services, materials, and techniques that are available. The name, city, and state appear at the left, and key information about each listing is indicated in the appropriate column to the right. A typical matrix will show which companies are in a particular area; whether the listee is a distributor, manufacturer, or studio; the principle materials and techniques that are used; if brochures or photographs are available; if telephone estimates are given, and the like.

Each section opens with a brief description of the material and ways in which it was used in the past; there are also some suggestions for possible future uses. This is followed by a section of Special listings covering associations, companies, or individuals that: (1) offer special information about the topic (such as the Portland Cement Association or American Concrete Institute); (2) are able to put you in touch with people who provide the services discussed in that section (Chicago Plastering Institute has names of ornamental plasterers in the area); or (3) provide unusual services directly related to the topic of that section (James Zielinski, of Bellerose, New York, has been handpainting awnings for thirty years; the Local Lumber Company of Oxford, Connecticut, stocks a large selection of carefully chosen, kiln-dried native lumber that is purchased green and cut to specification). Special listings are arranged alphabetically (by name), and do not appear in the matrix.

The listings within each section are arranged by region: Northeast, South, Midwest, and Rockies and Far West. Address abbreviations follow U.S. Postal Service practice. Several Canadian companies responded to magazine queries; they are included in the nearest geographical grouping.

Stainless steel lattice for wisteria. Indiana Bell Telephone Switching Center, Columbus, IN. Caudill Rowlett Scott, Architects, Houston, Texas. (Photo by Balthazar Korab, courtesy of Caudill Rowlett Scott)

Regions

Northeast
Connecticut (CT)
Delaware (DE)
Maine (ME)
Massachusetts (MA)
New Hampshire (NH)
New Jersey (NJ)
New York (NY)
Pennsylvania (PA)
Rhode Island (RI)
Vermont (VT)

South
Alabama (AL)
Florida (FL)
Georgia (GA)
Kentucky (KY)
Louisiana (LA)
Maryland (MD)
Mississippi (MS)
North Carolina (NC)
South Carolina (SC)
Tennessee (TN)
Virginia (VA)
Washington, D.C. (DC)
West Virginia (WV)

Midwest
Arkansas (AR)
Illinois (IL)
Indiana (IN)
Iowa (IA)
Kansas (KS)
Michigan (MI)
Minnesota (MN)
Missouri (MO)
Nebraska (NE)
North Dakota (ND)
Ohio (OH)
Oklahoma (OK)
South Dakota (SD)
Texas (TX)
Wisconsin (WI)

Rockies and Far West
Alaska (AK)
Arizona (AZ)
California (CA)
Colorado (CO)
Hawaii (HI)
Idaho (ID)
Montana (MT)
Nevada (NV)
New Mexico (NM)
Oregon (OR)
Utah (UT)
Washington (WA)
Wyoming (WY)

Some Notes on Horticulture

"Doctors bury their mistakes, architects put trees in front of them." As the old saying implies, planting is often an architectural afterthought. We felt that landscaping was beyond the scope of this book; nevertheless, many designers are already aware of the possibilities of this ancient form of architectural ornament.

The houses of Frank Lloyd Wright are probably the most famous recent examples of integration of architecture and decorative planting. This type of decoration can be as restrained as a window box of geraniums or as elaborate as the fabled Hanging Gardens of Babylon. In warmer climates ornamental planting serves a double purpose; it decorates and shields walls that are exposed to direct sun. With the proper earth cover, roof installations provide substantial insulation. In spite of the proddings of modernists like Le Corbusier, this valuable aspect of the relationship between architect and horticulturalist was largely ignored until rising energy costs reminded both client and architect of the thermal stability of earth.

The combination of fiber art and planting offers a chance to create a modern variation of espalier, the art of pruning plants into special shapes. Vines can be planted near a building and trained to follow a rope matrix. Trusses for vines can be made of wood, steel, or other materials in any form.

Yellow Pages Classifications

In an effort to help designers who want to find ornamenters in their immediate vicinity, but who live in an area that was not covered by our "grid" of cities, we have included the headings under which our categories appear in the Yellow Pages. Those requiring a bit of explanation are marked with an asterisk and explained immediately following the list. Certain "key" words appeared in the advertisements and were helpful in locating architecturally oriented companies; these are noted in parentheses.

Advertising-Outdoor*
Antiques (architectural)*
Awnings & Canopies
Brick-Clay-Common & Face (molded)
Bronze Ornamental Work (architectural)
Columns (wood, plastic)
Concrete Blocks & Shapes
Concrete Construction Forms & Accessories (ornamental, precast)*
Cupolas
Cornices-Building
Decalcomania (for windows, doors; custom; art staff)
Etching (glass, metals)
Fiber Glass Products (sculpture and architectural castings)
Foundries (sculpture casting)
Glass Beveling
Glass Block, Structural, Etc.
Glass-Carved, Ornamental, Etc.
Glass-Stained & Leaded (churches, synagogues, homes, windows)
Granite (fabricators, monument works)
Horticultural Consultants*
Iron Work (artistic, ornamental)
Letters-Sign (handcrafted, logos, custom)*
Millwork
Moldings (architectural)
Monuments (cornerstones, architectural, designers, names of individuals)*
Mosaic
Murals
Plaques (manufacturers, fiberglass, metals, portraiture, art department)*
Plaster Products-Ornamental (gargoyles, ornamental, fiberglass, architectural terms)*
Plastics-Reinforced (architectural)
Porcelain Products (panels and moldings)
Sculptors (architectural)
Sheet Metal Work (cornices, decorative, architectural)*
Signs (neon, various materials)*
Stenciling-Decorative*
Stone-Cast (architectural, ornamental, modular)
Stone-Natural (decorative, architectural trim)
Stucco Contractors (decorative, exterior)
Tile-Ceramic-Dlrs., Mfrs., & Distrs. (terracotta, mosaic, architectural, frostproof)
Truck Painting & Lettering*
Weathervanes
Wood Carving
Wood Turning (balusters, columns, stair railings)

Advertising. Outdoor. Many of these are billboard painters who can paint exterior murals from a scale drawing or photograph. If you want to design the mural yourself, you can hire one of the companies listed under this heading to execute it. However, check on the durability of the paints used; outdoor signs seldom have to last as long as murals.

Antiques. Many companies in this category deal in "left-over" architecture. (A more complete discussion, "Architectural Salvage," follows.)

Concrete Construction Forms & Accessories. These companies will make formwork for ornamental concrete panels or cast stone.

Horticultural Consultants. When familiar with outdoor planting, these consultants can be extremely helpful.

Letters. Sign. Many letter-making companies also do custom logos, castings in metals and plastics, and letters in different materials for outside use. They can often fabricate other items for exterior use as well.

Monuments. Monument and mausoleum carvers are often former architectural carvers, and are required to do elaborate granite and marble carving and fabricating. Many monument makers are skilled in sandblasting and incision carving and can make free-standing and bas-relief sculpture in addition to architectural elements to specifications.

Plaques. Bronze plaques are usually thought of as commemorating historic events, but one can put anything on a plaque, including decorative patterns. Some manufacturers cast fiber glass in addition to metals.

Plaster Products-Ornamental. Although plaster is not generally recommended for exposed exterior use, these particularly skilled craftsmen should not be overlooked. Plaster models are often used as guides for stone cutters or to make molds for casting fiber glass, cast stone, or metal. Most companies in this category also work in fiber glass and cast stone.

Sheet Metal Work. The few people who can still form metal cornices and brackets (or any other element you might design) are probably to be found under this category. They might also be found under *Cornices,* but we found that most companies under that heading removed rather than made cornices.

Signs. If you are interested in using neon ornamentally, look for *Neon* under this heading. Since almost all Signmakers' skills are seldom limited to lettering.

Stenciling-Decorative. Usually done indoors, but some stencilers are willing and able to work on exteriors.

Truck Painting & Lettering. Many trucks are skillfully and imaginatively decorated, and these same painters will sometimes work on buildings. They have the advantage of knowing about the durability of various paints in the local climate. Note: they seldom have rigger's licenses.

If you need information about what plants grow best in a specific region or façade orientation, or would like descriptions of plant habits, maintenance systems, or design services, look in the Yellow Pages under *Horticultural Consultants, Landscape Contractors, Landscape Designers,* and *Nurserymen.* Many companies under these categories supply plants, give technical information and offer design services. The key words to look for are "exterior" and "design."

If you would like to work with a landscape architect, contact:

American Society of Landscape Architects
Attn. Gayle Todsen, Program Director
Suite 750
1900 M Street N.W.
Washington, DC 20036
(202) 466-7730

The society has forty-three local chapters and two publications: *LAND* and *Landscape Architecture News Digest.*

Architectural salvage

Within the past decade, the awareness of the quality of workmanship that went into older buildings—as well as renewed respect for historical ornament of all kinds—has led to an increase in the number of places dealing in "leftover" architecture. These are the bits and pieces that are salvaged from demolished buildings. Salvage architecture can be as small as faceplates for light switches or ornamental hinges, and as large as whole cornices or cast iron façades.

Many companies deal with salvage, and the list that follows is just the tip of the iceberg. Stock changes regularly, so if there is a particular item you are interested in, we suggest that you get on the mailing lists, or contact them periodically.

Architectural Antiques Exchange
Attn. Mark Charry, Proprietor
709-15 N. Second Street
Philadelphia, PA 19123
(215) 922-3669

"Saloon and apothecary fixtures; salvage from Victorian buildings; nostalgia restaurant decor." Specializes in artifacts made between 1879 and 1920; items of all types and in all kinds of materials. A selection of pieces commonly on hand includes panelling, entryways and doors, stained glass windows and doors, neon signs, advertising memorabilia, columns, balustrades, wood carvings, iron gates and grilles, lighting fixtures, fretwork, and a variety of interior furnishings.

Art Directions
6120 Delmar Boulevard
St. Louis, MO 63112

Specialize in turn of the century and Art Deco items including columns, cornices, brackets. Contact them for information about their custom design service.

Bare Wood, Inc.
141 Atlantic Avenue
Brooklyn, NY 11201
(212) 875-3833

The majority of architectural elements carried by this company date from between 1840 and 1910. Boasts the "largest selection of Victorian doors in the U.S.A." Also offers hardware, columns, gates, spindels, fretwork, bannisters, newel posts, and a variety of interior details including wainscotting, panelling, and fireplaces. Items in stock may be sold "as is" or totally restored. Bare Wood also has a complete woodshop with "London-trained craftsmen" capable of modifying, repairing, or recreating "with integrity, almost any wood item required."

Briercliffe Imports
Attn. Louis Battistone
Suite 231
Long Reach Village Center
Columbia, MD 21045
(301) 596-4922
(301) 730-4737

An artifact firm that finds, catalogs, warehouses, and sells "unique artifacts from the past." Write or call for further information.

Great American Salvage Co.
3 Main Street
Montpelier, VT 05602
(802) 223-7711

A large, ever-changing selection of exterior and interior ornamental architectural elements including porch columns, stonework, ironwork, French doors, hardware, bars, etc. Primarily Victorian and colonial; specializes in leaded, stained, and beveled glass doors and windows. Will furnish photographs of specific items in response to a request, but recommends visiting the showroom/warehouse.

Irreplaceable Artifacts
Attn. Evan Blum
Executive Offices
526 E. 80th Street
New York, NY 10021
(212) 288-7397

(by appointment only)

Warehouse Outlet
259 Bowery
New York, NY 10012
(212) 982-5000

This company carries both interior and exterior architectural ornament in "almost all periods and styles." Specializes in high quality items, large quantities, and oversized pieces. Architects and designers can receive a quarterly newsletter and wholesale catalog listing what is available and suggested reuse of artifacts.

Old & Elegant Distributors
Bellevue, WA 98004

See listing under Metals.

Old Mansions Co.
1305 Blue Hill Avenue
Mattapan, MA 02126
(617) 296-0445

This company carries items from all periods of American history. A partial list of the inventory includes newel posts, unusual doors, windows, shutters, iron fences, ceramic tiles, leaded glass, plaster ornaments, fountains, timbers, ornamental stone, granite, and slate, ornamental grilles and window guards, columns, terracotta, and *objets d'art*.

Bradley Oliver
Box 246
Jim Thorpe, PA 18229
(717) 325-2859

This company has been restoring interior and exterior woodwork and furniture for several decades. In addition, offers metal fencing, urns and fountains, wood ornaments, moldings, etc., dating from 1840 to 1920.

Urban Archaeology, Ltd.
137 Spring Street
New York, NY 10013
(212) 431-6969

Specializes in Victorian and Art Deco exterior and interior architectural ornament, particularly stonework, ironwork, antique bars, and soda fountains.

Temporary ornaments

For temporary exterior nighttime ornament, a suggestion might be to use spotlights and templates to project shapes and colors on exterior walls. This combination is well known in stage lighting. A metal template with an etched pattern is inserted in an ellipsoidal reflector spotlight. Templates can be custom designed or selected from readymade patterns. The spotlight can be purchased or rented from stage lighting companies. These spotlights are not intended for outdoor use. However, if they are protected from bad weather, not exposed to high humidity for any length of time, and given adequate ventilation for heat build-up, they can be used outdoors. Technical advice is available from the stage lighting companies, found listed in the business directory under *Stage Lighting Equipment*. Two of the largest are:

Kliegl Brothers
32-32 48th Avenue
Long Island City, NY 11105
(212) 786-7474

Strand Century
20 Bushes Lane
Elmwood Park, NJ 07407
(212) 564-6910
and
5432 W. 102nd Street
Los Angeles, CA 90045
(213) 776-4600

Two template makers who make readymade and custom designs are:

Theatre Magic
1282 Nantucket Avenue
Columbus, OH 43220
(614) 459-3222

Great American Market
Attn. Andrea Tavil
P.O. Box 178
Woodland Hills, CA 91365
(213) 883-8182

AWNINGS

The origin of this word is obscure. At first it was used to describe a cover extending forward from the poop deck cabin, but, in 1624, Captain John Smith hung an awning from trees "to shadow us from the Sunne."

The decorative—and practical—advantages of awnings were still well understood in the early twentieth century. In our age of energy crises it is eye-opening to note that as late as the 1920s even large buildings were often fully fitted out with awnings. They are cheaper, infinitely more variable, and more efficient in terms of solar heat gain than the *brise-soleil* which modernism offers in their place. *Brises-soleil,* or "sun breakers," are made from tons of concrete and steel and are normally fixed to accommodate the worst possible sun condition. You are stuck if you do not want them on a cloudy day. Awnings are flexible; they can be put up or down, or anywhere in between. As they have no mass, they do not continue to radiate heat into a building once the sun has passed, as do *brises-soleil.* Remote controls for awnings are available if the windows cannot be opened. However, with operable windows coming back into vogue, standard retractable awning hardware will suffice.

Awnings add colorful, sculptural elements to a façade when seen from a distance and, depending on the choice of fabric and pattern, can provide details of greater refinement when seen close up. We were pleased and surprised to find that awnings are often used on high-rise apartment buildings—in Puerto Rico, for example. Even the most conventional awning, in a bright color and used repetitively, can be a powerful ornamental motif.

Another way of using awnings is to link several openings under one undulating form of varying depth and color, creating a building-sized sculpture. Awnings can also be painted or decorated with sewn appliques to make different designs. (See listings under Fiber Arts.) Wrought iron hardware and awning supports offer further possibilities for ornament.

Market Square, Vancouver, B.C. (Photo courtesy of Industrial Fabric Association, International)

A high percentage of the work done by most awning manufacturers is "custom" so many are equipped to make anything a designer might create. Some of them already fabricate the work of fiber artists; others expressed an openness to such work. This is indicated in the listings.

Designers who want to use banners, hangings, or fiber sculptures of their own design should contact one of the associations (see below, under "Special"). They will put you in touch with a local manufacturer who can advise about technical details concerning the durability and strength of fabric, construction methods, manufacturing techniques, and the like. You can also contact a local manufacturer directly. Companies with experience in fabricating banners are indicated in the matrix as well as the text.

The following materials are commonly used for awnings:

Duck (a form of canvas usually made of cotton. There are three weights of duck; from heaviest to lightest they are: "number" duck, "army" duck, and "ounce" duck. Duck is ordinarily treated to resist mildew and water when it is manufactured. It can also be made to meet U.S. Government specifications for fire resistance.)
Nylon and nywool (a nylon and wool mixture)
Painted sheet metal
Polycotton blends
Polyesters (both spun and filament)
Acrylics, solution dyed
Vinyl (electronically welded to ensure that it is waterproof) and other plastics
Vinyl-coated canvas

Bonanza Inn Book Store, San Francisco. Awning by Sullivan Awning Co. (Photo by Max Barbour)

According to the American Canvas Institute, a U.S. Department of Agriculture survey shows that canvas awnings last an average of 6.5 years in residential use and 5.1 years in commercial use. The life of the awning obviously depends on climate, design (if it is too flat, it collects rain), surface treatment, and proper care (do not leave them out in a hailstorm). To find out the exact properties and appropriateness of each material, contact one of the associations listed below or a local awning manufacturer.

Awning for Ariston. Designed by Donald Clever. Sullivan Awnings, San Francisco. (Photo courtesy of Sullivan Awnings)

Residential double awning with applique decoration by Marc Horovitz, Sidestreet Bannerworks, Denver, CO. (Photo courtesy of Marc Horovitz)

Painted awning with classical motif, New York City.

Special Listings

American Canvas Institute
10 Beech Street
Berea, OH 44017
(216) 243-0121

Gives suggestions and technical advice about use of material; also printed material. Can recommend fabricators and suppliers in your area. No charge for these services. Architects can get on mailing list by writing to the above address. Membership consists of fifteen fabric mills and wholesalers across the country.

The Astrup Co.
2937 West 25th St.
Cleveland, OH 44113
(216) 696-2800

A manufacturer of awning hardware systems and supplier of awning fabric.

John Boyle & Co., Inc.
Attn. John Bell, Jr., President
112 Duane Street
New York, NY 10007
(212) 962-4770

Founded in 1860, this company is one of the oldest and largest manufacturers and distributors of awning and other industrial fabrics (cottons and synthetics). It also manufactures a line of energy efficient fabrics for passive solar window coverings. Other services include:

Design and manufacture of custom awning hardware, including motorized and remote controls.
Recommendation of fabricators around the country with whom they have worked.
Occasional fabrication of large orders (over $100,000) or of unique pieces of fiber art (once fabricated a five-story inflated "leg" that was hung over the side of a building).
Advice on fabrics appropriate for specific projects, including length of life under various circumstances. (Has a file of flame retardancy specs for each state and recommend fabrics accordingly.)
Advice on proper paints to use for each type of fabric. (Their technical knowledge of paints can be linked with the talents of muralists to create painted awnings, canopies, etc.)

Industrial Fabrics Association International
350 Endicott Building
St. Paul, MN 55101
(612) 222-2508

It has a membership of 1,300 firms that make canvas products around the country. Can recommend fabricators in your area, give information about the durability of specific fabrics in specific climates, and give advice about common pitfalls people run into when working with this material. It has a limited amount of descriptive material; no newsletter. Will provide information on which fabrics are best for which regions.

James Zielinski
8738 252nd Street
Bellerose, NY 11426
(212) 347-5440

Mr. Zielinski has been designing and handpainting fine awnings and canopies for thirty years. One large awning contractor called him the "Czar of canvas painters." He measures on site but does all work in his studio. He prefers geometric patterns because pictorial work is too time-consuming. He is happy to work with an architect in developing a design or to create his own. Preliminary designs are shown to the client in elevation, perspective drawing, or model form. An expert on the best types of paint for different awning materials, he will also recommend the manufacturer whom he feels is the best for your particular job. If you would like awnings painted, and do not live in the area, they can be shipped to him. He has no brochure or photos but is pleased to provide a list of the locations of his work. Much of his work is for architects; he has done over 500 commissions in the past two years.

Regional Listings

Northeast

Cunningham and Upson
Attn. Gardner W. Hubbard, President
44-46 Hotchkiss Street
New Haven, CT 06511
(203) 777-2359

Canvas products in general; stock and custom.

New Haven Awning Co.
Attn. Philip Michelson or Jennifer Nelson
11 Edwards Street
New Haven, CT 06511
(203) 562-7232

Will fabricate anything in cloth including synthetics like Acrilan. Fabric and aluminum. Complicated custom work may require more detailed information than a rough sketch. Commercial and residential. "Any application where cloth is required."

Better Homes, Inc.
178 Harlow
Bangor, ME 04401
(207) 942-7373

Fabric and aluminum. Specializes in residential work.

Alfred G. Peterson and Sons, Inc.
Attn. Marianne L. Newhall, Vice President
491 West Main Street
Avon, MA 02322
(617) 588-8800

Custom designs can sometimes be produced from sketch; working drawing required depending on the complexity. Also does banners, sunscreens, and tents. Commercial and residential.

Pelletier Custom Decorators
65 Congress Street
Salem, MA 01970
(617) 745-4710

Works with all woven goods. Custom fabrication requires exact drawings and specifications. Commercial and residential.

Morgan Industries
335 Medford Street
Somerville, MA 02145
(617) 547-4152
(617) 374-0378

Fabricates "anything made of canvas" and aluminum to any design specification. Design, manufacture, and installation of European lateral arm systems. Commercial and residential.

Warren Strohmeyer
138 W. Pleasant Avenue
Maywood, NJ 07607
(201) 843-7990

Specializes in custom canvas awnings for all applications including patios, gazebos, etc. Also works with polyesters. Commercial and residential.

Canvas World
P.O. Box 81
Alplaus, NY 12008
(518) 399-2884

Works with canvas, nylon, acrylics, neoprene, and hypalon. Commercial and residential.

Acme Awnings Co. Inc.
514 Jackson Avenue
Bronx, NY 10455
(212) 292-9177

Residential and commercial installations in canvas, nylon, plastics, and plastic-coated fabrics. Custom work from working drawing only.

Armor Canvas Products
2194 Flatbush Avenue
Brooklyn, NY 11234
(212) 859-1271
(212) 859-0732

Specializes in canvas awnings. Commercial and residential.

King Awning & Shade Co., Inc.
5210 Fifth Avenue
Brooklyn, NY 11220
(212) 748-6900

"Anything in the way of canvas." Also works in vinyl-coated canvas, polyesters, and laminated fabrics. Custom work from measured drawings. They manufacture and install for residential and commercial buildings in metropolitan New York area.

William J. Mills
125 Main Street
Greenport, NY 11944
(516) 477-1500
TWX 510-220-6314

This company also makes sails, which would give them valuable experience in difficult fiber art applications that might have to withstand considerable strain from wind. It has a research and design division. Commercial and residential.

S. L. Doery & Son, Inc.
Attn. Arnold Doery
299 Rockaway Turnpike
Lawrence, NY 11559
(212) 327-1642
(516) 239-7852

Specializes in canvas awnings of all types—terrace, roll-up, canopy, marquees, etc. Prefers to take own measurements from site for custom fabrication. Works in canvas and vinyls.

Ace Banner and Flag Co.
107 W. 27th Street
New York, NY 10012
(212) 620-9111

Custom banners and flags in nylon, canvas, cotton, felt, and satin; can work from sketch or "suggestion." It has done banners for, among other large clients, Lincoln Center, in New York. Works with designers, advertising agencies, etc. Willing to fabricate any type of fiber art.

Art Flag Co., Inc.
Attn. David Annis
87 Fifth Avenue
New York, NY 10003
(212) 929-3035
(212) 473-8282

Established in 1929, this company's specialty is banners for businesses, museums, cities, etc. Has done banners for Lincoln Center and the Metropolitan Museum in NYC.

Continental Awnings & Canopies
342 E. 85th Street
New York, NY
(212) 988-0272

This company has an artist on staff who can do decorative work including silkscreening and handpainting of awnings. In addition to stationary awnings it does rollups, canopies, and marquees. Will make own designs or will fabricate the designs of others. Works in canvas, vinyl, plastics. Residential and commercial. Specializes in working with architects and contractors.

Jensen-Lewis Co., Inc.
98 Seventh Avenue
New York, NY 10011
(212) 929-4880

Specializes in custom work for architects and designers. Works in canvas and prefers doing custom work from a measured drawing. Residential and commercial.

Port Chester Shade and Awning Co.
60 Westchester Avenue
Port Chester, NY 10573
(914) 939-0441

Specialty: electronic welding of vinyl materials (50-foot electronic welding machine); this guarantees that the cover will be waterproof. Also all kinds of canvas work. Commercial and residential.

South

Dixie-Todd Awning Co.
215-17 Third Avenue W.
Birmingham, AL 35204
(205) 322-1859

Specializes in residential and commercial canvas applications.

Georgia Tent and Awning Co.
Attn. Robert M. Spooner, President
228 Margaret Street S.E.
Atlanta, GA 30315
(800) 241-5868
(404) 523-7551

Specialty: awnings, canopies, and other custom canvas products. Commercial and residential.

Coastal Canvas Products Co.
P.O. Box 1493
6A Industry Drive
Savannah, GA 31402
(912) 236-2416

Canvas, nylon, and plastic awnings and canopies. Custom from working drawings only.

The Carroll Awning Co.
Attn. James E. Carroll, Jr.
3108 Frederick Avenue
Baltimore, MD 21229
(301) 945-0022

Specializes in custom canvas products. Commercial and residential.

F. W. Haxel Co.
202 N. Pearl Street
Baltimore, MD 21201
(301) 539-5579

Specializes in custom canvas—of all shapes and sizes. Also manufactures flags and banners. Commercial and residential.

F. M. Stevenson Co., Inc.
2000 Asquith Street
Baltimore, MD 21218
(301) 243-2828

Works in canvas, nylon, plastics, and woven acrylics. In addition to awnings and canopies and "graphic panels," it does custom fabrication of industrial products. Specializes in custom fabrication. Commercial and residential. Preliminary design only from sketch.

Moran Canvas Products, Inc.
P.O. Box 8271
393 Wilmington Street
Jackson, MS 39204
(601) 373-4051

"Thirty years in the canvas world. If it's made of canvas, we make it." Moran also works in nylon, plastics, and metal.

Clark Art Shop, Inc.
300 Glenwood Avenue
Raleigh, NC 27603
(919) 832-8319

Specializes in custom canvas work from rough sketch, photo, or more detailed information. Residential and commercial.

Cool Temp Awning Co., Inc.
6005 Two Notch Road
Columbia, SC 29204
(803) 754-7416

Vinyl and aluminum awnings. Custom work from sketch, photo, or more detailed information. Residential and commercial.

Memphis Delta Tent and Awning Co.
P.O. Box 287
Memphis, TN 38101
(901) 522-1238

Specializes in canvas products. Also works in aluminum. Commercial and residential.

Anacostia-Suburban Awning and Shade Co.
1107 West Street S.E.
Washington, DC 20020
(202) 678-2210

Specializes in canvas awnings. Commercial and residential.

Beck's Home Improvements, Inc.
2902 Piedmont Road
Charleston, WV 25311
(304) 343-6316
(304) 925-4322

Specialty: canvas and vinyl sunshades. Also works in aluminum. Commercial and residential.

Midwest

Awnco, Inc.
Attn. Roy C. Schweinfurth, President
9301 S. Western Avenue
Chicago, IL 60620
(312) 239-1511

Awnco specializes in complicated custom work of all types. Commercial and residential.

The Canvas Smith, Inc.
165 N. Morgan Street
Chicago, IL 60607
(312) 666-0400

Speciality: "Commercial work of unusual or difficult nature." Will work in any fabric.

Custom-bilt Awning Co.
Attn. Frank J. Pobuda
116 Jackson Avenue N.
Hopkins, MN 55343
(612) 935-3545
(612) 941-1079

Fabric, aluminum, and fiber glass. Commercial and residential.

Canvas Products and Repair
Attn. John M. Matson
1139 Payne Avenue
St. Paul, MN 55101
(612) 771-2876

Works in canvas, nylon, and plastics. Commercial and residential.

Baker-Lockwood-Western Awning Co.
12918 Second Street
Grandview, MO 64030
(816) 761-2443

In business since 1870. Specializes in awnings and other canvas products. Commercial and residential.

Jefferson Tent and Awning Co.
2930 Gravois Avenue
St. Louis, MO 63118
(314) 776-0162

Specializes in canvas work of all types. Commercial and residential.

Canvas Products Co.
9100 Bank Street
Cleveland, OH 44125
(216) 524-5770

Custom work in canvas, nylon, vinyl, and neoprene. Commercial and residential.

Queen City Awning and Tent Co.
Attn. Robert P. Weingartner
318 E. Eighth Street
Cincinnati, OH 45202
(513) 241-0437

In business since 1877. Stationary and retractable awnings. Specializes in commercial installations, but will do residential too.

Columbus Tent and Awning Co.
593 S. Front Street
Columbus, OH 43215
(614) 224-4288

Canvas awnings; also flags, tents, and specialties. Residential and commercial.

American Tent and Awning Co.
Attn. Ralph Allen
1105 N. Cliff Avenue
Sioux Falls, SD 57103
(605) 332-3981

Specialty: custom awnings and canopies. Works in coated polyester, nylon, and canvas. Commercial and residential.

Dakota Awning and Siding Co.
Attn. Mal Hay, Sales Manager
321 N. Dakota Avenue
Sioux Falls, SD
(605) 334-2041

Works in canvas and aluminum. Commercial and residential.

Clanton's Quality Awning Co.
Attn. Calvin Walker
3111 N. Fitzhugh
Dallas, TX 75204
(214) 521-0424

"The canvas professionals." Commercial and residential.

American Awning and Shade Shop
Attn. Corky Sarvis
8310-A Speedway
San Antonio, TX 78230
(512) 344-6275

Specializes in residential and commercial custom canvas awnings.

Rockies and Far West

Sullivan Co.
245 S. Van Ness Avenue
San Francisco, CA 94103
(415) 861-4455

Specializes in commercial awnings and canopies.

Sidestreet Bannerworks
Denver, CO 80202

See listing under Fiber Art.

North Coast Canvas Products Co.
1916 N.W. Overton
Portland, OR 97209
(503) 227-2482

Custom awnings and canopies in canvas, nylon, and plastics. North Coast works from rough sketch or photo.

Pike Tent and Awning Co.
417 N.W. Third Avenue
Portland, OR 97209
(503) 226-4397

Works in canvas, nylon, acrylics, and dacron. Commercial and residential.

Key

See also Sculptors for artists who work in this material.

X Services, technique, or material is available
+ See listing for further information
* Sometimes offers this service

	Custom work from sketch	Custom work from working drawings	Materials: Canvas	Materials: Nylon	Materials: Plastics	Materials: Other	Brochure available	Will send samples	Telephone estimate	Banners
Northeast										
Cunningham and Upson New Haven, CT			X	X	X			X	X	
New Haven Awning New Haven, CT	X	X	X	X	X	X		X	X	
Better Homes Bangor, ME	X	X	X			X			X	
Alfred G. Peterson & Sons Avon, MA	X	+	X	X	X	X	X	X	*	X
Pelletier Custom Decorators Salem, MA		X	X	X		X	X	X	X	
Morgan Industries Somerville, MA	X	X	X	X		X	X	X	X	
Warren Strohmeyer Maywood, NJ	+	X	X		X			X	X	
Canvas World Alplaus, NY	X	X	X	X	X	X		X	X	
Acme Awnings Bronx, NY		+	X	X	X	X		X		
Armor Canvas Products Brooklyn, NY	X	X	X	X				X	X	
King Awning & Shade Brooklyn, NY		X	X		X	X				
William J. Mills Greenport, NY	X	X	X	X	X		X	X		
S. L. Doery & Son Lawrence, NY		+	X		X	X			X	
Ace Banner and Flag New York, NY	X	X	X	X		X			X	X
Art Flag New York, NY	X	X		X			X	X	X	X
Continental Awnings New York, NY	X	X	X		X			X	*	
Jensen-Lewis New York, NY		+	X					X		
Port Chester Shade and Awning Port Chester, NY	X	X	X	X	X			X	X	
South										
Dixie-Todd Awning Birmingham, AL	X	X	X	X	X		X		X	
Georgia Tent and Awning Atlanta, GA	X	X	X	X	X		X	X	X	

AWNINGS

Key

See also Fiber Art for artists who work in this material.

X Service, technique, or material is available
\+ See listing for further information
* Sometimes offers this service

	Custom work from sketch	Custom work from working drawing	Materials: Canvas	Materials: Nylon	Materials: Plastics	Materials: Other	Brochure available	Will send samples	Telephone estimates	Banners
Coastal Canvas Products Savannah, GA		X	X	X	X			X		
The Carroll Awning Baltimore, MD		X	X					X	X	
F. W. Haxel Baltimore, MD	X	X	X	X	X		X	X	X	X
F. M. Stevenson Baltimore, MD	+	X	X	X	X	+			X	
Moran Canvas Products Jackson, MS		X	X	X	X		X	X	X	
Clark Art Shop Raleigh, NC	X	X	X				X			
Cool Temp Awning Columbia, SC	X	X			X	+			X	
Memphis Delta Tent and Awning Memphis, TN	X	X	X	X	X	+		X	X	
Anacostia-Suburban Awning Washington, DC	X	X	X	X			X	X	X	
Beck's Home Improvements Charleston, WV	X	X	X	X	X	+	X	X	X	
Midwest										
Awnco Chicago, IL	X	X	X		X		X	X	X	
The Canvas Smith Chicago, IL	X	X	X	X		+	X	X	X	
Custom-bilt Awning Hopkins, MN	X	X				+	X	X		
Canvas Products and Repair St. Paul, MN	X	X	X	X						
Baker-Lockwood-Western Grandview, MO	X	X	X	X	X		X	X	X	
Jefferson Tent and Awning St. Louis, MO	X	X	X						X	
Canvas Products Cleveland, OH	X	X	X	X	X			X	X	
Queen City Awning Cincinnati, OH	X	X	X	X			X	X	X	
Columbus Tent and Awning Columbus, OH	X	X	X							
American Tent and Awning Sioux Falls, SD	X	X	X	X	X	+	X	X	*	

Key

See also Fiber Art for artists who work in this material.

X Service, technique, or material is available
+ See listing for further information
* Sometimes offers this service

	Custom work from sketch	Custom work from working drawing	Materials				Brochure available	Will send samples	Telephone estimates	Banners
			Canvas	Nylon	Plastics	Other				
Dakota Awning and Siding Sioux Falls, SD	X	X	X			+	X	X	X	
Clanton's Quality Awning Dallas, TX	X	X	X		X		X	X	X	
American Awning and Shade San Antonio, TX	X	X	X	X	X			X	X	
Rockies and Far West										
Sullivan San Francisco, CA	X	X	X	X	X			X		
Sidestreet Bannerworks Denver, CO	See listing under Fiber Art									
North Coast Canvas Products Portland, OR	X	X	X	X	X		X	X	X	
Pike Tent and Awning Portland, OR	X	X	X	X	X	+		X	*	

BRICK AND TERRACOTTA

Perhaps the earliest burned bricks were used in Babylonia nearly six thousand years ago. The practical-minded Romans perfected this material, introduced the kiln, and invented a variety of molded shapes. At Pompeii one can still see fluted columns of molded brick that were stuccoed and painted to look like marble.

In most of Europe brick-making went out with the Roman Empire and was revived only during the Middle Ages. By the seventeenth century it was again in vogue; London was rebuilt largely in brick after the Great Fire of 1666. Even before that time the first bricks had reached the New World; Dutch bricks were used to build on Manhattan Island in 1633.

Of the millions of bricks produced in this country in recent decades most have been laid in running bond, all stretcher courses in one plane. The result has been thousands of acres of characterless façades. Yet with minor changes even flat brick walls can be interesting. The back wall of the Fisher Building in Detroit looks as though it has attached pilasters, while in fact it is smooth as can be. This illusion is created by patterns made of different color bricks.

Other variables include mortar color (see Riverton Industries under "Special" below), surface textures, glazes, and type of pointing. Bas-relief patterns can be made by cantilevering or recessing bricks either singly or in groups. All of these can be done with readymade or custom bricks. Ventilating bricks, with small holes for air circulation, are also available.

Because it is modular, brick readily offers designers an opportunity to develop their own decorative systems by working with a few basic shapes that are combined in different ways. See the drawings of brick patterns from Yemen (from an unpublished manuscript by Alain and Marie Agnes Bertaud).

Many of the companies we list provide exceptional services to designers interested in executing original brickwork. They can match any sample in color, texture, and shape. Their stocks include shapes for making arches (with and without moldings), round entrances, cove bases, step treads, rosettes, keystones, watertables, squints, doglegs, radials, and date blocks. Wirecut brick and shapes for sills and copings are also available. Some manufacturers will produce large, single-unit panels, but advise working with a technical consultant during the design phase. Also, a number of companies, like the Glen-Gery Corporation, welcome small orders of handmade molded brick. Still others will permit artists to come into their factories to carve "green" brick (brick before it is fired) for murals; after firing, the brick is assembled by bricklayers on the site.

A number of companies have representatives around the country; to locate them, contact the home office. The brick industry itself also has representatives in principal cities. The two primary sources for locating a bricklayer who specializes in laying complex, ornamental patterns in your community are: (1) "mason contractors" (in business directory), and (2) the local bricklayer's union. The union will know which members have the skills to do your job. We were told that unions sometimes ask an older man to come out of retirement for particularly complicated work. Apprentice programs exist to teach ornamental work, but until the demand increases, these will lag behind.

Terracotta is an equally ancient material. A sixth-century

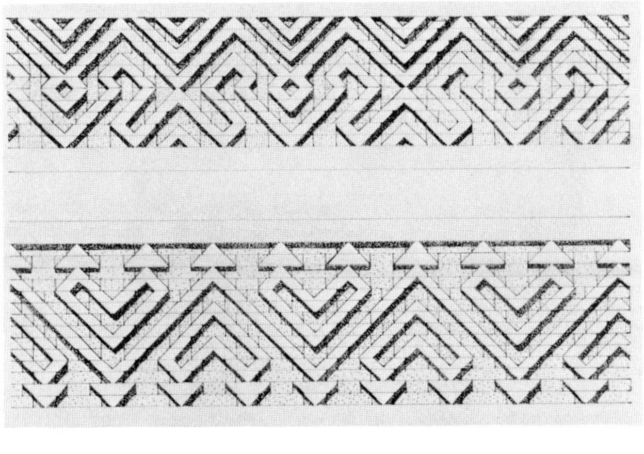

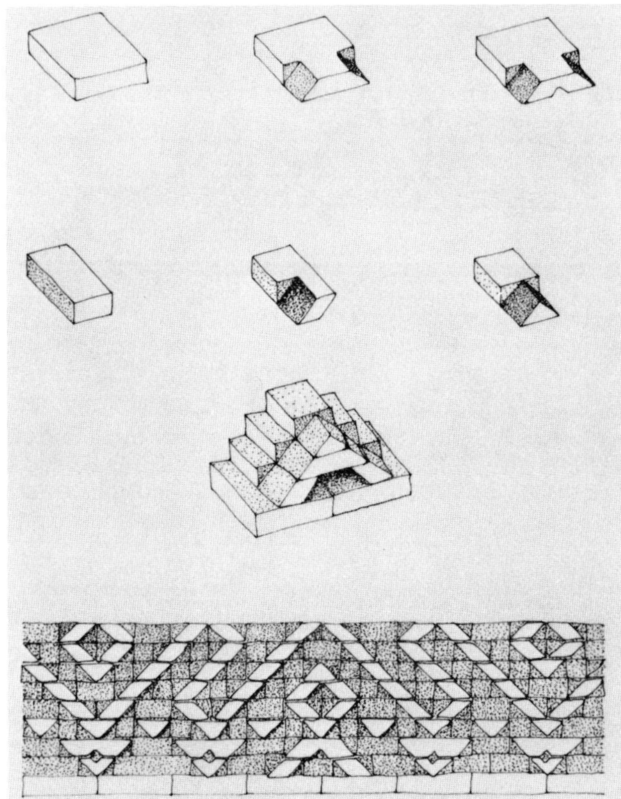

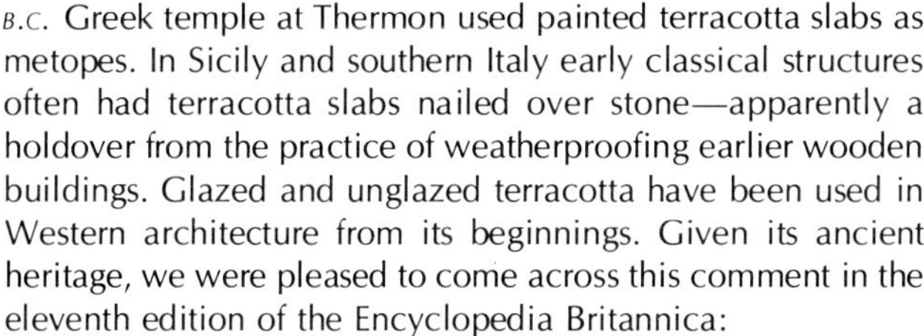

Brick patterns from Yemeni architecture. Because brick is modular and easily shaped before firing it has been used for millennia to create highly decorative patterns. The patterns shown here are a small selection of the traditional brick patterns found in North Yemen. The complexity of the designs belie the simplicity of the system that created them. The patterns are composed of six shapes (with one slight modification) made from two sizes of brick (a square and a half-square); these are used whole or cut in one of two ways. Square bricks similar to the type shown are available from several manufacturers listed. Similar decorative systems could be based on a standard brick. (Drawings courtesy of the artist, Marie Agnes Bertaud)

B.C. Greek temple at Thermon used painted terracotta slabs as metopes. In Sicily and southern Italy early classical structures often had terracotta slabs nailed over stone—apparently a holdover from the practice of weatherproofing earlier wooden buildings. Glazed and unglazed terracotta have been used in Western architecture from its beginnings. Given its ancient heritage, we were pleased to come across this comment in the eleventh edition of the Encyclopedia Britannica:

> The present method of constructing buildings of reinforced concrete, faced with glazed or unglazed terracotta, will afford architects of the twentieth century an unrivaled opportunity for the use of the materials.

It is not too late to start.

The decorative possibilities of terracotta are as varied as those of brick. In fact, it is the same material. Terracotta can be integrated into a structural or curtain wall, or used as an accessory—urns, planters, screens, lighting fixtures, fountains, etc. Terracotta is also surprisingly durable, even in harsh Northern climates. Cass Gilbert's Woolworth Building, in New York City, recently had extensive repairs on its terracotta exterior for the first time in over sixty years.

Gladding McBean, in California, is the only terracotta company in the United States now producing a variety of custom, decorative architectural elements. However, a representative of that company said that many defunct terracotta companies exist under other names, and can do repairs and small terracotta jobs.

Carved brick relief by Harold Balazs. Public Library, Richland, WA. Durham, Anderson & Freed, Architects. (Photo courtesy of Mutual Materials, Bellevue, WA)

Gladding McBean also told us that, while one-of-a-kind items are expensive to produce, the cost drops quickly as the mold is reused, so it is most economical to design repetitive ornament. This does not mean that the design need be all the same, however. A few shapes or patterns can be assembled in different ways to achieve considerable variety.

Special Listings

Brick Institute of America
Attn. C. N. Farley
1750 Old Meadow Road
McLean, VA 22101
(703) 893-4010

The Brick Institute has printed material about the use of brick and can refer you to fabricators and suppliers in your area. Some publications are for sale. They also have a masonry computer-analysis program. "Brick In Architecture," an eight-page, four-color magazine featuring noteworthy nonresidential brick architecture, is issued bimonthly.

The Bricklayers and Allied Craftsmen
Attn. John P. Joyce or Merlin L. Taylor
815 15th Street N.W.
Washington, D.C. 20005
(202) 783-3788

This organization represents a total of 135,000 bricklayers, stone masons, marble masons, tile setters, terrazzo workers, mosaic installers, plasterers, cast stone workers, cement masons, and stucco workers. Contact them to find a skilled mechanic in any of these areas; they will have the proper union local contact you with names, addresses, and phone numbers of the appropriate workers. They like to recommend seasoned mechanics to work along with younger ones so the latter can profit from contact with experienced workers. Many of the older workers are able to "improvise" a design if you give them something less than a detailed working drawing. They offer programs for upgrading members' skills, and train 10,000 apprentices each year in these fields.

The Riverton Corporation
Riverton, VA 22651
(800) 572-2480
(800) 336-2490 (outside VA)

This company produces, among other things, coloring for mortar. They have 800 colors from which to choose. Colored mortar has the remarkable ability to change the apparent color of the brick which it binds. As 20 percent of every brick wall is mortar, colored mortar has a decisive effect on the wall's appearance. It is possible to vary the color of the mortar in bands of horizontal courses to achieve a striped effect.

The Studio of Jack and Eva Grauer
Memphis, TN 38117

See listing under Sculpture.

Regional Listings

Northeast

Architectural Brick Co.
425 Washington Avenue
North Haven, CT 06473
(203) 239-2504

Distributor of Glen-Gery brick products. Specializes in ornamental designs, special shapes, date bricks; glazed and unglazed. Molded, wirecut, and pavers in many textures and colors.

Morin Brick Co.
Danville, ME 04223
(207) 784-9375

Manufacturer and distributor; hand- and machine-molded standard and custom shapes (from working drawing only). Morin can match color, texture, and shape of sample; and has done restoration work. Artist can carve green brick in factory.

Stiles & Hart Brick Co.
Cook Street
Box 367
Bridgewater, MA 02324
(617) 697-6928

Manufacturer making standard and custom shapes; machine- and hand-molded. Custom shapes from sketch, photo, or drawing. This company has done restoration work and can match a sample. Specializes in molded paving brick and molded waterstruck brick. Artists can come to the factory to carve green brick. Catalog of paving brick only.

Spaulding Brick Co., Inc.
120 Middlesex Avenue
Somerville, MA 02145
(617) 666-3200

Distributor. Can arrange for carving green brick in factory.

Kane-Gonic Brick Corp.
Attn. Walter W. Walsh
Winter Street
Gonic, NH 03867
(603) 332-2861

Manufacturer of Harvard Waterstruck Brick. Makes many sizes and special shapes (hand- and machine-molding). Custom shapes from working drawing only. Also flashed colors and various shades of reds to match old brick. Kane-Gonic manufactured brick for the South Street Seaport Restoration, in lower Manhattan. An artist can carve green brick in the factory.

Binghamton Brick Co., Inc.
P.O. Box 1256
Binghamton, NY 13902
(607) 722-0420

Manufacturer. Makes custom shapes with machine and hand molds, from working drawing only. Can match color, sample, and shape; can and have done restoration work.

A number of the brick manufacturers listed will let sculptors come to the factory to carve green brick; it is then put together on site by bricklayers. This work, being carved by Ken Williams at Summit Brick, was installed on Minnequa Elementary School, Pueblo, CO. Hurtig, Gardner & Froelich, Architects. (Photo by John Suhay)

Glen-Gery Corp.
Attn. Mr. Galgano
227 N. 5th Street
Reading, PA 19601
(215) 374-4011

Manufacturer. Glen-Gery was founded in 1890. It owns Alwine Brick, founded 1851, a company noted for its ability to produce handmade bricks (marketed under the name "Oxford"). Stock custom shapes include rosettes, cornices, Holy Water fonts, name bricks, corner curves, incised crosses, plus a variety of watertable shapes with interior and exterior corners. Also manufactures flat, circular, semicircular, elliptical, and segmental arches; wall copings; treads; and pavers of different shapes. Glen-Gery welcomes small orders of handmade bricks. Contact the company for a complete listing of the several hundred distributors around the country. Also produces concrete block.

Hanley Brick, Inc.
Administrative Office
Summerville, PA 15864
(814) 856-2181

Manufacturer. Specializes in glazed brick.

South

Palmer Brick and Tile
2304 Fourth Street
Tucker, GA 30084
(404) 934-7628

Distributor. Can arrange for artist to carve green brick in factory and can make bas-relief panels. Handles glazed and unglazed brick.

General Shale Products Corp.
212 South Park Road
Louisville, KY 40118
(502) 368-2551

Manufacturer. Makes custom shapes only; no custom colors.

Acme Brick Co.
7045 Read Boulevard
New Orleans, LA 70127
(504) 242-4950

This large manufacturer of extruded brick has several factories and sales offices in Arkansas, Kansas, Louisiana, Missouri, Oklahoma, Tennessee, and Texas. Call or write for a complete listing. Also distributes bricks from some smaller companies. Can match color, texture, and (sometimes) shape. Will make murals at some locations.

St. Joe Brick Works, Inc.
P.O. Box 400
740 Gause Boulevard
Slidell, LA 70459
(504) 643-2444

Manufacturer making custom, machine-molded shapes from a measured drawing. All shapes must fit within a standard brick mold. Special shape orders must be accompanied by a minimum 90,000 face brick order. Colors limited to certain pastels (dictated by native clay) and manganese gray to black shades. An artist can carve green brick in factory.

Pen Mar Co., Inc.
Attn. Benjamin J. Davis
1320 N. Monroe Street
Baltimore, MD 21217
(301) 523-5400

Distributor of molded bricks by Bickerstaff, Glen-Gery, and Old Carolina Brick Co.

Macon, Inc.
1220 Nebel Street
Rockville, MD 20852
(301) 881-2616

Manufactures terracotta chimney pots.

Potomac Valley Brick and Supply Co.
5515 Randolph Road
Rockville, MD 20852
(301) 770-3770

Distributor. Can match color and texture of a sample. Will accept any size order.

Victor Cushwa and Sons, Inc.
Attn. David K. Cushwa IV
P.O. Box 228
Williamsport, MD 21795
(301) 223-7700

Manufacturer. Manufacturers of "Calvert" sand-molded brick. Has been making molded brick since 1872 in standard and custom sizes, numerous shapes, machine- and hand-textured. Stock includes watertables, radials, jambs, angles, doorways (complete with pilasters, capitals, and bases), molded arches (flat, round, segmental, and elliptical), and surrounds (traditional and contemporary). Glazed (headers only) and unglazed.

Corbeled brick ornamental pattern. University of Chicago.

"Truck Driver" (8 by 3 inches). Brick sculpture by Richard S. Beyer, Mutual Materials, Bellevue, WA. (Photo by Art Holt & Assoc.)

Borden Brick & Tile Co.
Hoover Road
P.O. Box 11558
Durham, NC 27703
(919) 596-8241

Manufacturer. Standard shapes include watertables, sill and tread brick, and corners. Will make custom designs and give technical help in design process. Borden can generally match its own brick colors. Telephone estimates can be given but Borden prefers to make estimates from a sketch. Artists can come to the factory to carve green brick. Also, can recommend artists who will carve.

Boren Clay Products Co.
Attn. Bruce Benchler
Vice President of Sales and Marketing
Pleasant Garden NC 27313
(919) 674-2255

Manufacturer. Artists can carve green brick in the factory. Manufactures a variety of shapes: watertables, sills, sill returns, wall caps, ogee (headers, sills, corners, wall ends, post caps), bullnose, and arches.

Logo for Washington Mutual Savings Bank, Seattle, WA by the art staff of Mutual Materials, Bellevue, WA. (Photo by Art Holt & Assoc.)

Custom Brick Co.
1613 Old Louisburg Road
Raleigh, NC 27604
(919) 832-2804

Distributor; can match a sample.

Old Carolina Brick Co.
Rte. 9, Box 77
Majolica Road
Salisbury, NC 28144
(704) 636-8850

Manufacturer. An "unlimited variety" of custom shapes are available from this company. Artists can carve green brick in factory. Numerous hand-molded shapes available, including watertable, ogee, bullnose, cove, window sill, etc. Glazed and unglazed.

Ben Peters Brick, Inc.
P.O. Box 30686
Charleston, SC 29407
(803) 556-1922

Distributor; can match a sample.

United Materials and Services, Inc.
7117 Wimsatt Drive
P.O. Box 1446
Springfield, VA 22151
(703) 941-0200

Distributor. Machine- and handmade custom shapes from sketch. On request, will recommend an artist who can carve brick in the factory.

Midwest

Hoiss-Kuhn-Chuman Co.
2723 W. 47th Street
Chicago, IL 60632
(312) 927-6414

Distributor. Can match color, texture, and shape of sample. Can arrange for artist to carve green brick in certain factories.

Carved brick "Fish" mural (standard size brick). By Richard S. Beyer for the Newport Library, Newport, WA. Fabricated by Mutual Materials, Bellevue, WA. (Photo by Hugh N. Stratford)

"Turtles" (standard size bricks). By the art staff of Mutual Materials, Bellevue, WA. (Photo by Art Holt & Assoc.)

Mara Smith
Naperville, IL 60540

See listing under Sculpture.

Belden Brick Co.
P.O. Box 910
700 Tuscarawas Street W.
Canton, OH 44701
(216) 456-0031

Manufacturer selling through distributors. Hand- and machine-molded, glazed and unglazed custom shapes from sketch. Will match a sample in color, texture, and shape; and will make pieces for murals. Artists can go to the factory to carve green brick. Large, small, and one-of-a-kind orders.

The Galena Brick Co.
66 Holmes Street
Galena, OH 43021
(614) 965-1010

Manufacturer. Makes custom, unglazed shapes in hand molds from measured drawing only. Can match sample's color, texture, and shape. Has done restoration work. Accepts large, small, and one-of-a-kind orders.

Richland Brick
Division of Michigan Brick, Inc.
P.O. Box 457
Mansfield, OH 44901
(419) 884-1905

Manufacturers of hand-molded brick; standard and custom shapes (from working drawing only).

"Human Fly" (standard size bricks). By Richard S. Beyer. Fabricated by Mutual Materials, Bellevue, WA. (Photo by Art Holt & Assoc.)

Brick reliefs. By Ken Williams for the Minnequa Elementary School, Pueblo, CO. Hurtig, Gardner & Froelich, Architects. (Photo courtesy of Summit Pressed Brick and Tile Co.)

Superior Clay Products
Uhrichsville, OH 44683
(614) 922-4122

Manufacturer of terracotta chimney pots.

Ochs Brick and Tile Co.
15300 State Highway 5
Eden Prairie, MN 55344
(612) 937-9430

Distributor and manufacturer. Will match sample and can produce custom, hand-molded brick from working drawing only. Artists can carve green brick in factory.

Midwest Brick and Supply Co.
6530 Cambridge Street
Minneapolis, MN 55426
(612) 933-3889

Distributors of Bickerstaff and Cushwa. Has done restoration work.

Endicott Clay Products Co.
Box 17
Fairbury, NE 68352
(402) 729-3315

Manufacturer. Can recommend an artist to work with architect and arrange to have green brick carved in the factory.

Elgin-Butler Brick Co.
4000 Interregional Highway
P.O. Box 1947
Austin, TX 78767
(512) 453-7366

Manufacturer . Glazed and unglazed surfaces as well as structural glazed tile suitable for exterior use. Artists can carve green brick in the factory.

Rockies and Far West

Gladding McBean
P.O. Box 97
Lincoln, CA 95648
(916) 645-3341
and
P.O. Box 160448
Sacramento, CA 96816
(916) 444-9304

Extensive experience in all facets of ornamental terracotta architectural elements. Gladding McBean can match the shape and texture of any tile or terracotta ornament. The clay is naturally tan but, with additives, can match any color. Can also match the color of any glazed brick with glazed terracotta. Provides technical details of construction and installation methods.

Sculptor, draughtsmen, and glaze ceramicist on staff. Cus-

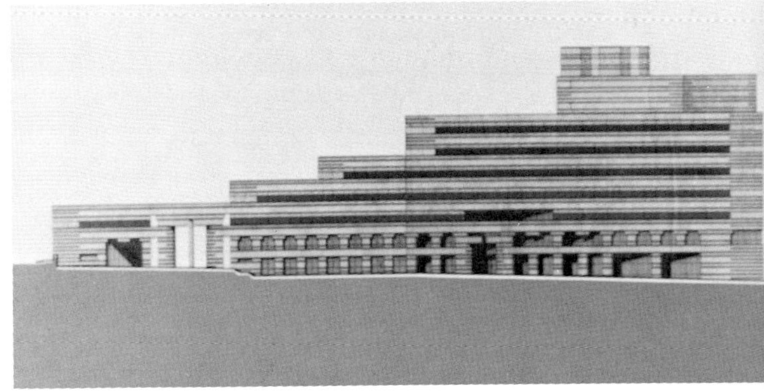

Banded brick used with clear and gray reflective glass. Prudential Building, Van Ness-Metro Center, Washington, DC. Hartman-Cox, Architects, Washington, DC. (Rendering courtesy of Hartman-Cox, Architects)

Arched pediment with brackets in molded brick. (Photo courtesy of Glen-Gery Brick Corp., Shoemakersville, PA)

tom designs from sketch, photo, or fragment. Only 10 percent of production is stock items; rest is custom work. Can fabricate bas-relief panels, sculpture, all types of moldings, pediments, pilasters, architraves, friezes, and cornices. The company recently completed an addition to the Hotel Utah, in Salt Lake City; they had provided the original cladding for this building in 1911. The extruded shapes are used as sills, jambs, belt courses, etc. Can produce almost any new shape. Can also provide copings for brick walls that will match any color brick.

Cameo Stone
7452 Varna Avenue
North Hollywood, CA 91605
(213) 982-2240

Manufacturer. Brick veneers which an artist could carve in bas-relief.

Summit Pressed Brick & Tile Co.
P.O. Box 533
Pueblo, CO 81002
(303) 542-8278

Custom, unglazed shapes, hand- and machine-molded. Can work from a sketch and, "sometimes," can match samples in color, texture, and shape. Artist can carve green brick in the factory. Also manufactures pavers, ceramic moldings and borders, and bas-relief panels—all frost resistant. Can put a relief pattern on a paver. No designer on staff, but Summit can recommend one to aid in the design of murals and special patterns.

Ken Williams
Pueblo, CO 81003

See listing under Sculpture.

Advance Brick Co.
2400 S. Highland
Las Vegas, NV 89102
(702) 386-0366

Distributor. Can match sample; has done restoration work. Can arrange for artists to carve green brick in factory.

Brooklyn Boat House, Brooklyn, NY. Exterior glazed terracotta by Gladding McBean, Lincoln, CA.

Detail of the Brooklyn Boat House, Brooklyn, NY. Exterior glazed terracotta by Gladding McBean, Lincoln, CA. (Photo courtesy of Gladding McBean)

Terracotta frieze from the nineteenth century.

Terracotta ornament; Bayard Building (formerly Condict Building). Louis Sullivan, Architect (1898).

Black-glazed brick used ornamentally to liven up the side wall of a New York City apartment building at 455 Park Avenue. Richard Mullen and Peter Palandrani, Architects (1981).

John Rogers
Portland, OR 97222

See listing under Sculpture.

Mutual Materials Co.
P.O. Box 2009
605 119th N.E.
Bellevue, WA 98009
(206) 455-2869

Manufacturer. Specialty: a variety of delightful and unusual hand-carved bricks. Some are single elements, others can be combined to make small (five or six bricks) or somewhat larger murals—abstract or realistic. Some possibilities are a truck driver, fish (recessed), semiabstract tortoises creeping up the wall, man and woman, and wrestlers. Any one of these would make an excellent near eye-level element to relieve an otherwise plain brick wall. Artists can carve green brick in factory. In addition to these small sculptures, Mutual provides other, more "standard" shapes including Roman, Econ, Norman, and a split face brick called Adobe. Also squints, doglegs, bullnose, and special jambs. Can recommend several artists with whom they have worked. Can match shape; possibly color and texture. They make custom shapes from working drawings only, but a sculptor hired by the client can do anything in the factory. Telephone estimates on one handling and firing only. They do a great many special shape orders.

Norm Warsmske
Bellevue, WA 98004

See listing under Sculpture.

Harold Balaz
Mead, WA 99021

See listing under Sculpture.

Richard S. Beyer
Seattle, WA 98112

See listing under Sculpture.

Clayburn, Inc.
8915 152 Avenue N.E.
Redmond, WA 98052
(206) 882-0484
and
P.O. Box 160
Abbotsford, British Columbia
Canada
(604) 859-5288

Manufacturer. Custom, unglazed, machine-molded shapes. Can match sample and will recommend artists (both in Seattle and Vancouver) who can carve green brick in their factory.

Key

See also Sculpture for artists who work in this material.

X Service, technique, or material is available
+ See listing for further information
* Sometimes offers this service

	Distributor	Manufacturer	Machine-molded	Hand-molded	Custom shapes from sketch	Custom shapes from measured drawing	Can match samples	Can make mural pieces	Brochure available	Telephone estimates	Terracotta
Northeast											
Architectural Brick North Haven, CT	X		X	X	X		X		X	X	
Morin Brick Danville, ME	X	X	X	X		X	X				
Stiles & Hart Brick Bridgewater, MA		X	X	X	X		X		+	X	
Spaulding Brick Somerville, MA	X					X	X		X	X	
Kane-Gonic Brick Gonic, NH		X	X	X		X	X				
Binghamton Brick Binghamton, NY		X	X	X		X	X				
Glen-Gery Reading, PA		X	X	X	X		X	X	X		
Hanley Brick Summerville, PA		X	X	X	X		X		X		
South											
Palmer Brick and Tile Tucker, GA	X			X	X		X	X	X	X	
General Shale Products Louisville, KY		X		X	X		X				
Acme Brick New Orleans, LA	X	X	X		X		X	X	X	X	
St. Joe Brick Works Slidell, LA		X	X			X	*		X		
Pen Mar Baltimore, MD	X		X	X							
Macon, Inc. Rockville, MD		X									X
Potomac Valley Brick Rockville, MD	X						X				
Victor Cushwa & Sons Williamsport, MD	X	X	X	X		X	X	X	X		
Borden Brick & Tile Durham, NC		X		X	X		+	X	X	+	
Boren Clay Products Pleasant Garden, NC		X	X		X		X	X	X		
Custom Brick Raleigh, NC	X						X			X	
Old Carolina Brick Salisbury, NC		X		X	X		X	X	X	X	

Key

See also Sculpture for artists who work in this material.

- **X** Service, technique, or material is available
- **+** See listing for further information
- ***** Sometimes offers this service

	Distributor	Manufacturer	Machine-molded	Hand-molded	Custom shapes from sketch	Custom shapes from measured drawing	Can match samples	Can make mural pieces	Brochure available	Telephone estimates	Terracotta
Ben Peters Brick Charleston, SC	X						X				
United Materials Springfield, VA	X		X	X	X		X	X			
Midwest											
Hoiss-Kuhn-Chuman Chicago, IL	X		X	X	X		X	X		X	
Mara Smith Naperville, IL	See listing under Sculpture										
Belden Brick Canton, OH		X	X	X	X		X	X	X	X	
Galena Brick Galena, OH		X		X		X	X				
Richland Brick Mansfield, OH		X		X		X			X	X	
Superior Clay Products Urichsville, OH		X									X
Ochs Brick & Tile Eden Prairie, MN	X	X		X		X	X	X			
Midwest Brick and Supply Minneapolis, MN	X		X	X		X			X		
Endicott Clay Products Fairbury, NE		X	X			X	X	X		X	
Elgin-Butler Brick Austin, TX		X	X	X	X		X	X	X	X	
Rockies and Far West											
Gladding McBean Lincoln, CA		X	X	X	X		X	X	X		X
Cameo Stone North Hollywood, CA		X		X					X		
Summit Pressed Brick Pueblo, CO		X	X	X	X	X	*	X		X	
Ken Williams Pueblo, CO	See listing under Sculpture										
Advance Brick Las Vegas, NV	X						X				
John Rogers Portland, OR	See listing under Sculpture										
Mutual Materials Bellevue, WA	X	X	X			+	+		X	+	

Key

See also Sculpture for artists who work in this material.

- **X** Service, technique, or material is available
- **+** See listing for further information
- ***** Sometimes offers this service

	Distributor	Manufacturer	Machine-molded	Hand-molded	Custom shapes from sketch	Custom shapes from measured drawing	Can match samples	Can make mural pieces	Brochure available	Telephone estimates	Terracotta
Norm Warsmske Bellevue, WA	See listing under Sculpture										
Harold Balaz Mead, WA	See listing under Sculpture										
Richard S. Beyer Seattle, WA	See listing under Sculpture										
Clayburn, Inc. Redmond, WA		X	X		X		X	X	X	X	

CAST STONE

Cast stone is made from Portland cement, water, and sand, plus marble chips or other types of stone to give the desired surface. Mica, for instance, is added for a touch of brilliance. The properties of cast stone are similar to those of concrete; but, because of the different finishes that can be attained by using exotic stone as aggregate, it creates a richer-appearing ornament than would be possible with ordinary concrete.

Through the use of different aggregates and coloring agents, cast stone can be given the appearance of such other materials as limestone, sandstone, and brownstone. Its ability to hold relatively fine detail in casting makes it appropriate for reproducing most elements and textures—modern and traditional. The only restrictions are that the details must not be too thin or too strongly undercut. Larger panels or decorative pieces are usually made up of several smaller segments.

Many ornamental plaster elements (suitable mainly for interiors) can be reproduced in cast stone for exterior use. Often an element which is produced in cast stone or plaster can also be made in fiber glass. Many of the manufacturers we mention in this section work in all of these materials, and can advise you about which one is best for your needs.

Special Listings

Chicago Plastering Institute
Attn. John Boland, President
5859 W. Fullerton Avenue
Chicago, IL 60639
(312) 237-6910

An organization formed by agreement between the unions and the employers for the purpose of promoting the trade of plastering (including stucco and cast stone). There are over twenty-five similar institutes around the country. They can give printed material, technical advice, and will recommend skilled plaster workers in their area. This Institute represents over 100 contractors in the greater Chicago area who will work anywhere in the region. There is no charge for any services.

Operative Plasterers & Cement Masons Institute of the U.S. & Canada
(OPCMI)
1125 17th Street N.W.
Washington, DC 20036
(202) 393-6569

This is the national headquarters for the 70,000-member union of plasterers, cement masons, casters, modelers, and shophands. They can give technical advice, suggestions on the use of their products, and will recommend skilled mechanics in your area. There is no charge for this service. The national headquarters has an on-the-job and classroom apprentice program. OPCMI can put you in contact with one of the forty or so lathe and plastering promotional bureaus around the United States. These bureaus have access to contractors, designers, materials dealers, building codes, and other information.

Portland Cement Association
Attn. Mario J. Catani
5420 Old Orchard Road
Skokie, IL 60077
(312) 966-6200

This association sells printed material and can give technical advice about the product; seven regional chapters in the United States, five in Canada.

Regional Listings

We list makers of small, decorative cast stone elements, as well as companies who do both small and large, precast concrete elements (panels weighing several tons or more). For additional sources of the latter, see also Concrete.

Northeast

Kenneth Lynch and Sons, Inc.
Wilton, CT 06897

See listing under Metals.

Art Cement Products
120 Old Boston Road
Wilbraham, MA 01095
(413) 596-9391

Produces all types of architectural elements. Art Cement replaced the terracotta on the Woolworth Building with cast stone elements. Can do bas- and high-relief elements. Estimates can be made from a sketch.

W. N. Russell and Co.
Attn. W. N. Russell, III, Vice President
34-60 Albertson Avenue
Westmont, NJ 08108
(609) 858-1057

Specializes in cast stone, including capitals (Doric and composite), moldings, gargoyles, arches, and cornices. Also does sandblasting and incising of cast stone. Preferred styles: Colonial, geometric, and modern. Will give technical advice and can make a pattern, working from a rough sketch or more detailed information. Russell has a sixty-page brochure showing a complete range of modern and traditional styles.

Longdino Stone Co., Inc.
3621 Provost Avenue
Bronx, NY 10466
(212) 324-1439

Balusters, cornices, coping stones, panels, and other architectural elements in a variety of textures and colors. Will give technical advice but does not install. Bas-relief patterns of all sorts, but not figural sculpture. Maximum single panel 4 by 8 feet (approximately four tons); can also do very small items. Longdino has done a great deal of restoration work.

Botanical study of Grandiflora Magnolia in cast stone (originally modeled in plaster) by Raymond Kaskey, Washington, DC. Mounted on exterior façade of new townhouses in historic Georgetown; Robert A. Bell, Architect, Washington, DC. (Photo by Max Hirshfeld)

Saldarini & Pucci
New York, NY 10012

See listing under Plastics.

Ornato Decors
Ridgewood, NY 11385

See listing under Stucco and Plaster.

Felber Studios
Ardmore, PA 19003

See listing under Plastics.

Tayssir Sleiman
Horsham, PA 19044

See listing under Stucco and Plaster.

South

Cut Art Stone Co.
109 W. Victory Drive
Savannah, GA 31405
(912) 234-7223

Company will do small and large jobs. Estimates given from working drawing only. Precasts all types of architectural elements. Can work from rough sketch, model, or working drawing. Casts in variety of colors and surface textures.

Six townhouses, historic Georgetown, Robert A. Bell, Architect, Washington, DC. Façades decorated with rondels by Raymond Kaskey. (Rendering courtesy of Robert A. Bell, Architect)

Albert Lachin and Assocs.
Attn. T. Lachin or J. Shubert, Jr.
2747 Perdido Street
New Orleans, LA 70119
(504) 821-5404
(504) 282-2054

Maker and distributor for four generations in New Orleans. Sells directly or through distributors. Makes all kinds of architectural elements: balusters, bas-reliefs, cornices, coping stones, fountains, etc., in a variety of surfaces. Can work from a sketch, and has their own modelmaker. Large selection of plaster rosettes and moldings, some of which can be made in cast stone. Maximum size is about 4000 pounds per item. Also makes a wide variety of decorative elements in plaster and cast stone including columns, capitals, ceiling domes, balustrades, finials, planters, and fountains. Custom work from sample, sketch, or photo. Can give technical, design, and installation advice. Models made in plaster and clay to architects' specifications. Items are reproduced in plaster and cast stone. They fill large, small and one-of-a-kind orders.

Florence Concrete Products, Inc.
Florence, SC 29502

See listing under Concrete.

Southern Cast Stone Co., Inc.
P.O. Box 1669
Knoxville, TN 37901
(615) 524-3615

Will cast bas-reliefs, cornices, coping stones, band courses, and panels. Variety of surface textures and colors. *(Also listed under "Concrete.")*

Studio of Jack and Eva Grauer
Memphis, TN 38117

See listing under Sculpture.

Midwest

C. G. Girolami
944 N. Spaulding Avenue
Chicago Il 60651
(312) 227-1959

Manufacturer selling directly. Gives technical, design, and installation advice. Models can be made to architects' specifications in plaster, clay, and wood, working from sketch, photo, sample, or working drawing. Will reproduce items from these casts in plaster, fiber glass, and cast stone. Balusters, bas-reliefs, cornices, and coping stones in various colors and surface textures. Fills large, small, and one-of-a-kind orders. No brochure, but has photos of past work.

Hendrix, Heikkilä, and Terry, Inc.
Norman, OK 73069

See listing under Murals.

Orlandini Studios, Ltd.
Decorative Plaster Supply Co.
Milwaukee, WI 53204

See listing under Stucco and Plaster.

Rockies and Far West

Leyva's J. P. Weaver Co.
917 Westminster Avenue
Alhambra, CA 91803
(213) 289-4364

Manufactures columns, balusters, cornice moldings and fireplace mantels in cast stone, fiber glass, and plaster. Modern and traditional designs. Specializes in custom designs; also does restorations.

Olympian Stone Co., Inc.
Box 685
Redmond, WA 98052
(206) 885-2833

Balusters, bas-reliefs, cornices, coping stones, panels; also does incising. Can do a variety of textures and colors with different aggregates. Minimum order. Gives technical advice.

Key

See also Sculpture for artists who work in this material.

- **X** Service, technique, or material is available
- + See listing for further information
- * Sometimes offers this service

	Readymade items	Custom design from sketch	Custom design from measured drawing	Brochure available	Balusters	Bas-reliefs	Cornices	Other architectural elements
Northeast								
Kenneth Lynch and Sons Wilton, CT	See listing under Metals							
Art Cement Products Wilbraham, MA		X	X		X	X	X	+
W. N. Russell Westmont, NJ	X	X	X	X	X	X	X	+
Longdino Stone Bronx, NY		X	X		X	+	X	+
Saldarini & Pucci New York, NY	See listing under Plastics							
Ornato Decors Ridgewood, NY	See listing under Stucco and Plaster							
Felber Studios Ardmore, PA	See listing under Plastics							
Tayssir Sleiman Horsham, PA	See listing under Stucco and Plaster							
South								
Cut Art Stone Savannah, GA	X	X	X		X	X	X	+
Albert Lachin New Orleans, LA		X	X	X	X	X	X	+
Florence Concrete Florence, SC	See listing under Concrete							
Southern Cast Stone Knoxville, TN	X		X			X	X	+
Studio of Jack and Eva Grauer Memphis, TN	See listing under Sculpture							
Midwest								
C. G. Girolami Chicago, IL	X	X	X	X	X		X	+
Hendrix, Heikkilä, and Terry Norman, OK	See listing under Murals							
Orlandini Studios, Ltd. Milwaukee, WI	See listing under Stucco and Plaster							
Rockies and Far West								
Leyva's J. P. Weaver Alhambra, CA	X	X	X	X	X	X	X	+
Olympian Stone Redmond, WA	X	X	X		X	X	X	+

CERAMICS

The range of ceramic ornament—in tiles, murals, plaques, and bas-relief sculpture—is unlimited. Texture, color, and shape are virtually without restriction. Size, too, is unlimited because large compositions can be made of small, easily manageable pieces. Ceramic ornament can be as restrained as a modest decorative plaque or identifying logo, and as aggressive as an undulating dragon who sips the condensation from an unfortunately placed air conditioner (see photo). If you create a two-dimensional pattern of your own, or find one you particularly like, it can be copied onto stock tiles. Designs can be applied by handpainting, silkscreening, or decal. We have noted the companies and ceramic studios that provide this service. Some manufacturers will also produce bas-relief or "dimensional" tiles.

The most common kinds of tiles are:

Ceramic mosaic tiles. These are glazed or unglazed and sold mounted on sheets. (Do not confuse these with glass mosaics which are much smaller and usually composed of irregular shapes.) Standard sizes (1/4-inch thick) are 1 by 1 inch, 2 by 2 inches, or 1 by 2 inches.

Glazed wall tiles. Made of clay combined with limestone, feldspar, or talc; glazed and fired. Normally comes 4 1/2 inches square, 4 by 6 inches, or 6 by 6 inches.

Pavers. These resemble quarry tiles and can be made of either ceramic or shale mixture, but they are pressed rather than extruded.

Quarry tile. Heavy duty, earthy red colors. Standard size, 6 by 6 inches. Traditionally made from clay and shale (hence the name "quarry"). Because quarry tiles are extruded, rather than pressed, they always have a square edge.

The simplest way of using tiles is to insert a small group of them—even one—as a "jewel" in an otherwise blank surface. Another way is to repeat a small pattern composed of a group of, say, four or six tiles. The same element can be grouped in different ways—horizontally, in courses, vertically, around windows and doors, as moldings or coins, in an overall pattern, or as frames or "pictures" in themselves—to create different effects. Finally, individual tiles can be handpainted to make large scale murals.

Depending on your geographical location, it may be important to ensure that exterior tiles are "frost-resistant." This means the tile has vitrified, and so is impervious to moisture and resistant to chipping and cracking from expansion and contraction of trapped moisture in extreme temperatures. Occasional freezing will not necessarily affect nonfrost-resistant tiles, but repeated freezings and thawings will probably destroy them. Local manufacturers, distributors, or ceramic studios will be able to give you reliable information about the durability of their products in your area.

Special Listings

Ceramic Tile Distributors of America
5315 E. Broadway Suite 204
Tucson, AZ 85711
(602) 747-8509

National headquarters for 300 tile distributors around the country. Can recommend suppliers in your area.

"119 Modules." A slip cast porcelain relief (24 by 4 by ½ feet). John Rogers, Portland, OR. (Photo courtesy of John Rogers)

Ceramic Tile Institute
700 N. Virgil Avenue
Los Angeles, CA 90029
(213) 660-1911

Complete technical services to architects, advice about installation, etc. Also a testing program which reviews and reports on new materials and installation techniques.

National Terrazzo and Mosaic Association
Attn. Edward A. Grazzini, Executive Director
3166 Des Plaines Avenue Suite 15
Des Plaines, IL 60018
(312) 635-7744
(800) 323-9736

This organization provides printed material, technical advice, and recommendations about fabricators in your area. No charge for these services. Architects can receive the newsletter by requesting to be put on the mailing list.

Tile Council of America, Inc.
P.O. Box 326
Princeton, NJ 08540
(609) 921-7050

Offers technical advice and printed material at no charge.

Regional Listings

Northeast

Ronald A. Schumann
244 Murphy Road
Hartford, CT 06114
(203) 246-5439

Distributes frost-resistant decorative tiles from Japan, Germany, Italy, and Holland. Also tiles from Mexico, Spain, and Portugal. Provides custom sizes, handpainted and bas-relief tiles; can make murals. Custom decorations manufactured in the United States. A designer on staff to recommend ornamental patterns for exterior use; can also recommend a specialty contractor for exterior murals and complicated decorative installations.

Torre Tile Inc.
237 Ledyard Street
Hartford, CT 06114
(203) 522-0507

Distributes frost-resistant tiles from Mexico, Spain, Japan, and Italy; and nonvitreous tiles from Korea. Has access to designer for decorative patterns; can recommend a specialty contractor for exterior installation of murals and decorative tiles.

Standard Tile Distributors of New Haven, Inc.
293 East Street
New Haven, CT 06511
(203) 777-3637

Distributes nonvitreous tiles from Mexico, Spain, Portugal, Korea, and frost-resistant tiles from Japan, Germany, Italy, and France. Can have custom decorations manufactured in the United States. Has access to a designer to recommend ornamental patterns, and can recommend a specialty contractor for exterior murals and complicated decorative work.

M. G. Martin
590 Upper Grassy Hill Road
Woodbury, CT 06798
(203) 263-3908

This studio does handpainted tiles, bas-relief tiles and panels, ceramic moldings and borders, and silkscreened patterns. Will make and install murals and can decorate ready-made commercial tiles. Can make frost-resistant tiles.

South Shore Tile Distributors, Inc.
Attn. Rick Smethurst
30 Liberty Street
Quincy, MA 02169
(617) 471-3210

Distributor. Can supply frost-resistant tiles and will give technical advice about exterior tile installation.

Top: "Ceramic Monster." An 11-foot-long ceramic wall sculpture designed to catch drips from the air conditioner. By M. G. Martin, Woodbury, CT. (Photo by Roger Barnes) *Left*: "Theodora." A raku-fried, grouted, framed wall piece with "pearls" (detail, 25 by 17 inches; entire piece, 46 by 36 inches). By Christine Sibley. Christine Sibley Pottery, Atlanta, GA. (Photo by Gary Bogue) *Above*: Glazed ceramic tile seal (approximately 44 inches in diameter) by Sim Shields, Houston, TX. (Photo courtesy of Sim Shields)

Detail showing a portion of a 277-foot-long glazed ceramic mural depicting a pre-Columbian heroic saga. Eight of the eleven colors are custom glazes. Edward R. Roybal Comprehensive Health Center, Los Angeles, CA. Daniel, Mann, Johnson, & Mendenhall, Architects, Los Angeles, CA. Mural by Franciscan Studio Ceramics, Los Angeles, CA. (Photo by Wayne Thom Assocs.)

Tile Internation, Inc.
319 Waverly Oaks Road (Rte. 60)
Waltham, MA 02154
(617) 899-8286

Distributes tiles from Japan and Italy. Custom decorations (handpainted or silkscreened) and shapes can be manufactured in Italy. Will recommend a specialty contractor for murals and decorative installations.

Albert F. Fitzgerald, Inc.
120 Commerce Way
Woburn, MA 01806
(617) 935-7821

Distributes tiles from Mexico, Spain, Italy, England, and Denmark; and frost-resistant tiles from Japan and Germany. Custom decorations and shapes can be manufactured in the United States or in any of the above-mentioned countries. Telephone estimates to the trade. Fitzgerald has a designer for decorative patterns.

Leon I. Nigrosh, Ceramic Designer
11 Chatanika Avenue
Worcester, MA 01602
(617) 757-0401

Does bas-relief tiles and panels and works in "photo clay" decorative technique. Makes ceramic murals and does installation; will decorate readymade commercial tiles.

Tile Fashions, Inc.
The Mall of New Hampshire
1500 S. Willow Street
Manchester, NH 03103
(603) 625-8989

Distributors of handpainted tiles, bas-relief tiles and panels, ceramic moldings and borders, and silkscreened tiles.

Terra Designs, Inc.
211 Jockey Hollow Road
Bernardsville, NJ 07924
(201) 766-3577

Manufactures several unique lines of "pre-Columbian and primitive Americana" tiles; also does custom designed ceramic tiles. All tiles handmade by American craftspeople. Because tiles are handmade, they vary in size and color intensity, and require "nonuniform installation." Colors: unglazed Terra Cotta, Mexicana, Tobacco, Sand. Will contract for custom designs, glazing, and handpainting; metallic lusters and sinage available. Average water absorbency 5 percent.

F. Joseph von Tury
11 Colonial Court
Metuchen, NJ 08840
(201) 549-0071

Von Tury is a well-known expert in ceramics, making tile panels, decorative tiles, mosaic murals, and sculptural ceramics. His works range from the ceramic tile dome of the Iranian Embassy in Washington, D.C., to the Great Seal of New Jersey, done for the Turnpike Authority; and includes handpainted and bas-relief murals. Can supply frost-resistant tiles. He will design his own murals, but also specializes in executing the designs of other artists and architects. He has extensive knowledge of the technical aspects of ceramic design and can, among other things, develop glazes for specific purposes.

Best Tile Distributors
1760 Central Avenue
Colonie, NY 12205
(518) 869-0219

Distributor. Can supply handpainted and decal decorated tiles.

Two prototype designs for ceramic balusters. Designed by Eva Zeisel, New City, NY. Manufactured by Westinghouse Electric Corporation, Industrial Ceramics Department, Porcelain Park, Derry, PA.

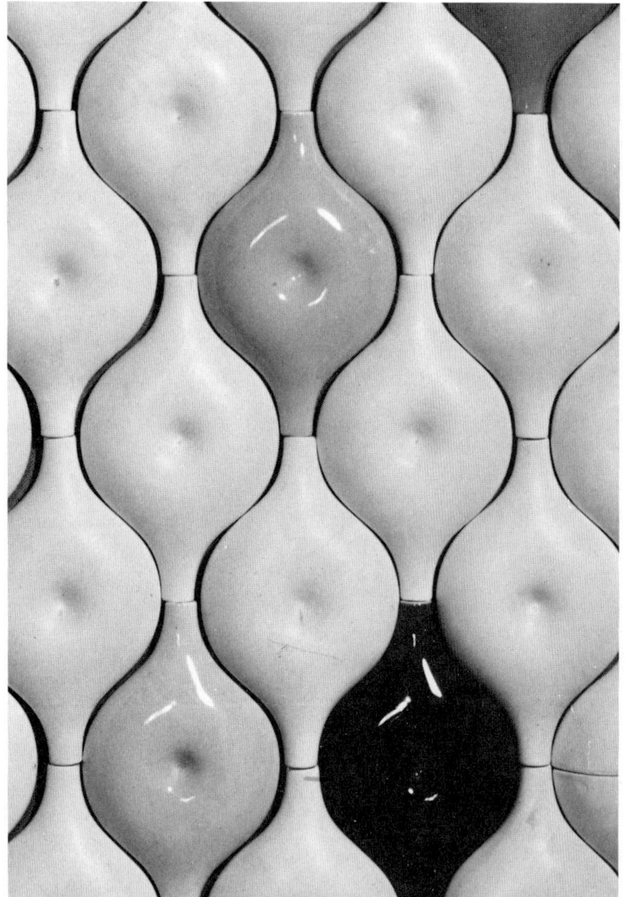

Stoneware wall covering (individual elements approximately 12 by 8 inches). Designed by Eva Zeisel, New City, NY. (Photo courtesy of Eva Zeisel)

Eva Zeisel
455 South Mountain Road
New City, NY 10956
(914) 634-2850
(212) 864-0341

Designer with extensive experience in mass production ceramics of all types including porcelain and stoneware suitable for exterior or interior use. Has a line of three-dimensional, architectural elements which can be produced in porcelain, stoneware, or cast stone, for use as balusters, screens, walls, etc. Photos available.

Amsterdam Tile Corp.
950 Third Avenue
New York, NY 10022
(212) 644-1350

This manufacturer, distributor, and studio can make pavers, quarry tile, glazed decorative tile, mosaic tile, ceramic moldings and borders, bas-relief tiles and panels—all frost-resistant. Will also impress a relief pattern on tiles. Amsterdam does handpainting as well as silkscreening, and has a designer on staff who can work from a rough sketch to make patterns, bas-reliefs, and murals. Also distributes frost-resistant tiles from Spain, Japan, Germany, Italy, and Holland. Brochure $2.50.

Blue Delft Co., Inc.
1201 Broadway
New York, NY 10001
(212) 679-7644

In production since 1661, these are among the most familiar and most beautiful decorative tiles. Their exquisite decorations are all traditional and come in either single or multitile *tableaux* of ship scenes, flowers, old Dutch interiors, and landscapes. Also makes custom decorations—decal, handpainted, or silkscreened. Blue Delft has a designer who can transform your measured drawing into a ceramic tile design.

Country Floors, Inc.
300 E. 61st Street
New York, NY 10021
(212) 758-7414

Distributor of imported tiles from Mexico, Spain, Portugal, Holland, and Israel; frost-resistant tiles from Finland and Italy. Can have custom decorations manufactured in the U.S. and other countries. Will recommend designer for ornamental patterns. Brochure $5.00. Telephone estimates given.

Benoit Gilsoul
New York, NY 10001

See listing under Murals.

Westchester Tile
170 Brook Street
Scarsdale, NY 10583
(914) 725-4355

Distributes frost-resistant tiles from Japan and Germany.

Agency Tile, Inc.
499 Old Nyack Turnpike
Spring Valley, NY 10977
(914) 352-7620

This distributor can have custom sizes and decorations made; distributes tiles from Mexico, Spain, Portugal, and Brazil, frost-resistant tiles from Japan, Germany, and Italy.

Crovatto Mosaics
Attn. Costante Crovatto
319 First Street
Yonkers, NY 10704
(914) 237-6210

A mosaic studio doing interior and exterior mosaic murals. Small or large orders. Designer on staff who can do custom work from sketch.

Twenty-nine story ceramic tile mural at the Hawaiian Village, Honolulu, Hawaii, Designer: Millard Sheets. Franciscan Studio Ceramics, Los Angeles. (Photo by Werner Stoy—Camera Hawaii, courtesy of Franciscan Studio Ceramics)

Ceramic tile mural at Disneyland, Anaheim, CA. Designer: Mary Blair. Franciscan Studio Ceramics, Los Angeles, CA. (Photo by Tri-Ads, courtesy of Franciscan Studio Ceramics)

Moravian Pottery & Tile Works
Swamp Road
Doylestown, PA 18901
(215) 345-6722

This manufacturer merits special mention. The Moravian Tile Factory, in Doylestown, is a registered National Historic Place, a "living" museum producing tiles by the same methods that were used at the turn of the century, when it was founded by a remarkable man, Henry Chapman Mercer (1856–1930). Mercer was dismayed at the loss of crafts—particularly the work of old Pennsylvania German potters—due to industrialization; so this Harvard-educated lawyer apprenticed himself to a potter. He ended up creating a working tile factory, the Moravian Tile Works. For many years it has hand-produced hundreds of patterns—rectangular tiles, individual figures to be inset in walls, mosaics, and separate elements that can be combined to make murals. Mercer's designs for these were derived from designs he saw in castles, monasteries, and abbeys in France and England, as well as from samples in his own collection.

The tiles—of local earthenware clay and fritted lead glazes—are all made by impressing clay with designed molds or, in the case of trim moldings and other bas-relief pieces, by pressing clay into mold cavities. Tiles are available in a range of glazes including a "smoked" finish, a natural terracotta red finish, and colored clay finishes. Mosaics are made by stamping clay onto molds, releasing the clay and then cutting apart the mosaic designs according to the impressed lines. The Pottery also produces borders of various types: half-rounds; rope twist; convex, concave, and step cornices. Given your particular situation, the Pottery's designer can create a decorative installation (mural, etc.) from their own tiles. Tiles are suitable for exterior use in northern climates but, the staff advises, "with caution." Brochure available.

"Birds of Great Kimble" (4-½ by 4-½-inch tile). The Moravian Pottery and Tile Works, Doylestown, PA. (Photo courtesy of The Moravian Pottery and Tile Works)

"Spinning Wool." Mosaic (25 by 25 inches) set in French quarry tile. The Moravian Pottery and Tile Works, Doylestown, PA. (Photo courtesy of The Moravian Pottery and Tile Works)

American Olean Tile Company
1000 Cannon Avenue
Lansdale, PA 19446
(215) 855-1111

Large manufacturer of quarry tile and frost-resistant mosaic tile, readymade only. Maintains a special staff of experts to help in all phases of (frost-resistant) mural design—from basic layout to technical advice about selection of proper tiles. Will work from a detailed drawing or from a rough sketch. Large or small orders. Brochure $1.00 (free to trade). Call or write for names of local representatives.

Design-Technics Ceramics, Inc.
RD 2 Box 2258
Stroudsburg, PA 18360
(717) 421-1230
(Showroom)
160 E. 56th Street
New York, NY 10022
(212) 355-3183

Several very attractive, textured, glazed tiles for exterior use. Can do custom ceramics and any type of bas-relief pattern. Can cast bas-relief panels; does glazed and unglazed tiles. Artists can carve clay tiles and do sculpture in the factory.

Eastern Tile Distributors
543 Atwood Avenue
Cranston, RI 02920
(401) 944-1300

Distributors of tiles from Mexico, Italy, Portugal, and the United States; frost-resistant tiles from Japan. Can have custom decorations made in the United States, and will recommend a specialty contractor for complex ornamental installations. Eastern can also design ceramic murals.

Bannon Tile Distributors, Inc.
160 Pearl Street
Providence, RI 02907
(401) 421-7292

Distributes decorative tiles from Spain, Japan, Germany, and Italy. Can have custom decorations and shapes manufactured in the United States. Staff designer can recommend ornamental patterns for exterior use. Bannon gives technical advice on the exterior installation of tiles and ceramic murals and can supply frost-resistant tiles.

Haskell Pottery
Attn. Jean or Paul Haskell
RD 1
East Highgate, VT 05459
(802) 868-2159

Studio doing custom, handpainted tiles in any style. Standard shapes are 4 by 4 inches and 6 by 6 inches, but custom shapes can be manufactured. Can also decorate ready-made commercial tiles.

South

Forms and Surfaces, Inc.
130 N.E. 40th Street
Miami, FL 33137
(305) 576-1880

Distributor. Can supply custom shapes and sizes, handpainted tiles, bas-relief tiles and panels, ceramic moldings and borders, and silkscreened patterns. Will supply ceramic murals and will supervise installation if contracted to do so. Also supplies cast panels, sculpture walls, porcelain bricks, and overglazed tiles.

Ceramic tile sign for the artist's showroom (3½ by 4 feet): Barbara Vantrease Beall, Torrence, CA. (Photo courtesy of Barbara Vantrease Beall)

Manufacturers Representatives
P.O. Box 370547
Miami, FL 33137
(305) 573-4506
Telex 6811211

This company represents several Italian tile manufacturers that make many different types of glazed decorative and quarry tiles, as well as glass mosaics. Custom decorations, shapes, and mosaics can be manufactured. Small and large orders. Several appealing color brochures.

Christine Sibley Pottery
845 Ashland Avenue N.E.
Atlanta, GA 30307
(404) 525-0595

This studio does custom decorations, sizes, and shapes, including bas-relief tiles. All decorative work is handpainted. Also produces ceramic murals, three-dimensional wall pieces, free-standing forms, and fountains. All can be frost-resistant, suitable for exterior use. Sibley does installation.

Zumpano Enterprises, Inc.
4197 Pleasantdale Road
Atlanta, GA 30340
(404) 449-3528
(404) 233-2943

This ceramic studio creates handpainted tiles, ceramic moldings and borders, and silkscreened patterns as well as designing and installing murals. Will match or create any design. Also distributes tiles from Mexico; frost-resistant tiles from Spain, Japan, Germany, Italy, Portugal, and Holland. Brochure $2.00.

Cameron Covert and Bruce Bobick
Carrollton, GA 30118

See listing under Murals.

Tile House, Inc.
4675 Granite Drive
Tucker, GA 30084
(404) 939-4370

Distributes tiles from Mexico, Japan, Italy, and Holland. Can have custom sizes and decorations manufactured in the United States, and will recommend a specialty contractor for complicated decorative installations.

Mees Distributors, Inc.
608 Locust Lane
Louisville, KY 40213
(502) 634-3606

Distributors of frost-resistant tiles from Mexico, Japan, Germany, and Italy. Also, tiles from Portugal and H. and R. Johnson tiles from England. Can have custom decorations manufactured in the United States, and will recommend a designer and specialty contractor for decorative and mural installations. Call or write for locations of outlets in Kentucky and Ohio.

"Egrets and Heron" (11 by 19½ feet). Ceramic tile mural, Seacliff Village, Huntington Beach, CA. Barbara Vantrease Beall, Torrence, CA. (Photo by Kent Oppenheimer, courtesy of Barbara Vantrease Beall)

Bolick Distributors, Inc.
Attn. A. Ganucheau
3940 Gravier Street
New Orleans, LA
(504) 488-0869

Distributes tiles from Mexico; frost-resistant tiles from Spain, Japan, Germany, and Italy. Can recommend a specialty contractor for exterior murals and special patterns.

Roubion Tile and Marble Co.
8204 Oak Street
New Orleans, LA 70118
(504) 866-3677

Distributes frost-resistant tiles from Mexico, Japan, Germany, and Italy; nonvitreous tiles from Portugal. Can have custom (silkscreened or handpainted) decorations made in the United States; also can supply custom sizes.

Maryland Tile Distributors, Inc.
5600-10 Old Frederick Road
Baltimore, MD 21228
(301) 747-1416

Distributes tiles from Mexico; frost-resistant tiles from Spain, Japan, Italy, and Brazil. Has access to a designer who can do ornamental patterns, and will recommend a specialty contractor for installation.

The Mosaic Tile Company of Maryland
5710 Erdman Avenue
Baltimore, MD 21205
(301) 483-2211

Distributes tiles from Spain, Portugal, Holland, England, and Brazil; frost-resistant tiles from Mexico, Japan, Germany, and Italy. Custom decorations and shapes can be made in the United States and Japan. The company has access to a designer for ornamental patterns, and can recommend a specialty contractor for installation.

Macon, Inc.
12201 Nebel Street
Rockville, MD 20852
(301) 881-2616

Distributes tiles from Mexico, Spain, Japan, Germany, Italy, Portugal, and Holland. Can have custom decorations and shapes manufactured in the United States, and has access to designer for decorations. Will recommend a specialty contractor for installation of decorative patterns. Also distributes Gladding McBean terracotta products.

B.J.'s Ceramic Tile Dist. Co., Inc.
512 Dexter Drive
Jackson, MS 39208
(601) 939-0111

Distributes tiles from Mexico, Spain, Italy, Portugal, Holland, and Brazil; frost-resistant tiles from Japan and Germany.

Can have custom decorations and shapes manufactured in the United States. B.J.'s has access to a designer for decorative patterns, and can recommend a specialty contractor for installation of murals and ornamental patterns.

MaryAnn Fariello
Rte. 1, Box 192
New Hope Road
Alexandria, TN 37012
(615) 529-2990

A manufacturer and studio artist working in porcelain and specializing in tiles. Each job individually considered according to needs of space. Exterior and interior, walls and floors. Will paint or silkscreen on commercial tiles; does bas-relief tiles, friezes, panels, ceramic moldings, double-faced tiles, and murals. Also, garden paths of ceramic tiles, tile/cement combinations, or exposed aggregate concrete. Some of her tiles are designed to be incorporated into brick walls. Custom designs from sketch or more detailed information. Gives technical advice for exterior tile and mural installation. Send stamped self-addressed envelope for brochure.

Mosaic Tile Co. of Virginia
8379 Terminal Road
Newington, VA 22122
(703) 550-9525

Distributors of frost-resistant tiles. Gives technical advice about exterior installation of tiles and murals.

Ademas
721 8th Street S.E.
Washington, DC 20002
(202) 547-5100

Distributes frost-resistant tiles from Mexico, Spain, and Italy (terracotta and glazed); other tiles from Portugal, Holland, Israel, and France. The frost-resistant tiles are mainly terracotta. Brochure $5.00.

Midwest

Korsin, Inc.
3836 N. Clark Street
Chicago, IL 60613
(312) 929-5410

Distributes frost-resistant tiles from Spain, Japan, Italy, and Korea.

Sunray Ceramics, Inc.
1507 Rand Road
Des Plaines, IL 60016
(312) 635-6300

Distributes frost-resistant tiles from Mexico, Germany, Italy, France, and the United States; nonvitreous tiles from Spain, Japan, Portugal, and Holland. Can have custom decorations and shapes manufactured in the United States and Mexico, and will recommend a specialty contractor for exterior murals and complicated decorative work.

Mid-America Tile Distributors, Inc.
1890 Lunt Avenue
Elk Grove Village, IL 60007
(312) 569-2628

Can supply frost-resistant tiles. Gives technical advice about murals and general exterior tile installation.

Century Supply Co.
747 E. Roosevelt Road
Lombard, IL 60148
(312) 495-2300

Distributes tiles from Spain, Japan, Italy, and Korea. Can have custom decorations and shapes manufactured.

International Materials Corp.
4585 Indian Creek Parkway
Overland Park, KS 66207
(913) 383-3383

Distributes tiles from Mexico, Spain, Italy, Portugal, Holland and Israel; frost-resistant tiles from Japan, Finland, and France. Has access to a designer who can recommend ornamental patterns, and will recommend a specialty contractor capable of installing exterior murals and special patterns.

Detroit Tile and Marble Co.
15308 E. Eight Mile Road
Detroit, MI 48205
(313) 839-6677

Distributes tiles from Italy; frost-resistant tiles from Mexico, Spain, Japan, Germany, and the United States. Can have custom decorations and shapes made in the United States. Will recommend a specialty contractor for exterior murals and decorative patterns. Estimates given on square footage of tile, not on installation.

Fred H. Blackwood
9599 104th Avenue
Zeeland, MI 49464
(616) 895-6729

A manufacturer, distributor, and ceramic studio making all types of custom tiles using "all types of firing media, some frost-free." Heat-absorptive solar tiles a specialty. Can put a relief pattern on pavers and press a pattern on quarry tiles. Will consult on solar uses of tiles and technical questions on ceramic mural installations. Designer on staff can do patterns, murals, large ceramic panels, graphics, and bas-relief tiles—from rough sketch or sample. Handpainting and silkscreened decorations. Blackwood distributes frost-resistant tiles from Spain, Japan, Germany, and Italy; nonvitreous tiles from Mexico, Portugal, Holland, Africa, England, Brazil, Korea, Canada, and other countries. Custom decorations and shapes can be manufactured in the United States, Germany, or Italy. Brochure $1.00.

Grazzini Brothers and Co.
620 16th Avenue
Minneapolis, MN 55404
(612) 336-7735

Ceramic studio making handpainted tiles, bas-relief tiles

and panels, ceramic moldings and borders, and silkscreened patterns in addition to custom shapes and sizes. Grazzini also makes and installs ceramic murals, and can decorate readymade commercial tiles. In business for over fifty years.

Ceramic Tile Services, Inc.
1610 Hampton Avenue
St. Louis, MO 63139
(314) 647-5132

Distributes tiles from Mexico, Spain, Portugal, Holland, and Israel; frost-resistant tiles from Japan, Germany, Italy, Denmark, and South Africa. The company has access to a designer who can advise about exterior ornamental patterns. Can also recommend a specialty contractor capable of installing exterior murals and special decorations.

Stark Ceramics, Inc.
Box 8880
Canton, OH 44711
(216) 488-1211
(800) 321-0662

The world's largest producer of structural glazed facing tile. A variety of colors and textures.

United States Ceramic Tile Co.
1375 Raff Road S.W.
Canton, OH 44711
(216) 477-8511

Manufacturer of glazed decorative tile, frost-resistant pavers, and mosaic tiles. A staff designer can do custom patterns and murals from rough sketch.

Ohio Tile and Marble Co.
Attn. Clyde L. Dowers
3809 Spring Grove Avenue
Cincinnati, OH 45223
(513) 541-4211

Can supply frost-resistant tiles. Gives technical advice about exterior installations of tiles and murals.

Summitville Tiles, Inc.
Summitville, OH 43962
(216) 223-1511

Manufactures pavers, quarry tiles, glazed, decorative, and mosaic tiles. Also, bas-relief panels and tiles. Can put a relief pattern on pavers or quarry tiles and make custom decorations on glazed decorative tiles (decal, handpainted, or silkscreened). There is a designer on staff for all custom decorative services who can work from rough sketch, pattern, sample, or working drawing. Summitville also does ceramic sculpture for exterior installation.

Hendrix, Heikkilä, and Terry, Inc.
Norman, OK 73069

See listing under Murals.

Monarch Sales Company, Inc.
37 N.E. 29th Street
Oklahoma City, OK 73105
(405) 525-0547

Distributes tiles from Mexico, Spain, Japan, Germany, Italy, Portugal, Holland, and the United States. Can have custom decorations and shapes made in the United States, and can recommend a specialty contractor to install decorative patterns.

Antiquestone, Inc.
Box 434
Bertram, TX 78605
(512) 355-2722

Manufacturer. Specializes in cast tile pavers; can make custom sizes and shapes—frost-resistant. Can put a relief pattern on a paver. A staff designer can create custom patterns and bas-relief panels.

American Glass Mosaics, Inc.
Dal-Tile Corp.
P.O. Box 17130
Dallas, TX 75217
(214) 398-1411

Distributor importing tiles from Mexico, and manufacturer producing glazed decorative tiles, frost-resistant pavers, and mosaic tiles in the United States. Can make handpainted or silkscreened custom decorations on glazed decorative tiles; the staff designer can work from sketch or sample. Can also make ceramic murals. Has a cheerful, rich-looking line of exterior tiles called Dal-Espania; and a series of exterior mosaic tiles, in a variety of blues and browns, which can be applied to curved surfaces.

Knox Tile Distributors
P.O. Box 59427
11232 Indian Trail
Dallas, TX 75229
(214) 243-6666

Ceramic studio and distributor. Knox can do handpainted tiles and ceramic moldings and borders. Also, will decorate readymade commercial tiles.

Sim Shields
6528 Westchester
Houston, TX 77005
(713) 862-6044
(713) 683-7138

Manufacturer and designer of bas-relief panels and tiles. Does handpainting and silkscreening and can create patterns to the customer's specifications.

Designer Tile and Imports, Inc.
Attn. Robert W. Carver, President
Suite 107
318 E. Nakoma
San Antonio, TX 78216
(512) 494-4148

Distributes tiles from Texas, Mexico, Spain, Brazil, and Italy. Tiles for exterior use include moldings and borders, glazed decorative, mosaic, and quarry.

Lexco Tile and Supply Co.
P.O. Box 312
5207 N. 125th Street
Butler, WI 53007
(414) 781-2420

Distributes exterior ceramic mosaics and "Monocuttura deco tiles." Standard sizes: 8 by 8 inches and 4 by 8 inches.

Butler Tile Sales, Inc.
746 N. 109th Street
Milwaukee, WI 53226
(414) 476-0970

Distributes tiles from Mexico, Japan, Germany, Italy, Portugal, Holland, France, and the United States. Can have custom decorations and shapes made depending upon the manufacturer. Butler has access to a designer for decorative patterns, and will recommend specialty contractors for decorative installations, including murals.

Childcrest Distributing, Inc.
6045 N. 55th Street
Milwaukee, WI 53218
(414) 462-9770

Distributes frost-resistant tiles from Japan, Germany, and Italy; other tiles from Mexico, Spain, Portugal, Holland, Brazil, and England. Can have custom decorations made in the United States. A staff designer can create ornamental patterns. Childcrest can recommend a specialty contractor for difficult installations.

Conrad Schmitt Studios, Inc.
New Berlin, WI 53151

See listing under Murals.

Rockies and Far West

Facings of America, Inc.
4121 N. 27th Street
Phoenix, AZ 85016
(602) 955-9217

A ceramic studio and distributor that can make hand-painted tiles, ceramic moldings and borders, and silkscreened patterns. Can create ceramic murals and supervise their installation. Also will supply custom sizes and decorate readymade commercial tiles.

Del Piso Tile Co.
Attn. Jim Banks
1637 S. State College Boulevard
Anaheim, CA 92806
(714) 771-0625

Distributes tiles from Mexico and the United States; frost-resistant tiles from Japan and Italy. Custom shapes and decorations can be manufactured in the United States. Has access to a designer for decorative patterns and specialty contractor for difficult installations.

Susan Tait
c/o The Tile Shop
1577 Solano Avenue
Berkeley, CA 94707
(415) 525-4312

This artist handpaints tiles and will work with the client to produce custom designs of the exact size, color, and effect desired. She often does address tiles; these are personalized by the incorporation of pictorial murals with the numbers. Some standard designs are also available. She does commercial and

Custom exterior ceramic tile (12 by 12 inches): Robinson's, Altamonte Springs, FL. Design-Technics, Stroudsburg, PA. (Photo by Jim Hedrich, Hedrich-Blessing, courtesy of Design-Technics)

"Fish Mural" (8 by 12 inches), handpainted white tiles. Designer: Susan Tait, The Tile Shop, Berkeley, CA. (Photo courtesy of Susan Tait)

residential installations; her designs vary from abstract patterns to highly realistic images. Tait produces three tile lines, one of which is suitable for exterior use.

The Tile Shop
1577 Solano Avenue
Berkeley, CA 94707
(415) 525-4312

The Tile Shop distributes tiles from Mexico, Spain, Italy, Taiwan, and the United States; frost-resistant tiles from Japan and Czechoslovakia. Can have custom decorations manufactured in the United States and Spain, and will recommend specialty contractors for exterior murals and decorative work. Sole outlet for ceramic artist Susan Tait.

Stan Bitters
25090 Auberry Road
Clovis, CA 93612
(209) 299-6441

A ceramic designer who does his own designs only, combining different materials and techniques. The designs include handpainted bas-relief tiles and silkscreened patterns. You can see what he does in his book, *Environmental Ceramics*, published by Van Nostrand Reinhold.

Franciscan Ceramics, Inc.
2901 Los Feliz Boulevard
Los Angeles, CA 90039
(213) 663-3361

Manufacturer of quarry tiles; will produce custom sizes, decorations (handpainted and silkscreened), and shapes from rough sketch, pattern, or sample. Can recommend a designer for murals.

Simpson Tile Co.
4904 Naples Street
San Diego, CA 92110
(714) 275-2464

A manufacturer specializing in glazed, decorative tiles—handpainted and silkscreened. A designer on staff can do patterns from your rough sketch. Also, can decorate readymade commercial tiles.

Tilecraft, Ltd.
101 Kansas - 226
San Francisco, CA 94103
(415) 552-1913

Distributes tiles from Mexico, Spain, Italy, and Portugal; frost-resistant tiles from Japan and Germany. Can have custom decorations manufactured in the United States. Tilecraft has access to a designer to help out with exterior ornamental patterns. Brochure $2.50.

Barbara Vantrease Beall Studio
23727 Hawthorne Boulevard
Torrance, CA 90505
(213) 378-1233

A well-known and rightfully acclaimed ceramic manufacturer and studio specializing in custom, handpainted tiles of the finest artistic quality. Will work to achieve designs reflecting the specific desires of the individual client. The studio's work is found all over the country, particularly in California and Hawaii. Commissions range from intimate residential panels to grand-scale compositions for hotels and shopping centers. There is also a less expensive line of silkscreened decorations of the same high design quality.

Designers Tile Gallery, Inc.
65 S. Colorado Boulevard
Denver, CO 80222
(303) 377-8886

Distributors of tiles from Mexico, Spain, Portugal, and Holland; frost-resistant tiles from Japan, Germany, Italy, and France. Supplies custom as well as standard sizes. Manufacturer of frost-resistant pavers, quarry tiles, glazed decorated tiles, mosaic tiles, and nonfrost-resistant ceramic moldings and borders. Can press a pattern into quarry tiles if order is large enough. Custom decorations are silkscreened, handpainted, or done with decals. Can recommend designer and specialty contractor for murals and special decorative patterns.

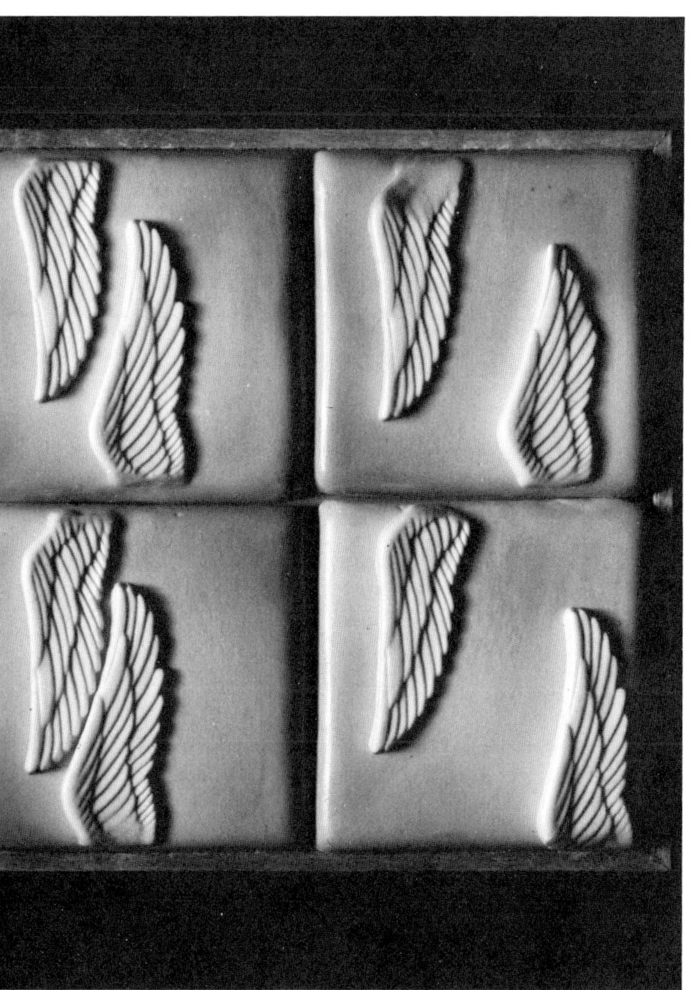

"Winged Tile" (4 by 4 inches), part of a series. MaryAnn Fariello (1979), Alexandria, TN. (Photo by Bobby Shatz, courtesy of MaryAnn Fariello)

Brimstone Tileworks
Attn. Garet Wohl
Box 833
Longmont, CO 80501
(303) 665-3380
(303) 532-3260

This studio makes handpainted and bas-relief tiles, ceramic moldings and borders, and silkscreened patterns (for interior use only). Brimstone makes and installs ceramic murals. Will decorate readymade commercial tiles.

Summit Pressed Brick & Tile Co.
Pueblo, CO 81002

See listing under Brick.

Central Pacific Supply Corp.
P.O. Box 29120
2855 Kaihikapu Street
Honolulu, HI 96820
(808) 839-1952
Telex 8378

Distributes tiles from Mexico, Spain, Japan, Germany, and Italy. Can have custom decorations manufactured in the United States, Philippines, and Japan. Supplies custom as well as standard sizes. Has access to a designer who can recommend ornamental patterns, and can direct you to a specialty contractor for exterior murals and special patterns.

Fox Hollow Pottery
30251 Fox Hollow Road
Eugene, OR 97405
(503) 344-1977

A ceramic studio offering custom decorations and shapes. Will do handpainted bas-relief tiles and panels, ceramic moldings and borders, murals, and ceramic animal sculpture. Will install or supervise installation. No brochure, but photos are available.

Design Tile Co.
5021 S.E. 26th Avenue
Portland, OR 97202
(503) 239-4030

Distributes tiles from Spain, frost-resistant tiles from Japan, Germany, and Italy. Can have custom decorations manufactured in the United States. Has access to a designer who can advise about ornamental patterns for exterior use, and can recommend a specialty contractor to install exterior murals and ornamental patterns. Also handles glazed and unglazed thin brick, imported mosaic tile, and glazed Summitville tiles. (See Summitville listing above.)

Lanzadoro Tile
3760 S.E. Division
Portland, OR 97202
(503) 238-0041

Distributes frost-resistant quarry and glazed decorative tiles from Italy. Can recommend a specialty contractor for exterior murals and special decorative installations.

Ceramic tile column capital by L. C. Tiffany. American Wing, Metropolitan Museum of Art, New York.

John Rogers
Portland, OR 97222

See listing under Sculpture.

Anne Storrs
7140 S.W. Virginia
Portland, OR 97219
(503) 244-6822

A ceramic studio making handpainted and bas-relief tiles and panels; can make tile murals (supervises installation). Can decorate readymade commercial tiles. Has made tiles for exterior use in Oregon climate. Mainly small orders.

Clay Pacific, Inc.
Willamina, OR 97396
(503) 876-4984

A manufacturer and ceramic studio making custom glazed and decorated tiles and bas-relief panels (frost-resistant). All decorations are handpainted. A designer on staff for custom patterns, bas-reliefs, and murals from rough sketch or sample. Will install. Small orders.

Trends in Tile
5206 Pinemont
Murray, UT 84107
(801) 266-9101

Manufacturers and distributors. Can do custom sizes, decorations, and shapes—frost-resistant.

Domestic-Import Tile & Marble
3650 S. 300 West
P.O. Box 15663
Salt Lake City, UT 84115
(801) 262-3033

Specialty: murals for high-rise buildings. Distributes tiles from Mexico, Spain, Italy Portugal, Holland, and England; frost-resistant tiles from Japan and Germany. Products include handpainted tiles, bas-relief tiles, and ceramic murals. Can have custom decorations manufactured in the United States and applied to commercial tiles. Access to a designer to recommend ornamental patterns for exterior use, and can recommend a specialty contractor for ornamental installations.

Uniq Distributing Corp.
3807 2nd South
Seattle, WA 98134
(206) 682-9470
and
E. 5814 Broadway
Spokane, WA 99206
(509) 535-4734

Distributes tiles from Spain; frost-resistant tiles from Japan, Germany, and Italy. Can have custom decorations manufactured in the United States. Uniq has access to designers who can advise about ornamental patterns for exterior use, and can recommend a specialty contractor for exterior murals and ornamental patterns. Also handles glazed and unglazed thin brick, imported mosaic tile, and glazed Summitville tiles. (See Summitville listing above.)

Key

See also Sculpture for artists who work in this material.

- **X** Service, technique, or material is available
- **+** See listing for additional information
- ***** Sometimes offers this service

Northeast	Manufacturer	Distributor	Studio	Custom decorations	Bas-relief	Frost-resistant	Brochure or photos available	Telephone estimates
Ronald A. Schumann Hartford, CT		X		X	X	X	X	X
Torre Tile Hartford, CT		X				X		
Standard Tile New Haven, CT		X				X	X	
M. G. Martin Woodbury, CT			X	X	X	X		
South Shore Tile Quincy, MA		X		X		X	X	X
Tile Internation Waltham, MA		X		X		X	X	
Albert F. Fitzgerald Woburn, MA		X		X		X	X	X
Leon I. Nigrosh Worcester, MA			X	X	X	X		
Tile Fashions Manchester, NH		X		X	X			X
Terra Designs, Inc. Bernardsville, NJ	X		X	X	X		X	
F. Joseph von Tury Metuchen, NJ	X		X	X	X	X	X	X
Best Tile Colonie, NY		X				X	X	X
Eva Zeisel New City, NY			X		X	X	X	
Amsterdam Tile New York, NY	X	X	X		X	X	+	
Blue Delft New York, NY		X		X			X	
Country Floors New York, NY		X		X		X	+	X
Benoit Gilsoul New York, NY	See listing under Murals							
Westchester Tile Scarsdale, NY		X				X		
Agency Tile Spring Valley, NY		X		X		X	X	
Crovatto Mosaics Yonkers, NY			X	+			X	
Moravian Pottery & Tile Doylestown, PA	X				X	+	+	X

Key

See also Sculpture for artists who work in this material.

X Service, technique, or material is available
\+ See listing for further information
* Sometimes offers this service

	Manufacturer	Distributor	Studio	Custom decorations	Bas-relief	Frost-resistant	Brochure or photos available	Telephone estimates
American Olean Tile Lansdale, PA	X					X	+	
Design-Technics Ceramics Stroudsburg, PA	X			X	X	X	X	X
Eastern Tile Cranston, RI		X		X				X
Bannon Tile Providence, RI		X		X		X	X	
Haskell Pottery East Highgate, VT			X	X	X	X	+	
South								
Forms and Surfaces Miami, FL		X		X	X	X	X	
Manufacturer's Reps. Miami, FL		+		X			X	
Christine Silbey Pottery Atlanta, GA			X	X	X	X	X	
Zumpano Enterprises Atlanta, GA		X	X	X		X	X	X
Cameron Covert and Bruce Bobick Carollton, GA	See listing under Murals							
Tile House Tucker, GA		X		X		X	X	X
Mees Distributors Louisville, KY		X		X		X	X	
Bolick Distributors New Orleans, LA		X				X		
Roubion Tile and Marble New Orleans, LA		X		X		X		X
Maryland Tile Baltimore, MD		X				X	X	X
Mosaic Tile of Maryland Baltimore, MD		X		X		X	X	X
Macon Rockville, MD		X		X		X	X	
B.J.'s Ceramic Tile Jackson, MS		X		X		X	X	X
MaryAnn Fariello Alexandria, TN	X		X	X	X	X	+	X
Mosaic Tile of Virginia Newington, VA		X				X	X	

Key

See also Sculpture for artists who work in this material.

- **X** Service, technique, or material is available
- \+ See listing for further information
- * Sometimes offers this service

	Manufacturer	Distributor	Studio	Custom decorations	Bas-relief	Frost-resistant	Brochure or photos available	Telephone estimates
Ademas Washington, DC		X				+	+	
Midwest								
Korsin Chicago, IL		X				X	X	
Sunray Ceramics Des Plaines, IL		X		X		X	X	X
Mid-America Tile Elk Grove Village, IL		X				X	X	X
Century Supply Lombard, IL		X				X	X	X
International Materials Overland Park, KS		X				X	+	X
Detroit Tile and Marble Detroit, MI		X				X		+
Fred H. Blackwood Zeeland, MI	X	X	X	X	X	X	+	X
Grazzini Brothers Minneapolis, MN			X	X	X	X	X	
Ceramic Tile Services St. Louis, MO		X				X	X	X
Stark Ceramics Canton, OH	X						X	X
United States Ceramic Canton, OH	X					X	X	X
Ohio Tile and Marble Cincinnati, OH		X				X	X	X
Summitville Tiles Summitville, OH	X			X	X	X	X	X
Hendrix, Heikkilä, and Terry Norman, OK	See listing under Murals							
Monarch Sales Oklahoma City, OK		X		X		X		X
Antiquestone Bertram, TX	X					X	X	
American Glass Mosaics Dallas, TX	X	X	X	X		X	X	
Knox Tile Dallas, TX		X	X	X		X		
Sim Shields Houston, TX	X			X	X			

Key

See also Sculpture for artists who work in this material.

- **X** Service, technique, or material is available
- **+** See listing for further information
- ***** Sometimes offers this service

	Manufacturer	Distributor	Studio	Custom decorations	Bas-relief	Frost-resistant	Brochure or photos available	Telephone estimates
Designer Tile and Imports San Antonio, TX		X				X	X	X
Lexco Tile and Supply Butler, WI		X		X	X	X		
Butler Tile Sales Milwaukee, WI		X			X	X	X	X
Childcrest Milwaukee, WI		X		X		X	X	X
Conrad Schmitt Studios, Inc. New Berlin, WI	See listing under Murals							
Rockies and Far West								
Facings of America Phoenix, AZ		X	X	X		X		X
Del Piso Tile Anaheim, CA		X		X		X	X	X
Susan Tait Berkeley, CA		X		X		X	X	
The Tile Shop Berkeley, CA		X		X		X	X	
Stan Bitters Clovis, CA			X	+	X	X	+	X
Franciscan Ceramics Los Angeles, CA	X			X			X	
Simpson Tile San Diego, CA	X			X		X		X
Tilecraft, Ltd. San Francisco, CA		X		X		X	X	X
Barbara Vantrease Beall Torrance, CA	X		X	X			X	
Designers Tile Gallery Denver, CO	X	X		X		X	X	X
Brimstone Tileworks Longmont, CO			X	X	X	X		
Summit Pressed Brick & Tile Pueblo, CO	See listing under Brick							
Central Pacific Supply Honolulu, HI		X		X		X		X
Fox Hollow Pottery Eugene, OR			X	X	X			X
Design Tile Portland, OR		X				X		X

Key

See also Sculpture for artists who work in this material.

- **X** Service, technique, or material is available
- **+** See listing for further information
- ***** Sometimes offers this service

	Manufacturer	Distributor	Studio	Custom decorations	Bas-relief	Frost-resistant	Brochure or photos available	Telephone estimates
Lanzadoro Tile Portland, OR		X			X	X	X	X
John Rogers Portland, OR	See listing under Sculpture							
Anne Storrs Portland, OR			X	X	X	*		X
Clay Pacific Willamina, OR	X		X	X	X	X	X	
Trends in Tile Murray, UT	X	X		X		X	X	
Domestic-Import Tile Salt Lake City, UT		X		X		X	X	
Uniq Distributing Seattle, WA		X				X		X

CONCRETE

The Romans first used concrete for walls around 500 B.C. By the time of Julius Caesar it was commonly used for floors and ceilings as well. The Pantheon (A.D.118) had a concrete dome 142 feet in diameter and 143 feet high. The secret of concrete died with the Empire and was rediscovered only in the nineteenth century. According to the *Oxford English Dictionary,* the first English language usage of the word "concrete" occurred in 1834.

Concrete—a simple mixture of cement, sand, aggregate, and water—has been used with so little imagination in contemporary architecture that we have forgotten how lively this material can be. In the first decades of our century concrete formwork was creative and skillful. Columns (including capitals), archivolts, dentil courses, and other quite complex shapes were routinely cast. When you read technical articles of that time, you realize that designers were well aware of how uninteresting concrete could be, so they spent a good deal of time exploring exciting ways to use it. Some standard ploys, such as sandblasting and acid-etching, are still used to show off the color of special aggregates. Decorative aggregate veneers were also applied using a "facing board." This was usually a sheet metal panel with spacers that held it an inch or so away from the inside face of the outside form. As the backup concrete was poured, the special aggregate mixture was sloshed into the 1-inch space between the facing board and the outside form. The board was then removed slowly, and the backup material compacted against the aggregate mixture. The veneer bonded with the backup material as they both cured.

In addition to decorative aggregates, concrete was often stained. This was done before pouring, by putting a coloring agent in the dry mix, or after the forms were removed. The former method generally gave more satisfactory results because the stain was uniform throughout the material.

Concrete was also painted. First, any lime that might have remained in the surface of the concrete was neutralized with a solution of zinc sulfate or magnesium fluorosilicate. Then the surface was "filled" with boiled linseed oil (with or without pigmentation). After this, a base stain was applied; the base stain was a combination of linseed oil, chinawood oil, and pigment (usually the background color of the design). The surface could then be painted like wood and sealed with varnish or shellac. This procedure was followed on exterior as well as interior concrete surfaces.

At its most sophisticated, the decorative concrete of the first decades of this century achieved remarkable effects. The technique devised by John J. Earley in the 1920s was used on a number of buildings including the Shrine of the Sacred Heart in Washington, DC. Techniques were refined to such an extent that rare onyx and marble aggregates could be placed precisely and different colors combined to create specific hues *à la* Pointillism. Aggregate sizes were carefully graded so that some panels retained their texture when seen from several hundred feet away while others lost theirs when seen from close up.

These early, usually eclectic extravagances were squelched by modernism, and for decades architects contented themselves with great expanses of bland, plywood-formed surfaces. Honest fare, to be sure, but dull. In the late 1950s things became somewhat more interesting. Paul Rudolph produced one of the better known examples of the "textured" look in his Art and Architecture Building at Yale. But the plastic qualities of concrete have not been touched in half a century.

Textures in precast paneling are still commonly produced by acid-etching for a "bright" finish. Acid-etching is restricted by government regulations in some locations. Sandblasting is employed for a matte finish. Both techniques are used to produce overall textures.

To achieve a more sophisticated level of ornament, inserts must be placed in the forms. "Contrary to common belief," in the words of Kurtz Precast Corporation of Denver, Pennsylvania, "sculpting of a precast wall unit does not involve a substantial premium, as long as there is sufficient repetition of the unit to keep mold costs within reason . . . especially if the sculpting adds to the unit's structural capacity." These inserts, or liners, can be made of a variety of materials depending on the type of ornament intended. Possible materials include wood, plaster, plastic, or rubber and they can take any shape that will not prevent the removal of the form. The inserts can be one-of-a-kind affairs—as you would expect of a sculptural mural, or reusable, such as the pans used to make coffered slabs. Inserts could easily have embossed textures or surfaces. In the 1920s, it was common to cast columns and other elements in reusable, hinged aluminum forms. Another way to create ornamental designs is to place a facing material into the molds—tiles, brick, even marble. Costs vary depending on the season, market, and location of the work. One fabricator groups the different types of ornament as follows, from least to most expensive:

1. Smooth finish
   Form liners
   Sandblasting
2. Retardation or water washing
   Acid-etching
3. Hammered ribs
   Tile facing
4. Cut stone facing

According to this assessment, the use of special form liners—offering the most potential for creating sophisticated ornament—is among the least expensive ways to ornament precast concrete.

"Blue-Eyed Devil Totem No. Two" (5 by 3 feet), directly carved concrete. Mary Fuller, Sculptor, Petaluma, CA. See listing under Sculpture. (Photo courtesy of Mary Fuller)

Special Listings

American Concrete Institute
Box 19150
22400 W. Seven Mile Road
Detroit, MI 48219
(313) 532-2600

Technical advice and printed material is offered, including a hefty catalog of literature on all aspects of concrete construction techniques and structural design. If you require additional information, the Institute will search it out for you. There is an hourly charge of $30/hour for members (minimum charge $45) and $45/hour for nonmembers (minimum charge $75); VISA and MASTER CHARGE are accepted. The searches normally take about three weeks. A monthly magazine is available to subscribers and members of the Institute.

National Precast Concrete Association
Attn. Robert W. Walton
825 E. 46th Street
Indianapolis, IN 46220
(317) 251-1214

Offers printed material, and can recommend fabricators in your area.

Owens Corning Fiberglas
Fiberglas Tower
Toledo, OH 43659
(419) 248-8832

This company produces alkali-resistant glass fibers and supplies them, with appropriate technology, to selected producers of architectural panels and other building components.

The Spanish Patio, Mission Inn, Riverside, CA. Reinforced concrete (1914). Arthur Benton, Architect.

Contact Owens Corning for a complete listing of companies that manufacture Fiberglas-reinforced concrete. The glass fibers function as crack arrestors at the micro level and eliminate the overall need for rebar in nonload-bearing cladding panels. This type of reinforcement has several advantages over traditional reinforcing bars when it comes to ornamental shapes. The more complicated shapes are less expensive in this type of concrete because the means of fabrication is considerably simpler than it would be by traditional methods. Rather than being poured, the concrete is sprayed on in a slurry, and so is more easily directed into the nooks and crannies of complex formwork. The other advantage, from an ornamental point of view, is that regardless of how complicated these panels become they remain lightweight because they are not solid. Fiberglas-reinforced panels with reveals of 5 or 6 inches need be only 3/8- or 1-inch thick at any point in the section, whereas a similar poured concrete panel would have to be solid throughout. Fiberglas-reinforced panels normally weigh only 10 percent as much as similar precast concrete panels. Thus, this technique makes possible deep reveals, curves, and complicated ornamental shapes that would be uneconomical because of weight and waste material in traditional methods.

Portland Cement Association
Attn. Mario J. Catani
5420 Old Orchard Road
Skokie, IL 60077
(312) 966-6200

An extensive array of information in several formats for sale: printed material, slide shows, motion pictures, and computer programs. Will give technical advice about cement. There are seven regional chapters in the United States and five in Canada.

The Riverton Corporation
Riverton, VA 22651

See listing under Brick.

Regional Listings

In the listings, "architectural elements" refers to the following: custom panels, railings, balusters, planters, spandrels, column cladding, and other such products.

You might also check the listings under Cast Stone. In general, the work of companies listed in this section is similar to—but larger than—work in cast stone. When a company has indicated that they do both small (balusters) and large (10 by 30 feet) elements, we have listed them under Concrete.

To get an indication of the minimum or maximum order, the questionnaire asked companies for their "effective range." The responses were given in terms of the minimum square footage for a job or the maximum weight of a single panel. Not all companies responded to this question. If the listing does not state an effective range, check directly with the company.

All companies listed below will give technical assistance to the architect during design of the precast element.

An arcade of reinforced concrete columns, constructed circa 1950. Riverside College, Riverside, CA.

Form fasteners and score lines ornament the rather Spartan surfaces of Louis I. Kahn's Salk Institute, in La Jolla, CA.

Northeast

Prefac Concrete Co., Ltd.
8501 Boulevard Ray Lawson
Ville d'Anjou
Quebec H1J 1K6
Canada
(514) 351-1060

Custom work from working drawings only. Prefabricated panels, railings, balusters, planters, spandrels, and column cladding available in variety of aggregates and colors. Has cast ornamental panels and sculpture. Gives technical advice. Effective range: 1,000,000 square feet per year.

Vibrek Inc.
CP. 7070
Charlesbourg Ontario
Quebec G1G 5E2
Canada
(418) 628-0440

Custom work from working drawing only. Does a variety of surfaces using various aggregates. Maximum panel size: 60 by 10 feet (70 tons). Gives technical advice. Effective range: 10,000 square feet and up.

Art Cement Products Co., Inc.
Wilbraham, MA 01095

See listing under Cast Stone.

Tecfab of New Jersey
2 Porete Avenue
North Arlington, NJ 07032
(201) 998-7600

Can cast bas- and high-relief surfaces, and can make all types of architectural elements. Effective range: 15,000 square feet and up.

Winkrete Precast
300 Longbranch Road
Syracuse, NY 13209
(315) 457-9116

Winkrete services the northeastern United States and Canada. Will fabricate large and small orders; bas- and high-relief surfaces. Estimates from sketch; brochure in preparation.

Kurtz Precast Corp.
Attn. Douglas L. Lorah, Sales Manager
Denver Road RD 3
Denver, PA 17517
(215) 267-3821

Custom panels, spandrels. Offers a variety of skills and techniques by which simple precast concrete surfaces can be made more ornamental: mold inserts, sandblasting, acid-etching, various facings, etc. Effective range: 5,000 to 100,000 square feet and up.

Reinforced concrete made to resemble clapboard to harmonize with this residential neighborhood. Whitney Avenue Fire Station, New Haven, CT (1963). Designer: Peter Millard; architect: Earl Carlin.

Durastone Flexicor Corp.
Attn. Raymond D. Flaherty, Estimator
Box 303
Higginson Avenue
Lincoln, RI 02865
(401) 723-7100

Specializes in precast architectural elements including columns, moldings, arches, etc. Will match an existing piece, but must work from a sample (unless a mold or full-size working drawing is supplied). Can also provide their own designs.

South

Castone Corporation
P.O. Box 747
Opelika, AL 36801
(205) 745-3571

Coping stones, band courses, and panels. Custom jobs from working drawings only. Large or small orders.

Cast-Crete Corp. of Kissimmee
P.O. Box 969
Kissimmee, FL 32741
(305) 847-5285

Will cast panels, spandrels, planters, and column cladding; bas- and high-relief surfaces. Effective range: above 20,000 square feet per contract.

Cochran Concrete Co.
Box 188
Sarasota, FL 33578
(813) 365-3953

Casts all types of architectural elements. Estimates from working drawings only.

Ornamental patterns in cast-in-place concrete. Mayfair in the Grove, Coconut Grove, FL. Kenneth Treister, Architect. (Photo courtesy of Kenneth Treister)

Florida Architectural Concrete
P.O. Box 16884
Tampa, FL 33687
(813) 621-5831

Will cast all types of architectural elements; bas- and high-relief surfaces. Effective range: above 12,000 square feet.

Florida Precast Concrete, Inc.
Attn. George Egalite, Vice President
P.O. Box 5707
Tampa, FL 33675
(813) 247-6663

Fabricates all types of architectural elements; bas- and high-relief surfaces. Most of this company's work is for commercial and institutional construction. Effective range: 40,000 square feet.

Cut Art Stone Co.
Savannah, GA 31405

See listing under Cast Stone.

Kendrick Concrete Products Co.
Attn. Fred A. Miller, Vice President
2600 Brookhaven Road
Columbus, GA 31906
(404) 687-0161

All types of architectural elements; bas- and high-relief surfaces. Effective range: above 25,000 square feet.

Tecfab of Maryland, Inc.
Attn. Curtis L. Jacobs, Jr., President
P.O. Box 435
10800 Hanna Street
Beltsville, MD 20705
(301) 937-4111

Fabricates all types of architectural elements; bas- and high-relief surfaces. Estimates given from sketch or working drawing. Effective range: 1,000 square feet per day.

F. S. Prestress, Inc.
Attn. Robert Jarrell
Rte. 7 Box 299X
Hattiesburg, MS 39401
(601) 582-4403

Produces custom panels, column cladding, and planters; bas- and high-relief surfaces. Any size job. Branch offices in Louisiana and Arkansas.

Florence Concrete Products, Inc.
P.O. Box 5506
Florence, SC 29502
(803) 662-2549

This manufacturer offers readymade and custom designs. Makes balusters, bas-relief panels, cornices, coping stones, band courses, and panels. Does incising. Custom designs from working drawings only. Can provide a variety of surfaces and colors. Maximum panel weight: 30,000 pounds.

Detail of ornament in cast-in-place concrete. Mayfair in the Grove, Coconut Grove, FL. Kenneth Treister, Architect. (Photo courtesy of Kenneth Treister)

Southern Cast Stone Co., Inc.
Knoxville, TN 37901

See listing under Cast Stone.

Featherlite Corp.
P.O. Box 13202
2615 Channel Avenue
Memphis, TN 38113
(901) 948-4578

Panels and spandrels; bas-relief surfaces. Effective range: 60,000 square feet.

Midwest

Wilson Concrete Co.
200 Commerce Drive
Red Oak, IA 51566
(712) 623-4978

All types of architectural elements—panels, railings, balusters, etc. Bas- and high-relief surfaces. Effective range: approximately 300,000 square feet per year.

Precast/Schokbeton, Inc.
3102 E. Cork Street
Kalamazoo, MI 49003
(616) 381-1550

Can cast bas- and high-relief surfaces. This company uses a method of casting concrete developed in the Netherlands about forty years ago. The mold is repeatedly shaken as the concrete is poured; this results in extremely dense concrete. As the final product is particularly strong, it is used most effectively as a load-bearing material. Size capabilities: 12 by 40 feet; shapes: "nearly unlimited." Estimates from working drawing only. Effective range: 10,000 square feet and up.

Spillman Company
Attn. Charles W. Styers, Vice President
P.O. Box 07847
1701 Moler Road
Columbus, OH 43207
(614) 444-2184

This company casts a variety of architectural elements.

Concrete Technology, Inc.
156 E. Mill Street
Springboro, OH 45066
(513) 224-1867

This company specializes in form-liner textures. Can make large signs as well as all types of architectural elements. Estimates made from sketches. Effective range: 30,000 square feet per job.

Concrete sculpture; cast separately and then applied. Mayfair in the Grove, Coconut Grove, FL. Kenneth Treister, Architect. (Photo courtesy of Kenneth Treister)

Sidley Precast
Attn. Ray L. Kennedy, Division Manager
P.O. Box 70
6900 Madison Road
Thompson, OH 44086
(216) 298-3232

This company processes its own materials, manufactures them in its own plants, and installs with its own crews. Produces any architectural element; stock panels come in a variety of sizes and different aggregate textures. No square footage limitations.

Belot Concrete Industries
P.O. Box 68
Tiltonsville, OH 43963
(614) 859-2191

Fabricates custom panels, planters, spandrels, and column cladding. Estimates based on working drawings only.

Featherlite Pre-Cast Corp.
Attn. Larch D. King, Sales Manager
P.O. Box 69
Austin, TX 78767
(512) 472-3171

Produces precast concrete, prestressed concrete, concrete block, lightweight aggregate, and limestone (from its own quarries in Texas). The precasting facilities offer complete freedom of size, shape, and choice of load-bearing or nonload-bearing panels. Bas- and high-relief surfaces.

The Featherlite Corp.
P.O. Box 17709
El Paso, TX 79917
(915) 859-9171

Panels, balusters, planters, spandrels, and column cladding—any precast or prestressed concrete.

TXI
Attn. Charles H. White, Sales Manager
P.O. Box 38
Katy, TX 77450
(713) 371-3116

Produces a variety of architectural elements in bas- and high-relief surfaces. Prefers giving estimates from working drawing but can from rough sketch. Effective range (per job): 15,000 square feet and up.

Rockies and Far West

Bordignon Construction, Ltd.
200–1200 Burrard Street
Vancouver, B.C. V6Z 2C7
Canada
(604) 684-7161

Panels, balusters, spandrels, column cladding, and planters; bas- and high-relief surfaces. Effective range: 6,000 square feet and up.

The Tanner Companies
Prestressed Concrete Division
Attn. Roger Tanner, Sales Manager
P.O. Box 20128
3052 S. 19th Avenue
Phoenix, AZ 85036
(602) 262-1360

Precast architectural panels from working drawings only. Can cast a variety of colors and surfaces using different aggregates.

Stanley Structures
7000 Broadway
Denver, CO 80221
(303) 427-5511

Cornices, coping stones, and panels. Can do a variety of surfaces and colors. Panel size: 4 by 4 feet to 10 by 30 feet. Minimum order required.

Hydro Conduit Corp.
Attn. Ben Snow, District Manager
P.O. Box 1609
Albuquerque, NM 87103
(505) 247-3725

Any size job; all types of architectural elements.

Central Premix Concrete Co.
Attn. Wes Westerman, Vice President
Box 3366 Terminal Annex
Spokane, WA 99220
(509) 534-6221

Produces panels, band courses, and coping stones. Can supply most kinds of precast architectural items with the exception of such small elements as balusters. Technical advice given; no minimum or maximum order.

Spanish Renaissance in concrete. Steeple of the First Congregational Church (1914), Riverside, CA. Myron Hunt, Architect. (Photo courtesy of Netta Brolin)

CONCRETE

Key

See also Sculpture for artists who work in this material.

X Service, technique, or material is available
+ See listing for further information
* Sometimes offers this service

	Panels	Spandrels	Column cladding	Railings	Balusters	Planters	Brochure available	Estimates from sketch	Estimates from working drawing
Northeast									
Prefac Concrete Quebec, Canada	X	X	X	X	X	X	X	X	
Vibrek Quebec, Canada	X	X	X				X	X	
Art Cement Products Wilbraham, MA	See listing under Cast Stone								
Tecfab of New Jersey North Arlington, NJ	X	X	X	X		X	X	X	
Winkrete Precast Syracuse, NY	X	X	X	X	X	X	X	X	
Kurtz Precast Denver, PA	X	X	X				X	X	
Durastone Flexicor Lincoln, RI		X	X	X	X	X			X
South									
Castone Opelika, AL	X								X
Cast-Crete Kissimmee, FL	X	X	X			X	X	X	
Cochran Concrete Sarasota, FL	X	X	X	X	X	X	X		X
Florida Architectural Tampa, FL	X	X	X	X	X	X		X	
Florida Precast Tampa, FL	X	X	X	X	X	X		X	
Cut Art Stone Savannah, GA	See listing under Cast Stone								
Kendrick Concrete Columbus, GA	X	X	X	X	X	X		X	
Tecfab of Maryland Beltsville, MD	X	X	X	X	X	X		X	
F. S. Prestress Hattiesburg, MS	X		X			X	X	X	
Florence Concrete Florence, SC	X	X	X	X	X				X
Southern Cast Stone Knoxville, TN	See listing under Cast Stone								
Featherlite Memphis, TN	X	X					X	X	

Key

See also Sculpture for artists who work in this material.

X Service, technique, or material is available
\+ See listing for further information
* Sometimes offers this service

	Panels	Spandrels	Column cladding	Railings	Balusters	Planters	Brochure available	Estimates from sketch	Estimates from working drawing
Midwest									
Wilson Concrete Red Oak, IA	X	X	X	X	X	X	X	X	
Precast/Schokbeton Kalamazoo, MI	X	X	X				X		X
Spillman Company Columbus, OH	X	X	X	X	X	X	X	X	
Concrete Technology Springboro, OH	X	X	X	X	X	X	X	X	
Sidley Precast Thompson, OH	X	X	X	X	X	X	X	X	
Belot Concrete Tiltonsville, OH	X	X	X			X			X
Featherlite Pre-Cast Austin, TX	X	X	X	X	X	X	X	X	
Featherlite El Paso, TX	X	X	X	X	X	X	X	X	
TXI Katy, TX	X	X	X	X		X	X		+
Rockies and Far West									
Bordignon Construction Vancouver, B.C., Canada		X	X		X	X		X	
The Tanner Companies Phoenix, AZ	X								X
Stanley Structures Denver, CO	X	X	X	X			X		X
Hydro Conduit Albuquerque, NM	X	X	X	X	X	X	X	X	
Central Premix Concrete Spokane, WA	X	X	X	X			X		X

CONCRETE BLOCK

Concrete block is often thought of as a "back wall" material—destined for the nether ends of supermarkets and warehouses. Nevertheless, this humble material is commonly rendered in a variety of decorative forms and colors. Some of the manufacturers listed below will make or match any color, shape, or surface.

At least half a dozen decorative concrete block surfaces are available at all times throughout the country. They fall into one of two categories: well-defined patterns formed in the molding process (vertical ribs or impressed "brick" patterns), and less precise textures created by breaking the molded block (split face). A split rib surface combines both techniques. As these decorative surfaces come in standard block sizes, they can easily be interchanged within one wall to make countless different patterns—from relatively simple to much richer textures to patterns combining decorative and flat blocks and colors.

There is also perforated block. This is most often found in the warmer climates because it permits breezes to pass through while offering relative privacy. Perforated blocks occur in a surprising variety of shapes which can be combined to form many different patterns.

It is also possible to use colored mortar to enhance this plebian material. The Riverton Corporation (see Special listing under Brick) supplies 800 different mortar colors.

Special Listings

The National Concrete Masonry Association
P.O. Box 781
Herndon, VA 22070
(703) 435-4900

This organization represents about 1,300 concrete block manufacturers, about 40 percent of whom make decorative concrete block. There are local branches in every state; national headquarters will put you in contact with the nearest association. The local branch will suggest manufacturers, give engineering advice, and recommend appropriate contractors for decorative installations. A list of the Association's members is available upon request.

The NCMA has in-house engineering capability and there is no charge for technical advice. However, there is a nominal charge for "structural design feasibility" studies, done with the aid of a computer. Printed materials are available, distributed through the membership.

Regional Listings

The manufacturers listed below will accept large and small orders unless otherwise stated. Those having minimum orders for custom shapes, surfaces, or colors are noted.

Ribbed and plain concrete block used inventively in the Robert T. Wolfe Apartments, New Haven, CT. Charles W. Moore Associates, Architects (1972).

Northeast

Milford Concrete Products, Inc.
Attn. Bob Honeck
Honek Street
Milford, CT 06460
(203) 878-3564

Various decorative surfaces, including embossed brick-face. Catalog shows decorative screen, split rib, and "brick" blocks. Can also make custom blocks, including bas-relief surfaces, in off-white, tan, and dark brown. Small and large orders.

Plasticrete Block & Supply Corp.
99 Stoddard Avenue
North Haven, CT 06473
(203) 239-4216

Scored, ground face, deep groove, ramblestone, hex, hex split. Also makes custom shapes and surfaces. Colors include umber, beige, brown, and white. Large and small orders.

Thames Permacrete Corp.
P.O. Box 382
Uncasville, CT 06382
(203) 848-9206

Split rib, split face, and round fluted; available in brown and buff; 16 and 24 inches long in standard widths. Special orders to specification. Custom shapes and surfaces.

Ideal Concrete Block Co.
Attn. Lawrence Nicola
232 Lexington Street
Waltham, MA 02154
(617) 894-3206

Split rib, split face, scored, and rake face. Earth tones: buff, light, medium, and dark browns. Carries 4-, 6-, 8-, 10-, and 12-inch blocks. Custom shapes and surfaces.

Connecticut Valley Block
Attn. Michael R. Kennedy, Sales Manager
55 Circuit Avenue
West Springfield, MA
(413) 781-0542

Limited custom surfaces and shapes. Split rib and split face. Earth tones and brown. Large orders only.

Foster Masonry Products, Inc.
22 Everett Street
Westwood, MA 02090
(617) 762-1622

Manufacturer and distributor with a large selection of decorative concrete blocks in stock. Over 4,000 items. "We manufacture and distribute the most extensive line of concrete products in New England." Foster offers more than twenty colors, and can make custom shapes and surfaces. Can give design advice on custom shapes.

Across the street from the Wolfe Apartments, the same ribbed concrete block used as a less decorative, overall texture.

Duracrete Block Co., Inc.
Attn. Joseph Conway
Box 416
Hooksett, NH 03106
(603) 625-6411

Split rib and split face. Light and dark brown. Custom shapes and surfaces.

Montrose Concrete Products, Inc.
Box 297
Montrose, NY 10548
(914) 737-0017

Split rib and split face; shadow and scored. White, tan, brown, and buff.

Angelo Lane, Inc.
12 W. Noblestown Road
Carnegie, PA 15106
(412) 279-1234

Custom work limited to shapes and surfaces.

Anthony A. Fizzano
1776 Chester Pike
Crum Lynne, PA 19022
(215) 833-1100

Split rib, split face, round fluted, striated, stri-face flute, machine flute. White, gray, tan, light brown, and dark brown. Custom faces and colors on orders of 25,000 or more units.

Turbotville Block Co., Inc.
348 Main Street
Turbotville, PA 17772
(717) 649-5181

Split face and screen block. White and gray.

South

Grasselli Concrete Products Co., Inc.
Attn. John C. Golightly, Jr.
4200 Jefferson Avenue S.W.
Birmingham, AL 35221
(205) 925-3617

Split rib and split face. Available in eleven colors.

Superock Block Co., Inc.
3301 27th Avenue N.
Birmingham, AL 35207
(305) 324-8624

Custom colors as requested.

Kingery Block Co.
3150 Pacific Avenue
Austell, GA 30001
(404) 941-1488

Split rib, split face, grooved split face. Kingery's "Holiday Hill Stone" is approximately 3 by 3 by 16 inches, with split face. Fifteen different colors. Large orders only.

Back River Supply, Inc.
810 Back River Neck Road
Baltimore, MD 21221
(301) 687-2075

Custom items of almost any size and shape in addition to block. Custom surfaces, colors, and shapes to order.

Peerless Block Company
P.O. Box 71
St. Albans, WV 25177
(304) 727-4301
(304) 736-8765

Split rib and split face. Custom surfaces.

Midwest

Potter Material Service, Inc.
Attn. N. B. Ochstein
3515 E. Washington Street
Indianapolis, IN 46201
(317) 356-6351

Split rib, split face, ground face. Black, brown, tan, and red. Custom shapes and surfaces.

Ideal Concrete Products Co.
3124 Spaulding
Omaha, NE 68111
(402) 451-0456

Split rib and split face. A variety of special sizes including 8 by 4 by 16 inches, 4 by 4 by 16 inches, and 4 by 4 by 8 inches.

Watkins Concrete Block
Attn. Robert E. Watkins
4215 R Street
Omaha, NE 68107
(402) 731-0900

Split rib and split face. Will make colors as ordered. Manufacturers of concrete block and interlocking pavers; Watkins also represents several brick companies. Both concrete block and clay brick can be manufactured in custom textures, shapes, and colors. Watkins says it is "essential" to be involved in the design process to make sure the product is produceable, and is "more than happy to attempt anything in the field."

Harter Concrete Products, Inc.
1628 W. Main Street
Oklahoma City, OK 73106
(405) 236-0491

Fluted, stri-face, and scored surfaces in stock; custom shapes and surfaces available. Twenty-five stock colors. Large and small orders.

J. Oscar Ward
Box 400
Arlington, TX 76010
(214) 638-8933

Split rib and split face. White, gold, tan, and brown standard colors; others on request. Also makes a lightweight block.

Eagle Lake Concrete Products, Inc.
P.O. Box 537
Hwy 90-A W.
Eagle Lake, TX 77434
(713) 234-3159

Split rib and split face. All colors and shapes available. Custom shapes and surfaces.

Bend Industries Inc.
Attn. John P. Meyers, Marketing Manager
N91 W17174 Appleton Avenue
Menomonee Falls, WI 53051
(414) 251-8330

Split rib and split face. All primary colors and earth tones. Estimates "if we know the situation." Custom shapes and surfaces.

Rockies and Far West

University Block Co., Inc.
Attn. Spencer Apple, General Manager
4623 E. University Drive
Phoenix, AZ 85034
(602) 967-1626

Split rib, split face, and round fluted in any color. Color, size, shape, and surfaces can all be custom made.

Pumice Products Co.
Attn. Loren E. Santo
1300 E. Franklin Road
Meridian, ID 83642
(208) 888-4050

This company has access to molds and, if quantity is sufficient, will make custom surfaces. Will make integral colors but recommend applying stain or paint after block is laid. Small or large orders. The block is made of pumice aggregate.

Dick Cloninger
1935 Parkson Road
Henderson, NV 89015
(702) 565-9751

Split rib and split face; brown and yellow. One hundred forty-nine different sizes of block available. Custom surfaces.

Robert G. Dawes
7265 E. Marginal Way S.
Seattle, WA
(206) 762-8681

Distributor. Split rib, split face, and round fluted. Buff, gray, and brown. Will do custom bas-relief surfaces on special orders.

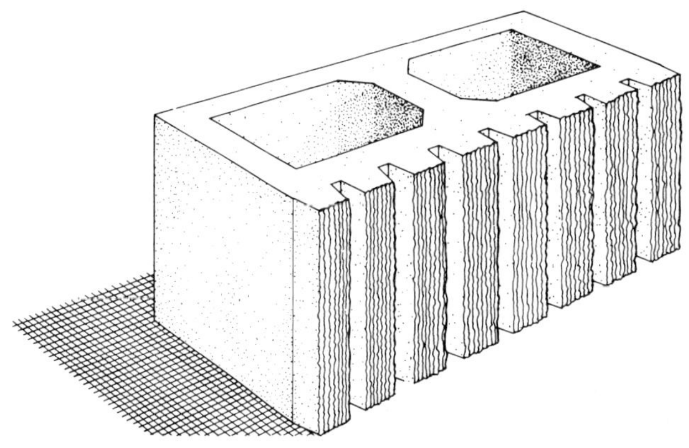

Eight-rib split block similar to the one used in the Wolfe Apartments. (Drawing courtesy of Milford Concrete Products, Inc., Milford, CT)

CONCRETE BLOCK

Key

X Service, technique, or material is available
+ See listing for further information
* Sometimes offers this service

	Manufacturer	Stock decorative surfaces	Custom decorative surfaces	Custom shapes	Stock colors	Custom colors	Telephone estimates
Northeast							
Milford Concrete Products Milford, CT	X	X	X	X	X		X
Plasticrete Block & Supply North Haven, CT	X	X	X	X	X		X
Thames Permacrete Uncasville, CT	X	X	X	X	X	X	
Ideal Concrete Block Waltham, MA	X	X	X	X	X	X	
Connecticut Valley Block West Springfield, MA	X	X	+	+	X	X	
Foster Masonry Products Westwood, MA	X	X	X	X	X	X	X
Duracrete Block Hooksett, NH	X	X	X	X	X	X	
Montrose Concrete Products Montrose, NY	X	X			X	X	
Angelo Lane Carnegie, PA	X	X	X	X			
Anthony A. Fizzano Crum Lynne, PA	X	X	X	X	X	X	
Turbotville Block Turbotville, PA	X	X			X		
South							
Grasselli Concrete Birmingham, AL	X	X			X	X	
Superock Block Birmingham, AL	X	X			+	X	
Kingery Block Austell, GA	X	X			X		
Back River Supply Baltimore, MD	X		+	+	+	+	
Peerless Block St. Albans, WV	X	X	X			X	
Midwest							
Potter Material Service Indianapolis, IN	X	X	X	X	X	X	
Ideal Concrete Products Omaha, NE	X	X			*		
Watkins Concrete Block Omaha, NE	X	X	X	X	X	X	

Key

X Service, technique, or material is available
+ See listing for further information
* Sometimes offers this service

	Manufacturer	Stock decorative surfaces	Custom decorative surfaces	Custom shapes	Stock colors	Custom colors	Telephone estimates
Harter Concrete Products Oklahoma City, OK	X	X	X	X	X		X
J. Oscar Ward Arlington, TX	X	X			X	X	
Eagle Lake Concrete Eagle Lake, TX	X	X	X	X	X	X	
Bend Industries Menomonee Falls, WI	X	X	X	X	X	+	
Rockies and Far West							
University Block Phoenix, AZ	X	X	X	X	X	*	
Pumice Products Meridian, ID	X	X	+		+	X	
Dick Cloninger Henderson, NV	X	X	X		X	X	
Robert G. Dawes Seattle, WA	+	X		X	X	X	

DECALS

Architectural ornament is not the first thing that springs to mind when you mention decals. This poor relative of hand-painting made an inauspicious entry into the world of decoration when English porcelain manufacturers began using paper transfer prints around the middle of the nineteenth century. The Encycolpaedia Britannica's eleventh edition (1910) refers to decals as "perhaps the most inappropriate decoration ever applied to porcelain."

Decals can be applied to any smooth, nonporous surface, so one obvious architectural application is as a pattern on tiles. The modern decal, or pressure-sensitive film, bears no comparison to its predecessor, the paper transfer. It is made in a variety of materials, several of which meet military specifications for exterior use; and its durability is attested to by use on frieght cars, trucks, and airplanes. Decals can be quite large (see photo of trailer truck); this makes them well-suited for murals and large graphics. Although they can be manufactured in at least 8-foot lengths, application is easier if you break large murals into several smaller pieces.

Perhaps the most familiar use of decals in modern architecture is as a safety device—something to catch the eye of the unwary so they will not walk through the glass wall that they think is an open door. People are not the only creatures to crash into these invisible barriers. The mirror-glass façade of Mercedes Headquarters in Montvale, New Jersey, had birds chasing their reflections and crashing into the glass. At the suggestion of the Audubon Society, the company applied decals in the shape of short-necked predatory birds to every other large pane. Fearing their natural enemies, the smaller birds gave the building a wide berth. The Audubon Society, however, says that any decal is better than none.

Decals can be produced in any color or pattern—including four-color printing. It is possible to transfer both color and black-and-white photographs to decals by the same screening process used to print continuous-tone photographs in maga-

"Vegetables." Four-color, exterior decal for Vons Supermarket trucks (approximately 8 by 15 feet). White Advertising, Merrilville, IN. (Photo courtesy of White Advertising)

"Venetian blind" pressure-sensitive transfer by The Meyercord Co., Carol Stream, IL. (Photo courtesy of The Meyercord Co.)

zines. Decals come in prismatic (reflective) or other surfaces and can be applied to particle board, plexiglass, hardwood, masonite, glass, etc. A number of different decal materials—including polyester, vinyl, mylar, and aluminum—are suitable for exterior application. Of course, decals can be applied to the inside of glass walls, so in many cases their ability to withstand weathering is irrelevant.

As with most mass-produced items, a one-of-a-kind job is expensive. However, White Advertising, one of the larger manufacturers of pressure-sensitive markings, says that some decals become economical in production runs of as few as ten.

Virtually all the companies listed below make custom designs. Most companies can make a surprising variety of sizes; one has a minimum size of 1/2 by 1/2 inch and a maximum size (for one piece) of 4 by 8 feet. Although we are accustomed to thinking of decals only in terms of lettering or as the "stars" architects found they had to put on glass walls so people would not walk through them, there are more imaginative uses of this product. One inventive and practical application is as a sunscreen. Their ability to block vision while transmitting light also enables them to afford privacy without materially lowering the level of brightness, so one can take advantage of natural light on ground floors without giving up privacy where needed. Photographic transfer techniques enable this timely idea to be executed in literally any design imaginable, from abstract patterns such as "matchstick" bamboo shades, window mullions, and venetian blinds (see photo) to the most realistic *trompe l'oeil* scenes showing office workers, window boxes full of flowers, etc. The possibilities are endless. Varying degrees of transparency can be achieved depending on the amount of privacy and solar protection needed—and all in full, four-color printing.

Application of "venetian blind" pressure-sensitive transfer by The Meyercord Co., Carol Stream, IL. (Photo courtesy of The Meyercord Co.)

Regional Listings

All companies listed below are manufacturers of decals. A note on sizes: when the company indicated a maximum and minimum size for one piece, we have listed the dimensions. When combined, of course, decals can make a design of unlimited size.

Northeast

Prest-On Products Corp.
110 W. 18th Street
New York, NY 10011
(212) 242-3783

Exterior and interior: polyester, vinyl, prismatic, mylar, and Scotchlite. Stock and custom designs; small and large orders.

Decal Techniques, Inc.
25 Mahan Street
West Babylon, NY 11704
(516) 491-1800

Decals for exterior and interior: nylon, polyester, vinyl, frosted, Scotchlite, and water applied. Stock and custom designs; small and large orders. Will install.

Delta Decal Co.
414 Long Island Avenue
Wyandanch, NY 11798
(516) 643-8001

Exterior and interior: vinyl, mylar, magnetic, and aluminum. Small and large orders. Custom designs. Minimum size, 2 by 2 inches; maximum size for one piece, 2 by 3 feet.

Rich-Art Graphics
1309 Vine Street
Philadelphia, PA 19107
(215) 922-1539

Exterior and interior: nylon, polyester, vinyl, prismatic, frosted, Scotchlite, and water applied. Custom designs; small and large orders.

Vermont Art Studio
Village Green
Pittsford, VT 05763
(802) 483-2368

Exterior and interior: polyester, vinyl, prismatic, frosted, Scotchlite, magnetic fluorescent, and water applied. Small and large orders. Also does all types of screen printing including direct screening on a vertical glass surface, in place. Maximum size for one piece, 20 by 27 inches (printed on clear mylar); 24 inches by any length (printed on white pressure sensitive vinyl).

Catozzi Signs
Rutland, VT 05701

See listing under Signs.

South

Alabama Labels & Graphics Corp.
P.O. Box 2025
2222 Fifth Avenue So.
Birmingham, AL 35201
(205) 328-0104

Exterior and interior: nylon, polyester, vinyl, Scotchlite, mylar, foil, laminated foil, and metal. Custom designs; small and large orders.

Central Advertising Co.
4505 Devine Street
Columbia, SC 29205
(803) 787-1211

Exterior and interior: vinyl, Scotchlite, water applied, metal, and "PFL of U.S. Plywood." Telephone estimates—"but they are difficult." Sizes from 1 inch square to 4 by 8 feet maximum. Custom and stock designs; small and large orders.

Art Display Co.
2315 18th Place N.E.
Washington, DC 20018
(202) 529-8884

Exterior and interior: vinyl, prismatic, Scotchlite, and water applied. Small, custom orders. Minimum size 2 inches square; maximum size for one piece, 4 by 8 feet.

Midwest

Rydin Sign and Decal Co.
P.O. Box 125
Bellwood, IL 60104
(312) 544-8000

Exterior and interior: polyester, vinyl, and Scotchlite. Custom designs; small orders.

The Meyercord Company
(Corporate Offices)
365 E. North Avenue
Carol Stream, IL 60187
(312) 682-6200

and

Pacific Coast Division
2915 S. Vail Avenue
Los Angeles, CA 90040
(213) 723-8661

Manufacturer of "Dri-Strip" window valance in simulated venetian blinds, and wrought iron (we were told that Meyercord used to make this in "glassblock," and could again for a special large order). The decal is applied to inside of glass, facing out, as a sunscreen and decorative element. Exterior and interior: clear and mirrorized polyester, reflective film, and vinyl. Application techniques include self-adhesive; water, solvent, and cement applied; heat transfer; and mechanical applications systems. (Stated five-year outdoor life of vinyl and solvent applied decals.) Nineteen branch sales offices around the country. Stock designs, custom designs from scaled sketch or drawing; large orders.

Labels and Decals, Inc.
4880 W. Grand Avenue
Chicago, IL 60639
(312) 622-3030

Exterior and interior: polyester, vinyl, prismatic, Scotchlite, acetate, rayon, satin, and laminated vinyl. Custom orders; small and large orders.

Midwest Decalcomania Co.
1100 W. Washington Boulevard
Chicago, IL 60607
(312) 829-0145

Exterior and interior: polyester, vinyl, prismatic, frosted, Scotchlite, water applied, and mylar. Custom designs; small and large orders. Maximum size 4 by 36 inches.

White Advertising Co.
Attn. Jana Gott, Sales and Marketing Coordinator
P.O. Box 8450
Merrillville, IN 46410
(800) 348-8968

and

625 109th Street
Arlington, TX 76011
(817) 261-1041

The Indiana office can direct you to the salesman or plant nearest you. White has designers on staff in four manufacturing plants, and salespeople in each state. "We reproduce intricate multicolored designs, graphics, and lettering on pressure-sensitive vinyl, using printing and thermal die cutting technology. Can be applied to virtually any surface: windows, walls, trucks, etc." Exterior graphics have a seven-year life. Custom designs; small and large orders.

The Artcraft Poster Display Inc.
14637 Meyers
Detroit, MI 48227
(313) 933-7400

Exterior and interior: polyester, vinyl, prismatic, frosted, Scotchlite, and water applied. Custom designs; small and large orders.

Continental Identification Products
140 E. Averill Street
Sparta, MI 49345
(616) 877-7341

Exterior and interior: polyester, vinyl, prismatic, Scotchlite, and water applied. Large custom orders.

A. M. Graphics, Inc.
521 S. Third Street
Minneapolis, MN 55415
(612) 341-2020

Exterior and interior: nylon, polyester, vinyl, frosted, Scotchlite, mylar, acrylic, and plexiglass. Custom designs; small and large orders.

C.O.B. Decals, Inc.
300 Westport Road
Kansas City, MO 64111
(816) 531-4400

Exterior and interior: polyester, vinyl, prismatic, frosted, and Scotchlite. Specializes in decals with cut out backgrounds (C.O.B.). The lines can be as thin as 1/16-inch. These would be excellent for murals on glass. Can reproduce photographs in color and black-and-white; customarily works in fifty-five-line screens. The C.O.B., or conventional, decals can be quite large; some of them are now on freight cars and trailer trucks. Custom designs; small and large orders.

Don Shafer Display, Inc.
1325 Park Avenue
Omaha, NE 68105
(402) 346-6140

Exterior and interior: polyester, vinyl, and Scotchlite. Maximum size 4 by 6 feet. Custom designs; small orders.

Fletcher Poster Co.
3174 Westerville Road
Columbus, OH 43224
(614) 471-9422

Exterior and interior: polyester, vinyl, Scotchlite, and water applied. Custom and stock designs; small and large orders.

Erd-Pirie, Inc.
3250 Monroe Street
Toledo, OH 43606
(419) 242-9545

Exterior and interior: polyester, vinyl, prismatic, frosted, Scotchlite, and plexiglass. Custom designs; small and large orders.

S & S Promotions
206 S.W. 30th
Oklahoma City, OK 73109
(405) 631-6516
(405) 631-8311

Exterior and interior: nylon, polyester, vinyl, and Scotchlite. Stock and custom designs; large orders. "Custom screen printing on most any surface."

Chroma-Tone, Inc.
3215 Oradell Lane
Dallas, TX 75220
(214) 385-1552

Exterior and interior: polyester, vinyl, frosted, Scotchlite, water applied, and aluminum. Small and large orders. Will supply samples of previously produced orders. Custom designed small and large orders.

Ad-Art Studios
813 Sixth Avenue
Fort Worth, TX 76104
(817) 335-9603

Exterior and interior; polyester, vinyl, Scotchlite, water applied, and mylar. Custom designed small and large orders. Also, hand-carved and sandblasted redwood signs.

Badger Decal, Inc.
407 E. Michigan
Milwaukee, WI 53202
(414) 273-1662

Exterior and interior: polyester, vinyl, Scotchlite, and water applied. Custom designs from sketch; small and large orders.

Pinter Grafix
224 W. Washington Street
Milwaukee, WI 53204
(414) 384-2311

Exterior and interior: nylon, polyester, vinyl, prismatic, frosted, Scotchlite, various foils, and water applied. Custom designed small and large orders.

Rockies and Far West

Signs by Fred
Anchorage, AK 99502

See listing under Signs.

Aztec Screen Print
Attn. Tony Schumway
333 S. Nina
Mesa, AZ 85202
(602) 833-3131

Exterior and interior: polyester, vinyl, frosted, and Scotchlite. Custom designs; small and large orders. Sizes: minimum, 1/2 by 1/2 inch, maximum, 4 by 8 feet. Also does silk screening of banners.

San Diego Silk Screen Inc.
7075 Mission Gorge Road
San Diego, CA 92120
(714) 286-4440

Exterior and interior: nylon, polyester, vinyl, prismatic, frosted, Scotchlite, and water applied. Also, solvent and cement applied, heat transfer, and mechanical applications systems. These decals can be applied to cloth. Custom designs; small and large orders.

Decals, Inc.
Box 208
Wheat Ridge, CO 80033
(303) 425-0510

Exterior and interior: polyester, vinyl, prismatic, frosted, Scotchlite, and water applied. Also, thermal die-cut prespaced legends and graphics. Custom designs; small and large orders. Telephone estimates when possible.

The Coble Company
1701 Broadway Avenue
Boise, ID 83706
(208) 344-7616

Exterior and interior: vinyl, prismatic, frosted, Scotchlite, water applied, and mylar. Small custom orders.

Masterscreen Products, Inc.
8225 S.E. Seventh
Portland, OR 97202
(503) 232-9104

Exterior and interior: polyester, vinyl, frosted, Scotchlite, aluminum, polycarbonate, and other rigid materials. Custom small and large orders. Maximum size, 20 by 28 inches.

Key

X Service, technique, or material is available
\+ See listing for further information
* Sometimes offers this service

	Fills small orders	Fills large orders	Stock designs	Custom designs	Brochure available	Telephone estimates
Northeast						
Prest-On Products New York, NY	X	X	X	X	X	X
Decal Techniques West Babylon, NY	X	X	X	X	X	X
Delta Decal Wyandanch, NY	X	X		X		X
Rich-Art Graphics Philadelphia, PA	X	X		X	X	X
Vermont Art Studio Pittsford, VT	X	X		X		X
Catozzi Signs Rutland, VT	See listing under Signs					
South						
Alabama Labels & Graphics Birmingham, AL	X	X		X		X
Central Advertising Columbia, SC	X	X	X	X		+
Art Display Washington, DC	X			X		X
Midwest						
Rydin Sign and Decal Bellwood, IL	X			X	X	X
The Meyercord Company Carol Stream, IL		X	X	X	X	
Labels and Decals Chicago, IL	X	X		X	X	X
Midwest Decalcomania Chicago, IL	X	X		X	X	X
White Advertising Merrillville, IN	X	X		X	X	
Artcraft Poster Display Detroit, MI	X	X		X	X	X
Continental Identification Sparta, MI		X		X	X	X
A. M. Graphics Minneapolis, MN	X	X		X		X
C.O.B. Decals Kansas City, MO	X	X		X	X	X
Don Shafer Display Omaha, NE	X			X		X

Key

X Service, technique, or material is available
+ See listing for further information
* Sometimes offers this service

	Fills small orders	Fills large orders	Stock designs	Custom designs	Brochure available	Telephone estimates
Fletcher Poster Columbus, OH	X	X	X	X		X
Erd-Pirie Toledo, OH	X	X		X		X
S. & S. Promotions Oklahoma City, OK		X	X	X		X
Chroma-Tone Dallas, TX	X	X		X	+	X
Ad-Art Studios Fort Worth, TX	X	X		X		X
Badger Decal Milwaukee, WI	X	X		X		X
Pinter Grafix Milwaukee, WI	X	X		X		X
Rockies and Far West						
Signs by Fred Anchorage, AK	See listing under Signs					
Aztec Screen Print Mesa, AZ	X	X		X	X	X
San Diego Silk Screen San Diego, CA	X	X		X	X	X
Decals Wheat Ridge, CO	X	X		X	X	*
The Coble Company Boise, ID	X			X		X
Masterscreen Products Portland, OR	X	X		X		

FIBER ART

Hangings are the simplest form of architectural fiber art. They are usually two-dimensional, sometimes with surface relief, and range in scale from intimate to monumental. Awnings, or awninglike structures that are painted, sewn together, or appliqued are a particularly useful type of fiber art (see "Awnings"). There are also three-dimensional creations that stand alone or are hung on rigid armatures and wander through plazas or interior spaces (see photo of the Kliot fiber sculpture). Banners, flags, and "windtubes" are yet another category, alternately two- and three-dimensional depending on the wind.

Some awning manufacturers will fabricate the work of fiber artists, so architects who want to design something along these lines can go directly to an awning maker for technical advice and fabrication.

We only asked our fiber artists about materials that are suitable for exterior use; many use other materials for interior pieces. The most durable outdoor materials for fiber art are the same as those for awnings: duck, canvas coated with vinyl, nylon, nywool, and other synthetics. Vinyl and heavyweight nylon are the only two that hold their color; canvas begins to fade noticeably in five to seven years depending on weather conditions. See introduction to Awnings for more detailed information about fabrics.

Different types of rope suitable for exterior pieces include nylon, dacron, polypropylene, and stainless steel wire. Ropes can be used as knotted hangings or perhaps in tension, as "trellises" for vines.

Monumentally scaled fiber sculpture by Jules and Kaethe Kliot, Berkeley, CA. (Photo by Jules Kliot, courtesy of Jules and Kaethe Kliot)

Special Listings

Gallery G
Attn. Carol Siegel, Director
408 Boulevard of the Allies
Pittsburgh, PA 15219
(412) 562-0912

Gallery G represents twelve fiber artists, two banner-makers, and one quilter—all of whom work in quite different styles. The range of their work includes hangings, free-standing fiber sculpture, and banners. Materials include nylon, duck, vinyl-coated canvas, spinnaker cloth, and nylon or stainless steel wire rope. The artists will supply preliminary sketches, estimates, and advice about maintenance; and they express a willingness to develop an idea with the architect. Gallery G specializes in what it calls "contract design" but which might also be called "turnkey" projects—planning, fabrication, and installation (as general contractor) of the entire project. All told, the Gallery represents sixty artists who—in addition to making banners, quilts, fiber sculpture, and three-dimensional fabric sculpture—work in plexiglass, metals, and wood. The technical staff includes a metal draftsman, structural engineer, and architect.

The Textile Conservation Center
Merrimack Valley Textile Museum
Attn. Jane K. Hutchins, Conservator
800 Massachusetts Avenue
North Andover, MA 01845
(617) 686-0191

Services include a laboratory for cleaning, chemical analysis, testing of fabrics, and photographic documentation before conservation steps are taken. Technical advice (written or oral) can be given on proper climate for preserving textiles and resistance of fabrics to types and levels of lighting, temperature, and humidity. The Center also cleans, stabilizes, and mounts older textiles. Michael Bogle's *Technical Notes*—a book covering problems of conserving a variety of natural and synthetic fibers, plus other, related topics—is available for $10.00 through the Museum.

Regional Listings

The following fiber artists do their own designs and will work with an architect to interpret the architect's ideas. Unless otherwise noted, each has either a brochure at no charge or photographs of his or her work. Also, we have listed some fiber artists who specialize in interior work, but who are interested in creating exterior pieces.

Northeast

Dawn MacNutt
5 Lyngby Avenue
Dartmouth, Nova Scotia
Canada B3A 3T5
(902) 469-4474
(902) 466-4792

Spinner, dyer, and weaver. MacNutt makes hangings, "trees," and other fiber sculpture—free-standing and hanging—including bird's nests, butterflies with 6-inch wingspans, and other delightful things. Has done large-scale hanging sculpture on steel frames. Also works in free-standing, woven wire sculpture—of trees and people—"about life-size."

Hanging sculptural trees in several "species" (8 feet to 12 feet high). Woven by Dawn MacNutt, Nova Scotia. In addition to the bird's nest, they are inhabited by a variety of small fauna such as butterflies and caterpillars (lower right of photo). (Photo courtesy of Dawn MacNutt)

Shirley Raphael
Canada Banner Company
Box 5371 St. Laurent Postal Station
Montreal, H4L 4Z9
Quebec, Canada
(514) 488-5548

Makes handpainted, parachute nylon banners; stock sizes 36 to 44 inches wide and up to 20 feet long. Material is colorfast and machine washable. Sketches are prepared first, with color swatches attached. Can incorporate words, writing, symbols, etc. Recommends hanging several together rather than sewing them to make a large piece. There are some stock designs but most are custom. Brochure and color slides available; there is a slight charge if many slides are required for examination. Price list available. Prices depend on the complexity of the final design.

Dolly Curtis
Architectural Textiles
35 Flatrock Road
Easton, CT 06612
(203) 372-4511

Hangings, free-standing sculpture, and "environmental fiber sculptures." Has done exterior work; uses ripstop nylon and duck. Can work in rope, and has made large, knotted rope hangings. Gives preliminary sketches, estimates, and advice on maintenance. Has interpreted an architect's ideas in fiber art.

Muriel Angelil
50 Lancaster Terrace
Brookline, MA 02146
(617) 566-2597

Does hangings and free-standing sculpture. "My work is inspired by underwater organisms and growths found in forests and on rocks. It is diaphanous and airy in character, but has a solid feel and touch." Uses rope, yarn, fabric, and found objects. Has done exterior pieces in sprang "netting," knotless netting, and rope macrame. Advises on maintenance.

Micala Sidore
15 Cedar Street
Northampton, MA 01060
(413) 586-4896

Tapestries (interior). Handwoven flat tapestry, 100 percent wool, highly representational—room interiors, landscapes, fruits, vegetables—to totally abstract. Gives preliminary sketches, estimates and advice on maintenance.

Kim Handschuh
29 Long Avenue
Mahwah, NJ 07430
(201) 529-3997

"Wall hangings, window coverings, chair backs, and seats designed to complement the aura of a room or area." Other projects taken into consideration. Handschuh works in jute, cotton, synthetics, feathers, shells, beads, wood, etc. Has done exterior pieces in nylon and nywool. Specializes in large, knotted rope or macrame hangings. Gives preliminary sketches, estimates, and advice on maintenance.

Paula Renee Hazlett
201 Serpentine Road
Tenafly, NJ 07670
(201) 568-3149

Interior hangings and murals; for exterior pieces would work in nylon, nywool, and rope. Her work emphasizes color and has strong textures; it is usually abstract, "often reminiscent of nature, with flowing lines and form." For interior pieces she uses wool, linen, cotton, silk, rayon, mohair, jute, chenille, ribbon, rope, Lurex (metallic), and fleece. A major emphasis on natural fibers, "often with unexpected combinations." Gives preliminary sketches, estimates, advice on maintenance.

Cindy Fornari
16 River Street, 2nd Floor
Chatham, NY 12037
(518) 392-4229
(518) 392-4582

Interior only. Handwoven, felted tile "squares" that can be grouped for hanging or to cover an entire wall. "Fiber tiles are modular wall pieces with the look of handmade paper. Each tile is made from two pieces of fabric, stitched together and felted with heat and abrasion. The felting process causes the wool fibers to 'lock' together, creating the 'deckled edge.' Other fibers used, such as cotton and silk, do not felt, and therefore provide a lovely contrast." Gives preliminary sketches and estimates. Might work with architect on the interpretation of an idea.

Jeanne Harris-McDonagh
168 Warburton Avenue
Hastings-on-Hudson, NY 10706
(914) 478-2322

Specializes in quilted "soft acrylic-batik" hangings. Unlike traditional batik, this artist prefers the spontaneity of painting directly on the fabric. "The finished works are colorful, three-dimensional, expressionist paintings of subjects taken from my environment." They are quilted and stuffed, thus "soft." Will also do banners. Gives preliminary sketches and estimates.

Ace Banner and Flag Co.
New York, NY 10012

See listing under Awnings.

Art Flag Co., Inc.
New York, NY 10003

See listing under Awnings.

Janet Goldner
611 Broadway #832
New York, NY 10012
(212) 677-3061

Interior hangings, free-standing pieces, and banners including—among other things—large, woven trees. "My fiber sculptures are woven on a loom and manipulated after weaving to create large, three-dimensional works. I enjoy the technical cleverness involved in using this traditional form in a nontraditional manner." Materials for interior pieces include wool, cotton, fiber glass, and metal wire. Also makes metal and fiber constructions. Could work in nylon, duck, wire, and rope for exterior. Gives preliminary sketch, estimates, and advice on maintenance.

Francoise Grossen
135 Greene Street
New York, NY 10012
(212) 777-1788

Two- and three-dimensional fiber constructions for large public spaces and residences. Uses sisal, paper, wick, rubber, etc.—natural and dyed. Braiding and/or knotting techniques; wall, floor, and pedestal pieces as well as miniatures. Hangings and free-standing sculpture. Has done exterior pieces in a variety of fabrics, as well as large (36 by 13 feet) pieces in rope. Gives preliminary sketch, estimates, and advice on maintenance.

Michele Lester
15 W. 17th Street
New York, NY 10011
(212) 989-1411

This studio can make "extremely large-scale and large quantity" interior tapestries. "I have worked for a long time with 'flat' tapestry, using landscape themes. Recently, extreme views—either closeups or aerials—have fascinated me. My experience of the Southwest is becoming part of the new pieces, too." Dyes wool by hand for custom work. For exterior, could work in nylon and nywool yarns or rope. Gives preliminary sketches, estimates, and advice on maintenance.

Jan Yoors Studio
108 Waverly Place
New York, NY 10011
(212) 533-8230

This studio produces tapestries in the Gobelin manner (interior only), using cotton warp and wool weft. Will translate your design into a tapestry. Gives preliminary sketches and estimates.

Bonnie Vierthalar
Whitehall
Smithville Flats, NY 13841
(607) 656-9413

Hangings, free-standing and suspended sculpture, and banners. Has done exterior work; can work in duck, nylon, nywool, vinyl-coated canvas, rubber, and plastic. Also uses different types of rope and would do large, knotted rope "hangings." Gives "rough" preliminary sketches, estimates, and advice on maintenance. Generally willing to work with an architect to interpret his or her idea; but she says it "depends on the idea."

Bakerworks
Sara L. Baker
1 E. Main Street
Westfield, NY 14787
(716) 326-2928

Tapestries typified by "spare, dramatic use of color to create asymmetrical, landscapelike elements with rich surfaces of

"Catenary Curves" (9¾ feet wide by 5 feet high by 5 inches deep); knotting, wrapping, and weaving; synthetic fiber, for interior or exterior use. Joan Michaels Paque (1980), Shorewood, WI (1980). (Photo by Henry P. Paque, courtesy of Joan Michaels Paque)

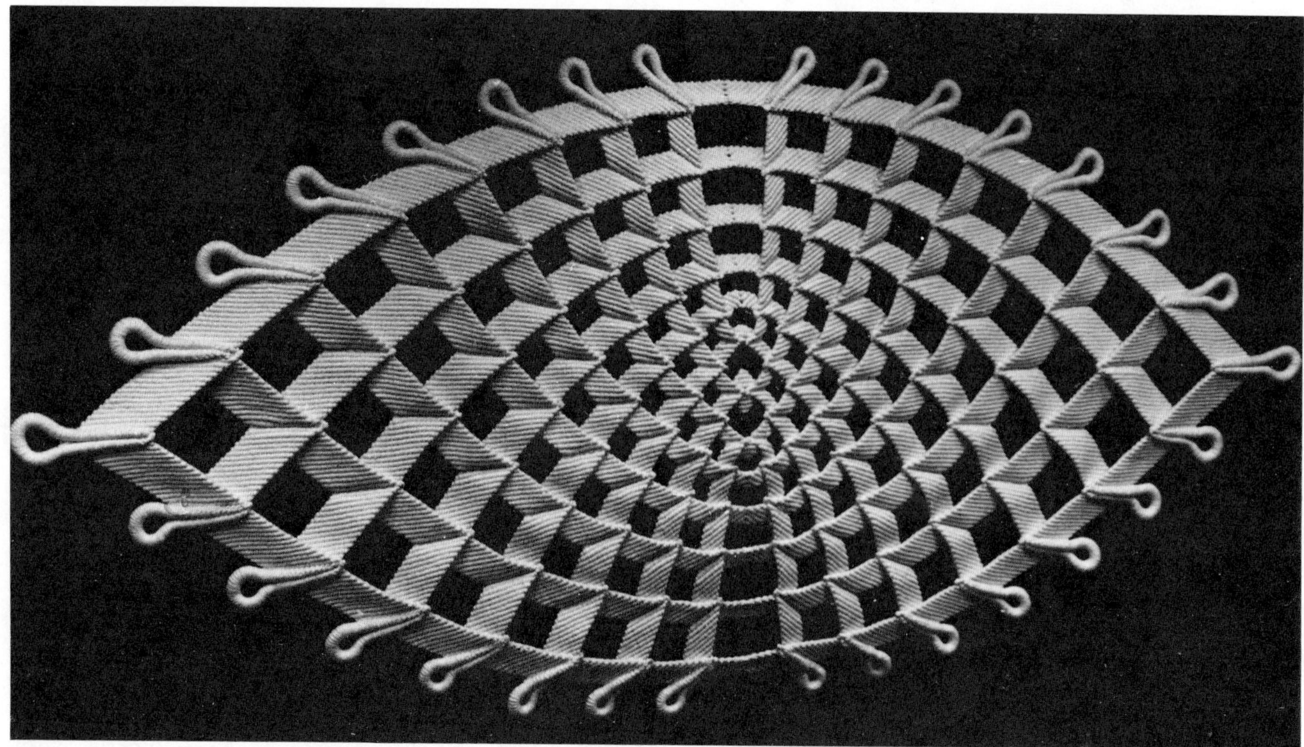

fine to coarse textures." Uses traditional and contemporary tapestry techniques, including selective painting of the piece while it is in the loom. Uses both natural and manmade materials. Has done exterior pieces in nylon and duck; hangings and three-dimensional, ceiling-hung (mobile) works; also able to do large rope pieces. Preliminary sketches, estimates, and advice on maintenance.

Michele Chenevert
RD 1, Box 930
Fox Road
Lebanon, PA 17042
(717) 274-5202

Woven textural tapestries "done as landscapes, modified into degrees of abstraction depending upon the client's desire." Works primarily in wool and linen, with cotton, synthetics, and unusual fibers. Interior hangings and free-standing sculpture. For exterior, would work in appropriate fabrics and rope; can make large rope "hangings." Gives estimates and advice on maintenance.

Karen Stoller
6038 Jackson Street
Pittsburgh, PA 15206
(412) 441-6158

Interior tapestries; can make large, knotted rope hangings. She works in "contemporary flat woven tapestries in 100 percent wool." Her approach is through "structural color," with special attention to the way in which each piece affects the space in which it is placed. Gives preliminary sketches, estimates, and advice on maintenance.

Anna M. Sunnergren
1231 Wightman Street
Pittsburgh, PA 15217
(412) 521-5702

Hangings, murals, and banners. Has done exterior pieces. Vivid banners with lettering and patterns, in realistic and abstract designs. Fabric "is always alive; moving, bending, wrinkling, stretching, shrinking, fading, fraying. The fact that all fabric originally was made from organic substances expands this 'living' quality in my thinking. Today's synthetics measure their success upon how well they can imitate wool, silk, cotton, linen, or leather. Fabric in combination with steel, granite, concrete, glass, etc., makes a perfect complement of the organic with the inorganic." For exterior work she uses "Sunbrella" awning fabric from Glen Raven Mills in North Carolina. Can use rope and do macrame hangings; gives preliminary sketches, estimates, and advice on maintenance.

Vickie Lieberman
Meadow House
Pocopson, PA 19366
(215) 793-1544

Lieberman's works are inspired by "the colors, movements, shapes, and lines of landscapes. From there I go inside the scene and express the feeling by transposing the colors and textures to fit the mood." Interior hangings, murals, and free-standing sculpture. Materials for large tapestry-hangings include wool, linen, mylar, rayon, and sisal. Gives preliminary sketches and estimates.

"Rainbow." Handwoven cotton yarns in rainbow spectrum (16 by 8 feet; each ribbon 21 feet by 7 inches). Architectural weaving by Dolly Curtis, Easton, CT. Installed, Richard Bergmann Architects, New Canaan, CT. (Photo by Victor Cromwell, courtesy of Dolly Curtis)

South

JoEl Logiudice-Clark
1005 Arthur Moore
Green Cove Springs, FL 32043
(904) 282-5937

"Life is a tactile experience. The textures, colors, and shapes that I incorporate into my fiber pieces reflect my love for the natural environment. For my large fiber pieces I manipulate handspun yarns, acrylics, and wool fibers to create abstract hangings with a sculptural relief quality." Interior hangings; willing to do exterior pieces in nylon and rope. Always gives preliminary sketches, often makes mock-ups. Gives estimates and advice on maintenance.

Martha C. Cowie
841 S. Johnson Avenue
Lakeland, FL 33801
(813) 683-4088

Interior hangings; for exterior, can work in nylon, duck, and vinyl-coated canvas. Large, handwoven fiber sculpture "for wall or ceiling treatments conducive to space, light, and shadow areas. Banded and solid—relative to movement." Oriented to enhance the simplicity of environment and to provide a sense of comfortable sensuality. Uses wool, linen, cotton, synthetics, aluminum, and wood. Gives preliminary sketches, estimates, and advice on maintenance.

Hélène Pancoast
Seagrape Designs, Inc.
3351 Poinciana Avenue
Coconut Grove, FL 33133
(305) 443-2653

Uses primarily natural materials in hangings: wool, linen, silk, and cotton. Direct dye applications through spraying, painting, and silkscreening; likes working on large-scale, abstract patterns. "My work is happy defining spaces visually, and often the pieces are equally interesting on both sides." Hangings and banners; has done exterior pieces using nylon and duck. Does large-scale fabric hangings and is interested in reaching clients with spaces suitable for her designs. Gives preliminary sketches, estimates, and advice on maintenance.

Ann Sams
3849 Leafy Way
Miami, FL 33133
(305) 444-1516

Exterior and interior banners; murals and hangings for interior. The artist has collaborated with designers and architects for over ten years. Fabrics dyed to order in vibrant colors. "I approach all surfaces as paintings, but I am no longer satisfied with a two-dimensional framed concept." Prefers the loose "construction of fabric which can be torn, twisted, and knotted—with color applied—the larger, the better." Gives preliminary sketches, estimates, and advice on maintenance.

Judith L. West
2959 Apalachee Parkway D-21
Tallahassee, FL 32301
(904) 878-6606

Interior hangings and "free-hanging sculpture." "My large hanging laces are a melting pot of architectural, structural, and natural imagery. I have worked with plastics, nylon cord, cotton, and rayon." Willing to do exterior work in nylon, duck, and rope. Preliminary sketches, estimates, and advice on maintenance. Possibly willing to interpret an architect's idea.

Ken Weaver
38 Inman Circle N.E.
Atlanta, GA 30309
(404) 892-7918

Interior hangings, murals, and banners. Specializes in "large-scale, woven, sculptural hangings for large spaces." For exterior, would work in nylon, vinyl-coated canvas, plexiglass, and rope. Gives preliminary sketches, estimates, and advice on maintenance.

Joanna Sunshine
RFD 1, Box 341-1A
Blacksburg, VA 24060
(703) 951-7234

Contemporary environmental works. Two- and three-dimensional constructions to support the physical environment. Small- and large-scale. Natural fiber and innovative explorations in materials. Has done exterior pieces; hangings, free-standing sculptures, and banners in duck, nylon, nywool, and vinyl-coated canvas. Can also do rope trellises, etc. Gives preliminary sketches, estimates, and advice on maintenance.

"Tulip," detail. Handweaving (50 by 80 inches) by April May, Weaving IV Design Studio, Venice, CA. (Photo courtesy of April May)

Phyllis Hazel Cullison
806 Westover Road
Richmond, VA 23220
(804) 353-9960

Loom-woven tapestries, tapestries woven into plexiglass, free-standing sculpture, and banners. Has done a series of twelve large panels, each 5 by 12 feet. "My handwoven tapestries convey a mood of restfulness. The subject matter ranges from Oriental landscape to abstract. The tapestries are finished by upholstering panels of homosote over thick dacron batting. They are lined on the back with muslin and serve as excellent sound-absorbers." Materials include silk, linen, cotton, rayon, metallic threads, blends, and wool. Gives preliminary sketches, estimates, and advice on maintenance.

Patricia McKenna Glavé
1725 Park Avenue
Richmond, VA 23220
(804) 353-4054

Hangings and free-standing sculpture. Has done exterior pieces and can work in nylon and rope. "My sculptural wall hangings and suspended pieces are knotted—usually in natural fibers, often hand-dyed, ranging from 2 to 8 feet long, from 2 to 5 feet wide, and from 1 1/2 to 3 1/2 inches deep." Style ranges from surrealistic to realistic. Materials include sisal, jute, coconut husk, horsehair, and large, braided yarns. Gives estimates and advice on maintenance.

Midwest

Virginia Boyd
11320 Southridge
Little Rock, AR 72212
(501) 227-0270

Interior hangings; could work in rope for exterior pieces. "I like to produce large and vibrantly colored fiber art in abstract design with strong textural emphasis. I want my work to be an integral part of the architectural design." Has used wool, cotton, synthetics, rope, leather, fur, and silk. Will create rope trellises, awninglike objects, and other fiber objects integral to buildings. Gives preliminary sketches, estimates, and advice on maintenance.

Charles Lupori
3735 W. 153rd
Midlothian, IL 60445
(312) 389-4828

Interior hangings, murals, and banners. All work is done by direct pigment application on natural fibers. For exterior would work with duck and vinyl-coated canvas. Produces limited additions of yardages for upholstery, etc. Gives preliminary sketches, estimates, and advice on maintenance.

Elaine Ball
RR #2
Mt. Vernon, IA 52314
(319) 895-8793

Current works are large, framed, wall pieces of handmade felt using natural and dyed wools. "The theme is basically of earth and sky." Banners and hangings; has done exterior pieces using duck, nylon, nywool, and vinyl-coated canvas; can use rope. She is also involved in production of handmade lamps with handthrown pottery bases and handwoven shades. Gives preliminary sketches, estimates, and advice on maintenance.

Robert L. Kidd Associates, Inc.
Attn. Robert L. Kidd
107 Townsend Street
Birmingham, MI 48011
(313) 642-3909

Free-form, three-dimensional, sculptured and woven wall hangings—primarily of wool, shaped and formed over a structured base. Interior hangings, murals, free-standing sculpture, and banners; would do exterior pieces in duck, nylon, nywool, and vinyl-coated canvas. Can work in all types of rope and would be able to make large rope hangings. Gives preliminary sketches, estimates, and advice on maintenance.

Linda Franzel-Annette
2331 E. 5th Street
Duluth, MN 55812
(218) 728-1563

Hangings, murals, free-standing sculptures, banners, textured walls, and ceiling pieces. Pieces to define such areas as entrances or exits or sitting areas in fiber and fabric forms. Has done exterior work in duck, nylon, nywool, and canvas. Can make large, knotted rope hangings. Gives sketches and estimates.

Nancy G. Miller
4728 York Avenue S.
Minneapolis, MN 55410
(612) 925-3989

Does mainly tapestries, with custom-dyed wool yarns; "very firm in hand (ruglike) and superior in use of color and texture. They are mostly two-dimensional, in a variety of sizes. The subject matter is often inspired by landscape, but the colors are not." She has done interior hangings and murals; can do large rope pieces. Gives preliminary sketches, estimates, and advice on maintenance. Miller also does commission work to specification. This work has included the following materials and methods: custom-dyed wool yarns (tapestry); custom-dyed cotton fabric (quilting, banners, etc.); nylon rope (large park sculpture); plus a variety of fabrics for upholstery, drapery, and floor coverings.

All Nations Capitol Flag & Banner Co.
118 W. 5th Street
Kansas City, MO 64105
(816) 842-8798

"Our primary business is selling flags, flag poles, and accessories. We custom make flags and banners in nylon and felt."

Athens Tapestry Works
Attn. Noreen Redding
Box 663
Athens, OH 45701
(614) 592-4319

An artists' cooperative designing and producing one-of-a-kind fiber hangings, wall sculptures, murals, and banners on a commission basis. A limited line of wholesale work also available. Standard procedure involves an analysis of the space in which the work will hang and the presentation of three to five designs from which the client chooses. The members have done exterior work, and can work in rope as well as in fabrics.

Carol Adams
2355 Main Street
Peninsula, OH 44264
(216) 657-2681

Wall sculptures are "abstract and highly textured. They are organic, with the shapes taken from nature." The edges and back of these sculptures are wired to make them bend away from the wall. Sometimes uses enamels on copper and wood to complement the fiber, but her sculptures are mainly woven and wrapped fiber forms.

John Winterich and Associates
Solon, OH 44139

See listing under Murals.

Blake Alexander
3004 Owenwood
Fort Worth, TX 76109
(817) 924-3975

Does hangings and possibly free-standing sculpture; has done knotted rope pieces. Incorporates "natural responses to fibers, using the simplest forms possible—such as squares or rectangles. I like to fold, drape, and pull the fabric to create a new identity for the forms and at the same time create a variety of dimensions." Works in cotton, wool, silk, rayon, linen, and clay. Would do exterior work in nylon or rope. Gives preliminary sketches, estimates, and advice on maintenance.

Joan Michaels-Paque
4455 N. Frederick Avenue
Milwaukee, WI 53211
(414) 962-2748

"My work reflects my interests in topology (study of warped surfaces) and constructivism and my attempts to use these in unique and unorthodox ways. I consider myself a sculptor whose medium is any flexible, linear material." Has done exterior work; materials she has used include metal sheeting and strips, wire, plastic, natural and synthetic fibers and fabrics, paper, plaster, and paint. Also works in rope—nylon, dacron, polypropylene—and can make large rope hangings. Sometimes gives preliminary sketches of her work, and might be willing to interpret an architect's ideas. Gives advice on maintenance.

Rockies and Far West

Wendy J. Black
11602 89th Street
Edmonton, Alberta
Canada T5B 3V2
(403) 477-7195

"My works are a reaction against mass-production and represent a desire to return to the exclusivity of handmade objects. While my inspiration is drawn from many sources, I never copy techniques but prefer to experiment with and expand upon them to attain an original juxtaposition of all fibers and all techniques for three-dimensional sculptural qualities." Hangings, murals, free-standing sculpture, and banners. Gives preliminary sketches, estimates, and advice on maintenance.

Lynn Murray
421 Clubhouse Drive
Aptos, CA 95003
(408) 688-8850

Hangings; for exterior pieces could use nylon, nywool, and pipe wrapped with rope. Can work in rope, and could make large, knotted rope hangings. Gives preliminary sketches (models when necessary), estimates, and advice on maintenance.

Richard Elliott
1269 Alcatraz #2
Berkeley, CA 94702
(415) 658-6210

"My work is abstract in design. It utilizes quite a bit of negative space (background) for a subtle, yet striking effect; generally in three or four colors." Elliott is interested in the "sensual, soft aspect of textiles as wall coverings or 'fiber paintings,' rather than very heavily textured fiber art. My pieces tend to look fragile, even aged, due to my affinity for primitive relics and artifacts. Actually, they are quite strong and durable." Works mainly in handmade felts (from wool fleece) used in combination with woven or netted elements, cheesecloth, sticks, yarns, threads, coconut husk, paper, satin, excelsior, upholstery piping, yak hair, and feathers. Does interior hangings and murals; could use various materials, including rope, for exterior work. Gives advice on maintenance.

Jules and Kaethe Kliot
2150 Stuart Street
Berkeley, CA 94705
(415) 843-7178

They have done quite large exterior pieces including an "event" involving thirty miles of sisal and manila rope in twenty-two sprang panels; this "event" was five stories high and surrounded three sides of the Transamerica Pyramid in San Francisco. Their murals, hangings, and lace tapestries are worked in jute, marlin, wax linen, wool, monofilament, copper wire, and sisal. "Each item and job demands its own fiber, and we do not limit ourselves in this." Gives preliminary sketches, estimates, and advice on maintenance.

Banner for Meadville Unitarian Church (approximately 15 by 7 feet). Anna M. Sunnergren, Pittsburgh, PA. (Photo by Photo-Graphic Arts, courtesy of Anna M. Sunnergren)

Lynden Keith Johnson
P.O. Box 1121
Cupertino, CA 95015
(408) 292-8071

Interior woven hangings and large, silkscreened panels. "Themes range from semiabstract animals to purely abstract—an aura of travelling through the universe." Could work in bound rope for large, knotted rope hangings. Gives preliminary sketches and estimates.

Alix Elizabeth Peshette
8622 Pershing Avenue
Fair Oaks, CA 95628
(916) 967-0239

"I weave surreal landscapes using traditional tapestry techniques. The materials are hand-dyed wool, silk, and cotton." Has not done exterior work before; but is moving into this area, and is well-versed in techniques that would work well for exterior pieces. Gives preliminary sketches and estimates.

Deborah Corsini
1342 Green Street #1
San Francisco, CA 94109
(415) 771-7996

Uses a "simple woven tapestry technique to create large, abstract, geometric designs. Line and color are important elements—defining space and conveying contrast, visual movement, illusion of volume." Uses linen warp and wool weft; normally uses 100 percent natural dyes and handspun yarns. Hangings and tapestries for interiors. Could use nylon and nywool for exterior pieces. Gives preliminary sketches, estimates, and advice on maintenance.

Danielle Hochman
690 Third Avenue
San Francisco, CA 94118
(415) 751-1424

Dye-painted wall hangings for interiors. Works primarily with silk and rayon yarns that have been dyed "in such a way that fading will not occur." All fiber works are "subjective, and all are created with physical durability in mind." Could work in exterior materials: nylon and ropes. Gives preliminary sketches, estimates, and advice on maintenance.

Christine Lardon-Rhone
Cultural Resource Management Center
78 Woodland Avenue
San Francisco, CA 94117
(415) 564-6711

Hangings, murals, and banners; has done exterior work. Could work in duck, nylon, nywool, and canvas. Gives preliminary sketches and estimates.

Toni A. Lowenthal
Limited Edition Textiles
1703 Paterna Road
Santa Barbara, CA 93101
(805) 965-1664

Weavings, "usually weft-faced, incorporating raw silk, ribbons, old trims, labels or 'exotic' yarns such as plastics, and metals. Most of my fabrics are laminated prior to cutting. I do not think of my pieces as 'wall hangings' but as panels or friezes inset into architectural settings." Gives preliminary sketches, estimates, and advice on maintenance.

"View Through Window." Weaving by Alix E. Peshette, Fair Oaks, CA. (Photo courtesy of Alix E. Peshette)

Bonita Diemoz
232 Potrero Street
Santa Cruz, CA 95060
(408) 426-2313

Large geometric patterns in high contrast and bright colors. Pieces are woven flat, and then pleated to add dimension and depth; 90 percent wool, 10 percent miscellaneous fibers. Has done interior hangings in nylon, jute, sisal, and manila fibers. Gives preliminary sketches, estimates, and advice on maintenance.

Richard D. Lyles
P.O. Box 635
Topanga, CA 90290
(213) 455-3038

Interior hangings, also stage design—interior and exterior. Can work in rope and make large hangings. Will interpret an architect's idea "within limits." Gives preliminary sketches and estimates.

Weaving IV Design Studio
April May
642 Venice Boulevard
Venice, CA 90291
(213) 823-3424

Her window art is a direct response to the effects of light—sunlight to moonlight—"a constant flow between illusion and reality." She derives most of her images from nature—seascapes, landscapes, birds, clouds, and flowers. Works in laid-in technique; wool, cotton, silk, and linen. Visits to studio by appointment only. Also macrame-type hangings. Gives preliminary sketches, estimates, and advice on maintenance.

Sidestreet Bannerworks
Attn. Marc Horovitz
1852 Blake Street
Denver, CO 80202
(303) 825-3186

Sidestreet's "textile graphics" are machine-sewn from colored fabrics, and can be used as banners, flags, hangings, awnings, space dividers, window coverings, "windtubes" (a colorful, giant sort of wind sock), etc. Interior or exterior. Prefers heavy nylon or cotton duck, although the methods can be applied to virtually any woven fabric. All work is "custom designed to suit the individual needs of the client." Gives preliminary sketches, estimates, and advice on maintenance.

Sharon La Pierre
2942 Chase Street
Denver, CO 80214
(303) 237-9116

Does interior hangings and free-standing sculpture. Could work in nylon and rope; would do large, knotted rope hangings. Gives preliminary sketches, estimates, and advice on maintenance.

Anne Edwards
2404 W. 2nd Avenue
Durango, CO 81301
(303) 259-3278

"Unique combinations of macrame and weaving techniques sculptured to fit any area. Made from natural fibers of many shades for use as doorways, room dividers, or window and wall coverings to complement any decor." Interior hangings; could do exterior pieces in nylon and rope. Gives preliminary sketches and advice on maintenance.

Jan McDole
10,000 Dryden
Reno, NV 89511
(702) 851-1115

Fiber hangings and pieces combining clay and fiber. McDole "emphasizes form, texture, and color through a handwoven process. The design of each piece is determined by what works with the existing environment. Themes vary from Indian motifs to 'moonscapes' to fairytale fantasies." Has done exterior work: duck, nylon, nywool, vinyl-coated canvas. Could make large, knotted hangings. Gives preliminary sketches, estimates, and advice on maintenance.

Alice Webb
P.O. Box 45
San Cristobal, NM 87564
(505) 776-8132

"Weaving for me is a creative meditation; an attempt to reflect the many paradoxes of the place in which I live. The quiet grandness of nature is what I wish to convey in my work." Interior hangings, banners, and free-standing sculpture. Materials include wool, linen, polyester, silk, cotton, jute twine, plexiglass, paper, and various metals. Prefers to make a preliminary model rather than a sketch; gives estimates and advice on maintenance.

Christina Bergh
711 Camino Corrales
Santa Fe, NM 87501
(505) 988-4893
(505) 983-3401

Her designs range from geometric patterns to semiabstract landscapes and cityscapes. Does tapestries only. Gives preliminary sketches, estimates, and advice on maintenance. Twenty-four page color catalog available on request.

Alice Van Leunen
P.O. Box 16
Marylhurst, OR 97036
(503) 245-6000

Does hangings, hanging sculpture, and banners. Her work falls in two categories: (1) abstract woven landscape/skyscape panels, many depicting water and land formations, and (2) three-dimensional folded and manipulated fabric strips forming wall reliefs and free-hanging or free-standing sculptures. Interior pieces are primarily wool; can do exterior pieces in nylon, metal wire, synthetic, weatherproof fabrics, and rope. Gives preliminary sketches, estimates, and advice on maintenance.

Diane Royal Dootson
16017 77th Avenue N.E.
Arlington, WA 98223
(206) 435-2755

Interior hangings, banners, murals, and rugs. "Three-dimensional or flat pieces, can do any size." All natural dyes or natural color of fiber; mothproofed. Works in wool, silk, cotton, feathers, and pottery beads. Can work in stainless steel wire rope as well as fabric for exterior pieces. Gives preliminary sketches, estimates, and advice on maintenance.

Bucky King
King Brothers Ranch
Box 371 Buffalo Star Route
Sheridan, WY 82801
(307) 672-5354

A spinner, weaver, stitcher, lacemaker, quilter, and metal thread-worker for twenty-five years. "Inspiration for my fiber works comes from the ranchland—its mountains, creeks, and landscapes." Does hangings, banners, and large, knotted rope hangings; has done exterior pieces. Can work in nylon, duck, and rope. Gives preliminary sketches, estimates, and advice on maintenance.

Key

X Service, technique, or material is available
+ See listing for further information
* Sometimes offers this service

Northeast	Hangings	Banners	Free-standing sculpture	Exterior pieces	Can work in rope	Estimates
Dawn MacNutt Nova Scotia, Canada	X		X	X	X	X
Shirley Raphael Quebec, Canada		X		X		X
Dolly Curtis Easton, CT	X	X	X	X	X	X
Muriel Angelil Brookline, MA	X		X	X	X	X
Micala Sidore Northampton, MA	X					X
Kim Handschuh Mahwah, NJ	X			X	X	X
Paula Renee Hazlett Tenafly, NJ	X				X	X
Cindy Fornari Chatham, NY	X					X
Jeanne Harris-McDonagh Hastings-on-Hudson, NY	X	X		X		X
Ace Banner and Flag New York, NY	See listing under Awnings					
Art Flag New York, NY	See listing under Awnings					
Janet Goldner New York, NY	X				X	X
Françoise Grossen New York, NY	X		X	X	X	X
Michelle Lester New York, NY	X				X	X
Jan Yoors Studio New York, NY	X					X
Bonnie Vierthalar Smithville Flats, NY	X	X	X	X	X	X
Bakerworks Westfield, NY	X		X	X	X	X
Michele Chenevert Lebanon, PA	X		X		X	X
Karen Stoller Pittsburgh, PA	X				X	X
Anna M. Sunnergren Pittsburgh, PA	X	X		X	X	X
Vickie Lieberman Pocopson, PA	X		X			X

Key

- X Service, technique, or material is available
- \+ See listing for further information
- * Sometimes offers this service

	Hangings	Banners	Free-standing sculpture	Exterior pieces	Can work in rope	Estimates
South						
JoEl Logiudice-Clark Green Cove Springs, FL	X				X	X
Martha C. Cowie Lakeland, FL	X					X
Hélène Pancoast Miami, FL	X	X		X		X
Ann Sams Miami, FL	X			X		X
Judith L. West Tallahassee, FL	X		X		X	X
Ken Weaver Atlanta, GA	X	X			X	X
Joanna Sunshine Blacksburg, VA	X	X	X	X	X	X
Phyllis Hazel Cullison Richmond, VA	X	X	X			X
Patricia McKenna Glavé Richmond, VA	X		X	X	X	X
Midwest						
Virginia Boyd Little Rock, AR	X				X	X
Charles Lupori Midlothian, IL	X					X
Elaine Ball Mt. Vernon, IA	X	X		X	X	X
Robert L. Kidd Birmingham, MI	X	X	X		X	X
Linda Franzel-Annette Duluth, MN	X	X	X	X	X	X
Nancy G. Miller Minneapolis, MN	X				X	X
All Nations Flag & Banner Kansas City, MO		X		X		X
Athens Tapestry Works Athens, OH	X	X	X	X	X	X
Carol Adams Peninsula, OH	X				X	X
John Winterich and Associates Solon, OH	See listing under Murals					

Key

X Service, technique, or material is available
+ See listing for further information
* Sometimes offers this service

	Hangings	Banners	Free-standing sculpture	Exterior pieces	Can work in rope	Estimates
Blake Alexander Fort Worth, TX	X				X	X
Joan Michaels-Paque Milwaukee, WI			X	X	X	X
Rockies and Far West						
Wendy J. Black Alberta, Canada	X	X	X			X
Lynn Murray Aptos, CA	X				X	X
Richard Elliott Berkeley, CA	X				X	X
Jules and Kaethe Kliot Berkeley, CA	X		X	X		X
Lynden Keith Johnson Cupertino, CA	X				X	X
Alix Elizabeth Peshette Fair Oaks, CA	X	X			X	X
Deborah Corsini San Francisco, CA	X					X
Danielle Hochman San Francisco, CA	X				X	X
Christine Lardon-Rhone San Francisco, CA	X	X		X		X
Toni A. Lowenthal Santa Barbara, CA	X					X
Bonita Diemoz Santa Cruz, CA	X				X	X
Richard D. Lyles Topanga, CA	X				X	X
Weaving IV Design Studio Venice, CA	X					X
Sidestreet Bannerworks Denver, CO	X	X		X		X
Sharon La Pierre Denver, CO	X		X		X	X
Anne Edwards Durango, CO	X				X	X
Jan McDole Reno, NV	X			X	X	X

Key

X Service, technique, or material is available
+ See listing for further information
* Sometimes offers this service

	Hangings	Banners	Free-standing sculpture	Exterior pieces	Can work in rope	Estimates
Alice Webb San Cristobal, NM	X	X	X		X	X
Christina Bergh Santa Fe, NM	X					X
Alice Van Leunen Marylhurst, OR	X	X	X		X	X
Diane Royal Dootson Arlington, WA	X	X			X	X
Bucky King Sheridan, WY	X			X	X	X

FOUNDRIES

Architects are often sculptors in their own right. Our aim in including foundries is to show architects where they can have their own decorative designs translated into bronze, stainless steel, aluminum, and other metals.

While foundries are customarily associated with sculpture, many will also cast plaques, letters, and other architectural elements. Decorative possibilities range from signs, logos, and directional graphics to repetitive decorative plaques to the sort of flamboyant metalwork for which Louis Sullivan was famous.

Regional Listings

Northeast

Renaissance Art Foundry, Inc.
250 Smith Street
Bridgeport, CT 06607
(203) 384-6363

Casts aluminum and bronze; free-standing and bas-relief sculpture. Can recommend a model-maker or an architectural sculptor. Estimates given from photo of original. Equipped for one-of-a-kind to large production runs.

Johnson Atelier
Technical Institute of Sculpture
743 Alexander Road
Princeton, NJ 08540
(609) 452-2661

This is a craft school with fifty-five sculptors teaching all technical aspects of sculpture and making these technical services available to the professional sculptor and architect. Can do modeling and enlarging; ceramic shell and sand mold-making; foundry; sand and wax casting; fabrication, chasing, and patination. They work in cast iron, stainless steel, aluminum, bronze, cupro-nickel, and plastics (polyester and epoxy resins). Can do one-of-a-kind or very small editions (bas-relief and free-standing). Will work from a model made in virtually any material or will make a model from a rough sketch or sample. Prefers to give an estimate based on the original model.

Roman Bronzeworks
Attn. Phillip Schiavo or John Schiavo
9618 43rd Avenue
Corona, NY 11368
(212) 429-4402
(212) 429-4403

The Schiavo family has operated this business since 1901. The company does casting and fabricating of ornamental metalwork including statuary, bas-relief sculpture, plaques, doors, and frames. Work is done in bronze, aluminum, white metals, gold, and silver. Can cast from models in any material or can make own model. Will manufacture to architect's specifications.

Sculpture House Castings, Inc.
38 E. 30th Street
New York, NY 10016
(212) 684-3445

Works in bronze, cast stone, and plastics—free-standing and bas-relief. Makes own models from sketch. Gives estimates based on sketch or more complete information. Any size order.

Sculpture Services, Inc.
9 E. 19th Street
New York, NY 10003
(212) 254-8585

Specialty: mold-making. Does cold-cast bronze and aluminum from any kind of model; can also make own model from sketch. Estimates given based on sketch. One-of-a-kind or small editions.

Wheeler Brothers Brass Founders, Inc.
2751 Fifth Avenue
Troy, NY 12180
(518) 272-8591

Specialty: aluminum and bronze plaques and tablets. Can do nonlettering designs, logos, coats of arms, and patterns of all types. "Our artist sculpts portraits, landscapes, buildings, etc., to go on plaques." Can work from models in most materials, photographs, or drawings. Estimates based on sketch. Any size order up to 15,000 pieces.

Donald Miller
Warwick, NY 10990

See listing under Sculpture.

Art Bronze and Manufacturing Co.
500 37th Street
Pittsburgh, PA 15201
(412) 621-1550

Specializes in bronze and aluminum castings—lost wax method and investment molding. Also works in copper and brass.

Paul King Foundry
92 Allendale Avenue
Johnston, RI 02919
(401) 231-3120

Aluminum, bronze, and yellow brass. Specialty: bronze sculpture casting. Can work from models in a variety of materials, and can recommend both model-maker and architectural sculptor. Estimates from photo or original. Any size order.

South

Lawler Machine and Foundry Co.
760 N. 44th Street
Birmingham, AL 35212
(205) 595-0596

Cast iron and aluminum; will do custom work to architects' specifications. Specialty: iron and aluminum castings made from aluminum matchplate and poured in sand molds. Can work from wood and metal models; estimates from sample only. Small editions and large runs. Catalogue $5.00.

All Bronze Foundry, Inc.
683 W. 26th Street
Hialeah, FL 33010
(305) 883-8484

Aluminum, bronze, and manganese; specializes in sand casting. Can make own models from sketch or sample, and can recommend an architectural sculptor. Estimates from sketch. Any size order.

Engineered Castings, Inc.
1025 S.E. 5th Street
Hialeah, FL 33010
(305) 887-9526

Specialty: aluminum and bronze bas-relief sand casting. Can make own models based on rough sketch. Estimates from sketch or spec sheet. Any size order.

United States Bronze and Aluminum Corp.
1065 E. 28th Street
Hialeah, FL 33013
(305) 836-2880

Specializes in casting bronze and aluminum plaques and statues.

"Nocturnus" (2 by 4 feet). Pierced nickel bronze bas-relief for Philadelphia Zoo. Donald Miller, Warwick, NY. (Photo courtesy of Donald Miller)

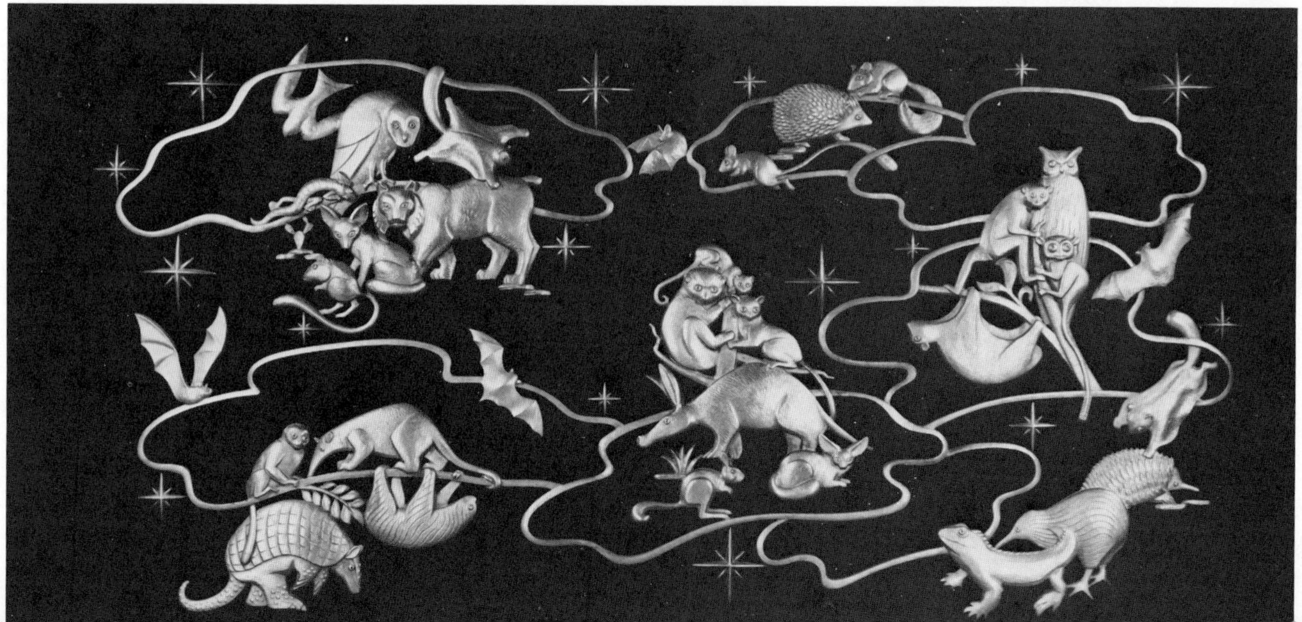

Midwest

Architectural Bronze and Aluminum Corp.
3638 W. Oakton Street
Skokie, IL 60076
(312) 539-0500
(312) 674-3638

Specializes in cast bronze, fabricated stainless steel, and acrylic baked enamel plaques, tablets, emblems, and letters (cast and cut out). Also does bas-relief work, etching, and modular graphics.

Experi-Metal or Plastics, Inc.
6345 Wall Street
Sterling Heights, MI 48077
(313) 977-7800

Metals: this company can produce drawn or die formed metal moldings and decorative castings in zinc and aluminum; can also do stamping and welding. Plastics: various types of molded plastics. The foundry (24,000-pound capacity) does plaster and sand casting and can reproduce any texture or grain. Design section and in-plant personnel are capable of decorative fabrications in all metals and various molded plastics. One-of-a-kind, small, and medium runs.

St. Paul Brass Foundry Co.
954 W. Minnehaha Avenue
St. Paul, MN 55104
(612) 488-5567

Manufactures bronze and aluminum plaques. Call or write for names of representatives in other cities.

Pasterchik Foundry and Iron Works
12806 Arrow Head Pass
Round Rock, TX 78664
(512) 258-6886
(512) 451-3419

Stainless steel, aluminum, bronze, fiber glass, and cast stone. Specialty: portraits and other original art works. Can work from models in a variety of materials or make own models from sketch. Estimates from sketch. Any size order.

Rockies and Far West

Franco Vianello
San Lorenzo, CA 94580

See listing under Sculpture.

Carter Casting Co., Inc.
9220 Atlantic Avenue
South Gate, CA 90280
(213) 566-5249

Bronze and aluminum. Can work from variety of model materials or can make own models from sketch. Estimates from sketch. Any size order.

West Coast Sculptors Foundry
1941 Pontius Avenue
West Los Angeles, CA 90025
(213) 473-4571

Bronze casting; specializes in limited editions. Can work from models in different materials. Can make own models from sample or photo, and can recommend a model-maker and architectural sculptor. Estimates based on sketch.

Tucker Enterprises
5555 Harlan
Arvada, CO 80002
(303) 423-5535

Works in bronze and white bronze. Specialty: free-standing sculpture. Models from variety of materials; can recommend model-maker. Estimates from sketch. One-of-a-kind and small editions.

Winner Foundries and Manufacturing, Inc.
5665 Marshall Street
Arvada, CO 80001
(303) 424-5509

Aluminum and bronze; bas-relief and free-standing. Can work from models in variety of materials or make own models from sketch. Estimates given on sketch. One-of-a-kind to large production runs.

Art Castings of Colorado, Inc.
511 8th Street, S.E.
Loveland, CO 80537
(303) 667-1114

Cast iron, aluminum, stainless steel, corten steel, and bronze. Specializes in bronze sculpture: bas-relief and free-standing. Can work from models in variety of materials; will recommend model-maker or architectural sculptor. Estimates from sketch or photo; any size order.

Oregon Brass Works
1127 S.E. 10th
Portland, OR 97214
(503) 232-7121

Specializes in architectural tablets and plaques, logos, and bas-relief portraits; can also do free-standing sculpture. Works in aluminum, bronze, nickel silver, and brass. Can make own models from photo or working drawing (sometimes from sketch or sample), depending on the item. Can recommend model-maker or architectural sculptor.

Northwest Bronze Foundry
Attn. George Bishop
2929 Lampman Road
Ferndale, WA 98248
(206) 384-1144

Aluminum and bronze casting; free-standing and bas-relief. Specialty: lost wax bronze casting for artists. Can work from models in different materials or can make own models from sketch. Estimates given from sketch. One-of-a-kind or small editions.

Key

See also Sculpture for artists who work in this material.

- X Service, technique, or material is available
- + See listing for further information
- * Sometimes offers this service

	Iron	Stainless steel	Aluminum	Bronze	Makes models	Recommends model-makers	Estimates from sketch	Brochure available
Northeast								
Renaissance Art Foundry Bridgeport, CT			X	X		X		
Johnson Atelier Princeton, NJ	X	X	X	X	X		+	X
Roman Bronzeworks Corona, NY			X	X	X		X	X
Sculpture House Castings New York, NY				X	X	X		
Sculpture Services New York, NY			X	X	X		X	X
Wheeler Brothers Troy, NY			X	X	X		X	X
Donald Miller Warwick, NY	See listing under Sculpture							
Art Bronze and Manufacturing Pittsburgh, PA			X	X	X			X
Paul King Foundry Johnston, RI			X	X		X	+	
South								
Lawler Foundry Birmingham, AL	X		X				+	+
All Bronze Foundry Hialeah, FL			X	X	X	X	X	
Engineered Castings Hialeah, FL			X	X	X		X	
United States Bronze Hialeah, FL			X	X	X			
Midwest								
Architectural Bronze Skokie, IL			X		X	X		X
Experi-Metal or Plastics Sterling Heights, MI					X		X	
St. Paul Brass Foundry St. Paul, MN			X	X	X			
Pasterchik Foundry Round Rock, TX		X	X	X	X		X	
Rockies and Far West								
Franco Vianello San Lorenzo, CA	See listing under Sculpture							

Key

See also Sculpture for artists who work in this material.
- **X** Service, technique, or material is available
- **+** See listing for further information
- ***** Sometimes offers this service

	Iron	Stainless steel	Aluminum	Bronze	Makes models	Recommends model-makers	Estimates from sketch	Brochure available
Carter Casting South Gate, CA			X	X	X		X	
West Coast Sculptors West Los Angeles, CA				X	X	X	X	
Tucker Enterprises Arvada, CO				X		X	X	
Winner Foundries Arvada, CO			X	X	X		X	X
Art Castings of Colorado Loveland, CO	X	X	X	X		X	X	
Oregon Brass Works Portland, OR			X	X	+	X	X	X
Northwest Bronze Foundry Ferndale, WA			X	X	X		X	

GLASS

Stained glass probably originated in the Middle East over 2,000 years ago, when pieces of colored glass were first imbedded in heavy matrices of stone or plaster. Leaded glass is more familiar in the West and dates from the Middle Ages.

The art of stained glass is in a period of lively revival. Perhaps one of the many reasons is because, as one of the studios told us, "private construction interests have discovered that the one percent of construction cost invested in stained glass increases sales values of a building by ten percent." The photographs we received ranged from the most traditional to the most contemporary and included stained, clear, textured glass, found objects, and the like. As with certain other types of ornament, such as mosaic, stained glass can be an effective decoration at many different scales; a large panel seems to be an impressionistic abstraction from a distance yet offers rewarding detail at close range. Although usually thought of as an art to be appreciated from the inside, stained glass is one of the few architectural ornaments equally successful from inside or outside. When lit at night its beauty is accessible to all.

"Stained glass" has become a catchall term for colored glass fastened in lead cames. The glass may be "pot-colored" (mixed with various chemicals while in a molten state so that its color is consistent throughout its thickness) or "stained" (painted with oxides and other chemicals which combine with the clear or pot-colored glass when fired to make different colors).

The most common stained glass technique involves fastening relatively small pieces of glass together by means of *lead cames.* These are strips of lead with an H-shaped section that slips around the edges of the glass. Putty is used to make the seal when the lead is bent around the glass. But this kind of joint cannot be guaranteed airtight, and the leakage from a large panel can be substantial. Therefore, depending on the climate and site, you might consider mounting the stained glass panel behind a sheet of clear glass or plastic. This also gives additional protection to the art work.

In the copperfoil technique, the pieces are held together by soldered copper strips instead of lead cames; this leaves a bead line of solder rather than a flat lead strip. Some artists recommend the copperfoil technique when the panel can be scrutinized from close-up, as they feel it permits finer detail; others take the opposite viewpoint. Some say, properly executed, copperfoil is stronger than leaded glass. This may be true, but either technique will require extra support when used in large panels. Both can be made watertight.

If there is a "sleeper" in the realm of ornamental glass techniques, it is beveling. It is a relatively young craft, having been in existence only about three hundred years. Although it is relatively modest compared to the extravagances of stained glass, beveling has an elegance and—depending on the exuberance of the design—a richness that can be quite impressive. Beveled glass has a pattern cut into its surface. Straight lines are done entirely by machine; for curved patterns, the glass must be guided by hand at the beveling machine. All beveling involves the following steps. Excess glass is first ground away at the proper angle (the cuts have a shallow V-section). The rough bevel is smoothed until translucent, then polished with pumice and water, followed by cerium oxide and water, to achieve the final finish.

Etching is another way to ornament glass. This involves

the controlled eating away of certain parts of the surface. Not only glass, but metals, plexiglass, stone, and wood are often etched. Etching can be done chemically or by directing a high-pressure stream of abrasive at a surface. This last technique, called sandblasting, works particularly well on glass and plexiglass, and can achieve refined and delicate results. The "blasted" portions of the design are translucent, which can be useful when privacy is needed without loss of light, as in a restaurant or other street-level, semipublic area.

Glass Block

If stained glass is most often associated with churches, glass block is most often connected with the modern movement in architecture. Like brick, another favorite choice of modernism, glass block is a pedestrian material. Such basic materials have advantages and disadvantages when it comes to decoration: they are cheap, but to make them ornamental you must use them inventively.

Glass block is customarily used in large panels, one of the least effective uses from our ornamental point of view because the decorative effect is diluted by repetition over a large area. Instead of large, even areas you might use fewer elements in stronger patterns—a zig-zag (two over, one up, two over, etc.) in an otherwise homogeneous surface. Glass block could also be used in small clusters. This could be particularly effective if the blocks themselves have a strong pattern. Or you can use the approach of Friday Architects/Planners, in Philadelphia, who took advantage of the way the material is put together, and the few available textures, to make a surprisingly rich-looking window out of very simple elements (see photo).

Window composed of glass block in three different patterns. Grays Ferry Community Center, Friday Architects/Planners, Philadelphia, PA (1976). (Photo by Peter Thaler, courtesy of Friday Architects/Planners)

The face of the block can also be decorated. **Philadelphia Art Glass** was one of the ornamenters we contacted that will etch or carve glass block. Solar reflective block offers yet another way to achieve a decorative effect.

Unlike brick, glass block is not porous. It does not absorb the water from mortar, and hence, has its own special structural requirements. Glass block should be laid by a mechanic who is familiar with it. If you do intend to use large panels, get technical advice from the manufacturer about how big an area can be laid before additional support is needed.

Special Listings

Stained Glass Association of America
1125 Wilmington Avenue
St. Louis, MO 63111

Stained Glass Journal (quarterly)

Regional Listings

Makers of stained glass often do their own installation. If they do not—or if they will design but not fabricate a piece—it has been indicated in the listing. However, most of these artists have also worked with framers whom they will recommend.

We have not listed distributors of glass block. If you are interested in this material, contact **Pittsburgh Corning** or **Bienenfeld Industries** for the names of distributors in your area.

All of the individuals and companies listed below will do large, small, and one-of-a-kind orders unless otherwise noted.

Northeast

Le Jardin de Verre Studios
Attn. Bebe Dring
197 Connecticut Avenue
New London, CT 06320
(203) 442-5579

Custom designs in stained, beveled, slab, etched, and mirrored glass. Can recommend a framer and can give technical advice about installation. Specializes in "designs that depict the function of the buildings they adorn." Also mosaics.

Studio Workshop
22 Bushy Hill Road
Simsbury, CT 06070
(203) 658-6374

Specializes in custom stained glass designs and antique restoration. Also does sandblasting.

Phoenix Studio, Inc.
374 Fore Street
Portland, ME 04101
(207) 774-4154

Custom stained, beveled, sandblasted, and etched glass. Restoration and repair of stained glass windows. Holds classes and lectures designed to acquaint people with the techniques the studio uses. Phoenix also works in porcelain enamel. One of the studio's commissions was design of a 90-by-7-foot mural depicting the Ascension of Christ for a church tower.

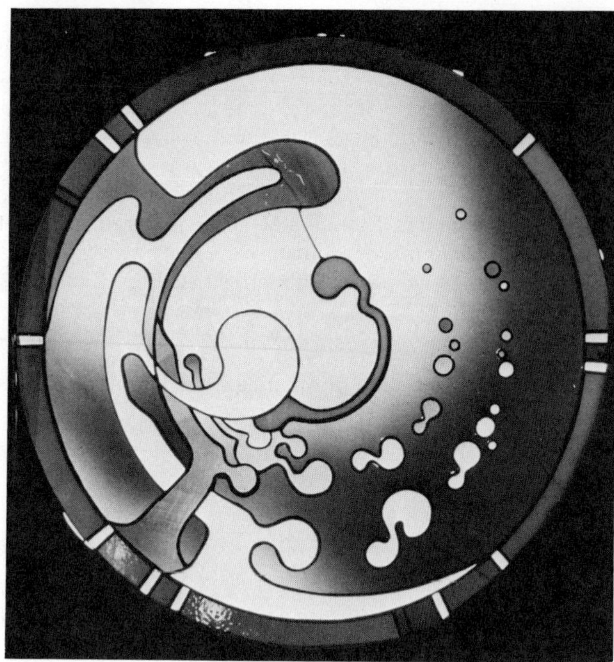

"Washing Machine Madness" or "The Front Loader" (30 inches in diameter). Dan Fenton, Oakland, CA. (Photo courtesy of Dan Fenton)

Bert Weiss Glass Studio
7 Fox Court
Portland, ME 04101
(207) 772-5828

Custom stained glass and sandblasting. Will install or recommend framer. Specializes in leaded glass seascapes and signs.

Osiris Glassworks
Attn. Robin Brailsford
90 West Street
Beverly Farms, MA 01915
(617) 927-0789

This designer does custom designs combining glass and metals (aluminum or cast bronze) in nontraditional ways, creating "architectural reliefs." He is also interested in epoxy-bonded, photo-realist panels and neon siteworks. One-of-a-kind works only.

Lieng Designs at The Piano Craft Building
Attn. John Tom or K. Brown
791 Tremont Street Studio E. #304
Boston, MA 02118
(617) 536-1215

Stained, beveled, and etched glass. Custom designs, specializing in one-of-a-kind large windows and screens.

Philip Stein
Such Happiness, Inc.
Box 32
Fitchburg, MA 01420
(617) 878-1031

Custom designs in stained, beveled, mirrored, and etched glass; does sandblasting and glass bending. He installs. Also sells restored antique windows. If you are looking for a window of a particular size, give him the dimensions and he will send color photos with dimensions and price list. If you want a custom window, send rough drawing indicating dimensions and color; prices and delivery date will be put in return mail.

La Roche Stained Glass, Inc.
214 Commercial Street
Malden, MA 02148
(617) 324-0396

Specialty: church windows. Custom stained, beveled, mirrored, and etched glass, as well as sandblasting. Large orders only. Will install.

Quantock Designers
50 Jersey Street
Marblehead, MA 01945
(617) 631-8761

Artist does own designs only in stained, beveled, and etched glass; also uses faceted, sandblasted, and laminating techniques. Will install. Does mural painting and mosaics as well.

Serpentino Stained and Leaded Glass
77 Charles Street
Needham, MA 02194
(617) 449-2074
(617) 444-9767

Stained and sandblasted glass. Specialty: custom stained and leaded glass for residential or commercial installation. Any size order. Provides Lexan covering for protection.

William Armstrong and Joseph Barberio
Craftsmen in Stained Glass
34 Liberty Street
Newburyport, MA 01950
(617) 465-2989

Custom designs in stained and beveled glass. Specialty: repair and restoration, including glass sagging and painting.

Cummings Studios
The Barn
182 E. Main Street
North Adams, MA 01247
(413) 664-6578

Specialty: stained glass consultation; particularly writing specifications. Own designs or can work from sketch for custom work. Stained and slab glass.

E. Settimelli and Sons, Inc.
24 Totman Street
Quincy, MA 02169
(617) 472-5050

Sandblasting of glass, granite, and marble; custom designs.

Pompei Stained Glass
455 High Street. (Rt. 60)
West Medford, MA 02155
(617) 395-8867

Readymade and custom designs in stained, beveled, sandblasted, and etched glass. Will do restorations; can install or can recommend a framer. Specializes in period reproductions.

Alfred Rucker
Pike, NH
(603) 989-3369

Artist/fabricator who does his own designs; readymade and custom commissions. Stained and slab glass; one-of-a-kind orders. Installs.

Stained Glass Creations, Ltd.
284 Fourth Avenue
Bay Shore, NY 11706
(516) 666-5599

Custom work in stained glass, also does beveling and sandblasting.

Carved Glass & Sign
Attn. Ike Shefts
767 E. 132 Street
Bronx, NY 10454
(212) 665-6240

Custom designs in stained glass. Specialty: ornamental glass carved by sandblasting; can also sandblast marble and granite. "New York is our brochure."

Ernest Porcelli
Stained Glass
123 7th Avenue
Brooklyn, NY 11215
(212) 857-6888

Works in leaded and copperfoil techniques as well as beveled and etched glass. Installs. Specializes in original pieces and restorations of stained glass.

George Sell
33 Flatbush Avenue
Brooklyn, NY 11217
(212) 875-1009

Sculptor working in various types of glass—stained, etched, beveled, mirrored, and frosted. Sell's works are three-dimensional. Gives estimates and will install.

Robert Sowers
303 DeGraw Street
Brooklyn, NY 11231
(212) 852-3265

An artist who does his own designs only. Stained and faceted glass for residential, ecclesiastical, and commercial installations. His style is abstract, sometimes with theme or visual metaphors. Has worked with architects; will recommend a framer. One-of-a-kind orders only. In addition to being a well-known maker of stained glass, Sowers has written extensively on the subject; his most recent book is *The Language of Stained Glass.* (Timber Press, Forest Grove, Oregon.)

Stained glass in the Dore Residence. Jim Furman (1980), Trumansburg, NY. (Photo courtesy of Jim Furman)

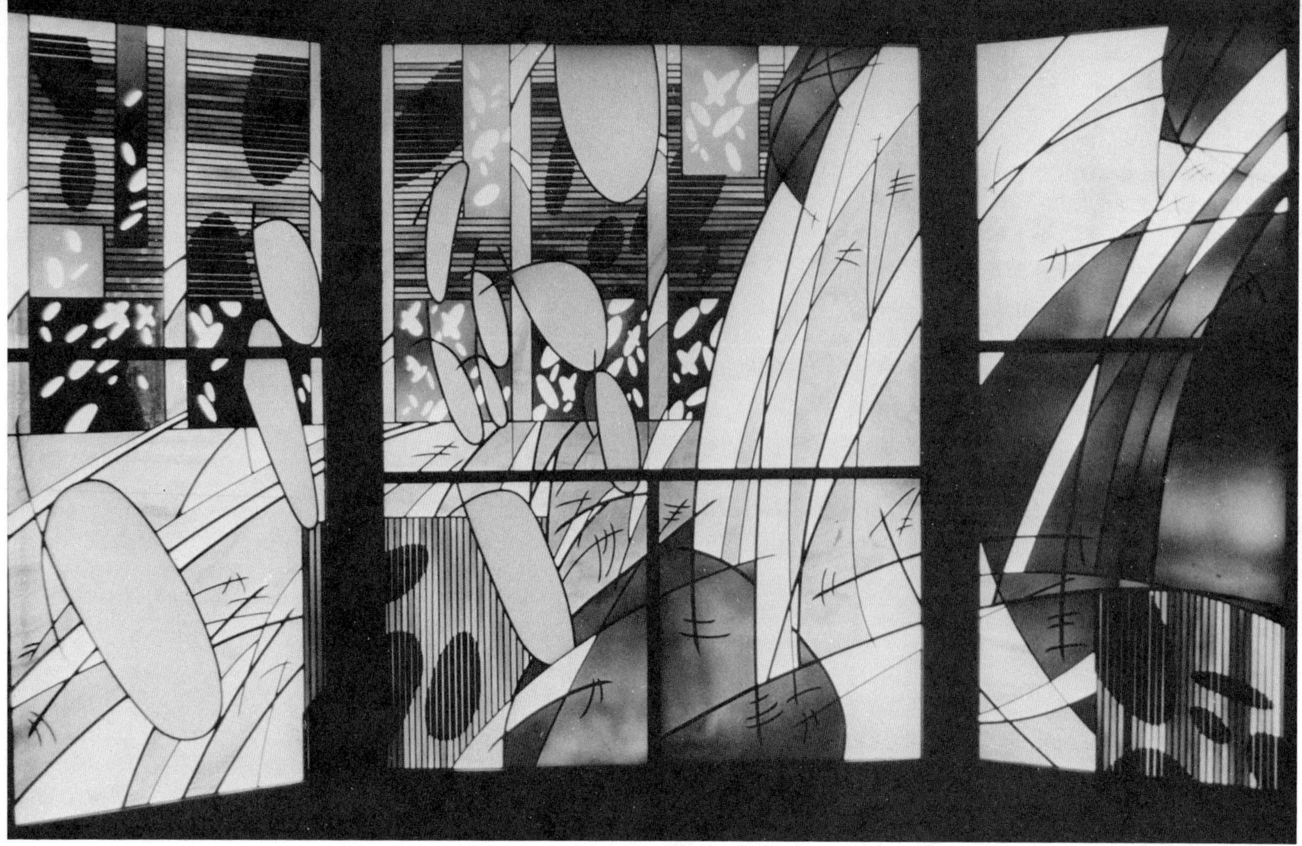

Artificially lit baywall (11 by 6 feet), Le Delice, Whippany, NJ. Marni Bakst, New York, NY. (Photo courtesy of Marni Bakst)

Manor Art Glass Studio
20 Ridge Road
Douglaston, NY 11363
(212) 631-8029

Artist/fabricator who does stained, beveled, and sandblasted glass; will install.

King Stained and Leaded Glass
1267 West Broadway
Hewlett, NY 11557
(516) 569-5511

Specializes in pictorial scenes, seascapes, landscapes, etc. Custom work in stained and beveled glass. Will install.

Joan Altabe
421 W. Olive Street
Long Beach, NY 11561
(516) 431-9156

Custom designs in stained, beveled, faceted, etched, painted, and sandblasted glass. Altabe does the designs, then works with a fabricator. Specialty: leaded glass. Has worked with architects before. Does install. Also does painted murals and mosaics. Preferred style: "stylization, hard-edge, or monochromatic realism." Will stencil or paint ornament on a building.

Durhan Studios, Inc.
Paul Coulaz, Proprietor
205 Sunrise Highway
Lynbrook, NY 11563
(516) 599-0440

Custom designs in stained, beveled, slab, and sandblasted glass. Will install.

Glass Crafters
369 Plandome Road
Manhasset, NY 11030
(516) 365-7404

Distributor, artist, and fabricator; custom and readymade designs in stained and beveled glass. Specializes in stained glass for residential and commercial.

Rohlf's Stained and Leaded Glass, Inc.
783 S. 3rd Avenue
Mount Vernon, NY 10550
(914) 699-4848
(212) 823-4545

Custom designs in stained, beveled, etched, slab, and sandblasted glass. Established 1920: "Complete liturgical art service." Specializes in design and manufacture. Rohlf's has done work in several of the major churches in the New York area including St. Patrick's Cathedral, Riverside Church, and Trinity Church. Extensive restoration and rehabilitation experience. Free consultation services, including estimates and full-color, scale drawings. Can install or can recommend a framer.

Richard Avidon
305 Riverside Drive
New York, NY 10025
(212) 866-1931

Works with stained, faceted, etched, bas-relief, and painted glass. Readymade and custom designs from sketch or more detailed information. Also works with mosaics.

Marni Bakst
Bakst Works
235 E. 5th Street No. 2
New York, NY 10003
(212) 533-2256

Artist doing her own designs only, in stained and sandblasted glass. She sometimes combines techniques, such as sandblasting and lead overlays, with traditional stained glass techniques. She is "a well-trained contemporary designer and a solid craftsman; makes each job blend smoothly with its architectural setting."

Peter Hans Felzmann
c/o Austrian Trade Commissioner
845 Third Avenue
New York, NY 10022
(212) 421-5250

Artist working with stained glass in a matrix of concrete or concrete with a plastic admixture. He has had extensive experience with large and small commissions for business and residences; will cooperate with the architect in the development of a design concept. Headquartered in Linz, Austria, but is expanding his work to include the U.S.

Benoit Gilsoul
New York, NY 10001

See listing under Murals.

The Greenland Studio
147 W. 22nd Street
New York, NY 10011
(212) 255-2551

Stained, beveled, slab, sandblasted, and etched glass. Custom designs in contemporary style. In addition, will fabricate the designs of others. Also works in mosaic.

New York Art Glass, Inc.
New York, NY 10010

See listing under Murals.

Stained Glass Studios at The Crafters
Attn. Royce John Fiske, III
Box 786 8 South Broadway
Nyack, NY 10960
(914) 358-9820

Beveled glass panel (approx. 42 by 48 inches), Cherry Creek Enterprises, Denver, CO. (Photo courtesy of Cherry Creek Enterprises)

Custom and readymade designs in stained, slab, beveled, and sandblasted glass. Can install or can recommend a framer.

Harriet Hyams
P.O. Box 178
Palisades, NY 10964
(914) 359-0061

Specialty: custom designs in stained glass. Also works in slab, sandblasted, and beveled glass. In addition, she works in wood, mosaic, marble, and metals.

Bienenfeld Industries
1539 Covert Street
Ridgewood, NY 11385
(212) 821-4400

Distributes Solaris Block, imported from Germany. It comes in clear or patterned surfaces, including some specifically intended to direct and diffuse light. Colors include warmtones or clear; warmtone blocks transmit approximately 60 percent of the light. Certain of the more decorative patterns are also supplied in light gray with black sidewalls—a rather elegant combination. Warmtone blocks come with white sidewalls. The following is a representative sample:

4 1/2 by 4 1/2 by 3 1/8 inches (115 by 115 by 80 mm)
7 1/2 by 7 1/2 by 3 1/8 inches (190 by 190 by 80mm)
9 1/2 by 9 1/2 by 3 1/8 inches (240 by 240 by 80mm)
11 3/4 by 11 3/4 by 4 inches (300 by 300 by 100mm)

Contact Bienenfeld to find a Solaris distributor near you. Bienenfeld also imports and distributes stained, sandblasted, slab, and mirrored glass.

Pike Stained Glass Studios, Inc.
Attn. Valerie O'Hara
180 St. Paul Street
Rochester, NY 14604
(716) 546-7570

Pike Stained Glass was founded by Ms. O'Hara's great-uncle in 1908, and taken over by her father with whom she is now in partnership. The studio has a "broad understanding of many different styles and techniques—skills handed down through the family." Pike has done architectural commissions for ecclesiastical, residential, and commercial installation. Custom and readymade designs in stained, faceted, etched, beveled, slumped (heating glass and letting it flow into a mold), and sandblasted glass. Estimates only on readymade designs.

David Wilson
RD 2, Box 121A
Fouett Road Farm
South New Berlin, NY 13843
(607) 334-3015

A well-known stained glass artist working in a contemporary style. Wilson does stained, faceted, carved, bas-relief, and sandblasted glass. He is also an experienced mural painter, and works in ceramics, mosaic, enameled metals, wood, concrete, and photomurals.

GLASS

The J. & R. Lamb Studios
30 Joyce Drive
Spring Valley, NY 10977
(914) 352-3777

Lamb says it is the oldest stained glass studio in continuous operation in the country—since 1857. Present owner is Don Samick who joined the studio in 1963. The four full-time artists represent a variety of styles; craftsmen on staff. The studio offers three grades of glass: Hand Blown, the most beautiful with the greatest range of color and texture; Cathedral Glass, machine-rolled and textured; Opalescent, a milky-appearing opaque glass used where light diffusion and opacity are needed. Stained, beveled, and etched glass. Will do their own designs or those of others. Call or write for names of representatives in other cities around the country.

James B. Furman
Glass Studio
27 W. Main Street
Trumansburg, NY 14886
(607) 387-4141

Stained, beveled, etched, faceted, bas-relief, and sandblasted glass. In addition to windows, he does autonomous panels in steel frames; these panels could be mounted as windows. Uses "a lot of found objects to stress three-dimensionality." Aims to make leaded glass surfaces sculptural. Uses found objects for bas-relief pieces.

Edward J. Byrne Studio
135 Cherry Lane
Doylestown, PA 18901
(215) 348-2577

Specializes in one-of-a-kind, larger commissions. Custom work in stained and carved glass; also does custom door sculpture.

The Emporium
Attn. Jack Roseman
RD 7, Box 381
Johnstown, PA 15905
(814) 288-2843

Contemporary designs in antique glass. Stained, sandblasted, fused, and raised glass (kiln-fired). Small and one-of-a-kind orders.

John Beirs Studio
45 S. Third Street
Philadelphia, PA 19106
(215) 923-8122

Stained, beveled, sandblasted, and etched glass. Will install.

Ray King
603 S. 10th Street
Philadelphia, PA 19147
(215) 627-5112

An artist doing own designs only. Specialty: free-standing pieces. Works in stained, etched, and sandblasted glass; also uses steel, aluminum, brass, and bronze.

Door and sidelight, Colt Commission (1979), stained, leaded glass. Gail J. O'Neill, Troutdale, OR. (Photo courtesy of Gail J. O'Neill)

Philadelphia Art Glass Co., Inc.
Attn. Tim Morand
948 Russell Street
Philadelphia, PA 19140
(215) 223-1200

Artist designs, then works with fabricator. Etched, beveled, sandblasted, laminated, and tempered glass. Specialty: multifaceted sandblasting of glass, mirrors, and glass block. Can do own design or designs of others; submit rough sketch indicating dimensions and tones desired and Morand will translate it into sandblasted glass. Will install.

Willet Stained Glass Studio
10 Morland Avenue
Philadelphia, PA 19118
(215) 247-5721

A large studio with thirty artists and master craftsmen working in stained, slab, carved, laminated, etched, and sandblasted glass. This studio often does commissions "combining faceted glass and sculpture and mosaics for inside and outside effects." Many of the artists have worked with architects before, and they specialize in "individually designed commissions of highest artistic value and workmanship."

Pittsburgh Corning
800 Presque Isle Drive
Pittsburgh, PA 15239
(412) 327-6100

Pittsburgh Corning is the only large-scale manufacturer of

glass block in the United States. Corning is open to "all considerations"; if a new mold is required they will quote a dollar figure for its cost or a volume figure indicating the production run necessary to cover the fabrication cost. Corning is planning to make some new, subdued colors—bronzes and grays—and is also open to producing different tints and colors. Also offering new shapes and sizes: a circular solid (6 1/2 by 2 inches) and a normal brick size (2 1/4 by 4 by 8 inches). Another option now available is a block with a light green fiber glass insert placed between the two halves before they are fused. Only one color insert—carefully devised to reduce glare—is now available. However, any color could be inserted, the only requirement is that the insert must be the same dimensions and thickness as the one now used. A pattern could be silk-screened onto the insert, but some experimentation with the amount of detail that could be seen would be necessary because the inserts are not presently put into clear glass blocks. We were told that clear glass could be used if it were essential to see fine detail. To find the names of Pittsburgh Corning's distributors in the United States, write Pittsburgh Corning.

Morgan Bockius Studios
1412 York Road
Warminster, PA 18974
(215) 674-1930

A studio employing several designers and craftsmen. Custom designs in stained, beveled, handpainted, etched, and carved glass. Also does bending, sandblasting and gold repoussé. Work includes windows (small and large), door panels, heraldry, sculpture, and lamps.

St. Luke's Studio
Belcourt Castle
Newport, RI 02840
(401) 846-0669

In continuous operation since 1896; custom stained glass windows designed in early European styles. St. Luke's will create and restore all types of leaded and stained glass, including Colonial leaded work, molded lead ornament, and Victorian windows. "Medieval and Renaissance styles, even intricate faces, matched to perfection." In addition, this studio can provide experts to do original and restoration work in molded plaster, wood carving, gold leafing, scagliola (marbleizing), stone carving, and metalwork.

Leaded, stained glass panel (34 by 53 inches). Ronald E. Lloyd, Artistry Stained Glass, Tempe, AZ. (Photo Copyright © 1978, Ronald E. Lloyd)

"New Year's Moon." Stained glass. Beverly Reiser, Oakland, CA. (Photo © 1980, Rob Super, courtesy of Beverly Reiser)

Classical Glass, Inc.
177 Church Street
Burlington, VT 05401
(802) 862-9422

Custom designs in stained, beveled, sandblasted, and etched glass. Will install.

Luminosity Stained Glass Studio
The Old Church
Rte. 100
Waitsfield, Vt 05673
(802) 496-2231

Specialty: custom stained glass canopies with wrought iron framework. Also does sandblasting.

South

Dupre Studio
169 N.E. 44th Street
Miami, FL 33137
(305) 576-7204

Specializes in sculptural stained glass (windows with bas-relief); artist does own designs only. Stained, beveled, and etched glass. Has done large, heavily sculptured walls with embedded, stained glass.

GLASS

Glassworks, Inc.
Attn. Jay W. Marden, President
18795 S.W. 216th Street
Miami, FL 33170
(305) 232-2464

Specializes in "unique signs and one-of-a-kind designs." Stained and sandblasted.

Rowe Studios
4768 S.W. 72nd Avenue
Miami, FL 33155
(305) 666-5164

Specializes in figural work and nature scenes—"extremely detailed." Stained, beveled, painted, and fired work.

Pharrmoors Studios
P.O. Box 6231
Orlando, FL 32853
(305) 423-5424
(305) 656-2538

Custom designs in stained glass. Specializes in Art Nouveau and Beaux-Arts styles—naturalistic floral designs. Also does some fiber glass ornament.

Art Glass Studio
5077 Peachtree Road
Atlanta, GA 30341
(404) 455-4447

Specializes in beveling glass and intricate copperfoil work; also stained and sandblasted glass. Artist does own designs only.

Southeastern Art Glass Studio/Windowcraft
100 Avondale Road
Avondale Estates, GA 30002
(404) 294-4296

Specializes in hand-beveled glass entrances. Custom and readymade designs; stained, beveled, sandblasted, and etched glass.

Fenestra Studios, Inc.
819 W. Main Street
Louisville, KY 40202
(502) 584-5433

Stained, beveled, laminated, and sandblasted glass. Also does mosaic. Specialty: liturgical designs. "Over four hundred major installations in twelve states and two foreign countries."

Penco Studios
1137 Bardstown Road
Louisville, KY 40204
(502) 459-4027

Custom designs in stained, beveled, etched, and sandblasted glass. Can install or can recommend a framer. Specializes in stained glass. Penco has been in the art stained glass business for over ninety years; these artists pride themselves on their craftsmanship.

Design for stained glass window, St. Patrick's Church, Baton Rouge, LA. David Wilson (1980). (Photo courtesy of David Wilson)

Oval window (44 by 36 inches) © 1981 by Narcissus Quagliata. Residence of John Demergasso, Incline, NV.

Dufour Glass Studio, Ltd.
P.O. Box 336
Baton Rouge, LA 70821
(504) 383-3671

Custom designs in stained, beveled, sandblasted, and etched glass. Other media: marble, mosaic, and bronze. Small and one-of-a-kind orders.

Chevy Chase Glass Co., Inc.
4933 Bethesda Avenue
Bethesda, MD 20014
(301) 654-2022

Fabricator of stained, beveled, mirrored, and etched glass. Can work from rough sketch. Will install.

Baltimore New Glass Studio
4140 Alesia-Lineboro Road
Millers, MD 21107
(301) 239-3545

Stained, etched glass and sandblasted work. Specializes in large (interior) art mirrors. Does not install, but can recommend a framer. Small orders only.

Andrews Art Glass Co.
14938 Main Street
Upper Marlboro, MD 20870
(301) 627-4660

Specializes in custom designed stained glass. Also does etching.

Pearl River Glass Studio
142 Millsaps Avenue
Jackson, MS 39202
(601) 353-2497

A group of seven stained glass artists. Stained, beveled, etched, and sandblasted glass. Specialty: custom designs for "architectural and individual" projects. The studio also has a retail store selling glass-working tools and supplies.

Stained glass windows, Monroe First Congregational Church (central panel 9½ by 4 feet). Diane Bonciolini and Gregg Mesner, Mesolini Glass Studio, Bainbridge Island, WA. (Photo courtesy of Mesolini Glass Studio)

Catherine N. Parrish
Parrish Glassworks
416 Chamberlain Street
Raleigh, NC 27607
(919) 821-5625 (before 10AM and after 7PM)

Stained, beveled, and etched glass, as well as sandblasting and laminating. Specializes in realistic scenes. Background in painting and portraiture; will do portraits in stained glass. Does not install but can recommend a framer.

Stained Glass Associates
P.O. Box 1531
Raleigh, NC 27602
(919) 266-2493

Custom and readymade designs; works in faceted and sandblasted glass. Uses epoxy to laminate stained to plate glass. Can install or can recommend a framer. Also embeds mosaic in faceted glass panels. Specializes in European style painted glass and restorations.

Charles Towne Glass Studios
1662 Savannah Highway
Charleston, SC 29407
(803) 766-3231

A "complete art glass studio" specializing in stained glass church windows; beveled, etched, and sandblasted techniques.

R. L. Roelse Stained Glass, Inc.
1030 B Highway 52
Goose Creek, SC 29445
(803) 797-6381

Stained, beveled, and sandblasted glass. Specializes in bent and stained glass; also manufactures insulated glass.

Mt. Airy Glass Co.
Box 541
Greer, SC 29651
(803) 877-7576

Specializes in custom and readymade beveled entrance doors, windows, transoms, and sidelights—combined with fine millwork. Engraving and sandblasting. Can install or can recommend a framer.

The Palmetto Mirror and Art Glass Co.
P.O. Box 1012
Greer, SC 29651
(803) 877-0040

This company does stained glass windows (custom designs and repairs) and beveled glass (custom hand-beveling and stock designs). Also, custom engraved glass and mirrors. Will install.

Classical Glass
#6 Stoneybrook Lane
Lexington, SC 29072
(803) 359-5818

Stained, etched, and beveled glass. Does restorations. Gives estimates based on square footage, and installs. Can fill large, small, or one-of-a-kind orders.

Series of stained glass windows, Church of St. Thomas More, Cherry Hill, NJ. Designed and executed by David Wilson (1980). Geddes, Brecher, Qualls, Cunningham, Architects. (Photo courtesy of David Wilson)

Saunders Stained Glass, Inc.
P.O. Box 177
Highway 51 N.
Brighton, TN 38011
(901) 476-7600

Custom work in stained, beveled, and etched glass. Specializes in church figure windows. Can install.

Sunlite Stained Glass Studio
Attn. Susan Cobb Zenni
11309 Sam Lee Road
Knoxville, TN 37922
(615) 690-5482

Small studio in business for ten years. Has produced over 250 glass panels for homes, restaurants, and municipal buildings. Specialty: "Clear, crystal, and etched glass. Also custom glass beveling." Also works in stained glass. Will install.

Bright Light Stained Glass and Beveling Co., Inc.
3616 N. Thomas Street
Memphis, TN 38127
(901) 357-1646
(901) 358-1574

Specializes in beveled and leaded glass; also uses slab, etching, and sandblasting techniques. The catalog shows nearly sixty shapes and sizes of stock beveled glass, including "house-shaped" pieces, "double-houses," triangles, squares, rectangles, diamonds, and lozenges.

Old Dominion Stained Glass Co., Inc.
Highway 1 and England Street
Ashland, VA 23005
(804) 798-5702

Specialty: "pure stained glass church windows," traditional and contemporary. Stained, faceted, sandblasted as well as mosaic. Large orders only.

Dieter Goldkuhle
11219 S. Shore Road
Reston, Va 22090
(703) 437-9315

A fabricator of stained glass; has collaborated with many artists. He specializes in restoration of Medieval pieces (for example, he worked on the cathedrals of Saint-Germain-des-Pres and Rouen), but can work in any style. Among other distinguished projects, he made the last rose window in the West façade of the National Cathedral in Washington, D.C. In addition to fabricating the designs of other artists, he can also complete a design from a rough sketch. Primarily small orders.

Cain-Powers Architectural Art Glass
414 N. 4th Street
Richmond, VA 23219
(804) 782-0910

A team of one artist and one craftsman, working in stained, carved, acid-etched, beveled, sandblasted, and painted glass. Have combined glass with copperwire sculpture, neon, and special lighting.

Fall Line Glass Co.
P.O. Box 8272
Richmond, Va 23226
(804) 288-2147

Does stained glass work, mostly "sun catchers" and window panels of original designs using copperfoil technique. Can recommend a framer.

Arthur Miller Studios Ltd.
105 N. Robinson Street
Richmond, VA 23220
(804) 353-6012

Custom designs in stained, beveled, and sandblasted glass. "We have fabricated interesting pieces from carved wood with stained glass inserts."

Grafton Studios
Box 314
Fayetteville, WV 25840
(304) 574-1042

Stained and faceted glass in epoxy matrix. Installs sometimes and will give technical advice about installation. One-of-a-kind pieces. "My works look like translucent mosaics."

Shobe's Stained Glass Studio
1529 4th Avenue
Huntington, WV 25701
(304) 522-0308

Specializes in one-of-a-kind pieces of stained, slab, etched, beveled, and sandblasted glass. Also works in wood and mosaic. Will install.

Midwest

Botti Studio of Architectural Arts
919 Grove Street
Evanston, IL 60201
(312) 869-5933

Specializes in ecclesiastical stained glass; also for commercial buildings. Works in stained, faceted, beveled, fused, sandblasted, glass mosaic, and copperfoil techniques. Also does sculpture and murals. Botti has a staff of artists and craftsmen for planning, design, fabrication, restoration, and installation.

Greg Spiess Building Materials
216 E. Washington
Joliet, IL 60433
(815) 722-5639

Custom stained and beveled glass; will install. Also deals in antique Victorian interior architectural items, saloon fixtures, and the like.

Regina Art Glass, Inc.
603 Roosevelt Road
Maywood, IL 60153
(312) 345-8338

Specialty: painted stained glass. Also beveled, slab, and etched glass, as well as copperfoil and sandblasting. Large orders; will install.

The Glassworks
1701-B Lakecliffe Drive
Wheaton, IL 60187
(312) 653-4043

Custom designs in stained and beveled glass; also copperfoil technique.

"A Touch of Color." Diane Bonciolini and Gregg Mesner, Mesolini Glass Studio, Bainbridge Island, WA. (Photo courtesy of Mesolini Glass Studio)

Studio window (detail, 3 feet wide). Robert Sowers (1980), Brooklyn, NY. (Photo courtesy of Robert Sowers)

The Crystal Cave
1141 Central Avenue
Wilmette, IL 60091
(312) 251-1160

Specializes in copperwheel engraving of glass. Custom and readymade designs. Does not install, but can recommend a framer. Will cut, bevel, engrave, or sandblast any kind of glass.

Der Glass Werks
835 E. Westfield Boulevard
Indianapolis, IN 46220
(317) 257-7603

Leaded, stained, beveled, sandblasted, slab, and etched glass; also copperfoil work. Specialty: original designs in leaded glass.

Studio Stained Glass
117 S. Main Street
Kokomo, IN 46901
(317) 452-2438

Leaded, stained, and beveled glass. Does installation.

C. Paul Stained Glass Studio
R.R. 1, Box 42
Lyons, IN 47443
(812) 659-3627

Specialty: contemporary, abstract design with handblown European glass; installs. Also works with beveled glass.

Adventist Hospital Chapel Window and Door, Portland, OR. Designed by Ed Carpenter (1977), executed by Tim O'Neill; door carving by Lu Hines; interior design by Howard Hermduschs Assoc. (Photo by Jack Sanders, courtesy of Ed Carpenter)

Sunburst Stained Glass Co.
P.O. Box 5
New Harmony, IN 47631
(812) 682-4065

Custom designs in stained and beveled glass, both leaded and copperfoil techniques. Do not install but can recommend a framer. Specializes in restoration.

Steven Frank Studios, Inc.
Attn. Don Carras
16352 E. Warren
Detroit, MI 48224
(313) 885-1362

Specialty: restaurant decor. Leaded and copperfoil; stained, faceted, and sandblasted glass. Does repairs and restoration.

Thompson Glass Co.
16520 Grand River Avenue
Detroit, MI 48227
(313) 273-5668

and

43726 Grand River Avenue
Novi, MI 48050
(313) 349-9393

Specializes in custom and readymade stained glass. Also does copperfoil, including memorials and medallions. Can do sandblasting and beveling. In business since 1929.

Trupiano Glassworks
Etched and Stained Glass Studio
13703 McClelland
Grant, MI 49327
(616) 834-8385

This studio accepts commercial and residential commissions. Specializes in etching by sandblasting—clear, stained, mirrored glass, and plexiglass. Designs and constructs stained glass windows and objects. Can install. In addition to glass, Trupiano works in wood, marble, and etched bronze.

ChinaHue Glassworks
728 Locust Street
Kalamazoo, MI 49007
(636) 344-4269

Custom and readymade designs in leaded, stained, faceted, beveled, and sandblasted glass. Also inlays tile in wood and marble, does glass mosaic, glass painting, and handblown three-dimensional objects.

Ice Nine Glass Design
1507 S. 6th Street
Minneapolis, MN 55454
(612) 375-9669

Will do custom designs; also has a selection of stock panels including thirty acid-etched patterns (many traditional in feeling) on 8-by-10-inch glass panels. Also in stock are realistic scenes, borders, monograms, and a series of 12-inch diameter ornamental designs that can be positioned on a pane of glass to

Stained glass windows, United Church of Christ, Forest Grove, OR. Designed by Ed Carpenter (1979); executed by Tim O'Neill; architect Zimmer, Ginsul, Frasca Partnership. (Photo by Karlis Grants, courtesy of Ed Carpenter)

your specifications. Ice Nine also has pattern glass of varying opacities for different degrees of privacy. Delightful catalog (includes price list) $2.00. Will do custom designs and can fill any size order.

John Eckley Sixth Street Studio
1501-07 S. Sixth Street
Minneapolis, MN 54545
(612) 339-2826

Stained, beveled, and faceted glass; also works with wood and mosaic. "Architectural art glass designed for commercial areas." Brochure $0.50. Will install.

Gaytee Stained Glass, Inc.
2744 Lyndale Avenue S.
Minneapolis, MN 55408
(612) 872-4550

Custom and readymade designs. Stained, slab, etched, beveled, and sandblasted glass. Will install.

Monarch Studios, Inc.
262 E. 4th Street
St. Paul, MN 55101
(612) 224-3170

Custom and readymade designs. Stained, beveled, and sandblasted glass. Will install.

Plaza Studio
4441 Main Street
Kansas City, MO 64111
(816) 531-6273

Custom designs in stained, beveled, and sandblasted glass. Specialty: interior and exterior applications for restaurants and bars (windows and lighting fixtures). Will install. Also does repairs and restorations.

Art Glass Unlimited, Inc.
412 N. Euclid
St. Louis, MO 63108
(314) 361-0474
(314) 361-0713

This company will bend glass up to 32 by 24 inches. Also works in stained and sandblasted glass. Will install. Specializes in "glass painting and staining." Beveled glass is ordered from stock houses.

Unique Art Glass Co.
5060 Arsenal
St. Louis, MO 63139
(314) 535-4200

The only licensed maker of Budweiser, Michelob, and Clydesdale stained and painted glass. Unique has been in business since 1880, and specializes in quality work and restorations. Works in stained, beveled, faceted, and sandblasted glass.

Boesen's Glasscrafts, Inc.
2203 N. 91st Plaza
Omaha, NE 68134
(402) 391-3419

Specialty: custom designs in stained glass. Does beveling, sandblasting, and faceted work as well as copperfoil technique.

The Stained Glass Workshop
615 9th Avenue S.
Fargo, ND 58103
(701) 293-9737

Custom and readymade designs in leaded and copperfoil stained glass; also does beveling and sandblasting. Will install.

Custom Mirror and Glass
2066 S. Taylor Road
Cleveland Heights, OH 44118
(216) 932-1390

Works in mirror glass; does carving and sandblasting.

Contemporary Glass
213-15 King Avenue
Columbus, OH 43201
(614) 299-7838

Specializes in contemporary stained glass designs, leaded and copperfoil; also sandblasting.

Franklin Art Glass Studios
222 E. Sycamore Street
Columbus, OH 43206
(614) 221-2972
(800) 848-7683 (outside Ohio)

Fabricators, artists, and distributors. This firm has been in business for over fifty years, and is being run by the third generation of the founding family. These designers and fabricators accept commissions on a nationwide basis, doing commercial and residential installations. Can work in stained, beveled, etched, and slab glass in leaded and copperfoil techniques. Will install. Large, small, or one-of-a-kind orders.

Leffler Studio
6943 Springfield
Holland, OH 43528
(419) 866-0258

Stained, sandblasted and beveled glass. Specializes in custom designed windows and lampshades.

Sherer's Stained Glass, Inc.
350 Holland Road Suite U
Maumee, OH 43537
(419) 893-2928

Specializes in beveled glass. Also does stained, fused, laminated, faceted, and sandblasted glass.

The House of DuValle
Attn. Robert G. Nitza
P.O. Box 358
North Olmsted, OH 44070
(216) 734-7493

Specializes in "problem" applications of glass. Works in stained, faceted, and sandblasted glass. Custom and readymade designs; will install.

John W. Winterich
Solon, OH 44139

See listing under Murals.

Stained glass panel (2 by 2 feet) by Garth Edwards (1978), Portland, OR. (Photo courtesy of Garth Edwards)

Hendrix, Heikkilä, and Terry, Inc.
Norman, OK 73069

See listing under Murals.

The Glass Farm
515 Main Street
Rapid City, SD 57701
(605) 348-6155

Artist designs, then works with a fabricator. Specializes in landscapes in glass. Works in stained, sandblasted, and beveled glass. Uses polished agates and rocks in these designs.

Phoenix Stained Glass, Inc.
4518 Burnet Road
Austin, TX 78756
(512) 459-0252

Custom designs in stained, beveled, and sandblasted glass. Works in both leaded and copperfoil techniques. Also does mosaics.

Renaissance Glass Co.
1003 W. 34th Street
Austin, TX 78705
(512) 451-3971

Readymade and custom stained, beveled, and sandblasted glass. Also does glass painting. Will install. Can supply photos (for a charge).

Mecaskey's 1912 Stained Glass Studio
12215 Coit Road 163
Dallas, TX 75251
(214) 661-8109
(214) 442-2811

Custom and readymade designs in stained, beveled, and faceted glass. Will install.

Thompson Art Glass
2311 Abrams Road
Dallas, TX 75214
(214) 824-3701

Specializes in beveling and custom stained glass. Also works in etched and sandblasted glass; custom and readymade designs. Will install.

Smith Stained Glass Studios
3209 Bryan Avenue
Fort Worth, TX 76110
(817) 926-5263

Custom designs in stained, beveled, and sandblasted glass. Also works in wood, mosaic, granite, marble, and metals.

Black's Art Glass Studio
3225 N. Flores
San Antonio, TX 78212
(512) 736-5201

Specializes in stained and slab glass. Also does beveling, etching, and sandblasting. Will install.

"Rose Window." Stained glass window by Valerie O'Hara, Pike Stained Glass Studios, Rochester, NY. (Photo courtesy of the Craftsman's Gallery, Scarsdale, NY. Design Copyright © 1977, Valerie O'Hara)

Brown's Stained Glass Studio
2411 Blanco Road
San Antonio, TX 78209
(512) 734-2653

Specializes in ecclesiastical painting on glass. Works in stained, beveled, slab, and sandblasted glass. Will install.

The Cavallini Co., Inc.
3410 Fredericksburg Road
San Antonio, TX 78201
(512) 733-8161

Stained, slab, beveled, and sandblasted glass. Custom designs; can fill large, small, or one-of-a-kind orders. Also has done many mosaic mural commissions.

PECO
Pat's Etcetera Co., Inc.
810 E. 1st Street
Smithville, TX 78957
(512) 237-3600

Basically a glass beveling studio, PECO specializes in readymade beveled glass designs for doors and windows. "As a convenience for our customers, we work with area craftsmen who provide doors and woodwork, sandblasting, etching, and cut brilliant work." Also does stained glass. Brochure $3.00.

Touchstone
Rte. 2, Box 198A
Smithville, TX 78957
(512) 237-2531

Specialty: sandblasted, etched doors and windows. Also works in glue chip and deep-etched glass. Other types of external ornament include ornamental wood, brass, and copper work. Will install.

Brandis Studio
1534 W. Rogers Street
Milwaukee, WI 53204
(414) 643-5066

Stained and beveled glass; custom and readymade designs. Will install. Will undertake any type of work with glass.

Dennis Pearson
P.O. Box 317
Spring Green, WI 53588
(608) 588-2001

Specialty: stained glass in bright colors and farm scenes; often uses roundels. Custom designs in stained, faceted, etched, and beveled glass; copperfoil technique. Also works with agate.

Chequamegon Bay Art Glass
Attn. Bob Adams
Rte. 1
Washburn, WI 54891
(No Phone)

Designs and fabricates windows, ceiling panels, room partitions, and lamp shades using stained, beveled, and etched glass. Works in Victorian, Art Nouveau, and Art Deco styles.

Can do repair and restoration church work. Specialty: working with antique and beveled glass. Can install.

Rockies and Far West

Art Glass of Arizona
1041 E. Camelback Road
Phoenix, AZ 85014
(602) 264-3115

Stained, beveled, sandblasted, and etched glass. Custom beveling, inside and outside curves.

The Glassworks Studio
2055 N. 16th Street
Phoenix, AZ 85006
(602) 253-7683

Glass specialists taking on unique problems in glass design. Works in stained, beveled, carved, etched, and sandblasted glass. Now developing a glass-blowing facility. Can do painting, slumping, repair, and restoration.

Maureen McGuire Designs
924 E. Bethany Home Road
Phoenix, AZ 85014
(602) 277-0167

Artist designs, then works with a fabricator. Stained, slab, and sandblasted glass. Also works in glass mosaic, stucco sgraffito, tapestries, church furniture. Considerable experience working with architects. Specialty: stained and faceted glass.

Artistry Stained Glass
225 W. University No. 101
Tempe, AZ 85281
(602) 966-6167

Stained, beveled, etched, carved, and sandblasted glass. Estimates "only a very general figure." Will install.

Robert Kehlman
2207 Rose Street
Berkeley, CA 94709
(415) 841-3898

Specializes in one-of-a-kind stained glass works. Also sandblasts plate glass; no size limitation. Artist does own designs only.

Looking Glass
Box 26
Davenport, CA 95017
(408) 423-2532

Beveled, faceted, etched, sandblasted, and blown glass. Custom work only. All types of glass or mirror (except tempered) can be combined with beveled, stained glass, copperfoil, etc. No size restrictions. Copies of slides available upon request.

Crowe Glass
1136 Industrial Avenue
Escondido, CA 92025
(714) 741-2069

Stained, beveled, etched, faceted, and sandblasted glass. Also works in wood.

Stained glass panel in Gothic style, designed by Donald Tinney. St. Lukes's Studio, Belcourt Castle, Newport, RI (1965). (Photo courtesy of St. Lukes's Studio)

Isaac's Stained Glass Studio
310 N. Vista Street
Hollywood, CA 91342
(213) 654-5205

Custom and readymade designs in stained, beveled, and etched glass. Also does faceting and sandblasting.

Jean Clyde Mason Design
2777 Woodshire Drive
Hollywood, CA 90068
(213) 464-2558
(213) 461-1872

Works with etched, slab, painted, and sandblasted glass. Artist is experienced in major Art Deco restorations and original designs. Also works in wrought iron and cast bronze. Can recommend a framer.

Adamm's Stained Glass
1437 Westwood Boulevard
Los Angeles, CA 90024
(213) 473-8303

Specialty: copperfoil work. Stained, beveled, etched, and sandblasted glass.

Beveled Glass Industries
900 N. La Cienega Boulevard
Los Angeles, CA 90069
(213) 657-1462

and

979 Third Avenue
New York, NY 10022
(212) 753-1380

Stock designs in a wide variety of shapes and sizes for doors and windows. Distributors in twelve states and Canada. Does custom work, and can fill large, small, or one-of-a-kind orders. Brochure $3.00.

Fairbanks and Fairbanks, Inc.
Los Angeles, CA 90065

See listing under Sculpture.

Salvatore Polizzi Stained Glass Studio
(Showroom)
706 N. La Cienega Boulevard
Los Angeles, CA 90069
(213) 657-2891

(Studio)
1067 N. Fairfax
Los Angeles, CA
(No phone)

Custom and readymade designs in stained, faceted, beveled, etched, and sandblasted glass.

Sunshine Glass Works
132 S. LaBrea
Los Angeles, CA 90036
(213) 935-0024

Sandblasted and etched glass; custom and readymade designs.

Stained glass window for Advent Christian Church, Peacedale, RI. Designed by Donald Tinney, St. Lukes's Studio, Belcourt Castle, Newport, RI (1979). (Photo courtesy of St. Lukes's Studio)

Ray Howlett
3918 Las Flores Canyon Road #6
Malibu, CA 90265
(213) 456-6550

Artist/sculptor making geometrical constructions with reflective glass; also sculpture using light. Has worked with architects before. Does install.

Linda McJunkin
Stained Glass Studios
14 Herrmann Drive
Monterey, CA 93940
(408) 375-6724

Works in stained, faceted, sandblasted, and beveled glass.

Fenton Stained Glass
486 49th Street
Oakland, CA 94609
(415) 655-9009

One-of-a-kind designs in stained glass. Also works in etched, sandblasted, and copperfoil techniques.

Peter Mollica
10033 Broadway Terrace
Oakland, CA 94611
(415) 655-5736

Artist does own designs only; one-of-a-kind pieces. Specializes in modern stained glass. Also does faceted glass work.

GLASS

Beverly Reiser
6979 Exeter Drive
Oakland, CA 94611
(415) 482-2483

Specializes in stained glass and ornamental graphic designs (sandblasted on clear glass), exterior façades at street level, interior glass walls, and space dividers. Also stained glass. Artist does own design only.

Stern Studios
Architectural Glass
1221 8th Avenue
Oakland, CA 94606
(415) 835-5162

Stern makes its own glass, and employs it in various techniques: stained, faceted, bas-relief, and sandblasted. Can do glass castings and custom sheet glass. Specializes in large, architectural glass commissions; also does ornamental work in wood, mosaic, and metals. "Understanding the design criteria of architects, designers, and clients is a major concern of mine."

John Wallis and Associates
2175 E. Foothill Boulevard
Pasadena, CA 91107
(213) 681-2387

Custom designs in stained glass.

Mark Adams
3816 22nd Street
San Francisco, CA 94114
(415) 648-5262

Stained, etched, and faceted glass. Adams also does murals, tapestries, mosaics, and paintings. Has designed doors, windows, and patterns carved in cement. Artist does own designs only.

The Glass House
131 Townsend Street
San Francisco, CA 94107
(415) 957-1329

Combines plate and other kinds of commercially manufactured glass with hand-blown glass. New reflective coatings are of particular interest. Custom designs in stained, etched, beveled, sandblasted, and painted glass.

Narcissus Quagliata and Studio
1550 Bryant Street
San Francisco, CA 94103
(415) 626-5976

Works in stained, faceted, etched, beveled, and sandblasted glass. Equipped to blow and slump glass. The studio does Quagliata's designs only.

Stan Hansen and Associates
300 W. Valley Boulevard
San Gabriel, CA 91776
(213) 576-0746

Established 1954. Design, fabrication, and repair of glass mosaics and stained, leaded, and faceted glass for churches, homes, and restaurants.

Prototype: Stern-Ruthglass cast architectural block. Santa Cruz, CA. Colors: light gray to darker purple. (Photo courtesy of Ruthglass)

Block grouping of prototypical cast glass blocks by Stern-Ruthglass. (Photo courtesy of Ruthglass)

John Bera Studios
774 N. Twin Oaks Valley Road
San Marcos, CA 92069
(714) 744-9282

Works in stained, leaded, faceted, etched, beveled, and sandblasted glass. Has worked extensively with architects.

Penelope Comfort Starr
Architectural Stained Glass
193 Mill Street
San Rafael, CA 94901
(415) 456-9345

Stained, beveled, etched, sandblasted, and painted glass. Specializes in contemporary leaded, stained glass. Brochure $5.00 (applied to first purchase). There is a minimum order. Starr is Executive Vice President of The Glass Depot, Inc., which operates a stained glass studio, retail sales outlet, and training programs. Her background is in architecture and city planning.

Hogan Stained Glass Studios, Inc.
151A Josephine Street
Santa Cruz, CA 95060
(408) 429-1371

Custom and readymade designs in stained, faceted, slab, etched, and sandblasted glass. Has worked with architects before. Specialty: contemporary art glass, sculpted slab glass. Also works in wood, mosaic, and mirror.

Ruthglass
328 Ingalls Street
Santa Cruz, CA 95060
(408) 425-5044

Artist, fabricator, and manufacturer specializing in hand-rolled architectural castings, often made with recycled bottle glass. Ruthglass produces sheets of rolled, multicolored glass (21 by 34 inches). This glass can be installed directly or used by other makers of stained glass. Also casts bas-relief glass sculpture. In addition to free brochure, Ruthglass offers a sample box ($10.00 postpaid). Can give technical advice about installation.

Richard Posner
16649 Superior Street
Sepulveda, CA 91343
(213) 892-9648

Specializes in "site-oriented work—integrating the image with the specific location." Works in stained, etched, faceted, sandblasted, and copperfoil techniques. He also works in wood, mosaic, and stone for exterior architectural ornament. Brochure $10.00.

Glass Menagerie, Ltd.
2070 Tulare Way
Upland, CA 91786
(714) 985-7719

Stained, beveled, etched, faceted, sandblasted, and painted glass. Free installation within 50 miles. Specialty: "traditional, scrolls, Victorian" glass work.

Boulder Art Glass Co.
Attn. Randall D. Leever
1920 Arapahoe Avenue
Boulder, CO 80302
(303) 449-9030

Complete stained glass studio services. Custom designed stained and leaded glass, contemporary and period work; painting, etching, custom beveling, brilliant cutting, intaglio engraving, sandblasting, and restorations. Boulder also manufactures glue chip glass for *dalles de verre*. Will install.

Line drawing for leaded glass design. John Beirs Studio, Philadelphia, PA. (Drawing courtesy of John Beirs Studio)

Cherry Creek Enterprises, Inc.
Attn. Martin Smerling or Lisa Smerling
937 Santa Fe Drive
Denver, CO 80204
(303) 892-1819

Specialists in hand- and machine-beveled glass. An extraordinary variety of texture and line is possible with this technique. Staff designers and craftsmen will create and fabricate their own designs as well as designs of others. In addition, Cherry Creek does stained, faceted, sandblasted, and glue chip glass.

First Impressions
Fort Collins, CO 80522

See listing under Metals.

Dimensions in Glass
Attn. Rollin McKim
2545 Youngfield Street
Golden, CO 80401
(303) 233-2492

Artist works with stained, etched, sandblasted, mirrored, and copperfoil glass. Installs and can recommend framer. Specializes in combinations of mirror and leaded, stained glass in contemporary style. There is a retail space for readymade works in his studio.

GLASS

Collins Stained Glass
8283 W. Iliff Lane
Lakewood, CO 80227
(303) 985-8081

This studio specializes in one-of-a-kind stained glass pieces. Custom designs in stained, beveled, etched, and sandblasted glass. Artist does own designs only. Also works in hardwoods; doors and screens with stained glass and laminated wood designs.

Creative Stained Glass Studio
2533 Kipling
Lakewood, CO 80215
(303) 232-1762

This studio has a staff of five artists and craftsmen, and specializes in custom design of stained, faceted, and flat glass. Also does painted, beveled, etched, and sandblasted glass.

G. Brittain M. Co.
Attn. Greg Monk
P.O. Box 537
Haleiwa, HI 96712
(808) 638-8158
(808) 531-2933

Custom designs in leaded and copperfoil stained glass; also does beveling and sandblasting.

Erica Karawina
3529 Akaka Place
Honolulu, HI 96822
(808) 988-3275

Stained (leaded and faceted) and *dalles de verre* (1-inch thick faceted glass in epoxy matrix). Also does painted glass. Style is "abstract and contemporary."

Kaleidoscope Art Glass Studio
Attn. Michael C. Booth
210 Bannock Street
Boise, ID 83702
(208) 344-5037

Leaded, sculptured, fused, and kiln-fired glass. Specialty: architectural and sculptural glass; traditional and contemporary designs. Also works in mosaics and metal.

Beal's Royal Glass and Mirror
1601 South Main
Las Vegas, NV 89114
(702) 384-0997

Stained, etched, beveled, slab, and sandblasted glass. Familiar with slumping techniques. Makes own glue chip glass. Specializes in large, commercial installations.

Creative Resources
11465 S. W. Canyon Road
Beaverton, OR 97005
(503) 641-2845

Specialty: carving glass by sandblasting. Also works with mirrored glass, wood, and marble. Estimates from sketch only.

Etched glass by Beverly Reiser, Oakland, CA. (Photo by Rob Super, courtesy of Beverly Reiser)

Ed Carpenter
3125 Van Waters
Milwaukie, OR 97222
(503) 635-5230

Artist does his own contemporary designs only. Stained, etched, sandblasted, and laminated glass. Does architectural commissions; estimates based on plans. Will also do mosaics. He has served as a consultant to architects and designers to locate artwork (in various media) appropriate for specific spaces.

Classical Glass
Attn. David Schlicker
823 S.E. 54th Street
Portland, OR 97215
(503) 231-9600

Custom and readymade designs in stained, beveled, sandblasted, and etched glass. Small and one-of-a-kind orders. Specializes in landscape windows.

Garth Edwards
3410 S.W. Water Avenue
Portland, OR 97201
(503) 223-5012

Artist/fabricator does own designs only. Stained, sandblasted, and etched glass. Accepts large, small, or one-of-a-kind orders. Gives estimates, and will install.

Gail J. O'Neill
Rte. 2, Box 1127A
Troutdale, OR 97060
(503) 661-6048
(503) 644-0160 ext. 4830 (work)

Artist fabricates her own designs for exhibition; commissions are fabricated by Inverness Glass Studio. Stained glass windows, free-hanging, movable panels, and sculptural wall pieces assembled with slumped glass, sandblasted glass, glass rods, and glass tubes.

Artistic Glass
315 E. 2100 South
Salt Lake City, UT 84115
(801) 484-8143

Design, manufacture, and repair of leaded, stained glass for churches, businesses, or residences by European-trained craftsmen.

Beehive Glass Co.
3070 E. 33rd Street South
Salt Lake City, UT 84109
(801) 486-4991

Distributor. Readymade and custom designs; stained, etched, beveled, and sandblasted glass. Mainly leaded, copperfoil on request. Will install. Large orders only.

Creative Glass, Inc.
703 S.W. Temple
Salt Lake City, UT 84101
(801) 328-4088

Custom, or readymade stained, etched, and beveled glass. Specializes in Tiffany-style lamps.

Mesolini Glass Studio
13291 N.E. Madison
Bainbridge Island, WA 98110
(206) 842-7133

Stained, etched, beveled, sandblasted, slumped, and cast glass. Will install. Specializes in leaded and copperfoil panels, reinforced if necessary.

Glassworks
12718 Northrup
Bellevue, WA 98005
(206) 455-4334

Custom designs in stained, faceted, etched, beveled, and sandblasted glass. Will install. Does one-of-a-kind or large orders.

Paul Marioni
4136 Meridian Avenue
Seattle, WA 98103
(206) 633-1901

and

1712 Elm Avenue
Richmond, CA 94805
(No phone)

Specializes in large-scale architectural glass in one-of-a-kind designs. Artist does own designs only. Stained, sandblasted, and cast bas-relief glass.

McGowan's Stained Glass Studio
12519 Lake City Way N.E.
Seattle, WA 98125
(206) 363-5678

Works in stained, faceted, etched, painted, and sandblasted glass. Specializes in painted, fired, and faceted glass church windows—original and restoration work. Has done windows for Mormon temples in Tokyo, Japan, and Bellevue, Washington.

Model of top of Tower Building, PPG Industries Corporate Headquarters, Pittsburgh, PA. Johnson/Burgee Architects (1981). (Photo by Gil Amiaga, courtesy of Johnson/Burgee Architects)

Key

X Service, technique, or material is available
\+ See listing for further information
* Sometimes offers this service

						Glass used							
Northeast	Artist	Artist/fabricator	Fabricator	Custom designs from sketch	Own designs	Stained	Beveled	Etched	Other	Rough estimates (by square foot)	Installs	Brochure or photos available	Glass block
Le Jardin de Verre New London, CT		X		X	X	X	X	X	+	X		X	
Studio Worshop Simsbury, CT		X		X	X	X		X	+	X	X	X	
Phoenix Studio Portland, ME		X		X	X	X	X	X	+	X	X	X	
Bert Weiss Glass Studio Portland, ME		X		X	X	X			+	X	X	X	
Osiris Glassworks Beverly Farms, MA		X		X	X	X	X	X	+	X	X	X	
Lieng Designs Boston, MA		X		X	X	X				X	X	X	
Philip Stein Fitchburg, MA		X		X	X	X	X	X	+	X	X	X	
La Roche Stained Glass Malden, MA		X		X	X	X	X	X	+	X	X	X	
Quantock Designers Marblehead, MA		X			X	X			+	X	X	X	
Serpentino Stained Glass Needham, MA		X		X	X	X			+	X	X		
Armstrong and Barberio Newburyport, MA		X		X	X	X	X		+	X	X	X	
Cummings Studios North Adams, MA		X		X	X	X			+	X	X	X	
E. Settimelli and Sons Quincy, MA		X		X	X				+	X		X	
Pompei Stained Glass West Medord, MA		X		X	X	X	X	X	+	X	X	X	
Alfred Rucker Pike, NH		X			X	X			+		X	X	
Stained Glass Creations Bay Shore, NY		X		X	X	X	X	X	+	X	X	X	
Carved Glass & Sign Bronx, NY		X		X	X	X		X	+	X	*		
Ernest Porcelli Brooklyn, NY		X		X	X	X	X		+	X	X	X	
George Sell Brooklyn, NY		X		X	X	X	X	X	+	X	X	X	
Robert Sowers Brooklyn, NY		X			X	X			+			X	
Manor Art Glass Studio Douglaston, NY		X		X	X	X	X		+	X	X	X	

Key

X Service, technique, or material is available
+ See listing for further information
* Sometimes offers this service

	Artist	Artist/fabricator	Fabricator	Custom designs from sketch	Own designs	Glass used: Stained	Glass used: Beveled	Glass used: Etched	Glass used: Other	Rough estimates (by square foot)	Installs	Brochure or photos available	Glass block
King Stained Glass Hewlett, NY		X		X	X	X	X		+	X	X	X	
Joan Altabe Long Beach, NY	+			X	X	X	X	X	+	X	X	X	
Durhan Studios Lynbrook, NY		X		X	X	X	X	X	+	X	X	X	
Glass Crafters Manhasset, NY		X		X	X	X	X		+	X	X	X	
Rohlf's Stained Glass Mount Vernon, NY		X		X	X	X	X	X	+	X	X	X	
Richard Avidon New York, NY		X		X	X	X		X	+	X	X	X	
Marni Bakst New York, NY		X			X	X			+	X	*	X	
Peter Hans Felzmann New York, NY		X		X	X				X		X	X	
Benoit Gilsoul New York, NY	See listing under Murals												
The Greenland Studio New York, NY		X	+	X	X	X	X	X	+	X	X	X	
New York Art Glass New York, NY	See listing under Murals												
Stained Glass Studios Nyack, NY		X		X	X	X	X	X	+	X	X	X	
Harriet Hyams Palisades, NY		X		X	X	X	X	X	+	X	X	X	
Bienenfeld Industries Ridgewood, NY						+			+			X	X
Pike Stained Glass Rochester, NY		X		X	X	X	X	X	+	+	X	X	
David Wilson South New Berlin, NY		X		X	X	X	X	X	+	X	X	X	
J. & R. Lamb Studios Spring Valley, NY		+		X	X	X			+	X	X	X	
James B. Furman Trumansburg, NY		X		X	X	X	X	X	+	X	X	X	
Edward J. Byrne Studio Doylestown, PA		X		X	X	X			+		X	X	
The Emporium Johnstown, PA		X		X	X	X			+			X	
John Beirs Studio Philadelphia, PA		X		X	X	X	X	X	+	X	X	X	

Key

X Service, technique, or material is available
+ See listing for further information
* Sometimes offers this service

	Artist	Artist/fabricator	Fabricator	Custom designs from sketch	Own designs	Glass used				Rough estimates (by square foot)	Installs	Brochure or photos available	Glass block
						Stained	Beveled	Etched	Other				
Ray King Philadelphia, PA		X			X	X		X	+		X	X	
Philadelphia Art Glass Philadelphia, PA	X			X	X		X	X	+	X	X	X	
Willet Stained Glass Philadelphia, PA		+		X	X	X	X	X	+	X	X	X	
Pittsburgh Corning Pittsburgh, PA									+			X	X
Morgan Bockius Studios Warminster, PA		X		X	X	X	X	X	+	X	X	X	
St. Luke's Studio Newport, RI		X		X	X	X				X	X	X	
Classical Glass, Inc. Burlington, VT		X		X	X	X	X	X	+		X	X	
Luminosity Stained Glass Waitsfield, VT		X			X	X		X	+	X	X	X	
South													
Dupre Studio Miami, FL		X			X	X			+	X	X	X	
Glassworks, Inc. Miami, FL		X		X	X	X	X	X	+	X	X		
Rowe Studios Miami, FL		X		X	X	X	X	X	+	X	X		
Pharrmoors Studios Orlando, FL		X		X	X	X			+	*		X	
Art Glass Studio Atlanta, GA		X			X	X	X	X	+		X		
Southeastern Art Glass Avondale Estates, GA		X		X	X	X	X	X		X	X	X	
Fenestra Studios Louisville, KY		X		X	X	X	X	X	+	X	X	X	
Penco Studios Louisville, KY		X		X	X	X	X	X	+	X	X	X	
Dufour Glass Studio Baton Rouge, LA		X		X	X	X		X	+	X	X	X	
Chevy Chase Glass Bethesda, MD			X	X	X	X			+	X	X	X	
Baltimore New Glass Millers, MD		X		X	X	X		X	+			X	
Andrews Art Glass Upper Marlboro, MD		X		X	X	X		X	+	X	X	X	

Key

- X Service, technique, or material is available
- \+ See listing for further information
- * Sometimes offers this service

	Artist	Artist/fabricator	Fabricator	Custom designs from sketch	Own designs	Glass used				Rough estimates (by square foot)	Installs	Brochure or photos available	Glass block
						Stained	Beveled	Etched	Other				
Pearl River Glass Jackson, MS		X		X	X	X	X	X	+	X	X	X	
Catherine N. Parrish Raleigh, NC		X		X	X	X	X	X	+	X	+	X	
Stained Glass Associates Raleigh, NC		X		X	X	X	X	X	+	X	X	X	
Charles Towne Glass Charleston, SC		X		X	X	X	X	X	+	X	X	X	
R. L. Roelse Goose Creek, SC		X		X	X	X	X	X	+	X	X	X	
Mt. Airy Glass Greer, SC		X		X	X		X	X	+	X	X	X	
Palmetto Art Glass Greer, SC		X		X	X	X	X	X	+	X	X	X	
Classical Glass Lexington, SC		X		X	X	X	X	X	+	X	X	X	
Saunders Stained Glass Brighton, TN		X		X	X	X	X	X	+	X	X	X	
Sunlite Stained Glass Knoxville, TN		X		X	X	X	X	X	+	X	X	X	
Bright Light Memphis, TN		X		+	X	X	X			X	X	X	
Old Dominion Ashland, VA	X		X		X			X	+	X	X	X	
Dieter Goldkuhle Reston, VA			+	X	X	X			+	X	X	X	
Cain-Powers Architectural Art Glass Richmond, VA		X		X	X	X	X	X	+		X	X	
Fall Line Glass Richmond, VA		X		X	X	X	X		+	X			
Arthur Miller Studios Richmond, VA		X		X	X	X	X	X	+	X	X	X	
Grafton Studios Fayetteville, WV		X		X	X	X				X			
Shobe's Stained Glass Huntington, WV		X		X	X	X	X	X	+	X	X	X	
Midwest													
Botti Studio Evanston, IL		X		X	X	X	X	X	+	X	X	X	
Greg Spiess Joliet, IL		X		X	X	X	X		+	X	X		

Key

- X Service, technique, or material is available
- + See listing for further information
- * Sometimes offers this service

	Artist	Artist/fabricator	Fabricator	Custom designs from sketch	Own designs	Glass used: Stained	Glass used: Beveled	Glass used: Etched	Glass used: Other	Rough estimates (by square foot)	Installs	Brochure or photos available	Glass block
Regina Art Glass Maywood, IL		X		X	X	X	X		+	X	X		
The Glassworks Wheaton, IL		X		X	X	X	X		+	X		X	
The Crystal Cave Wilmette, IL		X		X	X		X	X	+		+	X	
Der Glass Werks Indianapolis, IN		X		X	X	X	X	X	+	X	X	X	
Studio Stained Glass Kokomo, IN		X		X	X	X	X	X	+	X	X	X	
C. Paul Stained Glass Lyons, IN		X		X	X	X	X			X	X	X	
Sunburst Stained Glass New Harmony, IN		X		X	X	X	X		+	X	+	X	
Steven Frank Studios Detroit, MI		X		X	X	X	X	X	+	X	X	X	
Thompson Glass Detroit, MI		X		X	X	X	X	X	+	X	X	X	
Trupiano Glassworks Grant, MI		X		X	X	X	X	X	+	X	X	X	
ChinaHue Glassworks Kalamazoo, MI		X		X	X	X	X		+	X	X	X	
Ice Nine Glass Design Golden Valley, MN		X		X	X			X				X	
John Eckley Studio Minneapolis, MN		X		X	X	X	X		+	X	X	+	
Gaytee Stained Glass Minneapolis, MN		X		X	X	X	X	X	+	X	X		
Monarch Studios St. Paul, MN		X		X	X	X	X	X	+	X	X	X	
Plaza Studio Kansas City, MO		X		X	X	X	X	X	+	X	X	X	
Art Glass Unlimited St. Louis, MO		X		X	X	X	+	X	+		X	X	
Unique Art Glass St. Louis, MO		X		X	X	X	X	X	+	X	X	X	
Boesen's Glasscrafts Omaha, NE		X		X	X	X	X		+	X	X	X	
Stained Glass Workshop Fargo, ND		X		X	X	X	X		+	X	X	X	

Key

X Service, technique, or material is available
+ See listing for further information
* Sometimes offers this service

	Artist	Artist/fabricator	Fabricator	Custom designs from sketch	Own designs	Glass used: Stained	Beveled	Etched	Other	Rough estimates (by square foot)	Installs	Brochure or photos available	Glass block
Custom Mirror and Glass Cleveland Heights, OH		X		X	X				+	X	X	X	
Contemporary Glass Columbus, OH		X		X	X	X		X	+	X	X		
Franklin Art Glass Columbus, OH		X		X	X	X	X	X	+	X	X	X	
Leffler Studio Holland, OH		X		X	X	X	X		+	X	X	X	
Sherer's Stained Glass Maumee, OH		X		X	X	X	X	X	+	X	X	X	
The House of DuValle North Olmsted, OH		X		X	X	X	X	X	+	X	X	X	
John W. Winterich Solon, OH		X		X	X	X		X	X	X	X	X	
Hendrix, Heikkilä, Terry Norman, OK		X		X	X	X	X	X	X		X	X	
The Glass Farm Rapid City, SD		X		X	X	X	X	X	+	X	+	X	
Phoenix Stained Glass Austin, TX		X		X	X	X	X	X	+	X	X	X	
Renaissance Glass Austin, TX		X		X	X	X	X	X	+	X	X	+	
Mecaskey's Stained Glass Dallas, TX		X		X	X	X	X		+	X	X	X	
Thompson Art Glass Dallas, TX		X		X	X	X	X	X	+	X	X	X	
Smith Stained Glass Forth Worth, TX		X			X	X	X	X	+	X	X	X	
Black's Art Glass San Antonio, TX		X		X	X	X	X	X	+	X	X	X	
Brown's Stained Glass San Antonio, TX		X		X	X	X	X	X	+	X	X	X	
Cavallini San Antonio, TX		X		X	X	X	X	X	+	X	X	X	
PECO Smithville, TX		X		X	X	X	X			X		X	
Touchstone Smithville, TX		X		X	X			X	+	X	X	X	
Brandis Studio Milwaukee, WI		X		X	X	X	X		+	X	X	X	

Key

- **X** Service, technique, or material is available
- **+** See listing for further information
- ***** Sometimes offers this service

	Artist	Artist/fabricator	Fabricator	Custom designs from sketch	Own designs	Glass used: Stained	Beveled	Etched	Other	Rough estimates (by square foot)	Installs	Brochure or photos available	Glass block
Dennis Pearson Spring Green, WI		X		X	X	X	X	X	+	X	X	X	
Chequamegon Bay Art Glass Washburn, WI		X		X	X	X	X	X	+	X	X	X	

Rockies and Far West

	Artist	Artist/fabricator	Fabricator	Custom designs from sketch	Own designs	Glass used: Stained	Beveled	Etched	Other	Rough estimates (by square foot)	Installs	Brochure or photos available	Glass block
Art Glass of Arizona Phoenix, AZ		X		X	X	X	X	X	+	X	X	X	
The Glassworks Studio Phoenix, AZ		X		X	X	X	X	X	+	X	X	X	
Maureen McGuire Designs Phoenix, AZ	X				X	X		X	+	*	+	X	
Artistry Stained Glass Tempe, AZ		X		X	X	X	X	X	+	X	X	X	
Robert Kehlman Berkeley, CA		X			X	X		X	+				
Looking Glass Davenport, CA		X		X	X		X	X	+		X		
Crowe Glass Escondido, CA		X		X	X	X	X	X	+	X	X	X	
Isaac's Stained Glass Hollywood, CA		X		X	X	X	X	X	+	X	X	X	
Jean Clyde Mason Design Hollywood, CA		X		X	X			X	+	X	*		
Adamm's Stained Glass Los Angeles, CA		X		X	X	X	X	X	+	X	X		
Beveled Glass Los Angeles, CA			X	X	X		X			X		+	
Fairbanks and Fairbanks Los Angeles, CA	See listing under Sculpture												
Salvatore Polizzi Los Angeles, CA		X		X	X	X	X	X	+		X	X	
Sunshine Glass Works Los Angeles, CA		X		X	X	X	X	X	+	X	X	X	
Ray Howlett Malibu, CA		X			X				+	X	X	X	
Linda McJunkin Monterey, CA		X		X	X	X	X	X	+	X	X	X	
Fenton Stained Glass Oakland, CA		X		X	X	X		X	+	X	X	X	
Peter Mollica Oakland, CA		X			X	X			+	X	X	X	

Key

- X Service, technique, or material is available
- + See listing for further information
- * Sometimes offers this service

	Artist	Artist/fabricator	Fabricator	Custom designs from sketch	Own designs	Glass used				Rough estimates (by square foot)	Installs	Brochure or photos available	Glass block
						Stained	Beveled	Etched	Other				
Beverly Reiser Oakland, CA		X			X	X	X		+	X	*	X	
Stern Studios Oakland, CA		X		X	X	X			+	X	X	X	
John Wallis Pasadena, CA		X		X	X	X			+	X	X		
Mark Adams San Francisco, CA	X				X	X		X	+	X	+	X	
The Glass House San Francisco, CA		X		X	X	X	X	X	+	X	X	X	
Narcissus Quagliata San Francisco, CA	X				X	X	X	X	+		X	X	
Stan Hansen San Gabriel, CA		X		X	X	X	X		+		X	X	
John Bera Studios San Marcos, CA		X		X	X	X	X	X	+	X	X	X	
Penelope Comfort Starr San Rafael, CA		X		X	X	X	X		+	X	+	+	
Hogan Stained Glass Santa Cruz, CA		X		X	X	X	X	X	X	X	X	X	
Ruthglass Santa Cruz, CA			+		X	X			+			+	
Richard Posner Sepulveda, CA		X		X	X	X		X	+		X	*	
Glass Menagerie, Ltd. Upland, CA		X		X	X	X	X	X	+	X	X	X	
Boulder, Art Glass Boulder, CO		X		X	X	X	X	X	+	X	X	X	
Cherry Creek Denver, CO		X		+	X	X	X	X	+	X		X	
First Impressions Fort Collins, CO	See listing under Metals												
Dimensions in Glass Golden, CO		X		X	X	X		X	+	X	X		
Collins Stained Glass Lakewood, CO		X			X	X	X	X	+	X	X	X	
Creative Stained Glass Lakewood, CO		X		X	X	X	X	X	+		X	X	
G. Brittain M. Haleiwa, HI		X		X	X	X	X		+	X	X	X	
Frica Karwawina Honolulu, HI		X		X	X	X			+		X	X	

Key

X Service, technique, or material is available
+ See listing for further information
* Sometimes offers this service

	Artist	Artist/fabricator	Fabricator	Custom designs from sketch	Own designs	Glass used: Stained	Beveled	Etched	Other	Rough estimates (by square foot)	Installs	Brochure or photos available	Glass block
Kaleidoscope Art Glass Boise, ID		X		X	X	X		X	+	X	X	X	
Beal's Royal Glass Las Vegas, NV		X		X	X	X	X	X	+	X	X	X	
Creative Resources Beaverton, OR		X		X	X			X	+	+	+	X	
Ed Carpenter Milwaukie, OR	X				X	X		X	+		X	X	
Classical Glass Portland, OR		X		X	X	X	X	X	+	X	X	X	
Garth Edwards Portland, OR		X			X	X				X	X	X	
Gail J. O'Neill Troutdale, OR	+			X	X	X			+	X	X	X	
Artistic Glass Salt Lake City, UT			X	X	X	X							
Beehive Glass Salt Lake City, UT				X		X	X	X	+	X	X	X	
Creative Glass Salt Lake City, UT		X		X	X	X	X	X	+	X	+	X	
Mesolini Glass Studio Bainbridge Island, WA		X		X	X	X	X	X	+	X	X	X	
Glassworks Bellevue, WA		X		X	X	X	X	X	+		X	X	
Paul Marioni Seattle, WA		X			X	X			+		X	X	
McGowan's Stained Glass Seattle, WA		X		X	X	X	X	X	+	X	X	X	

IRON

Ornamental iron is used for grills, gates, finials, crestings, weather vanes, brackets, hardware, ornamental supports for awnings, and innumerable other architectural accessories. If the number of responses to our questionnaires is any indication, the blacksmith's art of hand-forging architectural iron is another craft in the midst of a major revival in this country. Hand forging—or hot forging—uses the traditional hammer and anvil to accomplish what is today more often done by cold bending and arc welding. Therefore, if you want authentic hand-wrought iron, look for "hot forging" as opposed to "cold bending" in these listings.

"In this country we've been in business twenty years. In the old country we were born with our job." So it was with many of the small companies we contacted. The majority of these can make up their own designs or those of an architect. In addition, many small companies fabricate large architectural elements using stock, interchangeable pieces from manufacturers such as Tennessee Fabricating.

The **Tennessee Fabricating Company, Julius Blum** (in New Jersey), and **Lawler Machine & Foundry** (in Alabama) are among several special cases listed below. These large, well-known companies produce a great variety of ornamental architectural accessories in cast iron and other metals. Their catalogs show hundreds of stock elements that can be assembled in countless different arrangements.

Regional Listings

Northeast

Butler Iron Works
Attn. Robert D. Butler
15 Main Street
Wethersfield, CT 06109
(203) 563-3136

Specialty: kinetic sculpture in iron. Makes such architectural elements as railings, weather vanes, and signs. Butler also works in brass, copper, and stainless steel.

Larson Forge Co.
Rte. 152, Box 97A
Cambridge, ME 04923
(207) 277-3254

Gates, railings, hardware, signposts. Brochure $0.50 (refunded with $10.00 purchase). Will give telephone estimates but prefers to estimate from site measurements. Additional charge for installation.

Capone Iron Works
15 Betty Street
Everett, MA 02149
(617) 387-3725

Custom designs; cold bending. Specialty; iron railings and fire escapes. Also produces iron furniture and some structural steel.

IRON

The Boston Blacksmith
47 Business Street
Hyde Park, MA 02136
(617) 364-1499

Specializes in decorative commercial and residential security grilles; also, gates, railings, etc.

Gino's Ornamental Iron Works
323 Commercial Street
Malden, MA 02148
(617) 324-2300

Produces gates, grilles, hardware, weather vanes, and other metalwork.

Superior Rail and Iron Works, Inc.
159 Mill Street, P.O. Box 506
Stoughton, MA 02072
(617) 344-9342

Specializes in railings of all types; iron and aluminum made by forming and cold bending.

Star Forge
Attn. Newton Millham
672 Drift Road
Westport, MA 02790
(617) 636-5437

This blacksmith specializes in eighteenth-century architectural hardware: exterior latches, knockers, shutter dogs, hinges, boot scrapers, and reproduction stair rails. Also, smaller items for hearth and lighting. Combines iron with brass and copper. Brochure $1.00.

Williamsburg Blacksmiths, Inc.
Goshen Road
Williamsburg, MA 01096
(413) 268-7341

Reproductions of early-American wrought iron hardware. No custom designs. Brochure $2.50.

Russell Pope
Water Street
Newmarket, NH 03857
(603) 659-2595

Specialty: medium and small custom ironwork and sculpture, wrought and joined using traditional methods. Combines iron with brass, copper, aluminum, wood, glass, stone, and ceramics. Also makes grilles, weather vanes, railings, etc.

Peter Happny
Contemporary Ironwork
66 Rock Street
Portsmouth, NH 03801
(603) 436-4859

Does fine forgings with a contemporary feeling: gates, railings, weather vanes, hardware, grilles, lighting, signs, and sculpture. Casts glass into iron forms; uses pottery, porcelain, fiber, cast brass, aluminum, and iron.

Scale model of forged iron "Merbird Gate" (15 by 12 inches; final size 5 by 4 feet). Christopher Ray (© 1979), Sculptor, Philadelphia, PA. (Photo courtesy of Christopher Ray)

Julius Blum & Co., Inc.
Carlstadt, NJ 07072

See listing under Metals.

Dinger Brothers Iron Works, Inc.
803 Liberty Street
Trenton, NJ 08611
(609) 396-1554

Railings, grilles, circular stairs, and fire escapes. Works in iron, brass, aluminum, and stainless steel. Installs, within fifty-mile radius.

Vestinian Craftsmen, Inc.
2966 Jerome Avenue
Bronx, NY 10468
(212) 295-0296

Specializes in ornamental wrought iron and wrought iron art. Does grilles, railings, doors, and entrances; works in white metal and copper as well.

Florentine Artistic Iron Works
1512 63rd Street
Brooklyn, NY 11219
(212) 331-4646

Specializes in gates and railings; custom only.

Hand-forged garden gate (5 by 5 feet). Schwartz's Forge & Metalworks, Deansboro, NY. (Photo courtesy of Joel A. Schwartz)

Schwartz's Forge and Metalworks
P.O. Box 205
Forge Hollow Road
Deansboro, NY 13328
(315) 841-4477

Beautifully designed forgings from cheese cutters to monumental grilles and railings. Particular attention paid to detailing. Has exhibited at the Museum of Contemporary Crafts in New York and at the Renwick Gallery of the Smithsonian Institute. Brochure $3.00 (free to trade).

Blythe Machine and Iron Works
Rte. 25A and Echo Avenue
Miller Place, NY 11764
(516) 473-2306

Specializes in ornamental iron railings and spiral staircases.

Deco Iron Creations
Attn. Harold Bisagn
170 W. 85th Street
New York, NY 10024
(212) 362-2206

Custom and readymade gates, railings, hardware, and grilles.

P. A. Fiebiger
462 Tenth Avenue
New York, NY 10018
(212) 563-5818

In business for over eighty years, this company specializes in fine restorations and executions of traditional design of "old world ironwork" for gates, railings, and other architectural accessories. Fiebiger has an extensive library of designs from which you can choose. Photos of the work can be seen on the premises. Has done work for the Frick Museum, Morgan Library, and the United States Capitol.

Koenig Iron Works
223 W. 19th Street
New York, NY 10011
(212) 924-4333

Does all kinds of custom work—railings, gates, ornamental grilles.

Richard Lichtenstein
237 Lafayette Street
New York, NY 10012
(212) 966-9799

See listing under Sculpture.

Particular Iron Works, Inc.
52 Greene Street
New York, NY 10013
(212) 226-5044

Railings, grilles, gates, and exterior hardware. Combines other materials—wood, plastic, brass, aluminum, and cast iron—with wrought iron.

Steve Kayne Hand Forged Hardware
17 Harmon Place
Smithtown, NY 11787
(516) 724-3669

Hardware, weather vanes, and grilles. Specializes in custom work hand-forged to customer's requirements. Household and builder's hardware: door knockers, latches, hinges, bolts. Works in iron, forged steel, brass, bronze, copper, etc. Three different brochures, $1.00 each. Installs in immediate area.

Victor Metals
Box 326
Unadilla, NY 13849
(607) 369-3395

and

4012 32nd Street
Mt. Rainier, MD 20822
(301) 779-3094

Distributor and fabricator. Grilles, railings, entrances, lettering (cast or cut plate).

Christopher T. Ray, Sculptor
Philadelphia, PA 19144

See listing under Sculpture.

Forged iron gate (approximately 5 by 5 feet), by Robert Owings, Point Reyes, CA. (Photo courtesy of Robert Owings)

Samuel Bird, Blacksmith
High Street
Block Island, RI 02807
(401) 466-2682

This blacksmith does a variety of hot forged work—railings, gates, weather vanes, etc.—including contemporary and Colonial reproductions. Has worked with a glass blower to make pieces combining glass and iron.

Jenison Ornamental Iron Works
334 Knight
Warwick, RI 02886
(401) 738-7711

Specializes in custom ornamental railings. Also does weather vanes, hardware, and gates; works in such other materials as brass, copper, gold, silver, and nickel plate. Repairs antique metalwork, including lead and cast iron.

Hubbardton Forge and Wood Corp.
SR, Bomoseen, VT 05732
(802) 273-2047

All work hand-forged, stock and custom designs. Price list and brochure of stock items is available; stock consists primarily of smaller pieces, including chandeliers, swing cranes, and utensils. Hubbardton accepts custom commissions for larger pieces, including gates, architectural screens, large wall hangings, and "huge lighting fixtures."

Robert Bourdon
Wolcott, VT 05680
(802) 472-6508

Does mostly custom work, primarily reproduction hardware. Also makes sundials, signs, and forged iron ski sculpture. Sometimes inlays brass or copper in smaller objects. Installs in immediate area when requested.

South

Cox Ornamental Iron Co.
P.O. Box 30081
452 N. 37th Street
Birmingham, AL 35222
(205) 324-4346

Specializes in custom gates, railings, spiral stairs, and light structural steel. Also works with brass.

Jones Valley Ornamental Iron Co.
3135 Jefferson Avenue S.W.
Birmingham, AL 35221
(205) 925-9591

Distributors and fabricators. Stairs (spiral and straight), columns, railings, and gates.

Detail of gate: opened bar, split into quarters, drawn and scrolled (4-inch diameter circle). Nol Putnam (1979), White Oak Forge, Madison, VA. (Photo courtesy of Nol Putnam)

Lawler Machine & Foundry
760 N. 44th Street
Birmingham, AL 35212
(205) 595-0597

This family-owned company, founded in 1933, employs over 125 workers making decorative cast iron and cast aluminum designs, as well as machine castings. Many of the designs are reproduced from original wood carvings that have been preserved through the years "because of their romantic or historical background." Lawler offers many different elements in many different styles that can be combined to create fences, enclosures, gates, grilles, crown designs, railings, porch brackets, and the like. Has about twenty different picket castings which fit on 1/2-inch-square picket rods and can be combined to create complex ornamental patterns.

Florida Ornamental Iron, Inc.
Attn. Paul E. Thibodeau, President
4305 E. 11th Avenue
Hialeah, FL 33013
(305) 688-3133

Weather vanes, railings, hardware, canopies, fences, etc. Will combine iron with such other metals as bronze, brass, or aluminum. Also does smaller items—wine racks and tables for example.

Artistic Ornamental Iron Co., Inc.
1977 College Avenue N.E.
Atlanta, GA 30317
(404) 373-6524

Specialty: fabrication of ornamental iron and miscellaneous metals along with light structural steel. Railings, gates, weather vanes, columns, etc. Metals combined with wood and plastics.

Dixie Ornamental Iron Co.
1930 Cheshire Bridge Road N.E
Atlanta, GA 30324
(404) 875-8088

Spiral stairs, gates, railings, security doors, and grilles. Combines metals with wood.

Bailey's Forge
Attn. Ivan Bailey
215 Whitaker Street
Savannah, GA 31401
(912) 233-2348

Bailey does a lot of work with architects. In addition to iron, can work with other metals, wood, and glass. Work includes "dolphin downspout boots" and a variety of other imaginative, detailed, architectural elements. Artist does own designs only: railings, weather vanes, lighting, signs, wall sculptures, gates—all made by hot forging.

Owens and Son Iron Works
Attn. Jimmy Owens
2106 Bolling Street
Savannah, GA 31404
(912) 236-4756

Makes railings and other architectural elements. Specialty: ornamental iron-work for porches.

Chas. Horrar
CPO 935
Berea, KY 40404
(No phone)

Hot forging only: railings, gates, hardware (including hinges), and grilles.

Farve Ornamental Iron Works
1701 20th Street
Kenner, LA 70062
(504) 466-9127

Ornamental ironwork, both readymade and custom, in the rich Southern tradition: railings, gates, weather vanes, hardware, porch enclosures, spiral stairs. Farve combines ironwork with aluminum, acrylic glazed panels, plexiglass, and mirror. Brochure $0.50.

J. Rothstein and Co., Inc.
Scott and Ostend Streets
Baltimore, MD 21230
(301) 539-8861

Grilles, railings, steel porches, and columns done in a variety of techniques including forming, bending, carving, and forging.

IRON

Ram's Forge
Randy McDaniel, Blacksmith
2501 E. Mayberry Road
Westminster, MD 21157
(301) 346-7873

Hot forging and forge welding using traditional techniques. Contemporary and colonial wrought iron including gates, railings, sign brackets, archways, grilles, and complete door hardware. Also works in copper. Does not install weather vanes.

Lawson's Welding
1008 Louis Street
Jackson, MS 39213
(601) 981-4761

Does mainly cast iron: grilles, railings, doors, windows, and entrances.

Charleston Awning and Metal Co., Inc.
P.O. Box 70146
3527 Meeting Street Road
Charleston Heights, SC 29405
(803) 744-3300

Specializes in gates and ornamental iron fences; also does grilles, railings, windows, doors, and entrances in iron and aluminum.

Fields Ornamental Iron and Welding
7192 Cross County Road
Charleston Heights, SC 29405
(803) 552-9432
(803) 553-5109

Readymade and custom designs of railings; hot forging and cold bending. Will install.

Dixie Iron Works
810 S. Edisto Avenue
Columbia, SC 29205
(803) 771-6534

Traditional designs only. Specializes in gates, grilles, and railings; also makes fascias, plaques, spiral stairs, etc. Works in bronze, aluminum, and stainless steel.

Wiggins Ornamental Iron and Welding
Rte. 2, Box 58
St. Stephen, SC 29479
(803) 723-5918
(803) 567-3223

Specializes in ornamental iron railings, columns, fences, stairs, and security grilles for doors and windows. Sometimes gives telephone estimates.

Tennessee Fabricating Co.
2366 Prospect
Memphis, TN 38106
(901) 948-3354

Extensive choice of readymade cast iron and aluminum decorative elements. These are specifically intended to be purchased separately and put together in a nearly-endless variety of ways. Many of the ironworkers listed in this section are familiar with Tennessee Fabricating products, and some specialize in installing them. Tennessee will recommend a fabricator in your area. Brochure $2.50.

Garden gate, forged iron (approx. 3 by 4 feet) by Nol Putnam (1979), White Oak Forge, Madison, VA. (Photo courtesy of Nol Putnam)

James Wallace
374 W. California
Memphis, TN 38106
(901) 775-1284

A blacksmith doing hot forged, custom designs: railings, gates, exterior hardware, weather vanes, signs, brackets, screens, etc. Can work from rough sketch or more detailed information. Specializes in contemporary ironwork; also provides complete restoration of iron to museum quality. Can combine iron with wood, brass, copper, bronze, aluminum, stainless steel, and glass.

White Oak Forge
Nol Putnam, Blacksmith
Rte. 657 RR #1, Box 109A
Madison, VA 22727
(703) 948-4379

Fine quality hand forgings: grilles, railings, gates, hardware, weather vanes, signs, and sign brackets. Specializes in forged architectural iron. Does restoration work as well. Combines iron with brass and copper. Brochure $2.00.

Goose Creek Metalworks
Brenny W. McLaughlin
P.O. Box 158
Montvale, VA 24122
(703) 947-5188

Railings, gates, grilles, and hardware; custom made, traditional styles only. Also makes fireplace and kitchen tools. Can work with brass, bronze, and stainless steel. Will install within 100 miles.

Accent Ornamental Iron Co., Inc.
1607 Altamont Avenue
Richmond, VA 23230
(804) 746-2524

Square tubing frames with cast or wrought iron designs. Also: windows, guards, railings, gates, and folding gates.

Armour Iron Works
1236 Mount Olivet Road N.E.
Washington, DC 20002
(202) 546-1333

Cast iron, wrought iron, aluminum, and steel; custom work from rough sketch. Specializes in ornamental wrought iron. Can manufacture pieces to architects' specifications, working from rough sketch or more detailed information.

Midwest

Jim Woods
Valley Forge
Rte. 1, Box 142
Barrington, IL 60010
(312) 381-5118

One-of-a-kind orders; custom made traditional designs using hot forging only. Will install.

Scott C. Fredenburg
The Iron and Forge Connection
508 S. Logan
Carbondale, IL 62901
(618) 453-3778
(618) 549-2530

Specialty: hot forging and fabricating metal. Railings, gates, hardware, weather vanes, and sculpture. Combines such other materials as glass, fiber, stone, and other metals with iron. Brochure $3.00.

Frank Alviani
Dragonfire Forge
1608 W. Morse
Chicago, IL 60626
(312) 386-8548
(312) 761-1297

Specializes in small, decorative hardware and house accessories. Traditional and contemporary designs.

Gateway Metal Products
11113 S. Western Avenue
Chicago, IL 60643
(312) 568-1020
(312) 928-3333

Works with bronze and aluminum as well as iron in making gates, grilles, fences, railings, and security doors. Also does casting.

Hand-forged hinges and hasp (each hinge approx. 20 inches high) by Peter Happny, Portsmouth, NH. (Photo courtesy of Peter Happny)

Railing with birds and cattails, detail. Ivan Bailey, Bailey's Forge, Savannah, GA. (Photo courtesy of Ivan Bailey)

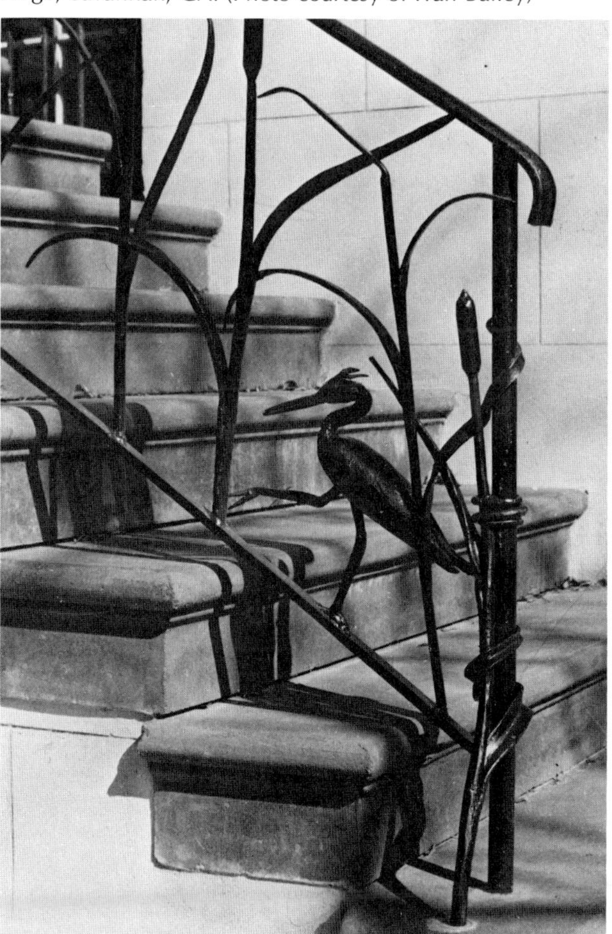

Lightning rod and finial ornament from the eighteenth century. Williamsburg, VA.

Iron balcony railing, detail (approx. 3½ feet high). Richard Lichtenstein, New York, NY. (Photo courtesy of Richard Lichtenstein)

New World Ornamental Iron Co.
2913 E. 10th Street
Indianapolis, IN 46201
(317) 636-0916
(317) 846-7854

Makes weather vanes, railings, gates, grilles, shutters, archways, etc. Also works with copper.

R. D. Hogg
Hogg's Forge
391 Ridgemont
Oxford, MI 38655
(313) 693-1746

Railings, hardware, weather vanes; specializes in grilles and gates. Also repairs general farm equipment.

Loftus Ornamental Iron
7100 Madison Avenue W.
Minneapolis, MN 55427
(612) 545-2669
(612) 929-2348

Specializes in ornamental ironwork of all types, including spiral stairs. Combines iron with wood.

Selby Ornamental Iron Works
Attn. Thomas Berry
1160 E. Seventh Street
St. Paul, MN 55106
(612) 778-0512
(612) 778-0314

Hot forging only. Railings, grilles, gates, window guards, and other architectural elements. Traditional and contemporary designs.

M. & M. Ornamental Iron
8614 N. 30th Street
Omaha, NE 68112
(402) 451-8144
(402) 571-1807

Custom railings and gates; cold bending.

Capitol City Ornamental Iron, Inc.
Attn. Richard Nathan
2030 Lovett Avenue
Bismarck, ND 58501
(701) 255-0124

Gates, stairways, and hardware.

Friend's Ornamental Iron Co., Inc.
3570 W. 140th Street
Cleveland, OH 44111
(216) 252-4740

Weather vanes, railings, gates, hardware, and "the unusual."

L. & L. Ornamental Iron
6024 State Route #128
Cleves, OH 45002
(513) 353-1930

Makes and distributes ornamental railings and gates—iron and aluminum, sometimes combined with wood.

Forged sign hanger (height approx. 15 inches). Richard Lichtenstein, New York, NY. (Photo by Marianne Dickinson)

Artcraft Ornamental Iron Co.
724 E. Hudson Street
Columbus, OH 43211
(614) 263-5668

Specialty: miscellaneous and structural steel. Railings, grilles, gates, and hardware.

Whiteside Ornamental Iron Co., Inc.
2514 Cleveland Avenue
Columbus, OH 43211
(614) 262-3388

Distributor and fabricator of railings, gates, security grilles, steel stairs, and many miscellaneous items. Whiteside fabricates special constructions from readymade iron items; will participate in the design phase.

Michael J. Bendele
907 1/2 E. Third Street
Delphos, OH 45833
(419) 445-5251
(419) 692-6268

Specializes in railings, gates, and dividers. Also does weather vanes, grilles, and lighting fixtures. Works with brass, copper and aluminum as well as with iron. Custom designs preferably from working drawings. Estimates from detailed information.

Finelli Ornamental Iron Co., Inc.
Attn. Mike Finelli or Frank Finelli
30815 Solon Road
Solon, OH 44139
(216) 248-0050
(216) 248-1645

Specializes in railings (aluminum or bronze top rails). Also does gates, spiral stairs, shutters, and window guards. Brochure $1.50.

Hayes Brothers Ornamental Iron Works, Inc.
1830 N. Reynolds
Toledo, OH 43615
(419) 531-1491

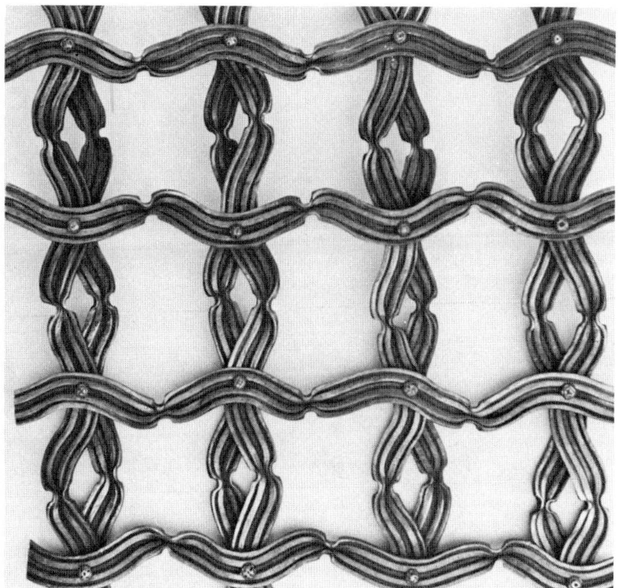

Forged iron grille (section shown: 18 by 18 inches). Schwartz's Forge & Metalworks, Deansboro, NY. (Photo courtesy of Joel A. Schwartz)

Specializes in custom rails and columns. Can combine iron with aluminum, brass, stainless steel, wood, and plastics.

Atlas Iron Masters, Inc.
Attn. George R. Shilling, Manager
5016 N.W. 10th
Oklahoma City, OK 73127
(405) 946-9973

Railings, gates, and weather vanes. All types of ornamental metal fabrication. Normally installs in metropolitan Oklahoma City; installation outside area possible by special arrangement.

Heritage Ornamental Iron Works
Attn. Jon Jerlow
3900 N. Geraldine
Oklahoma City, OK 73112
(405) 946-8929

Specializes in unique architectural items. Makes railings, gates, hardware, steel letters, custom logos, furniture, and spiral or straight stairs. Can mount carved wood panels in gates, etc.

House and Hanna Iron Works, Inc.
10565 Spangler Road
Dallas, TX 75220
(214) 556-0291

Distributor of railings, gates, and hardware. Can have custom work done.

South Side Ornamental Iron Works
3038 Bryan, at Berry Street
Fort Worth, TX 76110
(817) 926-0285

Railings, gates, grilles, stairs, and columns. Custom design and fabrication from working drawings only.

Forged iron window grille for residence, Brooklyn, NY (approx. 7 by 7 feet). Schwartz's Forge & Metalworks, Deansboro, NY. (Photo courtesy of Joel A. Schwartz)

Rivera Wrought Iron Works
7830 South Presa
San Antonio, TX 78221
(512) 533-2111

Specializes in fencing, railings, steel gates, window guards. Also works in aluminum, copper, and brass.

Carol G. Sakowski
The Unicorn Forge
Rte. 1, Box 50
Barneveld, WI 53507
(608) 795-4541 (after 6 pm)

Specializes in lighting devices and tools. Also does railings, gates, hardware, weather vanes, and grilles. Combines iron with copper, brass, bronze, aluminum, and glass.

John Graney
Bear Creek Forge
Rte. 2, Box 135
Spring Green, WI 53588
(608) 588-2032

This blacksmith does hot forging only of traditional and contemporary designs. Combines iron with stained glass, blown glass, brass. Specializes in window grilles and hardware; also does railings, gates, weather vanes, and other smaller items for homes. Brochure $0.50.

Rockies and Far West

A. and K. Ornamental Iron
Attn. Orian Osburn, Jr.
5849 Old Seward Highway, Suite C
Anchorage, AK 99502
(907) 349-1014

Specializes in railings and spiral stairs. Also does gates, hardware, and weather vanes; can use wood in conjunction with wrought iron.

Adobe Wrought Iron
4118 E. University Drive
Phoenix, AZ 85034
(602) 276-0011

In business since 1889. Specializes in ornamental iron. Entrances, grilles, gates, hardware, weather vanes, spiral stairs; can combine iron with stained glass, copper, and brass. "All ornamental iron, experts in design."

Wrought iron gate, Yale University (circa 1930).

Iron Design Co.
Attn. John A. Sinioris
2905 W. Lincoln
Phoenix, AZ 85009
(602) 269-9410

Railings, gates, hardware, weather vanes, spiral stairs, and other wrought iron architectural elements.

Valley Forge Blacksmith Shop
1829 E. Washington Street
Phoenix, AZ 85034
(602) 252-4768

Does forging, welding, and riveting, plus custom wrought iron. Also works in aluminum, stainless steel, and copper; subcontracts work in bronze, other metals, and wood.

Thomas G. Bredlow, Blacksmith
1827 E. Limberlost
Tucson, AZ 85719
(602) 323-2031

Specializes in a broad range of metalwork, mostly decorative iron but including tools and invention prototypes. Can combine iron with gold, silver, brass, or copper "where this is appropriate but not ostentatious." Railings, gates, hardware, weather vanes, grilles, fixtures, furniture, and sculpture.

Daly City Iron Works
7338A Mission Street
Daly City, CA 94014
(415) 992-4666

Specializes in iron gates. Also does grilles, balconies, railings, and hardware. Custom work only.

D. E. Bradley
3477 Old Conejo Road D-9
Newbury Park, CA 91320
(805) 498-9584

Specializes in authentically forged iron "of the period and country." Does railings, gates, grilles, hardware, weather vanes, signs, light brackets, and fixtures. Can do brass and bronze embellishment for ironwork. Small and one-of-a-kind orders. Samples available for viewing.

Robert Owings—Metal Design
615 Second Street
Petaluma, CA 94952
(707) 778-8261

Specializes in original designs in contemporary style and large-scale architectural works. Also does railings, gates, weather vanes, light fixtures, and other architectural elements. Can combine iron with glass.

Colonial Ornamental Iron Works
Attn. Jose Casillas
2702 Market Street
San Diego, CA 92102
(714) 234-1415
(714) 263-5854

Railings, gates, hardware and weather vanes. Can combine wrought iron with wood, cast iron, and other metals.

Jude Ornamental Iron Works
Attn. David Schwartz, Manager
3910 Mission Street
San Francisco, CA 94112
(415) 586-0914

Specializes in assembling readymade elements from Julius Blum & Co. (see listing under Ornamental Metals). Also works in brass and stainless steel.

Francis Whittaker
The Mountain Forge
Aspen, CO
(303) 925-3844
(303) 920-1265

One of our blacksmiths describes Whittaker as the "dean of American blacksmiths. He has the best knowledge of smithing of anyone in the country." He spends about half of his time conducting workshops for aspiring smiths. His specialty is very fine ornamental gates for private residences, churches, and public buildings. All work is hand-forged.

Ray Rantanen
Iron Anvil Forge
4043 S. I-25
Castle Rock, CO 80104
(303) 688-9428

Specializes in forging of small-scale hardware items. Railings, gates and weather vanes; also works in hammered brass.

This woodblock print will serve as a pattern for iron designs of Richard Lichtenstein, New York, NY. (Art work courtesy of Richard Lichtenstein)

Dufficy Iron Works, Inc.
Attn. John J. Dufficy
745 Decatur Street
Denver, CO 80204
(303) 534-8176
(303) 534-8177

Specialty: ornamental metalwork—railings, gates, hardware, weather vanes, and grilles. Also works with aluminum, brass, bronze, and stainless steel.

Klahm and Sons, Inc.
905 Isenberg Street
Honolulu, HI 96826
(808) 941-0045

Specializes in fancy gates and railings done by casting, forming, and bending.

M. O. Welding, Inc.
1924 Democrat Street
Honolulu, HI 96819
(808) 847-0445

Specializes in ornamental iron, marine trailers and repair; can do grilles, railings, and entrances.

Pacific Ornamental Iron, Inc.
8007 Mossy Cup Drive
Boise, ID 83709
(208) 362-4747

Specializes in custom railings and spiral stairs. Also does hardware and grilles. Can combine iron and wood; also works in stainless steel.

Rich Wrought Iron
7700 State Street
Boise, ID 83703
(208) 342-9341

Specializes in spiral stairs; also does railings, gates, and grilles. Custom designs from working drawing only.

Custom Ornamental Iron, Inc.
3082 Sheridan Street
Las Vegas, NV 89102
(702) 876-8775
(702) 876-8776

Railings, fencing, hardware, and grilles.

Fantasy in Iron, Inc.
2951 Westwood Drive
Las Vegas, NV 89109
(702) 735-3978

Specializes in custom ornamental iron, particularly stairs, security grilles, gates, gate openers. Some structural steel. Residential and commercial. Also works in aluminum and brass; does castings. Will give telephone estimates, but prefers having some detailed information.

A. & S. Steel, Inc.
Attn. Adolph Stuhmer
229 W. Fifth Avenue
Murray, UT 84107
(801) 262-6052

Wrought iron and everything for buildings (stairs, columns, heavy structural and miscellaneous structural steel). Also works with stainless steel and cast iron.

The Iron Anvil
Attn. Jay Wilson
1604 South 140 West
Salt Lake City, UT 84115
(801) 466-2053

Specializes in railings, gates, porch columns, and stairs.

Buser Ornamental Iron Works
Attn. Peter Buser
1107 N. 98th Street
Seattle, WA 98103
(206) 525-5624

Railings, gates, hardware, and weather vanes.

Fairway Ornamental Iron, Inc.
4501 Airport Way S.
Seattle, WA 98178
(206) 623-1441

Specializes in spiral stairs. Also does railings and gates.

Ironcraft
9415 Delridge Way S.W.
Seattle, WA 98106
(206) 763-2488

Specializes in ornamental iron railings, gates, grilles, and appropriate hardware.

Key

X Service, technique, or material is available
+ See listing for further information
* Sometimes offers this service

Northeast	Fabricator	Distributor	Readymade designs	Custom designs	Hot forging	Cold bending	Railings	Hardware	Weather vanes	Brochure or photos available	Telephone estimates	Will install
Butler Iron Works Weathersfield, CT	X			X	X		X		X	X	X	
Larson Forge Cambridge, ME	X		X	X	X	X	X	X		+	+	+
Capone Iron Works Everett, MA	X			X		X	X					X
The Boston Blacksmith Hyde Park, MA	X		X	X		X	X				X	X
Gino's Ornamental Iron Malden, MA	X		X	X	X	X	X	X	X		X	X
Superior Rail and Iron Stoughton, MA	X		X	X		X	X				X	X
Star Forge Westport, MA	X		X	X	X			X		+	X	
Williamsburg Blacksmiths Williamsburg, MA	X		X		X	X		X		+		
Russell Pope Newmarket, NH	X			X	X		X	X	X	X		X
Peter Happny Portsmouth, NH	X			X	X		X	X	X	X	X	X
Julius Blum Carlstadt, NJ	See listing under Metals											
Dinger Brothers Trenton, NJ	X			X	X	X	X					X
Vestinian Craftsmen Bronx, NY	X			X		X	X			X	X	X
Florentine Artistic Iron Brooklyn, NY	X			X	X	X	X			X	X	X
Schwartz's Forge Deansboro, NY	X			X	X		X	X	X	+	X	X
Blythe Machine and Iron Miller Place, NY	X			X		X	X					X
Deco Iron Creations New York, NY	X		X	X		X	X	X			X	X
P. A. Fiebiger New York, NY	X			X	X	X	X		X	+	X	X
Koenig Iron Works New York, NY	X			X	X	X	X	X		X	X	X
Richard Lichtenstein New York, NY	See listing under Sculpture											
Particular Iron Works New York, NY	X		X	X	X		X	X			X	X

Key

See also Sculpture for artists who work in this material.

X Service, technique, or material is available
\+ See listing for further information
* Sometimes offers this service

	Fabricator	Distributor	Readymade designs	Custom designs	Hot forging	Cold bending	Railings	Hardware	Weather vanes	Brochure or photos available	Telephone estimates	Will install
Steve Kayne Smithtown, NY	X		X	X	X	X		X	X	+	X	X
Victor Metals Unadilla, NY	X	X		X	X		X				X	X
Christopher T. Ray Philadelphia, PA	See listing under Sculpture											
Samuel Bird, Blacksmith Block Island, RI	X			X	X		X	X	X	X		
Jenison Ornamental Iron Warwick, RI	X		X	X	X	X	X	X	X	X	X	X
Hubbardton Forge and Wood SR, Bomoseen, VT	X		X	X	X		X	X		X		
Robert Bourdon Wolcott, VT	X		X	X	X			X	X		X	+
South												
Cox Ornamental Iron Birmingham, AL	X		X	X	X	X	X			X	X	X
Jones Valley Iron Birmingham, AL	X	X	X	X		X	X	X			X	X
Lawler Machine & Foundry Birmingham, AL	X	X	X				+			X	X	
Florida Ornamental Iron Hialeah, FL	X		X	X		X	X	X	X	X	X	X
Artistic Ornamental Iron Atlanta, GA	X	X	X	X	X	X	X	X	X	X	X	X
Dixie Ornamental Iron Atlanta, GA	X		X	X			X			X	X	X
Bailey's Forge Savannah, GA	X			X	X		X	X	X	X		X
Owens and Son Iron Works Savannah, GA	X		X	X		X	X	X		X	X	X
Chas. Horrar Berea, KY	X		X	X	X		X	X			X	X
Farve Ornamental Iron Kenner, LA	X		X	X	X	X	X	X	X	+	*	X
J. Rothstein Baltimore, MD	X		X	X	X	X	X				X	X
Ram's Forge Westminster, MD		X		X	X		X	X	X		X	+
Lawson Welding Jackson, MS	X		X	X			X					X

Key

See also Sculpture for artists who work in this material.

- **X** Service, technique, or material is available
- **+** See listing for further information
- ***** Sometimes offers this service

	Fabricator	Distributor	Readymade designs	Custom designs	Hot forging	Cold bending	Railings	Hardware	Weather vanes	Brochure or photos available	Telephone estimates	Will install
Charleston Awning and Metal Charleston Heights, SC	X			X		X	X	X	X		X	X
Fields Ornamental Iron Charleston Heights, SC	X		X	X		X	X					X
Dixie Iron Works Columbia, SC	X			X	X	X	X			+		X
Wiggins Ornamental Iron St. Stephen, SC	X		X	X	+	X	X	X	X	X	X	X
Tennessee Fabricating Memphis, TN	X	X	X							+		
James Wallace Memphis, TN	X			X	X		X	X	X	X		X
White Oak Forge Madison, VA	X			X	X		X	X	X	+	X	X
Goose Creek Metalworks Montvale, VA	X			X	X		X	X		X	X	X
Accent Ornamental Iron Richmond, VA	X			X		X	X					
Armour Iron Works Washington, DC	X			X	X	X	X	X		X		
Midwest												
Jim Woods Barrington, IL	X			X	X		X	X	X			X
Scott C. Fredenburg Carbondale, IL	X			X	X		X	X	X	+	X	X
Frank Alviani Chicago, IL	X		X	X	X			X			X	
Gateway Metal Products Chicago, IL	X	X				X	X			X	X	X
New World Ornamental Iron Indianapolis, IN	X		X	X	X	X	X	X	X		X	X
R. D. Hogg Oxford, MI	X		X	X	X	X	X	X	X	X		X
Lotus Ornamental Iron Minneapolis, MN	X		X	X	X	X	X		X	X	X	X
Selby Ornamental Iron St. Paul, MN	X		X	X	X		X	X		X		X
M. & M. Ornamental Iron Omaha, NE	X		X	X		X	X			X	X	X
Capitol City Iron Bismarck, ND	X		X	X		X	X	X		X	X	X

Key

See also Sculpture for artists who work in this material.
- **X** Service, technique, or material is available
- **+** See listing for further information
- ***** Sometimes offers this service

	Fabricator	Distributor	Readymade designs	Custom designs	Hot forging	Cold bending	Railings	Hardware	Weather vanes	Brochure or photos available	Telephone estimates	Will install
Friend's Ornamental Iron Cleveland, OH	X		X	X		X	X	X	X	X		X
L. & L. Ornamental Iron Cleves, OH	X		X	X		X	X				X	X
Artcraft Ornamental Iron Columbus, OH	X		X	X	X	X	X	X		X	X	X
Whiteside Ornamental Iron Columbus, OH	X	X	X	X	X	X	X			X	X	X
Michael J. Bendele Delphos, OH	X		X	+	X		X	X	X	X	+	X
Finelli Ornamental Iron Solon, OH	X		X	X	X	X	X			+		X
Hayes Brothers Iron Toledo, OH	X		X	X	X	X	X			X	X	X
Atlas Iron Masters Oklahoma City, OK	X	X	X	X	X	X	X	X	X	X	X	+
Heritage Ornamental Iron Oklahoma City, OK	X		X	X	X	X	X	X		X	X	X
House and Hanna Iron Works Dallas, TX		X	X	X		X	X	X				X
South Side Ornamental Iron Fort Worth, TX	X		X	X	X		X			X	X	X
Rivera Wrought Iron Works San Antonio, TX	X			X		X	X	X		X	X	X
Carol G. Sakowski Barneveld, WI	X			X	X		X	X	X	X		X
John Graney Spring Green, WI	X		X	X	X		X	X	X	+		X
Rockies and Far West												
A. and K. Ornamental Iron Anchorage, AK	X		X	X		X	X	X	X		X	X
Adobe Wrought Iron Phoenix, AZ	X		X	X	X	X	X	X	X	X	X	X
Iron Design Phoenix, AZ	X		X	X	X	X	X	X	X		X	X
Valley Forge Blacksmith Phoenix, AZ	X			X	X	X	X	X				
Thomas G. Bredlow Tucson, AZ	X		X	X	X		X	X	X		*	X
Daly City Iron Works Daly City, CA	X			X	X	X	X	X			X	X

Key

See also Sculpture for artists who work in this material.
X Service, technique, or material is available
\+ See listing for further information
* Sometimes offers this service

	Fabricator	Distributor	Readymade designs	Custom designs	Hot forging	Cold bending	Railings	Hardware	Weather vanes	Brochure or photos available	Telephone estimates	Will install
D. E. Bradley Newbury Park, CA	X		X	X	X		X	X	X			
Robert Owings Petaluma, CA	X			X	X	X	X	X	X		X	X
Colonial Ornamental Iron San Diego, CA	X		X	X	X		X	X	X	X	X	X
Jude Ornamental Iron San Francisco, CA	X		X	X	X		X	X			X	X
Francis Whittaker Aspen, CO	X			X	X		X	X		X		
Ray Rantanen Castle Rock, CO	X		X	X	X		X	X	X	X	X	X
Dufficy Iron Works Denver, CO	X			X	X	X	X	X	X	X	X	X
Klahm and Sons Honolulu, HI	X			X		X	X				X	X
M. O. Welding Honolulu, HI	X			X		X	X				X	X
Pacific Ornamental Iron Boise, ID	X		X	X		X	X	X		X		X
Rich Wrought Iron Boise, ID	X		X	X		X	X			X	X	
Custom Ornamental Iron Las Vegas, NV	X	X	X	X		X	X	X		X	X	X
Fantasy in Iron Las Vegas, NV	X	X	X	X	X	X	X	X	X	X	+	X
A. & S. Steel Murray, UT	X	X	X	X	X	X	X	X		X	X	X
The Iron Anvil Salt Lake City, UT	X	X	X	X	*	X	X	X	X	X	X	X
Buser Ornamental Iron Seattle, WA	X			X	X		X	X	X		X	X
Fairway Ornamental Iron Seattle, WA	X		X	X		X	X			X	X	X
Ironcraft Seattle, WA	X			X	X	X	X	X		X	X	X

METALS

Perhaps as a result of modernism's dislike of ornament, the term "ornamental metals" (bronze, brass, copper, iron, aluminum, stainless steel, etc.) has fallen into disfavor. A representative of one of the largest metal fabricators in the country told us that "some years ago we changed the name of our product from 'ornamental' metals to 'architectural' metals." This company found out that recent generations of architects have had a negative reaction to the word "ornament."

The companies listed below can make an enormous variety of products—delicate, stamped, gold-leafed foliage (to embellish wrought ironwork); copper and iron weather vanes; 4- by 8-foot embossed ceiling panels made from Civil War dies; huge formed sheet aluminum and copper steeples complete with finials, crockets, and moldings; monumental Art Deco hammered metal pediments; Spartan contemporary railings; and other hardware. The techniques used to produce these ornamental elements include, among others, bending, casting, forming, stamping.

The most impressive catalogs come from **Kenneth Lynch and Sons** in Connecticut and **Julius Blum** in New Jersey; they offer hundreds of pages of metal elements from which to choose. But with many of the companies listed, you are not limited to what the catalogs or brochures show; many also do custom work.

Special Listings

Architectural Metal Maintenance, Inc.
106 S. Early Street
Alexandria, VA 22304
(703) 751-1378

Refinishes bronze (oxidized to specified color), satin brass, aluminum, and stainless steel. Preventive maintenance contracts covering cleaning, refinishing, and repair of vandalism.

National Ornamental and Miscellaneous Metals Association
Suite 109
2996 Grandview Avenue N.E.
Atlanta, GA 30305
(404) 237-5334

This organization can recommend fabricators or suppliers of ornamental metal products in your area. Also publishes a magazine which might be of interest ($3/year or $5/two years). There are fourteen regional chapters; call or write for the chapter nearest you.

Regional Listings

While many of the companies listed below do work in iron, those companies specializing in ironwork are listed separately.

Northeast

Giza & Sons
50 Green Hill Road
Bethany, CT 06525
(203) 393-3704

Manufacturer of art figures and architectural display cases; can work from print or model. Works in bronze, aluminum, stainless steel, corten steels, iron, brass, copper; bending and welding. Specializes in highly polished metals.

Lappen's Fireside Centers
19 Main Street
Hartford, CT 06106
(203) 246-8851

Distributor of weather vanes; can have custom work in copper and gold leaf done from working drawing. Call for other locations in Connecticut. Brochure $1.00.

Washington Copper Works
Washington, CT 06793
(203) 868-7527

Specializes in custom and readymade copper lighting fixtures. Brochure $2.00.

Kenneth Lynch and Sons, Inc.
78 Danbury Road
Wilton, CT 06897

This company has an extraordinary range of capabilities. Lynch is able to produce exterior ornament in cast, stamped, and hammered metals; bronze, aluminum, stainless steel, iron, zinc, lead, and copper. A partial list of products includes grilles, railings, statues, fascias, plaques, street and wall clock bases and supports, sundials, spheres, shields, top scrolls, miters, marquee enrichments (including glass pendant frames), column capitals, modillions, brackets, keystones, panel ornaments, festoons, ribbons, crestings, urns, balusters, weather vanes, finials, moldings, scrolls, shells, corner ornaments, fountains (wall and free-standing), and more. Many of these come in traditional and contemporary (Art Deco-type) styles. In addition to the hundreds of designs shown in the catalogs, Lynch will fabricate any custom design in these materials.

This company also has an extensive array of cast stone elements including fountains, urns, finials, benches, and other architectural elements. Books describing Lynch's products can be ordered directly; titles include *Architectural Sheet Metal, Unusual Lighting Fixtures, Iron Work, Weather Vanes and Cupolas, Sundials and Spheres, Polychroming-Gesso, Park, Garden and Waiting Benches,* and *Art Gallery and Museum Supplies.* Hardcover $5.00; paper $2.50.

Abell Weathervanes
68 Robinson Avenue
Braintree, MA 02184
(617) 848-3728

Manufacturer of weather vanes; readymade (many different kinds of ships) and custom; copper, brass, and redwood. Brochure $0.25.

Part of a large steeple installed on a church in Georgia; metalwork by Campbellsville Industries, Campbellsville, KY. Internal framework of steel and aluminum; exterior is .032 aluminum skin with white, baked-on finish. Moldings, cornices, and modillions of aluminum; capitals are cast polyurethane. This company now uses cast aluminum components exclusively. (Photo courtesy of Campbellsville Industries)

E. G. Washburne and Co.
85 Andover Street, Rte. 114
Danvers, MA 01923
(617) 774-3645

Coppersmiths since 1853. Manufacturer of weather vanes; custom and readymade designs in copper—some handmade from antique molds. Also "rooster" and "fish" plaques for mounting; lanterns; outdoor furniture; and flagpoles. Call or write for other locations in Massachusetts.

Union Flag Co.
Lafayette Road
Hampton Falls, NH 03844
(603) 926-3007

Distributor of weather vanes. Readymade designs; may be able to have a custom design made from sketch or photo. Works in copper. Will install.

Wiendling Welding Works
33 W. Clinton Avenue
Bergenfield, NJ 07621
(201) 384-5874

A manufacturer specializing in ornamental work in cast iron, stainless steel, corten steel, and aluminum. Can do cast-

Stamped metal ceiling panels. Chelsea Decorative Metal Co., Houston, TX. (Photo courtesy of Chelsea Decorative Metal Co.)

Dolphin downspout, cast aluminum (length, approx. 8 inches). Ivan Bailey, Bailey's Forge, Savannah, GA. (Photo courtesy of Ivan Bailey)

ing of free-standing and bas-relief statues; can work from a model in clay, plaster, wood, or metal or make own model from rough sketch or more detailed information. Large, small, and one-of-a-kind orders.

Julius Blum & Co., Inc.
P.O. Box 292
Carlstadt, NJ 07072
(201) 438-4600
(212) 695-2236 (New York)
(800) 526-6293 (Alabama, Florida, Mississippi and Wisconsin, and states west of the Mississippi)
(800) 631-2827 (all other states east of the Mississippi)

In business since 1910, Julius Blum provides all types of ornamental metal components (to the architectural trades) in aluminum, stainless and pressed steel, cast and malleable iron, bronze, and PVC plastic. These are produced by casting, forming, extruding, rolling, and machining; stock items only. A hardbound, four-color catalog describes Blum's complete line of architectural metals in styles ranging from contemporary to traditional. In addition to the more familiar kinds of railings and grilles, this company makes rosettes; cups; husks and socket covers; leaves (acanthus, grape, oak, maple, and water); perforated and nonperforated moldings; and pickets. While the catalog is quite substantial, Blum advises that the company is continually adding to the line, so call or write for updates. Blum "solicits your inquiries for items not listed." Orders are shipped "within hours" after they are received.

Blum provides free technical assistance to architects, including "reviewing plans and drawings and making recommendations regarding railings, screens, and other architectural metalwork."

Interstate Architectural and Iron, Inc.
247 Laird Avenue
Cliffside Park, NJ 07010
(201) 941-0393

Railings, hardware, gazebos, etc. This company has a "rolling shop" in form of a 40-foot trailer, and prides itself on being able to do out-of-the-ordinary fabrications. Works in bronze, aluminum, stainless steel, and iron (including cast).

J. W. Fiske Architectural Metals
111 Pennsylvania Avenue
Paterson, NJ 07503
(201) 684-2888

One of the oldest and largest manufacturers of architectural metalwork. Manufactures all types of custom architectural elements in bronze, aluminum, stainless steel, and iron; railings, grilles, soffits, fascias, doors, windows, entrances.

Empire Stove and Furnace Co.
795 Broadway
Albany, NY 12207
(518) 449-5189
(518) 499-2590

Distributor. Specialty: railings. Also makes doors, windows, and grilles in aluminum and iron.

Lang Stamp Works, Inc.
18 Green Street
Albany, NY 12201
(518) 434-2121

Specializes in cast bronze plaques.

Brainum-Shanker Steel
70–32 83rd Street
Glendale, NY 11385
(212) 894-5581

Specializes in manufacturing pressed plate ornament and ornamental metal ceilings. If properly sealed, these would work in protected outdoor areas.

Allied Bronze Corp.
25–11 Hunterspoint Avenue
Long Island City, NY 11101
(212) 361-8822

A large manufacturer of all custom ornamental and architectural products: grilles, railings, soffits, fascias, plaques, doors, windows, entrances, column covers, wall panels, stairs, canopies, signs, and sculpture. Can do custom work for banks, restaurants, and offices. Works in bronze, aluminum, and stainless steel; casting, forming, and bending.

All-State Metal Stamping, Inc.
305 E. 86th Street
New York, NY 10028
(212) 876-7543

This company does many different kinds of stock, small-scale ornamental stampings in plating quality heavy-gauge steel. Also works in brass. Products include flowers, rosettes, leaves, canopies, bobêches, and husks; this type of ornament is often used in conjunction with wrought iron. Some of the designs are Colonial or French; others are contemporary.

Carroll Studio
694 Third Avenue
New York, NY 10017
(212) 682-1316
(212) 986-0786

Manufactures and distributes etched products. Works in bronze, aluminum, stainless steel, glass, glass backed with silver, brass, copper, zinc, plexiglass, gold, and silver. Specialty: plaques and etching. Large and small orders.

Richard Lichtenstein
New York, NY 10012

See listing under Sculpture.

Academy Fence Co.
660 Jericho Turnpike
St. James, NY 11780
(516) 265-3577

Fabricator of weather vanes; sells directly. Readymade designs in aluminum, copper, and bronze. Installs on residential buildings.

Forged grille (30 by 20 inches). Scott Fredenburg, Carbondale, IL. (Photo courtesy of Scott Fredenburg)

Donald Miller
Warwick, NY 10990

See listing under Sculpture.

Hankison Corp.
1000 Philadelphia Street
Canonsburg, PA 15317
(412) 745-1555

Manufactures soffits, fascias, and stair risers in aluminum, steel, and stainless steel. Specializes in press brake forming.

Art Bronze & Manufacturing Co.
500 37th Street
Pittsburgh, PA 15102
(412) 621-1550

Casting of bronze and aluminum; grilles, doors, windows, entrances, plaques, and statues.

Designers Forge
Pittsburgh, PA 15217

See listing under Sculpture.

South

Bailey's Forge
Savannah, GA 31401

See listing under Iron.

United States Bronze and Aluminum Corporation
1065 E. 28th Street
Hialeah, FL 33013
(305) 836-2880

Specializes in casting bronze and aluminum plaques and sculpture. Will install.

Campbellsville Industries
P.O. Box 278
Campbellsville, KY 42718
(502) 465-8135

Specialists in custom fabricated steeples, towers, spires, cupolas, and crosses; also does grilles, railings, balusters, urns, and fascias. Works in sheet and cast aluminum with baked-on finishes.

F.S.S.I.
Box 9327
Columbia, SC 29209
(803) 776-2658

Specialty: stainless steel grilles and railings. Also works in aluminum and iron.

Armour Iron Works
Washington, DC 20002

See listing under Iron.

Midwest

Sytsma Sheet Metal, Inc.
7530 W. 90th Street
Bridgeview, IL 60455
(312) 430-1400

Fabricators of fascias and soffits; specializes in standing seam, batten seam, concave, and flat soldered decks. Can also do inlaid gutter and cornice work.

Scott Fredenburg
Carbondale, IL 62901

See listing under Iron.

Chicago Wire Iron and Brass Works
2411 W. Belmont Avenue
Chicago, IL 60618
(312) 935-6676

Grilles, railings, entrances, doors, cupolas, and weather vanes; bronze, aluminum, stainless steel, and iron. Produces a selection of decorative wire meshes—some with a contemporary look, some traditional (brite basic wire and galvanized wire). Readymade grilles and weather vanes; everything else custom from sketch or more detailed information.

Albert J. Wagner and Son
3762 N. Clark
Chicago, IL 60613
(312) 935-1414

In business since 1894, this company specializes in restoration quality architectural sheet metal work. Can do handmade decorations. One-of-a-kind work; all fabrication done with break and molds. Works with galvanized iron, copper,

"American Song" (bronze, 7 feet tall). Sculpture by Eric Parks, Unionville, PA (copyright 1976). Philadelphia '76, Inc., Living History Center, Independence Mall, Philadelphia, PA. (Photo courtesy of Eric Parks)

Wall relief in steel, after Picasso's "Bathers" (approx. 3½ by 4½ feet). Richard Lichtenstein, New York, NY. (Photo courtesy of Richard Lichtenstein)

lead-coated copper, brass, and terne metal. Will do almost all architectural sheet metal work, including cornices, except stampings. Experienced in restoration; has done work on several Frank Lloyd Wright houses.

Architectural Bronze and Aluminum Corp.
3638 W. Oakton
Skokie, IL 60076
(312) 674-3638

Can etch bronze, aluminum, stainless steel, brass, copper, and zinc. Large and small orders.

J. C. Lauber Co.
504 E. La Salle Avenue
South Bend, IN 46617
(219) 234-4174

Founded in 1890 and servicing the Great Lakes area, J. C. Lauber specializes in sheet metal and fiber glass fabrication. Can make architectural monuments. Does steeple work and renovation in such materials as slate, tile, copper, stainless steel, corten steel, and brass. Will also do gilding and will apply corrosion-resistant coatings. Can fabricate cornices, moldings, finials, domes, and gutters (including built-in), among other things. Often called upon to do restoration work.

Giese Sheet Metal
2125 Kerper Boulevard
Dubuque, IA 52001
(319) 588-2023

Manufactures cornices in galvanized iron, fiber glass, stainless steel, copper, and aluminum. Giese has a stamping machine, and can make handmade decorations. Will install.

Linder Manufacturing and Welding
19490 Metcalf
Stilwell, KS 66085
(913) 681-2394

Custom work of all kinds—grilles, railings, and the like—

Formed metal crows camouflaging bathroom roof vents (height, approx. 8 inches); Chief Plenty Coups Museum, Pryor, MT. Eugene Padanyi-Gulyas, Architect. (Photo by Denes G. Istvanffy, photo courtesy of Eugene Padanyi-Gulyas)

in aluminum, stainless steel, and iron. Specializes in spiral stairs. "Often the things other people don't want to attempt."

Special Fabricators, Inc.
31649 Stephenson Highway
Madison Heights, MI 48085
(313) 564-6624

Specializes in custom railings; also does soffits, fascias, decorative screening, panels, planters, church crosses, and fixtures. Works in bronze, aluminum, stainless steel, and plastics.

ERS Corporation
668 Jenks Avenue
St. Paul, MN 55106
(612) 774-9528

Specialty: ornamental fencing and spiral stairways; also does grilles, railings, and other architectural elements. Works in bronze, aluminum, stainless steel, and iron.

St. Louis Lightning Protection Co.
515 S. Vandeventer
St. Louis, MO 63110
(314) 535-2810

Custom designs of weather vanes from working drawing only. Also makes brass hardware. Materials: aluminum, copper, bronze. Will install and give telephone estimates.

Usona Manufacturing Co.
3512 Chouteau
St. Louis, MO 63103
(314) 664-8000

Manufacturer specializing in railings; also makes grilles, soffits, plaques, and fascias. Works in bronze, aluminum, stainless steel, and iron. Installs on some jobs; telephone estimates on simple jobs.

Steeple by Campbellsville Industries, Campbellsville, KY. (Photo courtesy of Campbellsville Industries)

Jimstar Masonry Decor
601 Parkview Avenue
Bryan, OH 43506
(419) 636-3253

Makes and distributes cast aluminum "stars" ("cloudburst" and four- to nine-points; 7 and 9 inches in diameter) that can be fixed to any masonry wall. These stars require a ⅜-inch hole, and are easily interchangeable.

Newman Brothers, Inc.
5609 Center Hill Avenue
Cincinnati, OH 45216
(513) 242-0011

Does custom stainless steel column covers, grilles, railways, fascia, and trim; bronze doors and trim; aluminum solar screens, canopies, and curtain walls. Also works in iron.

"Flora & Fauna of Europe." Drawing for cast bronze doors, the Washington Cathedral (height, approx. 12 feet). Donald and Harriet Miller, Warwick, NY. (Drawing courtesy of Donald and Harriet Phillips Miller)

Columbus Metalcraft Co.
146 S. Yale Avenue
Columbus, OH 43222
(614) 279-3207

Specialty: stairs and miscellaneous ironwork. Works in bronze, aluminum, stainless steel and iron.

Hendrix, Heikkilä, and Terry, Inc.
Norman, OK 73069

See listing under Murals.

John Winterich and Associates
Solon, OH 44139

See listing under Murals.

Chelsea Decorative Metal Co.
6115 Chena Drive
Houston, TX 77096
(713) 721-9200

This company produces embossed metal ceiling panels.

Stainless steel column capital, Piazza d'Italia, New Orleans. Charles Moore, Architect, with Urban Innovations Group, and August Perez, Associates, Architects. (Photo by Norman McGrath)

The panels are stamped from original dies (some of which date back as far as the Civil War) and vary in style from rococo to Art Deco. There are eighteen patterns from which to choose, including 2-foot, 1-foot, 6-inch, and 3-inch pattern modules. All come in 2-by-8-foot sheets with a silvery tin finish. The finish can be left as is or painted (with oil-base paint). Properly painted, these panels would be usable in such protected outside areas as the undersides of porch roofs. Metal cornices (ten different styles are shown in the brochure) come in 4-foot lengths but widths vary. Will install in Houston.

Hoffmann Architectural Metals
Box 494
Tyler, TX 75701
(214) 595-1314

Specializes in manufacturing custom ornamental metals for contractors. Can do grilles, railings, soffits, fascias, doors, windows, entrances, column covers, paneling, canopies, and the like; works in bronze, aluminum, and stainless steel. In addition to forming and bending, Hoffmann does welding and polishing. Call or write for names of representatives in other cities.

Rockies and Far West

La Haye Bronze, Inc.
1346 Railroad Street
Corona, CA 91720
(714) 734-1371

Cast bronze columns and gates, Calvary Cemetery. La Haye Bronze Co., Corona, CA. (Photo courtesy of La Haye Bronze Co.)

Manufacturer specializing in bas-relief bronze and aluminum letters, plaques, and larger architectural elements such as columns, pilasters, and friezes.

Standard Cabinet Works, Inc.
1936 Staunton Avenue
Los Angeles, CA 90058
(213) 749-7278

Manufactures grilles, railings, soffits, and other architectural elements; works in bronze, aluminum, stainless steel, and iron. Specializes in hotel and store fixture equipment.

Architectural Sheet Metal Corp.
927 W. MacArthur Boulevard
Oakland, CA 94608
(415) 655-7900

This company works with copper in addition to bronze, aluminum, stainless steel, and iron. Manufactures soffits, fascias, plaques, wall coverings, and fireplace coverings.

Newly erected, (formed) metal marquee; 250 Mercer Street, New York City (1981). Designed by JCS Design Associates from element by Kenneth Lynch and Sons.

W. G. Ehmcke Sheet Metal Works
404 14th Street
San Diego, CA 92101
(714) 233-6484

Distributor and manufacturer. Specialty: architectural sheet metal, siding, decking, mansard roofing. Does forming, bending, embossing, and rolling. Works in copper, zinc, bronze, aluminum, stainless steel, and iron.

L. Ph. Bolander and Sons
P.O. Box 24134
San Francisco, CA 94124
(415) 648-5611

Distributor of weather vanes; readymade designs. Can have custom designs made from sketch or photo; copper only. Telephone estimates given only on stock items.

Castle Craft
19605 Ventura Boulevard
Tarzana, CA 91364
(213) 345-7711

Manufacturer of weather vanes; sells directly. Aluminum, wrought iron, and brass. Residential installation only. Also does plaques, house signs, and custom mailboxes.

First Impressions
P.O. Box 2261
Fort Collins, CO 80522
(303) 484-7604

Specialties: custom doors inlaid with copper or clad in formed copper; fountains; and waterfalls. First Impressions can combine hand-formed copper and brass (or welded steel) with leaded, stained glass; also can combine hand-formed metals with wood. Works in stained, beveled, etched, faceted, and sandblasted glass; carved and fabricated wood, and fiber glass.

Art Deco metal detailing, 330 W. 42nd Street, New York City.

Wasco Sheet Metal and Manufacturing
P.O. Box 8243
Boise, ID 83707
(208) 375-3809

Specialty: stainless steel; mainly railings. Also works in bronze, iron, and aluminum.

Imperial Steelcraft, Inc.
13910 S.W. Tualatin Valley Highway
Beaverton, OR 97005
(503) 644-2626

Distributor and manufacturer. Does grilles, railings, soffits, fascias, entrances, skylights, etc. Works with brass, bronze, aluminum, stainless steel, and iron; can do forging and welding.

Ray F. Becker Co.
2345 N. Ross Avenue
Portland, OR 97227
(503) 288-5341

Specializes in fabrication of custom architectural sheet metal wall and roof systems including soffits and fascias. Does roll forming; works with prepainted sheet metal.

Old and Elegant Distributors
10203 Main Street Lane
Bellevue, WA 98004
(206) 455-4660

Antique and custom items. Distributors of weather vanes; the "Northwest's largest collection of weather vanes." Old and Elegant offers nineteen styles of cupolas with copper roofs, and a variety of furnishings including handmade tiles, etched glass windows, terracotta wall friezes, carved doors, and architectural gingerbread.

Key

See also Sculpture for artists who work in this material.

- X Service, technique, or material is available
- \+ See listing for further information
- * Sometimes offers this service

			Materials												
Northeast	Distributor	Manufacturer	Bronze	Aluminum	Stainless steel	Iron	Casting	Forming	Bending	Carving	Brochure or photos available	Telephone estimates	Will install	Weather vanes	Miscellaneous
Giza & Sons Bethany, CT		X	X	X	X	X			X				X		+
Lappen's Fireside Hartford, CT	X										+			X	
Washington Copper Works Washington, CT		X									+	X			
Kenneth Lynch and Sons Wilton, CT		X	X	X	X	X	X	X	X		X			X	+
Abell Weathervanes Braintree, MA	X										+			X	
E. G. Washburne Danvers, MA		X									X	X		X	
Union Flag Hampton Falls, NH	X										X	X	X	X	
Wiendling Welding Works Bergenfield, NJ		X		X	X	X	X		X		X				
Julius Blum Carlstadt, NJ	X	X	X	X	X	X	X	X	X		X				+
Interstate Iron Cliffside Park, NJ			X	X	X	X		X	X		X	X	X		+
J. W. Fiske Paterson, NJ		X	X	X	X	X		X	X				X		+
Empire Stove and Furnace Albany, NY	X			X		X						X	X		
Lang Stamp Works Albany, NY		X	X				X				X	X			
Brainum-Shanker Steel Glendale, NY		X									X	X			+
Allied Bronze Long Island City, NY		X	X	X	X		X	X	X		X		X		
All-State Metal Stamping New York, NY		X						X			X	X			+
Carroll Studios New York, NY	X	X	X	X	X						X				+
Richard Lichtenstein New York, NY	See listing under Sculpture														
Academy Fence St. James, NY		X		X									+	X	
Donald Miller Warwick, NY	See listing under Sculpture														

Key

See also Sculpture for artists who work in this material.

- **X** Service, technique, or material is available
- **+** See listing for further information
- ***** Sometimes offers this service

			Materials												
	Distributor	**Manufacturer**	**Bronze**	**Aluminum**	**Stainless steel**	**Iron**	**Casting**	**Forming**	**Bending**	**Carving**	**Brochure or photos available**	**Telephone estimates**	**Will install**	**Weather vanes**	**Miscellaneous**
Hankison Canonsburg, PA		X		X	X			X	X			X			
Art Bronze & Manufacturing Pittsburgh, PA		X	X	X			X				X			X	
Designers Forge Pittsburgh, PA	See listing under Sculpture														
South															
Bailey's Forge Savannah, GA	See listing under Iron														
U. S. Bronze & Aluminum Hialeah, FL		X	X	X			X				X	X	X		
Campbellsville Industries Campbellsville, KY		X		X			X	X	X		X	X	X		
F.S.S.I. Columbia, SC		X		X	X	X		X	X				X		
Armour Iron Washington, DC	See listing under Iron														
Midwest															
Sytsma Sheet Metal Bridgeview, IL		X		X	X	X		X	X				X		+
Scott Fredenburg Carbondale, IL	See listing under Iron														
Chicago Wire Chicago, IL		X	X	X	X	X	X	X	X		X	X	X	X	+
Albert J. Wagner and Son Chicago, IL		X				X		X	X		X	X	X		+
Architectural Bronze Skokie, IL		X	X	X	X										
J. C. Lauber South Bend, IN		X						X	X		X	X	X		+
Giese Sheet Metal Dubuque, IA		+			X	X		+							+
Linder Manufacturing Stilwell, KS		X		X	X	X		X	X		X	*	X		
Special Fabricators Madison Heights, MI		X	X	X	X			X	X			X	X		
ESR St. Paul, MN		X	X	X	X	X			X		X	X	X		
St. Louis Lightning St. Louis, MO		X	X	X								X	X	X	

Key

See also Sculpture for artists who work in this material.

- **X** Service, technique, or material is available
- **+** See listing for further information
- ***** Sometimes offers this service

	Distributor	Manufacturer	Bronze	Aluminum	Stainless steel	Iron	Casting	Forming	Bending	Carving	Brochure or photos available	Telephone estimates	Will install	Weather vanes	Miscellaneous
			Materials												
Usona Manufacturing St. Louis, MO		X	X	X	X	X	X	X	X		X	+	+		
Jimstar Masonry Decor Bryan, OH		X		X			X				X	X			
Newman Brothers Cincinnati, OH		X	X	X	X		X	X	X		X				
Columbus Metalcraft Columbus, OH		X	X	X	X	X		X	X		X	X	X	X	
Hendrix, Heikkilä, and Terry Norman, OK	See listing under Murals														
John Winterich and Associates Solon, OH	See listing under Murals														
Chelsea Decorative Metal Houston, TX		X									X	X	X		+
Hoffmann Metals Tyler, TX		X	X	X	X			X	X		X		*		+
Rockies and Far West															
La Haye Bronze Corona, CA		X	X	X			X				X	X	X		
Standard Cabinet Works Los Angeles, CA		X	X	X	X	X		X	X				X		
Architectural Sheet Metal Oakland, CA		X	X	X	X	X		X	X				X		
W. G. Ehmcke Sheet Metal San Diego, CA	X	X	X	X	X	X		X	+			X	X		+
L. Ph. Bolander and Sons San Francisco, CA	X											+		+	
Castle Craft Tarzana, CA		X		X		X							+	X	
First Impressions Fort Collins, CO		X				+	X	X	X		X	X	*		+
Wasco Sheet Metal Boise, ID		X	X	X	X	X		X	X				X		
Imperial Steelcraft Beaverton, OR	X	X	X	X	X	X	X	X	X		X	X	X		
Ray F. Becker Portland, OR		X						X	X		X	X	X		+
Old and Elegant Bellevue, WA	+	X												X	+

MURALS

Murals are a magical kind of ornament, regardless of the medium: a few gallons of paint, or a few square yards of glass and ceramic chips can make a solid masonry wall seem to dematerialize before your eyes.

While our subject is exterior architectural ornament, we have had to acknowledge several gray areas where interior and exterior cannot easily be separated. This is one such category. Murals are often installed on the inside but are intended to be seen from the outside too. Therefore we are listing muralists who do interior as well as exterior work.

Two types of muralists are listed below. The first, and more traditional kind, is the individual artist who executes his own designs. The second is the community muralist. This is an individual (or group) who works directly with the community to create a work expressing that particular community's feelings about a particular subject. This category has two subgroups: the artist (or artists) who designs and paints a theme of his own, the content and images of which come from his feelings about the community; and the artist (or artists) who provides technical advice and supervision to a community that has its own ideas and may even help with the painting.

Stone mosaic panel (4 by 7 feet). By Nini Jennings, Aspen Mosaics, Aspen, Co. (Photo courtesy of Nini Jennings)

Painting

Painting may be the oldest form of architectural decoration; the first murals were probably painted some 30,000 years ago in the caves of southern France. The longevity of painted murals depends on several factors. Among the most important are climate and the amount of pollution in the air. Exposure to sunlight fades colors, thus a mural on a south-facing wall will

Mural in Novacolor and Liquitex acrylics (12 by 45 feet). By Kent Twitchell. Los Angeles (1971). (Photo courtesy of Kent Twitchell)

deteriorate more quickly than one facing north. Airborne, chemical pollution (from car exhaust and industry) can break down the paint chemically. The condition of the wall surface is also critical; the more durable the material, and the better it takes the paint, the longer the paint will adhere to the surface. Lastly, the original surface and the final mural must be properly sealed.

There is considerable discussion among muralists as to the best paint. Many of the muralists we contacted gave very high marks to Politec Mural Acrylic. It seems to be particularly popular in the West because it is readily available there. Richard Haas, perhaps the best-known painter of architectural murals, prefers a German medium called Keim paint. It was invented in 1878; and it is extremely durable, permeating unsealed masonry in much the same way fresco paint sinks into moist plaster. The Keim catalog shows the houses around the marketplace of Stein am Rhine, a small German town. These houses were painted with Keim in 1885, and the finish still looks fresh.

From an entirely different point of view, some muralists ask whether they should even try to make their work permanent. This question may continue to be pondered by future generations of muralists and theoreticians. However, we cannot help but observe that many who profess a preference for transient, self-effacing art nevertheless regret that da Vinci did not take more care while mixing his paint.

Architects who would like to have a mural painted should contact the muralists listed below and ask for photographs of their work. Some architects may want to develop an idea with a muralist; others might prefer to design their own. Those who prefer the latter approach have several alternatives. One choice is to find a muralist who is willing to execute a finished design. Some are, some are not. Another method is to contact a sign painter (see your Yellow Pages under Advertising-Outdoor). If you do this, be sure to discuss the type of paint they intend to use, as signs are generally not intended to last for long periods of time. Also, these craftsmen are not used to producing finished work from a rough sketch; you must give them detailed, scale drawings.

If the project involves smaller-scale work, such as painting or stenciling decorative designs on a building (around windows or doors, for example), you can contact the muralists listed below who say they will do this work. You might also contact sign painters or truck painters, as they will often paint buildings as well. (Rigging licenses and insurance are usually required for scaffold work, so special arrangements might have to be made for someone like a truck painter who must work above the first floor.)

Marbleizing, Graining, and other Ornamental Painting

Before you turn the page out of embarrassment at being asked to consider blatant fakery, listen to the following story. We visited the Milan Cathedral a few years ago, when we still considered the idea of honesty of materials an unquestionable design tenet. We had not been inside for long before several busloads of tourists forced us out of the giant nave, and for some time we wandered in the side aisles. Looking up, we noticed what seemed to be extraordinary marble vaulting. Only after examining the vaults through a telephoto lens did we realize that it was not marble at all but painted plaster. Our immediate reaction was annoyance at having been fooled. But this feeling soon changed to mild amusement, and then admiration, as we marveled at the skill that had gone into this gentle deception.

While it is often more satisfying to use genuine materials, particularly when you can get close enough to actually touch them and examine their texture, there are times when it makes little difference whether the marble (or wood or limestone) is real or the product of a craftsman's inventive eye and hand. In fact, some marbleized stucco, such as that in the Bavarian Cathedral of Ottobeuren, is more breathtaking than natural marble. And it takes a good eye to tell the difference.

Mosaic

The art of mosaic involves creating an image by combining thousands of tiny chips (tesserae) of glass, ceramics, stone, or other material. We were surprised to learn that mosaics decorated some of the bases of the marble columns of the Erechtheum (fifth century B.C.) on the Acropolis of Athens, that bastion of pristine whiteness. According to Pliny, the Romans took over the practice of decorating their floors "after the fashion of painting" from the Greeks. Roman mosaics were often composed of extremely small (from ½- to ¼-inch square) tesserae, which indeed made them look like paintings from a distance. Later Medieval mosaic pavements, particularly those in Italy, were usually made of larger tesserae of different kinds of marble. Some of the best examples are in Venice's Cathedral of St. Mark.

In the United States, mosaic remained a fairly common architectural embellishment well into this century, due largely to the continuing influx of European artisans. Today, mosaics are again being done in a variety of materials and styles.

The skills of the muralists listed below encompass a broad range of techniques including fresco, fresco secco, oil on canvas, ceramics, stencilling, painted glass, various types of mosaic, lacquer on silver leaf, enameled metals, photography, and combinations of the above. The styles in which these muralists work are equally diverse.

Special Listings

Evergreene Painting Studios, Inc.
Jeff Greene
365 W. 36th Street
New York, NY 10018
(212) 239-1322

This company will execute a mural designed by someone else, but can also do its own designs. If you have an idea for a mural, this company can realize it, working from sketch, photo, or measured drawing—even from life models. Size is no object. Evergreene recently executed a Richard Haas mural over twenty stories high and covering all four sides of a building in Chicago.

Jeff Greene says his aim is to make murals that will last a century. Accordingly, the exterior work is usually done in Keim paint. (See the discussion of Keim paint in the introduction to this section.)

The size of the staff at Evergreene Studios varies depending on the work to be done. Normally, there are six full-time muralists. Greene is in touch with painters all over the country and, when he travels to other locations, he often hires local muralists to complement his own crew.

His preferred style is architectural trompe l'oeil paintings with human figures; subject matter can be symbolic, allegorical, historic, narrative, etc. The studio works in fresco, fresco secco, oil on canvas, ceramics, mosaic, enameled metals, sandblasted metal, plastic, glass, stencils, egg tempera, and sgraffito. Can also do bas-relief and three-dimensional constructions. Miscellaneous skills include woodgraining, marbleizing, airbrush techniques, gold leafing, wall hangings, and encaustic or hot wax paintings (exterior hot wax in Southern climates only). Does restoration work, is fully insured, and has a rigging license.

Murals Newsletter
Attn. Tim Drescher, Editor
P.O. Box 40383
San Francisco, CA 94140
(415) 285-6192

Detail of mural by Kent Twitchell (1979) showing painted (right) and real palm tree, in progress when photo was taken. (Photo courtesy of Kent Twitchell)

Offers printed material, technical and design advice. Can recommend muralists in your area. No charge for these services.

National Society of Mural Painters
Attn. Helen Treadwell, President
41 E. 65th Street
New York, NY 10021
(212) 988-7700

The Society, incorporated in 1895, can provide you with a listing of members in your area. It has printed materials describing the Society's history, mural techniques, the relationship of muralist to architect, and other information.

Regional Listings

Northeast

Sandra Kopell
Box 383
Greens Farms, CT 06436
(203) 255-6004

Works in painted glass and wood, also "sturdy" papier-mâché bas-relief sculpture (to be seen from the outside). Usually works in a fairly realistic style, but sometimes does more stylized work. Also does lettering.

"2-D, 3-D" (detail): trompe l'oeil wall painting. On The Wall Productions, St. Louis, MO (Copyright © 1980). (Photo courtesy of Bob Fishbone)

Jennifer D. Crane
247 St. Ronan Street
New Haven, CT 06511
(203) 624-8075

Works in fresco secco, acrylic murals on plaster, and large cloth applique wall hangings—all interior. Wall hangings usually abstract; murals usually representational. Preferred subject matter: nature forms, animals, people.

Jim Peters
39 Depot Road
Uncasville, CT 06382
(203) 848-0609

Fresco secco, oil on canvas, and egg-oil emulsion tempera on gesso panels. Life-size figures (which interact with pictorial and real space) and architectural backgrounds.

Richard Layton
2600 W. 19th Street
Wilmington, DE 19806
(302) 654-2115

Preferred medium: oil on canvas; also works in egg tempera on gesso panel, watercolor, pen and ink, and medallion design. Prefers painting realistic landscapes. Photos of work available on loan only. Does trompe l'oeil.

John S. Coles
28 Whittmore Street
Arlington, MA 02174

Oil on canvas and arcylics. Preferred style: realism. Preferred subject matter: landscapes and animals. Painted murals for Storham Zoo. Does trompe l'oeil.

Center for Public Design
Massachusetts College of Art
Attn. Al Gowan, Director
364 Brookline Avenue
Boston, MA 02140
(617) 731-2340 Ext. 18

The Center for Public Design is a "faculty consulting office" within the college and is directed at public design projects of all sorts. The Center represents virtually every media (including fresco, oil on canvas, ceramics, stainless steel, stained glass, painted glass, mosaic, and latex or enamel or acrylic on brick or masonry) and all styles and directions in the arts today. The Center stresses, however, that the works be "site-oriented." A softcover book, *Nuts and Bolts,* by Al Gowan, is available; it documents case studies in public design from around the country. (Public Design Press, 80 Orchard Street, Cambridge, MA 02140.)

John Manship
10 Leverett Street
Gloucester, MA 01930
(617) 283-1915

Fresco, fresco secco, oil on canvas, and mosaic. Also does restoration. Relief sculpture in bronze and epoxy. Preferred style: "figurative."

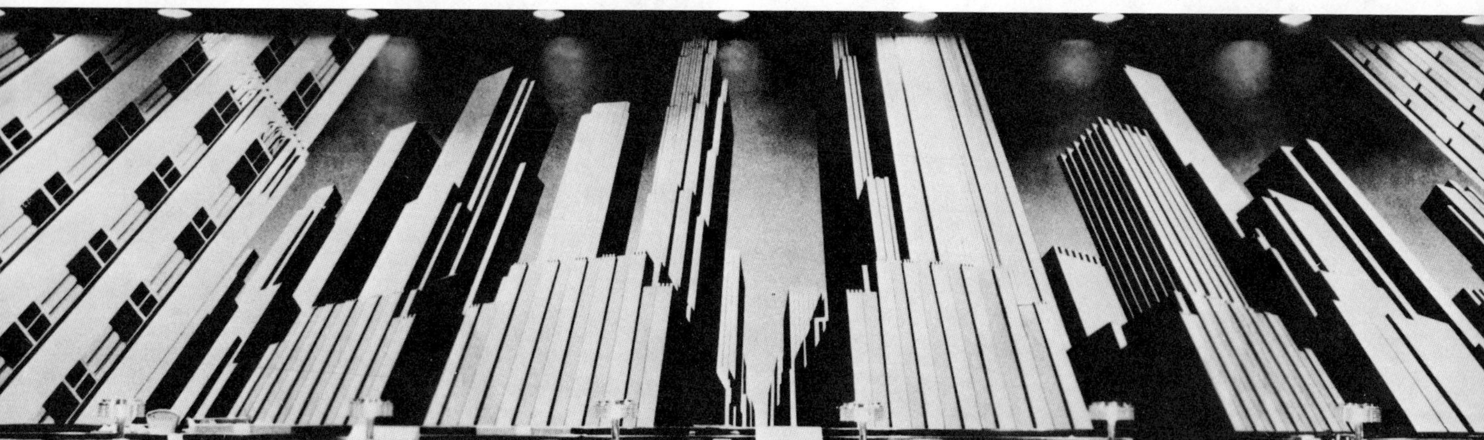

Art Deco mural for Chembank branch office in New York. Concept by Claude Langworth; executed by Evergreene Painting Studios, Inc., New York City. (1978). (Photo courtesy of Evergreene Painting Studios)

K. M. Cousineau
West Road No. 25
Westfield, MA 01085
(413) 562-0697

Stenciled acrylics on walls, canvas, and textiles. Although she has done mainly interior work, "because most of New England is entrenched in tradition," she is willing and able to do exterior stencilling. Prefers early American style, but will do any kind of stenciling except Op or Pop. Subject matter: plant life, geometrics, and scroll borders.

Lawrence N. Jensen
Box 482
Woods Hole, MA 02543
(617) 548-4329

Works in acrylics and collage; prefers architectural designs. "Semi-realism." Does own installations.

Andree Lisette Herz
65 N. Main Street
Allentown, NJ 08501
(609) 586-6883

Oil on canvas, painted glass, mosaic, enameled metals, and acrylic polymer on gessoed walls, canvas, or wood. Will paint any modern or historical subject in a style that suits the situation. Does trompe l'oeil and could stencil or paint ornament on buildings.

Cathy Santucci
22 Grove Street
Lincoln Park, NJ 07035
(201) 694-7608

Oil on canvas, painted glass, acrylic on plexiglass and canvas. Subject matter includes allegory and landscape, rendered in styles from realistic to impressionistic to abstract. Will do both trompe l'oeil and painting of ornament on buildings.

Phillip I. Danzig
86 Edgemont Road
Upper Montclair, NJ 07043
(201) 746-0709

This architect/muralist works in fresco secco, ceramics, and ceramic mosaic. Bas-relief sculpture in ceramics and sand-cast concrete. Preferred style: "graphical." Preferred subject matter: allegorical. Experienced in community mosaic murals.

Philip S. Read
Box 204
Brookhaven, NY 11719
(516) 286-3349
(305) 832-6632

Oil on canvas, lacquer on silver leaf, wood assemblages, and acrylic painted murals. Prefers realism and trompe l'oeil. "History, eighteenth century, decorative, scenic and still life" are preferred subjects. Does architecturally decorative painting including foliage, trellises, animals, landscape scenes, seascapes, historical cityscapes, surrealistic scenes, giant vegetables, marbleizing, false tiling, etc.

Hank Prussing
1603 11th Avenue
Brooklyn, NY 11215
(212) 788-2389

Oil on canvas, mosaic, acrylic on plaster, and "exterior house paint for outdoor murals." Bas-relief sculpture with pigmented cement. "Realistic renderings, dry-brush, scumbling, wet modelling, and glazing combined." Subject matter: "people, buildings, and other manmade environments—I often work with photographs." Does trompe l'oeil. Would stencil or paint ornament on a building if it was part of a total mural concept.

Susan Kaprov
149 Willow Street
Brooklyn Heights, NY 11201
(212) 624-2775

Works in fresco, oil on canvas, oil and enamel on aluminum, painted glass, mosaic, and enameled metals. Also photo murals (interior and exterior). Semiabstract to abstract. "I use realistic images as well as abstract forms." Will stencil or paint ornament on buildings and does install.

Christian Thee
39 Columbia Place
Brooklyn Heights, NY 11201
(212) 834-1513

Specializes in trompe l'oeil; acrylics on wood or canvas, which is then fixed to the walls. Likes doing windows (looking in or out) and doorways (as architectural elements). He will work in any historical style.

James Penney
312 College Hill Road
Clinton, NY 13323
(315) 853-5676

Oil on canvas or panels. Nature, figures, historical scenes, symbolism in simplified or abstracted realism. Penney's work is shown at the **Kraushaar Galleries, 1055 Madison Ave., NYC 10028** (212) 535-9888.

Michael Thornton-Smith
141–57 71st Avenue
Flushing, NY 11367
(212) 544-0742

Works in fresco; acrylic for interior, oil base paint for exterior. Prefers representational style and does trompe l'oeil. Preferred subject matter: "naturalistic birds and trees"; also does geometric abstractions.

Robert P. Archer
South Street
Greenville, NY 12083
(518) 966-8015

Works in fresco secco and oil on canvas. Preferred style: "academic, impressionistic." Preferred subject matter: figures, landscapes. Does own installations.

Tibor Freund
34–57 82nd Street
Jackson Heights, NY 11372
(212) 335-2119

Mosaic, acrylic on canvas and masonite, oil on aluminum and wood ridged surfaces. The originator of "motion painting" and "moving murals." Geometrical abstractions and "4-D" geometrical optical illusions. Does trompe l'oeil.

Anthony Toney
16 Hampton Place
Katonah, NY 10536
(914) 232-4312

Fresco, fresco secco, oil on canvas, and mosaic. Preferred medium: oil on canvas. Preferred style: "creative realism." Any subject matter. Does trompe l'oeil.

Oil sketch for "Momentous Events in American History." Frank Mason, New York, NY. (Photo courtesy of Frank Mason)

Alton S. Tobey
296 Murray Avenue
Larchmont, NY 10538
(914) 834-6197

Fresco secco and oil on canvas; also bas-relief sculpture. Usually works with historical subjects in realistic or abstract style and on a grand scale. Tobey did the "Evolution of Shipbuilding" for the rotunda of the American Bureau of Shipping Building. Also "sculpts" metal in an interesting technique. Does trompe l'oeil.

Joan Altabe
Long Beach, NY 11561

See listing under Glass.

Yaffa Yael Stec-El
358 Massachusetts Avenue
Massapequa Park, NY 11762
(No phone)
or
43 Lincoln Avenue
Massapequa, NY 11758
(516) 541-8266 (evenings)

Fresco secco, oil on canvas, and mosaic. Preferred medium: fresco secco *in situ*, oil, or acrylics. Preferred style: realism, with expressionism and "conceptual perceptions of contemporary expressions." Any subject matter approached "humanistically." Does trompe l'oeil and will paint or stencil ornament on a building.

Jack Beal
c/o Allan Frumkin Gallery
50 W. 57th Street
New York, NY 10019
(212) 757-6655

Mural-scale oil on canvas paintings. Preferred style: "realism." Preferred subject matter: "people doing good."

Cityarts Workshop
Attn. Kathleen S. Gupta, Executive Director
525 E. 6th Street
New York, NY 10009
(212) 673-8670

Founded in 1969, this nonprofit arts organization is interested in the creation of "community responsive" interior and exterior murals. The work is executed by artists connected with this organization who work in consort with the community. Workshop artists can operate with greater or lesser amounts of community participation. Can also do bas-relief sculpture: concrete with mosaic. Preferred style: representational murals, decorative and representational mosaics. Will install. The Resource Center on Public Art—part of the organization—holds workshops on murals, rents slide shows, and gives lectures and mural tours. Variety of literature, slides, postcards, and posters available.

Eva Cockcroft
280 Lafayette Street #3A
New York, NY 10012
(212) 966-0007

Oil on canvas, mosaic, and painted murals. Also does bas-relief, cast cement mosaics. Preferred style: realism. Preferred subject matter: "narrative, figurative history, or current realities." She also does community participation projects.

Allyn Cox
165 E. 60th Street
New York, NY 10022
(212) 838-4092

This artist works in fresco, oil on canvas, stained glass, and mosaic. Style: traditional. Will do trompe l'oeil; will paint ornament on a building if it is part of a general scheme. Did a series of murals for the U.S. Capitol Building.

Benoit Gilsoul
231 W. 29th Street, Room 807
New York, NY 10001
(212) 868-8414
(212) 695-0787

Oil on canvas, stainless steel, painted glass, mosaic, enameled metals, stained, slab, and sandblasted glass. Works in mosaic, terracotta, metals, and does bas-relief sculpture in stone and wood. Also ceramics: custom patterns, bas-reliefs, and murals. Style: contemporary. Scale: monumental.

Lloyd Lozes Goff
P.O. Box 1144
Ansonia Station
New York, NY 10023
(212) 874-6029

Fresco secco, oil on canvas, mosaic, and acrylic. Representational style, any subject matter. Preferred medium: acrylic. Would stencil or paint ornament on buildings.

The Greenland Studio
New York, NY 10011

See listing under Glass.

Richard Haas
81 Greene Street
New York, NY 10012
(212) 431-9579

Richard Haas is the best known architectural muralist today. He has done everything from storefront murals in New York's Little Italy to the four façades of a Chicago skyscraper. Oil and Keim paint on brick, cement, stucco, cinder block; also painted glass and (interior) oil on canvas. Preferred medium: Keim paint on unpainted brick or stucco. This artist prefers subjects from "Occidental architecture of the last 5,000 years" including a wide variety of ornamental and environmental forms. His specialty is trompe l'oeil or "architectural illusionism." He will work only where he can control both the design and execution of the project.

G. Hunter Jones
15 Gramercy Park S.
New York, NY 10003
(212) 475-2528

Works in oil on canvas and painted glass. Preferred media: oil or water base paint. Does realistic or expressionist paintings of "historical, pictorial, period, or religious subjects." Can do own installations "if applicable." Much experience in trompe l'oeil and painting and stenciling ornament.

Let There Be Neon
New York, NY 10012

See listing under Signs.

Cile Lord
42 E. 12th Street
New York, NY 10003
(212) 228-6030

Oil on canvas and Japan-paint on any nonglossy surface (wood, plaster, paint, etc.). Classic stenciling, any period, any scale. Flowers, leaves, geometric patterns are specialties. Does site work if necessary. Would stencil or paint ornament around windows or doors.

Frank Herbert Mason
385 Broome Street
New York, NY 10013
(212) 226-7033

Oil and tempera on canvas. Contemporary and historical figures in a "classical" style. Preferred subject matter: "figures in classical or modern landscapes." He has a series of paintings of St. Anthony of Padua hanging in the Church of S. Giovanni di Malta, in Venice.

Marcus Matson
332 E. 91st Street, Apt. 1E
New York, NY 10028
(212) 427-4205

Fresco, oil on canvas, stainless steel, and mosaic. Preferred medium: oil on canvas or wall. Willing to work with any subject, "loose realism to abstract." Does trompe l'oeil; would paint decoration on a building.

Ronald Millard
548 Hudson Street
New York, NY 10014
(212) 675-6465

Fresco secco, oil on canvas. Also does freehand decoration, gilding, graining, marbleizing, etc. Bas-relief sculpture in Plasteline for casting in plaster, fiber glass, etc. Preferred style: traditional. Any subject matter. Sometimes does own installations. Will do trompe l'oeil.

New York Art Glass
Attn. J. Castagna
920 Broadway, Suite 701
New York, NY 10010
(212) 673-3733

Specialty: custom designs and contracting. Oil on canvas, ceramics, glass, metals, semiprecious stones, woods, marble, and inlaid marble. Also stained, slab, sandblasted, beveled, and illuminated glass work. Preferred media: glass, metal, and stone. Works with most any subject matter in contemporary or classical style. Does own installations; larger jobs subcontracted to specialists.

Elemer Polony
777 Sixth Avenue
New York, NY 10001
(212) 924-8879

Fresco, fresco secco, oil on canvas, ceramics, painted glass, mosaic, and marble inlay. "Nonobjective or figurative." Does trompe l'oeil.

Rambusch Decorating Co.
40 W. 13th Street
New York, NY 10011
(212) 675-0400

Founded in 1898, this company maintains a staff of designers and craftsmen who work in mosaic, stained glass, wood carving, painted murals, porcelain enamel, repoussé, chased bronze, metal casting, and exterior lighting. Likes to develop an architect's idea from the early stages; to give design suggestions and cost estimates for various media; and take the project through the final design, fabrication, and installation. Also does a great deal of restoration work. Past work ranges from metalwork and exterior murals at the 1939 World's Fair to fabricating the mammoth stained glass mural for the American Airlines Terminal at Kennedy Airport (Robert Sowers, artist). Branch office in Toronto, Canada.

Topps Decorating Co., Inc.
701 Seventh Avenue
New York, NY 10036
(212) 246-9473

Fresco, fresco secco, oil on canvas, ceramics, mosaic, gold leafing, marbleizing. Can do trompe l'oeil and painted decoration on own installations.

Nitza Tufino
533 E. 11th Street, Apt. 5N
New York, NY 10009
(212) 533-5242

Oil on canvas, ceramics, enameled metals, bas-relief ceramic sculpture. Prefers ceramic tile. Style and subject matter depend on site and circumstances.

Stuyvesant Van Veen
320 Central Park W.
New York, NY 10025
(212) 787-2136

Oil on canvas, fresco secco, liquid plexiglass on plexiglass, formica marquetry. "Traditional or simplified representational style; industrial, historical, or purely decorative subject matter." Does trompe l'oeil.

Jacques Maloubier
2675 Henry Hudson Parkway
Riverdale, NY 10463
(212) 543-8754

Oil on canvas, acrylic, lacquer on silver leaf, bas-relief painted plastic paste. Prefers "stylized, semiabstract expressionism," any subject matter. Does trompe l'oeil and would stencil or paint ornament on a building.

1211 N. LaSalle, Chicago—before mural.

1211 N. Lasalle, Chicago—after mural. Designed by Richard Haas; executed by Evergreene Painting Studios, Inc., New York City. Only the windows on this façade are real. Everything else, including the "bay" windows, are painted on a flat façade. (Photo by François Robert)

Bernard Caster
P.O. Box 154
South Butler, NY 13154
(315) 365-2248

Works in a variety of media including paint, enamel on steel, mosaic panels, and copper and wood sculpture. Enameled mosaic panels of various sizes. Style best described as "fantasy: stylized animals, fish, flowers, birds, and people, with a tapestrylike effect."

David Wilson
South New Berlin, NY 13843

See listing under Glass.

Shirley Rosenthal
Contemporary Enamels
Williamsville, NY 14221

See listing under Porcelain Enamel.

Kenneth Stern of Woodstock
Chestnut Hill Road
Woodstock, NY 12498
(914) 679-9250

Oil on canvas, painted glass, tissue and clear lacquer on glass, and sgraffito. Preferred medium: paint on sealed plaster, gesso panel, or canvas. Preferred style: "traditional imprimatura painting." Preferred subject matter: "comedic, ironic, or lyrical period evocations of architecture in nature, figures, or still life." Specialty: trompe l'oeil. Will stencil or paint decoration.

James Sulkowski
220 1/2 Orchard Avenue
Canonsburg, PA 15317
(412) 746-3624

Works in oil on plaster walls and canvas. "Traditional realism"; any subject matter.

Justine Presha DeVan
1305 N. Frazier Street
Philadelphia, PA 19131
(215) 878-1861
(215) 849-6891

Enameled metals, oil on canvas, stainless steel. Also bas-relief sculpture—copper and brass repoussé, cast bronze, aluminum, welded metals. Preferred style: "realistic, semirealistic, symbolic." Subject matter: "mythology, the Bible, astrology."

Rudolph N. Rohn Co., Inc.
Attn. Rolf Rohn
807 Crane Avenue
Pittsburgh, PA 15216
(412) 561-2266

This company has twenty-five artists who work in many media: fresco, fresco secco, oil on canvas, ceramics, painted glass, mosaic, lacquer on silver leaf, enameled metals, etched glass, sculpture in all materials. Styles range from traditional to contemporary. Does mainly religious and institutional work. Can do hand-cut and painted stenciling.

Linder and Associates
151 S. Baringer Avenue
Silverdale, PA 18962
(215) 257-2792

Enamels and lacquers on masonite, wood, and plastic. Painted backgrounds, bas-relief foregrounds. Subject matter: "landscapes with geographical connotations—South Seas, western, oriental, etc." Does trompe l'oeil.

South

Hollis Holbrook
1710 S.W. 35th Place
Gainesville, FL 32608
(904) 377-7719
(904) 372-4979

Fresco, oil on canvas, egg tempera, and acrylics. Bas-relief sculpture in polyester and fiber glass. Contemporary, figurative, and abstract style; any subject matter. Installs.

Bill J. Hammon
Box 952
Islamorda, FL 33036
(305) 664-9391
(305) 664-4649

Fresco, fresco secco, oil on canvas, ceramics, stainless steel, painted glass, mosaic, enameled metals. Free-standing sculpture in metal and concrete; bas-relief sculpture in concrete, clay, brick, and metal. Works in whatever medium best suits the architecture. Generally abstract style but determined by "surrounding area." Will stencil or paint ornament on buildings depending on subject matter and design. Can do trompe l'oeil.

Cameron Covert and Bruce Bobick
Art Department
West Georgia College
Carrollton, GA 30118
(404) 834-1235
(404) 834-7345

Covert is a ceramicist; Bobick is an artist. They combine their skills to make ceramic murals in stoneware, porcelain, and terracotta. Preferred style: abstract; any subject matter. Can do restoration or duplication of terracotta elements, working from sketch or sample.

Anthony DiMarco
New Orleans, LA 70119

See listing under Sculpture.

Monique Goss
Visual Impact
2505 Pinebrush Avenue
Baltimore, MD 21209
(301) 358-9737

Latex murals, oil on canvas, ceramics, painted glass, and mosaic. Preferred style: abstract. This artist directed the Baltimore Mural Project, a series of eighty murals created with the help of local residents and executed by local artists. She now heads a consulting and designing company called Visual Impact.

Sally Price
7416 Aspen Avenue
Takoma Park, MD 20012
(301) 891-2488

Fresco, fresco secco, and oil on canvas. Prefers figurative subject matter. Price assisted Allyn Cox on the murals for the U. S. Capitol Building.

Roger Allen Nelson
P.O. Box 526
Linville, NC 28646
(No phone)

Fresco and oil on canvas. Describes style as "intricate realism." Preferred subject matter: human form, movement, water. Does own installations.

Maryann Fariello
Rte. 1 Box 192
New Hope Road
Alexandria, TN 37012
(615) 529-2990

Porcelain panels, murals, and bas-relief tiles. Can, but normally does not, install. Will do trompe l'oeil and stencil or paint ornament on buildings.

D. Hall Robertson
723 Barkley Drive
Fredericksburg, VA 22401
(703) 786-2924

Oil on canvas. Traditional style; religious and historical subjects. Installs.

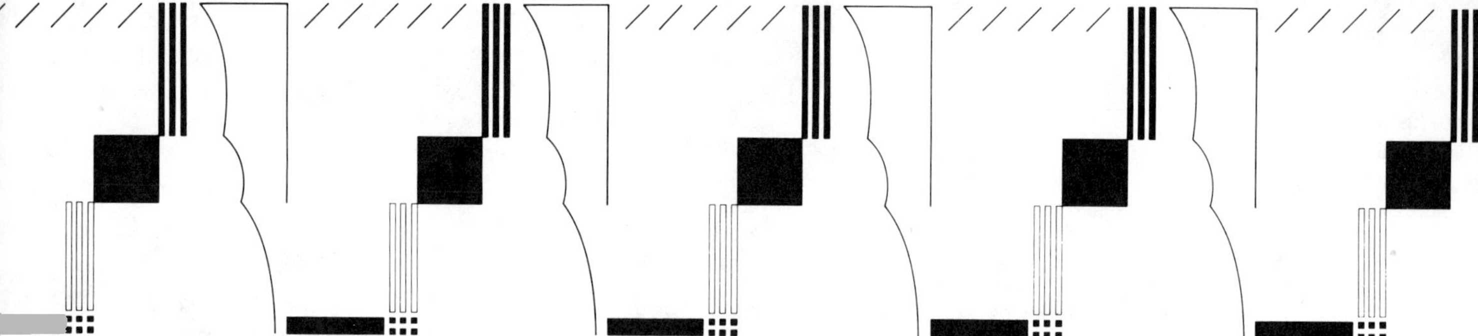

Cartoon for stencil, executed on walls of Sunar furniture showroom, New York; 5-by-5-inch module (1981). Designed by Michael Graves, Architect, Princeton, NJ. For possible future use, the module would be enlarged to approximately 7 by 7 inches. (Drawing courtesy of Michael Graves)

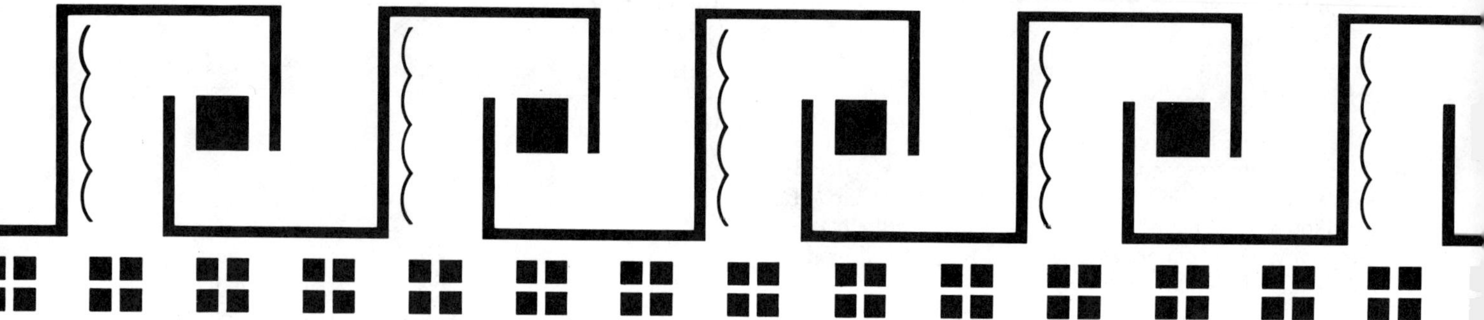

Cartoon for stencil, executed on walls of Sunar furniture showroom, New York; 5-by-5-inch module (1981). Designed by Michael Graves, Architect, Princeton, NJ. For possible future use, the module would be enlarged to approximately 7 by 7 inches. (Drawing courtesy of Michael Graves)

Midwest

The Community Mural Project
Chicago Mural Group
Attn. John Pitman-Weber, Executive Director
2261 N. Lincoln Avenue
Chicago, IL 60614
(312) 871-3089
and
4830 N. Springfield
Chicago, IL 60625
(312) 583-9890

Extensive experience in community-participation murals (over 100 completed). In addition to painted murals, can do mosaic, concrete relief, and multicolor sgraffito. Gives longevity estimates for both indoor and outdoor work. Can travel to other locations to organize and supervise a community mural. Preferred style: allegorical. Preferred subject matter: political issues, neighborhood-related themes, historic events. Other services offered by this group include technical advice, recommendations about fabricators and suppliers in the area, and printed material relating to murals. Fees for consulting on site survey and analysis; complete mural proposals, including budget, time line, and design; and slide shows; and tours. Membership in the organization is $20.00, and is open to architects. You must join to be on the mailing list.

Jose Guerrero
4340 W. Kamerling
Chicago, IL 60651
(312) 342-4191

Painted glass and mosaic; bas-relief in cement mosaic. Preferred subject matter: "neighborhood scenes."

Harold Haydon
5009 Greenwood Avenue
Chicago, IL 60615
(312) 285-7614

Fresco, oil on canvas, ceramics, mosaic, and porcelain enamel.

Kathryn Kozan
1421 West Hood
Chicago, IL 60660
(312) 743-4478

Oil on canvas; also paints on other surfaces and works in ceramics. Any style, any subject matter. She often organizes mural projects for schools and community groups (interior and exterior, painting and ceramics). Does trompe l'oeil.

John Pitman-Weber
4830 N. Springfield
Chicago, IL 60625
(312) 583-9890

Does his own designs and will supervise community murals. Works in paint, ceramic tile, mosaic, concrete relief, and multicolor sgraffito. Preferred style: realistic and allegorical. Preferred subject matter: "neighborhood, feminist, third world and related issues, people, nature, historical." Is open to suggestions from architect. Shows preliminary sketches; gives cost and longevity estimates. Can travel to other locations and organize a community mural.

Public Art Workshop
Attn. Mark Rogovin, Director
5623 W. Madison Street
Chicago, IL 60644
(312) 626-7713

A community-based mural workshop started in 1972, it does murals on a variety of different subjects. Has done fixed and portable murals (for exhibitions). In addition to planning and executing murals, the Workshop offers resource material and art classes to the community. Maintains an extensive library on "the current mural renaissance, great Mexican murals, and the WPA era." If you come to them with a mural you would like done, the Workshop can give you technical advice, warn you about the common pitfalls, and recommend fabricators in your area. (Fee for these services is negotiated at the time.)

Mark Rogovin, Director
Public Art Workshop
5623 W. Madison Street
Chicago, IL 60644
(312) 626-7713

A muralist whose preferred themes include political and neighborhood issues, cityscapes, and people. He will do his own designs or the community's. (See listing for Public Art Workshop.)

Beth Shadur
7352 N. Winchester
Chicago, IL 60626
(312) 761-4832

Mosaic, paint (latex, acrylic latex, or oil enamel), and cast concrete. Fairly realistic style; prefers subjects related to the community in which the murals are to be placed.

Mira Jedwabnik Van Doren
Chicago, IL 60605

See listing under Porcelain Enamel.

Mira Jedwabnik Van Doren
Chicago, IL 60605

See listing under Porcelain Enamel.

Williams and Meyer Co.
630 S. Wabash Avenue
Chicago, IL 60605
(312) 322-9800

Black-and-white photographic murals made in one piece (sizes up to 52 by 160 inches). Larger murals are made in sections and precisely matched for installation. These can be printed on "Duochrome" colored paper (in red, green, blue, yellow, metallic gold, and silver) for special effects.

Larry Day
Day by Day Graphics
Box 50
607 South Melvin
Gibson City, IL 60936
(217) 784-4702
(217) 784-5550

Painting and hand lettering. Representational style; any subject matter. Will stencil or paint ornament on a building.

Tom Edwards
1810 Oxford Street
Rockford, IL 61103
(815) 964-4445

Interior and exterior murals, stencils, painted plywood cut-outs, illustrated signs, and commissioned paintings and drawings. Will work anywhere in the Midwest. Can do trompe l'oeil.

Howard Orr
4565 Lawn Avenue
Western Springs, IL 60558
(312) 246-4829

Acrylics and oil on canvas; gold leaf on canvas, wood, and glass; lacquer on gold and silver leaf. Bas-relief sculpture in wood and light metals. Custom designed clock faces; miniature dock, street, and period scenes, all three-dimensional. Prefers historic and controversial issues as subject matter, rendered in unusual assemblages. Uses "patch-sewn" canvases.

G. Dorthea Tomlinson Marquis
4111 Ingersoll Avenue, Apt. 616
Des Moines, IA 50312
(515) 277-1745

Genre style—people and landscape. Oil on canvas.

Stanley James Herd
300 E. Mulberry
Dodge City, KS 67801
(316) 225-2851

Oil and acrylic on canvas, stainless steel, enameled metals; also experienced in painting on stucco, brick, and other exterior surfaces. Bas-relief, limestone sculpture. Preferred style: contemporary Western. Subject matter: Western historical or any historical work. A native of this part of the country, he researches his subject very carefully. Among other projects is a 306-by-10 foot mural on metal panels. It depicts the history of Dodge City, Kansas, and was commissioned by the Hyplains Dressed Beef Company. Does trompe l'oeil.

The Detroit Mural Artists Guild
Attn. Ruth Loring Janes or Nathan Andrew Thomas
14961 Oakfield
Detroit, MI 48227
(313) 838-4751
(313) 224-3482

They will paint any subject; preferred style: "humanistic abstractions; enjoy both contemporary and traditional imagery and techniques." Work in enamel on concrete, acrylic on masonite, mounted on any surface; also painted glass and lacquer on gold and silver leaf.

Jerry Hunt
4263 Cass #2
Detroit, MI 48201
(313) 833-1727
(313) 832-1042

Works in oil, acrylic, and latex on canvas. Extensive experience in relief with cut board and concrete. Preferred style: nonobjective, geometric abstraction. Preferred subject matter: "growth-form-crystals-visual illusion-music-intuitive representation-toroidal shapes-matter-anti-matter."

The Popular Arts Workshop
Attn. Gary Andrews, Director
P. O. Box 15052
Lansing, MI 48901
(517) 882-7972

The Popular Arts Workshop does community-based murals as well as bas-relief sculpture in a variety of media. The organization is made up of many different people—not only artists—from the Lansing area.

Thomas Cappuccio
Department of Art & Design
Northern Michigan University
Marquette, MI 49855
(906) 227-2194

Oil on canvas; acrylics on board and canvas. Preferred style: "simplification from reality, surrealism." Preferred subject matter: "development of communications, flying machines, the earth from afar."

Susan McDonald
Wall Painting Artists, Inc.
1056 13th Avenue S.E.
Minneapolis, MN 55414
(612) 378-2571

Acrylic latex murals on exterior walls; spray or brush technique. Any subject matter.

William Saltzman Studio
5140 Lyndale Avenue S.
Minneapolis, MN 55419
(612) 822-7077

Works in oil on canvas and stained glass. Does sheet copper (relief or full round) and wood bas-relief sculpture. Semi- to complete abstractions; subjects are related to building site, purpose, or architectural design.

Sidney Larson
2025 Crestridge Drive
Columbia, MO 65201
(314) 445-2058

Oil on canvas; acrylic on any suitable surface. Abstract or representational style. Does trompe l'oeil. Also specializes in restoration and conservation of murals.

Tracy Montminy
1506 Paris Road
Columbia, MO 65201
(314) 442-4093

Fresco, oil on canvas (previously attached to wall), acrylic on concrete. Prefers painting the human figure, semi-abstracted. Will stencil or paint ornament on a building.

Ravenna Mosaic Co.
Rte. 2 Box 512
Fredericktown, MO 63645
(314) 783-5066

"Byzantine smalti (deep blue) glass and marble mosaics" for exterior and interior; will work in any style.

Eric James Bransby
401 E. 54th Street
Kansas City, MO 64110
(816) 363-3407

or

University of Missouri
Kansas City, MO 64110
(816) 276-1501

Works in fresco, fresco secco, mosaic, lacquer on silver leaf, egg tempera, polymer tempera, and ethyl silicate (on exterior concrete). Makes portable polyptich panels. Also does bronze bas-reliefs. "Semiabstract (cubist-derived) to representational." Prefers mythological or historical subject matter; does trompe l'oeil. Will install.

On the Wall Productions, Inc.
Attn. Sarah Linquist or Bob Fishbone
2023 Arsenal
St. Louis, MO 63118
(314) 773-9220

Acrylic paint on brick, concrete, and other outdoor surfaces, sometimes in combination with wood, etc., to create three-dimensional effects. Also does mosaic. Preferred style: "combined real and surreal." Will often include remnants of past "history," including faded signs and neon lighting. This company has been designing and executing murals since 1974. Linquist and Fishbone pride themselves on adapting their work to the particular space rather than working in one, identifiable style. They have worked with small community groups and also with architects. They will travel to do a mural.

Edmond J. FitzGerald
6585 Lisa Lane
Cincinnati, OH 45243
(513) 791-6939

Oil on canvas and ceramics. Representational style. Preferred subjects: historical, wildlife, and maritime scenes.

John W. Winterich and Associates
31711 Solon Road
Solon, OH 44139
(216) 248-2900

A large studio employing craftsmen who work in stained glass, marble, granite, slate, mosaic, wood, metals and tapestries as well as painters and muralists. Has done over 1700 major remodeling and building projects since World War II. Commercial and ecclesiastical stained glass for over four generations. Specializes in stained and faceted glass murals.

Hendrix, Heikkilä and Terry, Inc.
118 West Main Street
Norman, OK 73069
(405) 360-5823

Staff of three glaziers working in stained, cast, bas-relief, sandblasted, and beveled glass. This studio does other work besides glass; reproductions or original designs of gargoyles, capitals, and caryatids (in concrete, plaster, and fiber glass), ironwork, enameling, ceramics, gilding, woodwork restoration, and landscape design. Can do complete restorations of ornate altars and accessory pieces including sculpture.

Harry Worthman
2867 Stoney Brook Drive
Houston, TX 77063
(713) 782-5832

Oil on canvas; stylized and realistic treatments of historical subjects. Supervises installations. Will do trompe l'oeil and will stencil or paint ornament on buildings.

Marjorie Kreilick
2713 Chamberlain Avenue
Madison, WI 53705
(608) 238-7528

Preferred medium: marble mosaic. Also does bas-relief sculpture in bronze with mosaic inlay. Installs.

Conrad Schmitt Studios, Inc.
2405 S. 162nd Street
New Berlin, WI 53151
(414) 786-3030

This studio has been working with different media since 1889—"liturgical and commercial art." The work is extremely varied. Murals in fresco, fresco secco, oil on canvas, ceramics, painted glass, mosaic (contemporary, traditional, Byzantine), lacquer on silver leaf, and enameled metals. The studio also does stained glass, sculpture, lighting design, and screens. Has done many major restorations in different styles. One of the most impressive is the Paramount Arts Centre, Aurora, Illinois, with a magnificient Art Deco interior.

Caryl Yasko
Wisconsin Mural Works
136 Whiton Street
Whitewater, WI 53190
(414) 473-2273

Works in fresco, fresco secco, oil on canvas, ceramics, enameled metals, hand-molded concrete, cast concrete,

Trompe l'oeil painting of pavillion on the sea. The pavillion is trimmed by tiny lights, actually fiber optics, as are the wave tops. Windows are translucent, revealing silhouettes of dancing couples (pavillion is 2 feet high). Christian Thee, Brooklyn Heights, NY.

wood, egg tempera, and sgraffito. Preferred style: "representational abstraction." Preferred subject matter: "figures, the human condition, social comment, power, and relevance."

Rockies and Far West

Michael Schnorr
730 First Avenue
Chula Vista, CA 92010
(714) 422-4580
(714) 276-7599 (tie-line from San Diego)

Fresco, fresco secco, oil on canvas, and acrylic murals. Also does bas-relief sculpture in wood and plastics. Preferred style: "realistic, with freedom"; any subject. Installs.

Kay Whitcomb
La Jolla, CA 92037

See listing under Porcelain Enamel.

Roderick Sykes
4830 St. Elmo Drive
Los Angeles, CA 90019
(213) 931-3409

Oil and acrylic on different surfaces. Any style that fits the situation. Subject matter: children, free-form abstract.

Kent Twitchell
2160 Sunset Boulevard
Los Angeles, CA 90026
(213) 483-6268

Fresco secco, oil on canvas, and acrylics on walls or gesso panels. Style: "superrealism" (40-foot-high figures, etc.). Prefers painting the human figure but is open to other subject matter. Does trompe l'oeil.

Joseph Young, Director of Design
Art in Architecture
1434 S. Spaulding Avenue
Los Angeles, CA 90019
(213) 933-1194

A muralist working in many media: fresco, fresco secco, oil on canvas, ceramics, stainless steel, mosaic, enameled metals, tapestries, weaving, stained glass, cast bronze, fabricated aluminum, marble, granite, sandblasted glass, cast concrete, carved wood, corten steel, and photomurals. West Coast residents can see fourteen of his bas-relief panels as a frieze in the UCLA Math Sciences Auditorium.

K. Free and Art Grant
154 Ethel Avenue
Mill Valley, CA 94941
(415) 383-1340

Fresco, oil on canvas, ceramics, painted glass, and mosaic. They also do bas-relief wood carvings and work in concrete and bronze. Preferred subject matter: "human beings."

Florinda Leighton
Riverside, CA 92506

See listing under Porcelain Enamel.

The central skyscraper in this photo is painted: Crossroads Building, 42nd Street and Broadway, New York, with funds from H.U.D., lighting paid for by Marine Midland Bank. Designed by Richard Haas, executed by Evergreene Painting Studios, Inc., sponsored by the 42nd Street Redevelopment Corporation.

Raúl Martinéz
1161 York Street
San Francisco, CA 94110
(415) 647-6507

Murals in acrylics and enamels (brush and air-brush). Preferred style: "dynamic, hard-edged, thrusting movements." Preferred subject matter: "La Raza and third world cultural themes."

Frances Valesco
301 Chenery Street
San Francisco, CA 94131
(415) 585-2074
(415) 648-1221

Oil on canvas, acrylic murals, screen printing, photo printing, etching, and xerox. Preferred style: "figurative, photographic, calligraphic."

Ashley Wolff
1824 Baker Street
San Francisco, CA 94115
(415) 567-3867

Paints in oil on wood or masonry. Preferred style: "extremely realistic trompe l'oeil." Preferred subject matter: "animals and portraits." Will stencil or paint ornament on buildings.

L. K. Wittman
Wittman Arts
1286 Main Street
Santa Clara, CA 95050
(408) 249-7774

Oil on canvas and acrylics on panel. Bas-relief sculpture in wood assemblage. Representational or abstract style. Preferred subject matter: "stylized figures."

Judith F. Baca
685 Venice Boulevard
Venice, CA 90291
(213) 822-9560

Painted murals in a variety of styles (realistic, allegorical, abstract) and on a variety of themes (neighborhood, feminist, and third world issues; nature, cityscapes, people, and purely decorative subjects). Open to suggestions from the architect as to both theme and style. She can travel to another location to organize and supervise a community mural; can also recommend community artists. Cost estimates given. Will advise on ensuring community acceptance of public art projects; paint application for durability; restoration of murals; toxicity of acrylic paint systems; learning through the arts, and public art projects for youth. Also available for touch-ups and maintenance.

Social and Public Art Resource Center (SPARC)
Attn. Judy Baca or Linda Eber
685 Venice Boulevard
Venice, CA 90291
(213) 822-9560

Can give suggestions for the use of murals, can offer technical advice, and can recommend muralists in your area. The Center has printed material, "portable murals" (8 by 12 feet and 8 by 24 feet, crated), slides of public art from around the world, and slide films on mural painting. Also available is a nine-minute documentary film entitled "The Great Wall of Los Angeles"; it explains the reasons behind the 1/3-mile-long "History of California Mural" in Los Angeles (design and supervision by Judy Baca). There is a negotiable charge for some of these services.

Nini Jennings
Aspen Mosaics
330 E. Main Street
Aspen, CO 81611
(303) 925-7884

Creates her own designs in mosaic. She incorporates a variety of materials including mirror, stone, and glass. Much of the work is done in panels of varying sizes (ranging from 4 by 4 feet to 4 by 8 feet). The panels can be installed in walls, floors, doors, etc.

Wallternatives, Inc.
Attn. Lynda Watkins
2724 Vita Drive
North Las Vegas, NV 89030
(702) 649-5345

Large murals, graphics, and fine art to meet client's needs. Oil on canvas; enamel, oil, latex, and acrylic on most exterior or interior wall surfaces. "Artistic styles include graphics, optical illusions, theme work, color coding, impressionistic realism, photorealism, and patterns." Does trompe l'oeil and will paint decoration on a building. Wallternatives charges by the square foot for work ranging from simple graphics to complex realistic murals.

Kaleidoscope Art Glass
Boise, ID 83702

See listing under Glass.

Erica Karawina
3529 Akaka Place
Honolulu, HI 96822
(808) 988-3275

This artist works in *dalles de verre* (1-inch-thick faceted glass in an epoxy matrix), in an "architectural" style—abstract and contemporary.

Niki Glen
117 S. 9th Street
Livingston, MT 59047
(406) 222-3658

Fresco, ceramics, and mosaics. Extensive experience in exterior murals. Prefers realistic subject matter. Also does bas-relief sculpture in hand-molded and cast concrete or bronze. Would collaborate with other artists on stone, wood, or metal sculpture. Will install.

Key

- X Service, technique, or material is available
- \+ See listing for further information
- * Sometimes offers this service

Northeast	Painting in various media	Mosaic	Bas-relief	Other	Installs	Brochure or photos available	Trompe l'oeil	Community murals
Sandra Kopell Greens Farms, CT	X			+	X	X	X	
Jennifer D. Crane New Haven, CT	X			+		X		
Jim Peters Uncasville, CT	X				X	X		
Richard Layton Wilmington, DE	X		X	+		+	X	
John S. Coles Arlington, MA	X					X		
Center for Public Design Boston, MA	X	X	X	+		X		X
John Manship Gloucester, MA	X	X	X	+	X	X		
K. M. Cousineau Westfield, MA	+			+	X	X		
Lawrence N. Jensen Woods Hole, MA	X				X	X	X	
Andree Lisette Herz Allentown, NJ	X	X			X	X	X	
Cathy Santucci Lincoln Park, NJ	X				X	X	X	
Phillip I. Danzig Upper Montclair, NJ	X	X	X	+	X	X		
Philip S. Read Brookhaven, NY	X			+			X	
Hank Prussing Brooklyn, NY	X	X	X	+	X	X	X	
Susan Kaprov Brooklyn Heights, NY	X	X		+	X	X		
Christian Thee Brooklyn Heights, NY	X						X	
James Penny Clinton, NY	X				+	X		
Michael Thornton-Smith Flushing, NY	X				X	X	X	
Robert P. Archer Greenville, NY	X				X	X		
Tibor Freund Jackson Heights, NY	X	X			+	X		
Anthony Toney Katonah, NY	X	X			X	X	X	

Key

X Service, technique, or material is available
+ See listing for further information
* Sometimes offers this service

	Painting in various media	Mosaic	Bas-relief	Other	Installs	Brochure or photos available	Trompe l'oeil	Community murals
Alton S. Tobey Larchmont, NY	X		X		X	X	X	
Joan Altabe Long Beach, NY	See listing under Glass							
Yaffa Yael Stec-El Massapequa, NY	X	X			X			
Jack Beal New York, NY	X					X		
Cityarts Workshop New York, NY	X	X	X	+	X	X	X	X
Eva Cockcroft New York, NY	X	X	X			X		X
Allyn Cox New York, NY	X	X		+		X	X	
Benoit Gilsoul New York, NY	X	X	X	+	X	X		
Lloyd Lozes Goff New York, NY	X	X				X		
The Greenland Studio New York, NY	See listing under Glass							
Richard Haas New York, NY	X				*		X	
G. Hunter Jones New York, NY	X				X	X		
Let There Be Neon New York, NY	See listing under Signs							
Cile Lord New York, NY	X			+	X	X		
Frank Herbert Mason New York, NY	X				X	X		
Marcus Matson New York, NY	X	X		+	X	X	X	
Ronald Millard New York, NY	X		X		*	X	X	
New York Art Glass New York, NY	X	X		+	X	X		
Elemer Polony New York, NY	X	X		+		X	X	
Rambusch Decorating New York, NY	X	X	X	+	X	X	X	
Topps Decorating New York, NY	X	X		+	X	X	X	

Key

X Service, technique, or material is available
+ See listing for further information
* Sometimes offers this service

	Painting in various media	Mosaic	Bas-relief	Other	Installs	Brochure or photos available	Trompe l'oeil	Community murals
Nitza Tufino New York, NY	X	X	X		X	X		
Stuyvesant Van Veen New York, NY	X			+			X	
Jacques Maloubier Riverdale, NY	X		X	+		X	X	
Bernard Caster South Butler, NY	X			+				
David Wilson South New Berlin, NY	See listing under Glass							
Shirley Rosenthal Williamsville, NY	See listing under Porcelain Enamel							
Kenneth Stern Woodstock, NY	X			+	X	X	X	
James Sulkowski Canonsburg, PA	X					X		
Justine Presha DeVan Philadelphia, PA	X		X	+		X		
Rudolph N. Rohn Pittsburgh, PA	X	X	X		X	X	X	
Linder and Associates Silverdale, PA	X		X		X	X	X	

South

	Painting in various media	Mosaic	Bas-relief	Other	Installs	Brochure or photos available	Trompe l'oeil	Community murals
Hollis Holbrook Gainsville, FL	X		X	+	X	X		
Bill J. Hammon Islamorda, FL	X	X	X	+	X	X	X	
C. Covert and B. Bobick Carrollton, GA	X		+	+	X			
Anthony DiMarco New Orleans, LA	See listing under Sculpture							
Monique Goss Baltimore, MD	X	X	X		X	X		
Sally Price Takoma Park, MD	X					X	X	
Roger Allen Nelson Linville, NC	X				X	X	X	
Maryann Fariello Alexandria, TN			X	+	+	X		
D. Hall Robertson Fredericksburg, VA	X				X	X		

Key

X Service, technique, or material is available
\+ See listing for further information
* Sometimes offers this service

	Painting in various media	Mosaic	Bas-relief	Other	Installs	Brochure or photos available	Trompe l'oeil	Community murals
Midwest								
The Community Mural Project Chicago, IL	X	X	X	X	X	X	X	X
Jose Guerrero Chicago, IL	X	X	X			X	X	
Harold Haydon Chicago, IL	X	X		+		X		
Kathryn Kozan Chicago, IL	X		X		X	X		X
John Pitman-Weber Chicago, IL	X	X			X	X		X
Chicago Mural Group Chicago, IL	X	X	X		X	X		X
Mark Rogovin Chicago, IL	X				X	X		X
Beth Shadur Chicago, IL	X	X	X			X		X
Mira Jedwabnik Van Doren Chicago, IL	See listing under Porcelain Enamel							
Williams and Meyer Chicago, IL				+		X	+	
Larry Day Gibson City, IL	X			+	X			
Tom Edwards Rockford, IL	X			+	X	X	X	
Howard Orr Western Springs, IL	X		X	+	X	X		
G. Dorthea T. Marquis Des Moines, IA	X				X	X		
Stanley James Herd Dodge City, KS	X		X	+	X	X	X	
Detroit Mural Artists Detroit, MI	X				X	X		
Jerry Hunt Detroit, MI	X		X		X	X		
Popular Arts Workshop Lansing, MI	X		X	+	X	X		X
Thomas Cappuccio Marquette, MI	X				X	X		
Susan McDonald Minneapolis, MN	X				X	X		

Key

X Service, technique, or material is available
+ See listing for further information
* Sometimes offers this service

	Painting in various media	Mosaic	Bas-relief	Other	Installs	Brochure or photos available	Trompe l'oeil	Community murals
William Saltzman Studio Minneapolis, MN	X		X	+	X	X		
Sidney Larson Columbia, MO	X				X		X	
Tracy Montminy Columbia, MO	X				+	X		
Ravenna Mosaic Fredericktown, MO		X			X	X		
Eric James Bransby Kansas City, MO	X	X	X		X	X	X	
On The Wall St. Louis, MO	X	X			X	X	X	X
Edmond J. FitzGerald Cincinnati, OH	X				X	X		
John W. Winterich Solon, OH	See listing under Glass							
Hendrix, Heikkilä, and Terry Norman, OK	See listing under Glass							
Harry Worthman Houston, TX	X				+	X	X	
Marjorie Kreilick Madison, WI		X	X		X	X		
Conrad Schmitt Studios New Berlin, WI	X	X		+	X	X		
Wisconsin Mural Works Whitewater, WI	X	X	X	+	X	X		X
Carol Yasko Whitewater, WI	X	X	X	+	X	X		X
Rockies and Far West								
Michael Schnorr Chula Vista, CA	X		X		X	X	X	
Kay Whitcomb La Jolla, CA	See listing under Porcelain Enamel							
Roderick Sykes Los Angeles, CA	X							
Kent Twitchell Los Angeles, CA	X				X	X	X	
Joseph Young Los Angeles, CA	X	X	X	+	X	X	X	
K. Free and Art Grant Mill Valley, CA	X	X	X			X		

Key

X Service, technique, or material is available
+ See listing for further information
* Sometimes offers this service

	Painting in various media	Mosaic	Bas-relief	Other	Installs	Brochure or photos available	Trompe l'oeil	Community murals
Florinda Leighton Riverside, CA	See listing under Porcelain Enamel							
Raúl Martinéz San Francisco, CA	X				X	X		
Frances Valesco San Francisco, CA	X				X	X		
Ashley Wolff San Francisco, CA	X					X	X	
L. K. Wittman Santa Clara, CA	X		X		X	X		
Judith F. Baca Venice, CA	X				X	X		X
SPARC Venice, CA	X				X	X		X
Nini Jennings Aspen, CO		X				X		
Wallternatives Denver, CO	X				X	X	X	
Kaleidoscope Art Glass Boise, ID	See listing under Glass							
Erica Karawina Honolulu, HI				+				
Niki Glen Livingston, MT	X	X	X		X	X		

PLASTICS

For decades, the gamut of designers—from mundane corporate architects to supersophisticated modernists—have been using plastics on the inside of buildings. However, this family of materials has yet to overcome the stigma attached to it in terms of exterior use. Until now, plastics have been found only in the architectural netherworld: thousands of miles of vacuum-formed commercial sinage, not to speak of MacDonald's golden arches. Although it is less well known, plastics have also been used to match castings of other materials with little sacrifice in the rendering of detail. The building shown in the photo, at Broadway and 29th Street in New York, had several of its damaged cast iron panels replaced with fiber glass reproductions cast from latex molds of the originals. The fiber glass copies show every detail, right down to screw heads, with faithful color.

The prejudice against plastics is beginning to break down. Several manufacturers now offer finely detailed moldings, pediments, cornices, and other elements in lightweight polymers; these are worked with standard carpenter's tools, and withstand weathering at least as well as painted wood. Needless to say, while most of these elements are in traditional forms, plastics can easily take any shape the designer can imagine.

Often, an element that can be produced in cast stone or plaster can also be made in fiber glass. Many of the manufacturers we mention in this section also work with other materials, and can advise you about which material is best for your needs.

A note on materials. Owens Corning (see Special listing under Concrete) produces a material under the registered trademark Fiberglas. Fiber glass is the generic term for a material consisting of extremely fine filaments of glass that are either chopped up and mixed with a resin or woven into yarn or cloth, and applied with resin. Layers of this combination are either laid or sprayed into a mold, and the material can be given any color.

Several variations—using different additives—have evolved from this technique. One such variation is a product called Bonded Bronze (bronze powder is mixed into the fiber glass resin and placed into the mold first). Other metal powders, such as brass powder, could be substituted. Still another variation involves the use of stone. A number of companies that supply sculpture materials stock stone and metal powders that can be combined with resins. You can replicate black "Belgian" marble, pure white "Cararra" marble, plus other stone and metal finishes. The appearance of marble veining is achieved by painting streaks of sienna on the inside of the mold; these streaks bleed into the surface when the resin is applied.

The main advantages of fiber glass-based materials are that they are cheaper (using only a fraction of the material they replicate) and they weigh less than the "original" materials, so supporting structures can be lighter. Each of these combinations can be brought to a high polish. The variations are probably more durable than fiber glass alone because of the additional strength lent by the stone or metal powders.

Certain cities have fire codes specifying degrees of fire retardancy of plastics. Normally, this applies to interior finishes, but check your local fire laws to determine the exterior requirements in your area as well. There are also corrosion problems that can be solved by using corrosion-resistant resins. Questions about corrosion should be directed to the individual companies.

Special Listings

The Society of the Plastics Industry, Inc.
Reinforced Plastics Composites Institute
Attn. Joseph S. McDermott, Manager
355 Lexington Avenue
New York, NY 10017
(212) 573-9400

Has printed material, can give technical advice, and can recommend fabricators and suppliers in your area.

Regional Listings

All the companies listed manufacture with fire-resistant and corrosion-resistant resins.

Northeast

Duro Fiber
Attn. Jack Hatfield
239 Andover Street
Wilmington, MA 01887
(617) 657-4205

Specializes in all types of architectural elements, from new building panels to restorations and duplications of such traditional elements as cornices and finials. Custom work from rough sketch or more detailed information.

Quality Prefabrication, Inc.
P.O. Box 90
Toms River, NJ 08753
(201) 349-0565

Specialty: fiber glass and wood carvings; restoration. Also cornices, exterior panels, domes, canopies, balconies, planters, and cupolas. Standard designs and custom work from rough sketch or more detailed information.

Lawrence Wittman and Co., Inc.
1395 Marconi Boulevard
Copiague, NY 11726
(516) 842-4770

Manufacturer of fiber glass products for exterior architectural use: façades, cornices, panels, planters, etc. Also pre-fab buildings. Can make designs from sketch, sample, or photo. Specialty: design consulting and custom molding to architects' specifications.

Alpha One Manufacturing Co., Ltd.
90–A Alpha Plaza
Hicksville, NY 11801
(516) 822-4141

Makes cornices, exterior panels, planters, shelters, play cubes, and other elements. Specializes in custom fiber glass molding.

This cast iron façade at Broadway and 29th Street in New York City has had several of its bays replaced by fiber glass. The fiber glass castings were made from latex molds, and are true to the original cast iron down to the smallest screw head. Fiber glass by Saldarini and Pucci, New York.

Saldarini & Pucci
Attn. Gabriel Petrella
156 Crosby Street
New York, NY 10012
(212) 673-4390

Specialty: fiber glass and plasterwork of all types. Can fabricate virtually any type of architectural element for exterior (or interior) use including: capitals, brackets, cartouches, cornices, panels, etc. Standard designs available; will make any custom design from rough sketch or more detailed information, or can fabricate something of their own design. Everyone in the shop is a model-maker and skilled at fabricating all types of architectural ornament. They can make plaster models for stone carvers to copy (as they did for the stone capitals of the new addition to the Frick Museum), or for latex molds from which castings can be made. Also manufactures custom cast stone balusters, bas-reliefs, cornices, etc. Can produce a variety of surfaces and textures and, "to a certain extent," various colors. Technical advice given. Maximum size for single cast stone panel: 4 by 4 feet (larger elements are made from several panels).

Maquette for wall fountain, epoxy resin (27 inches high) by Raymond Kaskey, Washington, DC. (Photo courtesy of Raymond Kaskey)

High density polyurethane pediment, overdoor, and cornice moldings by Focal Point, Inc., Atlanta, GA. (Photo courtesy of Focal Point, Inc.)

Ornato Decors
1663 Grove Street
Ridgewood, NY 11385
(212) 456-9424

Custom designs in plaster, cast stone, and fiber glass. Can make models to architects' specifications. Has molds available from which castings can be made. Considerable experience in preservation and landmarks work; able to match any ornament. Gives design, technical, and installation advice. "Can make anything your heart desires, as long as it's ornamental."

Felber Studios
110 Ardmore Avenue
Ardmore, PA 19003
(215) 642-4710

Distributor and maker selling directly; does custom work and can copy a sample. Makes models in a variety of materials; can work from rough sketch but prefers sample or working drawing. Can make designs in plaster, cast stone, and fiber glass. Specializes in fiber glass for exterior use, and installation and reconstruction of antique plaster. Also does scale models in cooperation with architects and designers. Stocks an extensive array of exterior and exquisite interior ornamental designs including ceiling moldings, cartouches, shell niches, cornices, and center medallions. Brochure $10.00.

Gitco, Inc.
P.O. Box 73
Clifton Heights, PA 19063
(215) 622-5777

Specializes in custom molding for construction, industry, marine, etc.

Fypon, Inc.
108 Hill Street
Stewartstown, PA 17363
(717) 993-2593

Specializes in Colonial and Victorian trim: moldings, various types of pediments, fans, etc., manufactured in high-density polyurethane. All well-suited to exterior use. "Will not warp or rot. Are impervious to insects. Can be nailed, drilled, or sawed with field carpenter tools; patched or repaired with wood filler materials or exterior glues."

Don Ray Fiberglass
100 Pulaski Street
West Warwick, RI 02893
(401) 822-0170

Specializes in custom tooling for molding plastics.

South

Dimensional Plastics Corp.
1065 E. 26th Street
Hialeah, FL 33013
(305) 691-5961

Manufactures exterior architectural panels; standard designs. Can produce custom panels from sketch. Specializes in curtain wall applications, "stained" (glass) plastic, casting, cast laminating, and cast compression. Manufactures "Krinklglas"—a patterned, multicolored facing material for solar energy collectors, and "decorative" vandalproof panels.

Entol Industries, Inc.
8180 N.W. 36th Avenue
Miami, FL 33147
(305) 696-0900

Manufacturers of decorative doors, panels, and ceiling; uses high-density urethane—stock and custom designs. "Every week we do something different." Entol's "Art Carved" line—doors, moldings, and medallions— consists of urethane panels that are cast from hand-carved wood reliefs. The line comes in five hand-rubbed finishes; special finishes available. Paneled ceilings on 2-foot grids are available in twenty-four stock designs, traditional and contemporary, that accommodate grilles, lighting, diffusers, sprinklers, and mirror panels.

Focal Point
Attn. Irene K. Moore
2005 Marietta Road
Atlanta, GA 30318
(404) 351-0820

Preengineered moldings, overdoor pieces, niche caps, domes, ceiling medallions, brackets, and trellis pieces in lightweight polymers. These elements can be installed on the exterior if they are protected in the same way you would protect exterior woodwork. Brochure $1.00. "Architectural artwork from the past, engineered for today."

Mid-Atlantic Distributors, Inc.
6212 Reisterstown Road
Baltimore, MD 21215
(301) 358-8550

Distributes stock designs only; exterior panels.

Giannetti Studios
Brentwood, MD 20722

See listing under Stucco and Plaster.

Studio of Jack and Eva Grauer
Memphis, TN 38117

See listing under Sculpture.

Installation of pigmented fiber glass finial (height, approx. 7½ feet). The top piece is threaded and screws over the bottom piece. Rosettes are cast individually and bolted to the body of the finial. Architects: Endevor, Inc., Boston, MA. Fiber glass fabricated by Duro Fiber, Wilmington, MA. (Photo courtesy of Miguel Gomez-Ibanez)

Midwest

C. G. Girolami
Chicago, IL 60653

See listing under Cast Stone.

J. C. Lauber Co.
South Bend, IN 46617

See listing under Metals.

The Stone Center
3200 Brannon Avenue
St. Louis, MO 63139
(314) 771-1000

Produces custom designs only; cornices, exterior panels, and planters, in fiber glass.

Cincinnati Fiberglass, Inc.
4174 Half Acre Road
Batavia, OH 45103
(513) 221-8058
(513) 724-6111

Manufacturer producing fiber glass products for exterior architectural use.

Fischer and Jirouch Co.
Cleveland, OH 44103

See listing under Stucco and Plaster.

Fiber glass dormers being installed. Molds were made from the original metal dormers. Architects: Endevor, Inc., Boston, MA. Fiber glass fabricated by Duro Fiber, Wilmington, MA. (Photo courtesy of Miguel Gomez-Ibanez)

Detail showing the installation of new fiber glass dormers before slate roof was laid. Note that the new dormer is self-flashing. Architects: Endevor, Inc., Boston, MA. Fiber glass fabricated by Duro Fiber, Wilmington, MA. (Photo courtesy of Miguel Gomez-Ibanez)

Aleph Plastics
2398 Wood Avenue
Columbus, OH 43221
(614) 486-2629

Custom job shop doing resin transfer molding and open-sprayed hand layup.

R. L. Industries
P.O. Box 324
5885 State Rte. 128
Miamitown, OH 45041
(513) 353-1800

Custom designs only: cornices, exterior panels, and planters. Specializes in large structural components.

Owens Corning Fiberglas
Toledo, OH 43659
(419) 248-8832

See listing under Concrete.

Hendrix, Heikkilä, and Terry, Inc.
Norman, OK 73069

See listing under Murals.

Rockies and Far West

American Fiberglass
701 N. 22nd Avenue
Phoenix, AZ 85009
(602) 257-0521

Manufactures all types of architectural elements: exterior and interior planters, fascias, cornices, panels, signs, emblems, etc. Can imitate stamped metal, concrete, wood, stone, and other materials; custom and standard designs.

Leyva's J. P. Weaver Co.
Alhambra, CA 91803

See listing under Cast Stone.

Parabam, Inc.
3017 E. Las Hermanas
Compton, CA 90221
(213) 537-1771

This company uses a variety of manufacturing techniques to make fiber glass products ranging from curved projection screens to auto bodies, domes, and transportable instrument housings. An experienced engineering staff, as well as machine and electrical shops, for custom work. "Prototype or quantity to meet military or commercial standards."

Triangle Industries (Noble Division)
1919 Vineburn Avenue
Los Angeles, CA 90032
(213) 223-1201

Manufactures building accessories including cornices, exterior panels, and planters. Standard designs; can make custom designs from sample or working drawing. Specializes in products made of various types of plastics, wood, and decorative metals.

DFG Corporation
P.O. Box 127
Auburn, WA 98002
(206) 939-3633

Colonial style structural "duraglass" columns; readymade designs. "No splits, no rots, no termites, ever." Guaranteed for thirty years from time of installation.

Key

See also Sculpture for artists who work in this material.

- **X** Service, technique, or material is available
- **+** See listing for further information
- ***** Sometimes offers this service

	Distributor	Manufacturer	Standard designs	Custom designs from sketch	Custom designs from working drawing	Brochure available	Telephone estimates	Fiber glass reinforced plastic	Other materials	Panels	Cornices	Other architectural elements
Northeast												
Duro Fiber Wilmington, MA		X		X	X		X	X		X	X	X
Quality Prefabrication Toms River, NJ		X	X	X	X	X	X	X	+	X	X	X
Lawrence Wittman Copiague, NY		X	X	X	X	X	X	X		X	X	X
Alpha One Manufacturing Hicksville, NY		X	X	X	X	X	X	X		X	X	X
Saldarini & Pucci New York, NY		X	X	X	X		+	X	+	X	X	X
Ornato Decors Ridgewood, NY		X		X	X			X	+		X	X
Felber Studios Ardmore, PA	X	X	X	X	X	+		X	+		X	X
Gitco Clifton Heights, PA		X		X	X			X		X	X	X
Fypon Stewartstown, PA		X	X	X	X	X	X		+		X	X
Don Ray Fiberglass West Warwick, RI		X	X	X	X		X	X		X		
South												
Dimensional Plastics Hialeah, FL		+	X	X	X	X	X	X	+	X		X
Entol Industries Miami, FL		X	X			X	X		+			X
Focal Point Atlanta, GA		X	X	X	X	+			+		X	X
Mid-Atlantic Distributors Baltimore, MD	X					X	X	X		X		
Giannetti Studios Brentwood, MD	See listing under Stucco and Plaster											
Studio of Jack and Eva Grauer Memphis, TN	See listing under Sculpture											
Midwest												
C. G. Girolami Chicago, IL	See listing under Cast Stone											
J. C. Lauber South Bend, IN	See listing under Metals											
The Stone Center St. Louis, MO	X	X		X	X			X		X	X	X

Key

See also Sculpture for artists who work in this material.

- **X** Service, technique, or material is available
- **+** See listing for further information
- ***** Sometimes offers this service

	Distributor	Manufacturer	Standard designs	Custom designs from sketch	Custom designs from working drawing	Brochure available	Telephone estimates	Fiber glass reinforced plastic	Other materials	Panels	Cornices	Other architectural elements
Cincinnati Fiberglass Batavia, OH		X		X	X			+				
Fischer and Jirouch Cleveland, OH	See listing under Stucco and Plaster											
Aleph Plastics Columbus, OH		X		X	X			+	X	X	X	X
R. L. Industries Miamitown, OH		X		X	X	X	X	+		X	X	X
Owens Corning Fiberglas Toledo, OH	See Special listing under Concrete											
Hendrix, Heikkilä, and Terry Norman, OK	See listing under Murals											
Rockies and Far West												
American Fiberglass Phoenix, AZ		X	X	X	X		X	+		X	X	X
Leyva's J. P. Weaver Alhambra, CA	See listing under Cast Stone											
Parabam Compton, CA		X			X	X	X	+		X	X	X
Triangle Industries Los Angeles, CA		X	X		X	X	X	+	X	X	X	X
DFG Corporation Auburn, WA		+	X			X	X	+				X

PORCELAIN ENAMEL

Porcelain enamel is usually baked onto steel panels for large architectural installations. Smaller murals and inserts often have a copper backing. Porcelain enamel has a remarkable range of ornamental possibilities; almost anything that can be photographed can be made into a porcelain enamel panel, and virtually any color is possible. One company, **Wolverine Porcelain Enameling,** offers about forty stock colors as well as different textures and embossed patterns.

Line drawings or designs with broad areas of solid color are most easily reproduced in porcelain enamel. Designs are applied by silkscreening liquid porcelain onto a panel that was previously fired with a porcelain enamel background color. One silkscreen is required for each color. The alignment (registration) of succeeeding colors can be held to relatively close tolerances. Continuous-tone designs, with gradual shadings from light to dark, require the same kind of dot screen used to print photos in magazines and newspapers. Techniques are quite refined, and huge enlargements can be made without appreciable loss of detail.

Porcelain enamel is a durable material. It is acid-, scratch-, and abrasion-resistant; most markings are easily wiped off. Even aerosol paint can be removed without damaging the finish. Exterior porcelain enamel panels are almost maintenance free. Rainwater is usually sufficient to clean the surface.

In the past, porcelain enamel has usually been used for one-color, curtain wall applications; but there have been bolder approaches. More and more often it is used as a medium for murals. The exciting designs of Robert Venturi's Best Products Co. (see photo) are a welcome relief from the typically timid approach we often see.

A refreshingly bold approach to ornament. Porcelain enamel panels, Best Products Co. Venturi, Rauch & Scott-Brown, Architects. Fabricated by Ervite Corporation. (Photo courtesy of Venturi, Rauch & Scott-Brown, Architects)

"Kyoto Excursion." By Kay Whitcomb, La Jolla, CA. Champleve enamel on copper door viewer (8 by 12 inches)—peep hole in center. (Photo courtesy of Kay Whitcomb)

The artists and artist/fabricators who are listed in this section will do their own designs, or develop your design and have it fabricated. Manufacturers will fabricate your design. If they do not have a designer on staff, they usually require finished artwork (painting, drawing, photograph, etc.). Most can recommend an artist with whom they have worked.

Special Listings

Porcelain Enamel Institute, Architectural Division
Attn. Bill Weeks
1911 N. Fort Myer Drive
Rosslyn, VA 22209
(703) 527-5257

The Institute has some printed material giving information about porcelain enamel, and can give some technical advice. In addition, the Institute can recommend fabricators in your area.

Regional Listings

Unless otherwise noted, the companies listed below will give technical advice about the best ways to realize an idea and advice about installation.

Northeast

Phoenix Studio, Inc.
Portland, ME 04101

See listing under Glass.

"Song of Prometheus," enamel (2 by 3 feet). Shirley Rosenthal, Williamsville, NY. (Photo courtesy of Shirley Rosenthal)

Andree Lisette Herz
Allentown, NJ 08501

See listing under Murals.

Appco Porcelain Co., Inc.
6525 S. Crescent Boulevard
Pennsauken, NJ 08105
(609) 663-9010
(215) 925-7232

Distributor representing Wolverine Porcelain Enameling (see listing below). Can supply, in addition to murals, various architectural elements including fascias, copings, and formed ground stops. Custom designs can be hand-executed or silk-screened; line, continuous-tone, single color, or multicolor. A staff designer can work from your rough sketch or detailed drawing to develop a design in porcelain enamel. Will also design a mural from photos, drawings, or other graphic material. Maximum panel size: 5½ by 11½ feet. Can also process an artist-designed mural. Small or large orders.

Susan Kaprov
Brooklyn Heights, NY 11201

See listing under Murals.

Benoit Gilsoul
New York, NY 10001

See listing under Murals.

Nitza Tufino
New York, NY 10009

See listing under Murals.

Bernard Caster
South Butler, NY 13154

See listing under Murals.

David Wilson
South New Berlin, NY 13843

See listing under Glass.

Shirley Rosenthal Contemporary Enamels
76 Fenwick Road
Williamsville, NY 14221
(716) 632-4813

"Best Friends," enamel (2 by 3 feet). Shirley Rosenthal, Williamsville, NY. (Photo by Don Weigel Studio, courtesy of Shirley Rosenthal)

Artist doing enamel-on-copper wall panels, "both abstract and abstracted figures." Works with architects to create one-of-a-kind and limited-run commissions.

Ervite Corporation
4000 W. Ridge Road
Erie, PA 16505
(814) 838-1911

Large manufacturer of porcelain enamel on steel murals, maps, graphics, and graphic arts. Can do single panels up to 5 by 12 feet.

Justine Presha DeVan
Philadelphia, PA 19131

See listing under Murals.

Rudolph N. Rohn, Co., Inc.
Pittsburgh, PA 15216

See listing under Murals.

South

Bill J. Hammon
Islamorda, FL 33036

See listing under Murals.

Porcelain, Inc.
P.O. Box 18938
3835 Viscount, Suite 13
Memphis, TN 38118
(901) 795-3060

Distributors for American Valve and Enameling Corp.; Cement Enamel Corp.; Ferro Enameling Co.; Span Metals Corporation; Glasweld International; KoolShade Corporation. Can supply murals, decorated panels (silkscreened or hand-painted), and architectural elements. Can design a mural from drawings, photos, etc.

Midwest

Mira Jedwabnik Van Doren
Jedwabnik and Co.
410 South Michigan Avenue
Chicago, IL 60605
(312) 427-8593 (office)
(312) 475-1882 (studio)

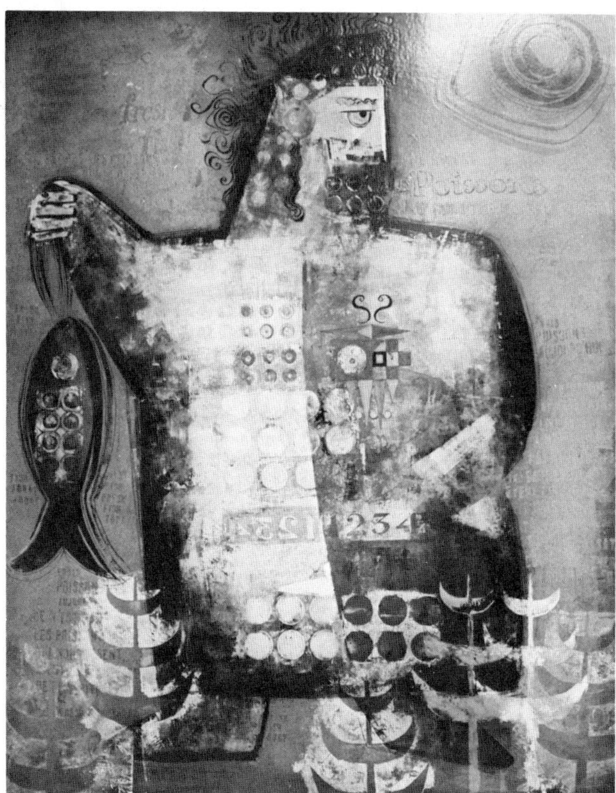

"The Fisherman," enamel on steel (36 by 45 inches). Kay Whitcomb, La Jolla, CA. (Collection of Mr. and Mrs. Alfred King, Austin, TX, photo courtesy of Kay Whitcomb)

This artist specializes in architectural porcelain enamel designs on steel. Among her many commissions are 250 pairs of elevator doors for the Hyatt Regency Hotel chain. She can do hand-painted or silkscreened custom designs and can work from a rough sketch. Large or small orders. She subcontracts the fabrication, and works in the factory while the panels are made. The maximum size for a single panel is 4 by 10 feet. Prefers large, architectural commissions.

Wolverine Porcelain Enameling Co.
3350 Scotten Avenue
Detroit, MI 48210
(313) 897-7727

A large-scale manufacturer that has been producing architectural porcelain enamel for the past sixty years. Products include architectural wall systems; Wolverine has done murals and graphics for subway systems in New York City, Boston, and Washington, DC. Custom designs can be hand-executed or silkscreened; line, continuous-tone, single color, or multicolor. Can process artist-designed murals. In addition to approximately forty colors, Wolverine offers a number of different textures (smooth, ripple, multicolor mottle, and aggregate [U.S. & Foreign Patents]), plus embossed patterns in any finish or color. Laminated panels of uncoated stainless steel, aluminum, and other facings also available. One hundred percent architecturally oriented in manufacturing facilities.

Elevator mural based on printed circuits. Porcelain enamel (approx. 5 by 7 feet) at M.I.T. Jedwabnik & Co., Chicago, IL. (Photo by Margo Foote, courtesy of Jedwabnik & Co.)

PEFCO
3207 Labore Road
St. Paul, MN 55110
(612) 484-1814

This manufacturer works directly with architects in the five-state area around St. Paul. For work outside this area, write to PEFCO for a list of their representatives. Fabricates porcelain enamel on steel: murals, panels, soffits, fascias, gravel stops, coves, and other architectural elements. PEFCO fabricated half of the porcelain enamel panels for the New York City and Boston subway systems. Custom designs from measured drawing or finished artwork; can also give design suggestions. Line, continuous-tone, and multicolor designs. Installation advice given to architects. All size orders taken.

Hendrix, Heikkilä, and Terry, Inc.
Norman, OK 73069

See listing under Murals.

American Porcelain Enamel Co. of Dallas
Attn. John P. Hampton
3506 Singleton
Dallas, TX 75212
(214) 637-4775

Manufactures various types of architectural elements including panels, fascias, copings, and ground stops. Also does murals and decorative panels. Can do hand-painted or silkscreened custom designs from measured drawings only. Can design a mural from photographs, etc.; will process artist-designed murals.

American Porcelain Enameling, Inc.
Attn. C. J. Cook, Vice President
1130 West Loop N.
Houston, TX 77055
(713) 869-3731

A manufacturer that can fabricate panels and various architectural elements such as fascias and copings. Also fabricates custom panels; does silkscreened or hand-painted decorative designs; can process an artist's work. Will fabricate your design from measured drawing.

Conrad Schmitt Studios, Inc.
New Berlin, WI 53151

See listing under Murals.

Caryl Yasko
Whitewater, WI 53190

See listing under Murals.

Rockies and Far West

Kay Whitcomb
1631 Milmulus Way
La Jolla, CA 92037
(714) 454-0590

An artist and fabricator whose enamel on steel and copper work ranges in size from a few inches square to a 9-by-96-foot mural for the United Arab Emirates airport (made from 9-by-45-foot sections). She can do panels, murals, and architectural elements including fascias. The panels are hand-painted or silkscreened; designs can be continuous-tone, line, single color, or multicolor. She can design a mural from photos or other graphic material. Gives installation advice. One-of-a-kind orders only.

Joseph Young
Los Angeles, CA 90019

See listing under Murals.

Florinda Leighton
5432 Glenhaven Avenue
Riverside, CA 92506
(714) 682-2309

Primarily murals in enamel on copper, some monumental in scale (6 by 24 feet). Also works in acrylics. Realistic and stylized. "I do everything and anything my clients want, from people to animals to symbolic things, even flora and fauna of the desert." Supervises installation.

D & W Construction
Attn. Dieter Walter
3596 S. 300 W. 13
Salt Lake City, UT 84115
(801) 261-4078

Represents American Porcelain Enamel (see listing above). Can supply various architectural elements, plus hand-painted or silkscreened custom designs. Can have a mural designed from your graphic material; can have artist-designed murals processed.

Pioneer Enamel Manufacturing Co., Inc.
5531 Airport Way S.
Seattle, WA 98108
(206) 762-7540

Manufacturer and artist fabricator. Can produce murals, panels, and architectural elements such as fascias. Can supply custom shapes and custom designs on panels (silkscreened and hand-painted). Staff designer can provide you with a design or realize yours from a rough sketch; can also design a mural from drawings, photos, or other material. Pioneer does not give technical or installation advice.

Key

See also Sculpture for artists who work in this material.

- **X** Service, technique, or material is available
- **+** See listing for further information
- ***** Sometimes offers this service

	Distributor	Manufac-turer	Artist	Murals	Architectural elements	Custom shapes	Custom designs	Will design	Brochure or photos available
Northeast									
Phoenix Studio Portland, ME	See listing under Glass								
Andree Lisette Herz Allentown, NJ	See listing under Murals								
Appco Porcelain Pennsauken, NJ	X			X	X	X	X	X	X
Susan Kaprov Brooklyn Heights, NY	See listing under Murals								
Benoit Gilsoul New York, NY	See listing under Murals								
Nitza Tufino New York, NY	See listing under Murals								
Bernard Caster South Butler, NY	See listing under Murals								
David Wilson South New Berlin, NY	See listing under Glass								
Shirley Rosenthal Williamsville, NY			X	X		X	X	X	X
Ervite Corporation Erie, PA		X		X	X	X	X	X	X
Justine Presha DeVan Philadelphia, PA	See listing under Murals								
Rudolph N. Rohin Pittsburgh, PA	See listing under Murals								
South									
Bill J. Hammon Islamorda, FL	See listing under Murals								
Porcelain Memphis, TN	X			X	X	X	X	X	
Midwest									
Mira Jedwabnik Van Doren Chicago, IL			X	X	X	X	X	X	X
Wolverine Porcelain Detroit, MI	X				X	X	X	+	X
PEFCO St. Paul, MN		X		X	X	X	+		X
Hendrix, Heikkilä, and Terry Norman, OK	See listing under Murals								
American Porcelain of Dallas Dallas, TX	X			X	X	X	*		

Key

See also Sculpture for artists who work in this material.

- **X** Service, technique, or material is available
- **+** See listing for further information
- ***** Sometimes offers this service

	Distributor	Manufac-turer	Artist	Murals	Architectural elements	Custom shapes	Custom designs	Will design	Brochure or photos available
American Porcelain Houston, TX		X			X	X	X		
Conrad Schmitt Studios New Berlin, WI	See listing under Murals								
Caryl Yasko Whitewater, WI	See listing under Murals								
Rockies and Far West									
Kay Whitcomb La Jolla, CA			X	X	X	X	X	X	X
Joseph Young Los Angeles, CA	See listing under Murals								
Florinda Leighton Riverside, CA			X	X				X	X
D & W Construction Salt Lake City, UT	X			X	X	X	X		
Pioneer Enamel Seattle, WA		X		X	X	X	X	X	

SCULPTURE

It is possible that the first Western architecture was actually a kind of sculpture. Whatever their original purpose, the eerie stone menhirs of Great Britain and the northwestern coast of Europe are simple—if gigantic—sculptural devices that define space in a minimal, modernist sort of way. Our reason for including listings of sculptors should be obvious: since its beginnings, architecture has been embellished by free-standing and bas-relief sculpture in every imaginable material from delicate wood and terracotta to the more durable metals to the relatively immutable limestone, marble, and granite.

The sculptors listed below work in many styles and materials. A number of them are willing to develop an idea with the architect. We should mention that artists who have referred to themselves as "sculptors" are listed below; in other sections such as ceramics, iron, and wood, there are artists who can execute bas-relief and free-standing sculpture and who qualify as sculptors in everything but title. So check these other sections as well.

Regional Listings

Northeast

Stanley Bleifeld
27 Spring Valley Road
Weston, CT 06883
(203) 227-0490

One of the relatively few sculptors who does architectural terracotta. Also works in marble, wood, bronze, cast stone, bonded bronze, and corten steel. Specializes in representational figures and landscapes. Makes own molds for cast work.

Richard Fisher
U.S. Bells
P.O. Box 73
Prospect Harbor, ME 04669
(207) 963-7184

A maker of "wind bells," large and small constructions made of finely crafted wood and cast bronze. The bells are rung by clappers activated by the wind pushing against a balanced "fin." Bells range in size from around 6 inches to 4 or 5 feet high. The larger pieces are free-standing; smaller ones hang or can be fixed to walls. Some serve as doorbells. Inquiries are invited concerning works in progress and commissions.

Mico Kauman
23 Marion Drive
Tewksbury, MA 01876
(617) 851-4220

Does sculpture in any traditional or modern material. Works in ceramics, marble, bronze, cast stone, and limestone. Bas-relief and medallions.

A. Monti Granite Co., Inc.
Quincy, MA 02169

See listing under Stone.

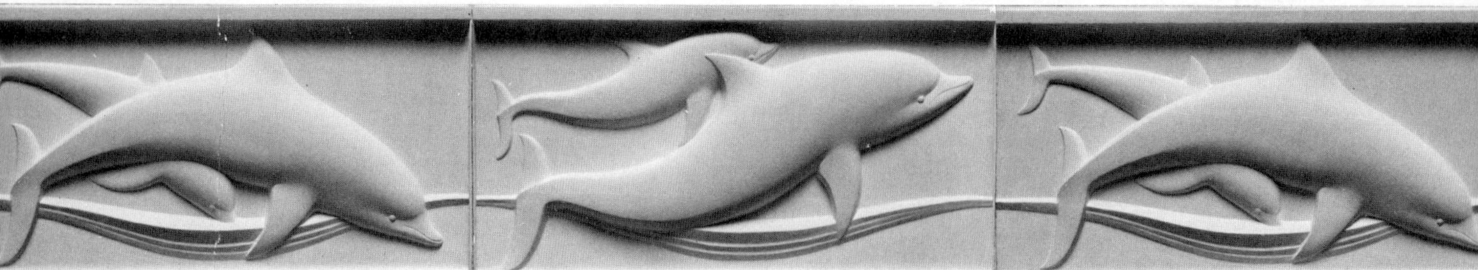

Dolphin frieze; cast bronze. John Edward Svenson, Upland, CA.

George Ciocher, Inc.
5184 71st Street
Guttenberg, NJ 07093
(201) 861-3150

A sculptor doing forging, welding, and casting. Works in wrought iron, steel, bronze, copper, plastics, wood, marble, and cement. Can interpret an architect's idea.

Anthony Notaro
14 Brookfield Way
Mendham, NJ 07945
(201) 543-7094

Marble, wood, bronze, cast stone, limestone, brass, copper, and bonded bronze. Style: "representational sculpture in the Great Tradition." Free-standing and bas-relief.

Roland Roberge
491 Rosedale Road
Princeton, NJ 08540
(609) 924-6329

A stone carver and sculptor working in marble; does bas-relief, statues, gargoyles, etc., in "figural" style. He can provide his own designs or execute an architect's, from a rough sketch or more detailed information. Will travel to carve "in place." In addition to stone, he carves wood, models clay, is a mold-maker and casts in plaster and bronze.

Michael Gressel
Gressel Place
Armonk, NY 10504
(914) 273-3282

Carver and sculptor. Works in marble; carves Doric, Ionic, and Corinthian capitals; gargoyles; arches; and moldings (including egg and dart). Does bas-relief and free-standing sculpture. He can help in the design or provide his own designs; works in floral, figural, geometric, and modern styles. Gives technical advice about stone; can make a pattern; and can work from a rough sketch or more elaborate information.

George Sell
Brooklyn, NY 11217

See listing under Glass.

Schwartz's Forge and Metalworks
Deansboro, NY 13328

See listing under Iron.

Alton S. Tobey
Larchmont, NY 10538

See listing under Murals.

Michael J. Colonna
79–12 Metropolitan Avenue
Middle Village, NY 11379
(212) 326-1166

Granite and marble; can do cutting, carving, and sandblasting of bas-relief and free-standing sculpture and moldings. Works in floral and figural styles. Can make a pattern for stone cutting from sketch or sample.

Renata M. Schwebel
36 Silver Birch Drive
New Rochelle, NY 10804
(914) 632-6523

Wood, bronze, plastics, lucite, bonded bronze, corten steel, stainless steel, and aluminum. Specializes in welded metal constructions. Free-standing and bas-relief. Schwebel's work is shown at the **Sculpture Center, 167 E. 69th Street, New York, NY** (212) 737-9870.

Mitzi Cunliffe
200 Central Park S.
New York, NY 10019
(212) 246-3777

Specializes in large, abstract architectural sculptures for mass production; figurative carving for "one-of-a-kind." Has worked in marble, bronze, concrete, limestone, and fiber glass. Willing to interpret an architect's idea. Does free-standing and bas-relief designs, carved and cast. Commissions range from a 4-ton carved stone bas-relief with heraldic devices to large-scale sculptural wall patterns composed of mass-produced fiber glass modules. Brochure $5.00.

Domenico Facci
248 W. 14th Street
New York, NY 10011
(212) 929-6142

Works in marble, wood, bronze, cast stone, limestone, terracotta, plaster, and bonded bronze. He does all types of sculpture—"from monumental to miniature." Free-standing and bas-relief.

Richard Lichtenstein
237 Lafayette Street
New York, NY 10012
(212) 966-9799

Lively, voluptuous, sculptured grilles, gates, railings, bas-relief panels, sign hangers, gazebos, weather vanes, and any other object (large or small) that can be made in iron or steel. Hot forging; custom designs. Will fabricate architect's designs from rough sketch, photo, or sample. He has also interpreted paintings in metal. Large, small, or one-of-a-kind orders. Estimates: prefers to have some detailed information. Also works in stainless steel, brass, and copper; inlays pewter in wood, steel, and other materials.

Ivan Olszewski
140 W. Houston Street
New York, NY 10012
(212) 777-8837

Incision, burning, and bas-relief wood carving. Sculptures, panels, murals and moldings. Advises about installation.

The Sculpture Studio, Inc.
Attn. William Bowie
441 Lafayette Street
New York, NY 10003
(212) 777-1414

Sculpts in a variety of metals but recommends stainless steel for exteriors. Specializes in wall-hung sculpture; has readymade pieces. Color brochure.

"Wissahickon Valley Gate," forged iron (8 by 8 feet). Installed, Chestnut Street Park, Philadelphia, PA. Christopher Ray, Sculptor, Philadelphia, PA (1979). Photo courtesy of Christopher Ray)

Ned Smyth
14 Harrison Street
New York, NY 10013
(212) 966-7431

Does mosaic and tapestries as well as bronze and cast stone sculpture. Works in variety of styles to suit situation: figurative, floral, abstract, realistic, architectural. Only original work. Free-standing and bas-relief. Smyth's work is shown at the **Holly Solomon Gallery, 392 West Broadway, New York, NY** (212) 925-1900.

George Gách
212 Willow Street
Roslyn Heights, NY 11577
(516) 621-5946

Marble, wood, bronze, cast stone, plastics, brass, lucite, bonded bronze, and steel. Prefers figurative, realism, and church symbols.

Clemente Spampinato
36 Littleworth Lane
Sea Cliff, NY 11579
(516) 671-5037

Specializes in sport and western sculpture, free-standing, bas-, and high-relief pieces. Marble, bronze, limestone, and copper; makes own molds for cast work.

Thomas G. Lomedico
60 Main Street
Tappan, NY 10983
(914) 359-2361

Works in brass, marble, wood, and bronze. Variety of styles from classical to contemporary. Free-standing, bas-relief, and medallions.

H. J. Schaller
P.O. Box 145
Valhalla, NY 10595
(914) 949-3240

Works in limestone, granite, and marble; floral, figural, geometric, or modern styles. Has photos of work. Free-standing and bas-relief.

Donald R. Miller
RD 2, Box 229
Warwick, NY 10990
(914) 258-4461

Specializes in animal sculpture in marble, wood, bronze, limestone, terracotta, and a variety of mixed media. He is willing to work with an architect to interpret an idea and will travel to carve stone "in place." Among other commissions, he has carved several gargoyles for the Washington Cathedral. His works can be seen in the **Fisher Galleries, 1509 Connecticut Avenue, N.W., Washington, DC 20036** (202) 265-6255.

Frudakis Gallery
1829 Chestnut Street
Philadelphia, PA 19103
(215) 567-5777

Evangelos Frudakis: classic realism; Zenos Frudakis,

Philip Schrenker, and Gerd Hesness: contemporary realism. These sculptors do free-standing and bas-relief in marble and bronze. Will work with an architect to interpret an idea.

Maddalo Enterprises
256 W. Erie Avenue
Philadelphia, PA 19140
(215) 426-8900

Plastics and neon art sculpture.

Christopher T. Ray, Sculptor
315 E. Wister Street
Philadelphia, PA 19144
(215) 438-7129

Specializes in energetic, lively, wrought iron sculpture for architectural settings: wrought iron gates with fantastic animals and wrought bronze sculpture. Also works with carved wood.

Designers Forge
2366 Eldridge Street
Pittsburgh, PA 15217
(412) 421-5112

Work executed in brass, copper, stainless steel, and corten steel; free-standing and bas-relief.

Jozef Stachura
2306 Marbury Road
Pittsburgh, PA 15221
(412) 241-9002

Welding, casting, stone carving, and hammered metalwork. Materials include granite, marble, limestone, wood, bronze, copper, wrought iron, and steel. Does modern figures or abstract style. Can interpret an architect's idea.

Clifton A. Prokop
815 Clay Avenue
Scranton, PA 18510

Free-standing and bas-relief sculpture in a contemporary style; metals (cast and welded), woods, and plastics. Maquettes in bronze on display at **HOM Gallery, 2121 P Street N.W., Washington, DC 20037** (202) 466-4076.

Eric Parks
Green Valley Road
Unionville, PA 19375
(215) 486-0426

Bronze, steel, and corten steel. Makes own molds for cast work. Skillfully done, extremely lifelike portraits, figures, animals—life-size and larger than life-size. He did a 9-foot-high memorial of Elvis Presley. Most subjects (judging from the catalog) come from contemporary life, but often with historical overtones. Free-standing and bas-relief.

Edward Fenno Hoffman III
353 Oak Terrace
Wayne, PA 19087
(215) 688-5270
(215) 688-4279

"World Tree," carved brick relief by Mara Smith (15 by 18 feet). Loews Anatole Hotel, Dallas, TX. (Photo by Grace Williams, courtesy of Mara Smith)

Brass, bronze, marble, bonded bronze, and limestone. Free-standing and bas-relief. Showroom.

Giuliano Cecchinelli
RD 4
Barre, VT 05641
(802) 479-0339

Fabricator, carver, and sculptor. Cutting and carving—including sandblasting and incising—of capitals (Doric, Ionic, Corinthian, and composite), moldings, gargoyles, and arches. Does bas-relief and free-standing sculpture of his own design. Works in limestone, granite, and marble; floral, figural, geometric, and modern styles. Can advise during design process; can make a pattern from sketch or more detailed information. Will travel to carve "in place."

Frank C. Gaylord
P.O. Box 464
Barre, VT 05641
(802) 476-6711

Marble, wood, bronze, plastics, bonded bronze, and granite. Prefers carving granite in a representational, figurative style; free-standing and bas-relief. Will travel to carve "in place."

South

Julian H. Harris
177 5th Street N.W.
Atlanta, GA 30313
(404) 892-6513

Works in marble, wood, lucite, bonded bronze, corten steel, and limestone. Makes own molds for cast work. Free-standing and bas-relief.

Thomas H. Williams
22 E. Andrews Drive
Atlanta, GA 30305
(404) 233-7578

Creates carved doors and large, bas-relief panels, figures, furniture. Does free-standing, abstract objects in wood and bronze.

Barney Bright
2031 Frankfort Avenue
Louisville, KY 40206
(502) 895-7107

Bronze, brass, steel, lead, aluminum, and other metals. Prefers realistic figures—human and animals—and will do portraits. Free-standing and bas-relief. Has showroom.

Anthony DiMarco
2948 Gr. Rte. St. John
New Orleans, LA 70119
(504) 948-3128

Marble, wood, cast stone, limestone, plastic, and bonded bronze. Specializes in direct carving. Has showroom. Free-standing and bas-relief. Also does murals.

Carved cedar stump; play sculpture. Richard Beyer, Seattle, WA. (Photo courtesy of Richard Beyer)

Ralph Ransome De Witt
404 W. Battimon Street No. 11
Baltimore, MD 21201
(301) 685-5940

"Restoration artist/relief sculptor." Plastics, lucite, copper, bonded bronze, and epoxy. Specializes in relief portraits. Willing to interpret an architect's idea. Showroom visits by appointment only.

Giannetti Studios
Robert L. Giannetti
3806 38th Street
Brentwood, MD 20722
(301) 927-0033

Works in epoxy and plaster (interior only). Will also duplicate and repair old plasterwork. Has showroom. Free-standing and bas-relief. Brochure $3.00 (refundable with first order).

Hal McWhinney
The Thought Gallery
10111 Frederick Avenue
Kensington, MD 20795
(301) 942-3554

Works in plastics, marble, wood, and cast stone. Style: abstract; free-standing and bas-relief. Visits to gallery by appointment.

Carved wood bas-relief (6 by 8 feet) commemorating the work of the Sisters of Providence and the growth of Alaska over the past seventy-eight years. Providence Hospital, Anchorage, AK. John E. Svenson, Sculptor, Upland, CA. (Photo courtesy of John E. Svenson)

Studio of Jack and Eva Grauer
1261 W. Perkins Road
Memphis, TN 38117
(901) 683-9540

Free-standing and bas-relief sculpture. The studio also produces a variety of architectural elements in cast stone, including balusters, bas-reliefs, and cornices. They do castings in a variety of materials for reproduction of their own designs and the designs of others; can work from sketch, photo, clay or plaster model, and produce the final work in a variety of surfaces. The Grauers also make molds for brick manufacturers and manufacture brick themselves, specializing in restoration work.

Ted Guenther
Rte. 1, Box 10
Rocky Gap, VA 24366
(304) 325-8715

Laminated wood, brass, bronze, copper, cast and built up cement, stainless steel, and corten steel. Makes own molds for cast work. Has showroom. Free-standing and bas-relief.

"Winged Tile" series (4 by 4 inches). By MaryAnn Fariello, Alexandria, TN. (Photo by Jane Porter, courtesy of MaryAnn Fariello)

Raymond Kaskey
2221 Hall Place N.W.
Washington, DC 20007
(202) 337-2305

Works in bronze, bonded bronze, and cast stone; free-standing and bas-relief. Makes own molds for cast work. Specializes in realistic figural and botanical subjects, and is willing to work with an architect to interpret an idea. Has photos of work.

Don Turano
2625 Connecticut Avenue N.W.
Washington, DC 20008
(202) 462-5044

Sculpts in marble, wood, bronze, limestone, and plastics. Free-standing and bas-relief.

Harold C. Vogel
Wood & Stone, Inc.
5920 Old Saw Mill Road
Fairfax, VA 22030
(703) 830-8806

A carver who apprenticed in Germany; carves mainly limestone (sometimes granite) and wood. Will do his own designs, "more contemporary," or carve the designs of others in any style. Worked on the Washington Cathedral for ten years and carved "hundreds" of gargoyles. Does cutting, carving, incising, bas-relief, statues, and architectural elements—arches, moldings, rustication, gargoyles, and all types of column capitals. Can work from a rough sketch, photo, sample, or measured drawing. Will travel to carve "in place." Vogel will supply, on request, a list of architects for whom he has worked and the locations of his carvings. Brochure available for carved lettering.

Skip Roberts
P.O. Box 269
Bethany, WV 26032
(304) 829-4818

Works in steel, iron, wood, and bronze. Prefers welded steel constructions with mixed media; "nonfigurative—formal abstraction, site specific." Free-standing only. Brochure $1.00.

Silvana Cenci
13C Harmony Route
Spencer, WV 25276
(304) 927-4679

Cenci has developed an innovative technique using controlled explosions to shape stainless steel sculptures. "I can actually explode entire walls in stainless steel and burn gold on some parts of the surface to give a glowing patina. My work is very suitable for outside façades since it is practically indestructable and vandal-proof." Free-standing and bas-relief sculpture; also fountains. Some reliefs are composed of modular elements and so can vary in size.

Bill Hopen
Hopen Studio
268 North Hill
Sutton, WV 26601
(304) 765-5611

Marble, wood, bronze, cast stone, limestone, and brass. Cement work is ferro cement carved and cast. Preferred style: figurative. Can carve any stone, any size, specializing in bas-relief. Can interpret architect's idea but would like to have some artistic input. Has a showroom and working studio open to customers. Free-standing and bas-relief.

Midwest

Gast Monuments, Inc.
4806 N. Clark Street
Chicago, IL 60640
(312) 561-0427

Bronze, Bedford stone, granite, and fiber glass. Makes own molds for fiber glass work. Free-standing and bas-relief sculpture. Showroom.

Mara Smith
227 Spring Avenue
Naperville, IL 60540

A sculptor working in stoneware and brick; free-standing and bas-relief. The brick relief sculptures are carved in the factory while the brick is "green," fired and then assembled at the site. She will work in any style, any subject matter. Supervises large installations.

Ferdinand Rebechini Studio
928 Busse Highway
Park Ridge, IL 60068
(312) 945-9188

Marble, wood, bronze, bonded bronze, stainless steel, and corten steel. Free-standing and bas-relief; does casting and welding. Prefers contemporary style but will do realistic subjects. Has showroom.

Richard Bauer
RR 5 Box 121
Columbus, IN 47201
(812) 342-3795

Wrought iron, bronze, copper, and steel. Style: contemporary; free-standing and bas-relief.

Warner Williams
Geodesic Dome Studio
Culver, IN 46511
(219) 842-2593

Specializes in bronze medallions. Can interpret an architect's idea from a rough sketch. Has showroom.

Joseph N. DeLauro
7560 Bircklan Drive
Canton, MI 48187
(313) 453-4498
(313) 963-6112 (ext. 494)

Marble, wood, bronze, cast stone, steel, plastics, and other materials; figurative, abstract, and geometric styles. Will develop an architect's idea based on rough sketch or more detailed information. This sculptor has also created a variety of sculpted blocks to be used as solar screens; some form a flat plane; others are more three-dimensional. They are based on 12-inch module and use a lightweight aggregate. Will also be available in aluminum, bronze, and plastic.

Raubar Granite Co., Inc.
9455 W. Fort Street
Detroit, MI 48209
(313) 841-3991

Executes sculpture of all kinds in granite, marble, bronze, and limestone—free-standing and bas-relief. Specialty: realistic sculpture in stone and bronze. Can also do cornerstones and architectural elements. Raubar has a showroom but no brochure.

Eyrie Studios
Attn. Marty Eichinger
220 Mill Street
Lansing, MI 48933
(517) 485-0101

Plastics, bronze, cast stone, bonded bronze, and silicone ("for tactile sculpture"). Does own molds for cast work. Specializes in large-scale "fluid and rhythmic forms." Would work with an architect to interpret an idea. Also does custom bronze plaques. Brochure $1.50.

Marshall M. Fredericks Studio
4113 N. Woodward Avenue
Royal Oak, MI 48072
(313) 549-3666

Marble, wood, bronze, cast stone, limestone, plastics, copper, steel, granite, and aluminum. Prefers "personal stylizations of natural forms." Free-standing and bas-relief.

Reno Studios, Inc.
Attn. Reno Gastaldi
6905 Manchester Avenue
St. Louis, MO 63143
(314) 781-2382
(314) 991-1461

Normally works in clay, from which model is made and then translated into bronze or stone. Also makes cement castings in his studio; he can make plaster models as patterns for stone cutting or casting in other materials. Mainly realistic works, but also does work in other styles. Brochure (free to dealers). Free-standing and bas-relief.

Herring Coe
2554 Gladys
Beaumont, TX 77702
(713) 832-7386

Works in marble, wood, bronze, cast stone, limestone; makes clay and plaster models for execution in any material. Specializes in figures; free-standing and bas-relief. Brochure; will also lend photos of work.

Prof. Heri Bert Bartscht
Sculptor Studio-Gallery
1125 N. Canterbury Court
Dallas, TX 75208

Wrought iron, marble, wood, bronze, cast stone, limestone, brass, copper, and steel. Free-standing and bas-relief; figurative and ornamental.

Larry M. Ludtke
10127 Whiteside
Houston, TX 77034
(713) 468-0769

Works in marble and bronze; makes own molds for cast work. Brochure shows skilled, realistic figure sculpture, including a moving Pieta located in St. Mary's Seminary, Houston. Is willing to interpret an architect's idea. Free-standing and bas-relief.

Richard Herr
c/o Art Independent Gallery
222 Broad Street
Lake Geneva, WI 53147
(414) 248-3612

"Contemporary, nonobjective" sculpture in wood, plastics, bronze, copper, cement, steel, and bonded bronze; free-standing and bas-relief. Makes own molds for cast work. Is willing to interpret an architect's idea.

Al Blaukschien
1479 N. Farwell
Milwaukee, WI 53202
(414) 276-8686

Sculpture with neon and other media connected to sign-maker's trade.

Rockies and Far West

James Greenburg
27289 Sleepy Hollow Avenue S. No. 104
Hayward, CA 94545
(415) 782-9310

Sculpts in plastics, brass, bronze, cast stone, stainless steel, and corten steel. Creates "solar sculptures" using heliostats (solar trackers), prisms, and lenses for the daytime projection of colored light. These range in size from garden sculptures to mountaintop works projecting over forty miles. Specialties: "modern, monumental, nonrepresentational, and traditional representational." Willing to work with an architect. Free-standing and bas-relief.

Lyons & O'Haver, Inc.
8180 Parkway Drive
La Mesa, CA 92041
(714) 463-7156

This company produces sandcastings exclusively; specializes in murals that can be made in sections for large installations. All castings are made of high-density plaster, reinforced throughout with fiber glass strands with a permanent natural silica sand surface. These can be used outdoors if properly treated. A selection of stock pieces. Will do custom work from sketch or more detailed information.

Fairbanks and Fairbanks, Inc.
1204 San Fernando Road
Los Angeles, CA 90065
(213) 222-0126
(213) 222-0127
(213) 221-6442

Wood, bronze, cast stone, brass, copper, and steels. Specialty is open-face bronze reworked with heliarc. Free-standing and bas-relief. This company also works in glass. Will do stained, faceted, etched, beveled, and sandblasted glass; also does three-dimensional faceted glass, casting own slabs.

Mary Fuller
2955 Sonoma Mountain Road
Petaluma, CA 94952
(707) 795-4612

Specializes in direct carving of concrete. Large sections are poured and carved with knife or ax while still wet, then finished with a wood rasp. "The shapes are abstract animals or anthropomorphic forms drawn from fantasy and mythology." She also works in bronze. Can interpret an architect's idea.

Spero Anargyros
2503 Clay Street
San Francisco, CA 94115
(415) 931-7171

Works in marble, wood, bronze, cast stone, limestone, copper, brass, and granite. Style: "traditional-representational." This sculptor has done architectural ornament in the past. Free-standing and bas-relief.

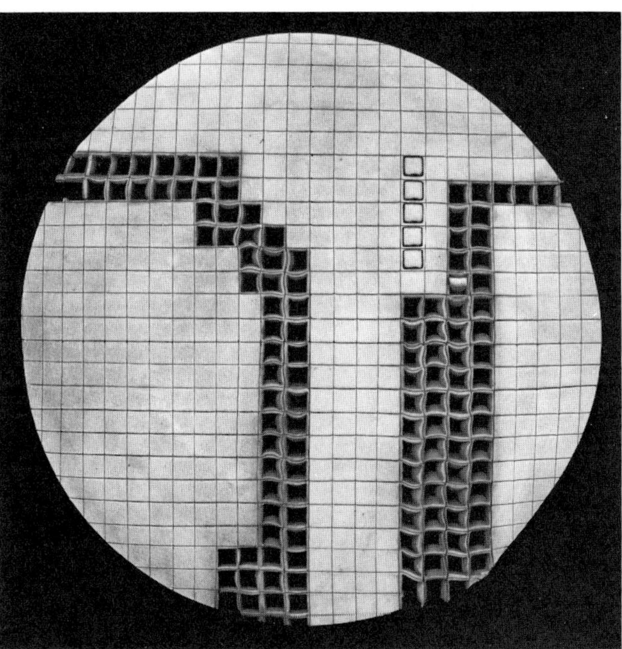

Porcelain wall relief (18-inch diameter, convex.) By John Rogers, Portland, OR. (Photo courtesy of John Rogers)

Anthony Stellon
1670 15th Street
San Francisco, CA 94103
(415) 621-0660

Marble, wood, bronze, cast stone, plastics, brass, bonded bronze, stainless steel, and corten steel. Prefers realistic sculpture but is happy to work with architect's preference. Showroom. Free-standing and bas-relief.

Franco Vianello
Art Bronzes
P.O. Box 186
2584 Grant Avenue
San Lorenzo, CA 94580
(415) 278-0520

Bronze bas-relief and free-standing sculpture. Specialty: original statuary bronzes, small to monumental, in realistic style. Makes own models; can do small or large runs.

Jacques Overhoff, Architectural Sculptor
333 Margarite Drive
San Rafael, CA 94901
(415) 885-0675

Free-standing and bas-relief sculpture in wood, brick, precast concrete, bronze, and steel; makes his own molds for cast work. He aims at achieving "integral relationships between forms and spaces in permanent architectural environments." Does own designs only. Installs; has California contractor's license.

Catherine Brant
Brantscroft
7165 E. Hurlbut Avenue
Sebastopol, CA 95472
(707) 823-1259

She has done hangings, murals, and other sculptural pieces combining stoneware and fiber. Also stoneware sculpture including free-standing pieces and entire fireplaces.

Enrique de la Vega
4507 Atoll Avenue
Sherman Oaks, CA 91403
(213) 981-0185

Marble, wood, bronze, cast stone, limestone, plastics, brass, bonded bronze. Also does slate carving. Portraiture in bronze. Will do both figurative and abstract work. Free-standing and bas-relief.

John Edward Svenson
2480 Vista Drive
Upland, CA 91786
(714) 981-1865

Marble, wood, bronze, cast stone, brass, copper, plastics, and bonded bronze. Makes his own molds for casting. Specializes in sculpture of marine life, animals, birds; also does complex, narrative historical panels. Free-standing and bas-relief.

Hal Reed
20914 Pilar Road
Woodland Hills, CA 91364
(213) 884-6278

Bronze, cast stone, plastics, and bonded bronze. Prefers realistic bas-relief.

Roy Erickson
Erickson Memorial Co.
920 Speer Boulevard
Denver, CO 80204
(303) 571-5151

Marble, limestone, and granite. Mainly memorials; also free-standing pieces and sundials.

Ree Gorshow
3701 W. First Avenue
Denver, CO 80219
(303) 936-2809

Works in marble, wood, bronze, plastics, brass, copper, and steel. Contemporary style, "fountains are a favorite." Also does sundials. Free-standing and bas-relief. Showroom only.

Robert Tully
615 Quitman Street
Denver, CO 80204
(303) 534-0976

Works in wood; free-standing and bas-relief pieces. Can interpret an architect's idea. Preferred style: abstract and geometric patterns.

Ken Williams
Sangre de Cristo Art Center
210 N. Santa Fe
Pueblo, CO 81003
(303) 543-0134

Specialty is brick murals that are carved "green" in the factory (glazed or unglazed). Works with Summit Brick for these murals; with Sangre de Cristo for ceramics. Preferred style: abstract, symbols, figures, animals. Sometimes does installations. Can do frost-free ceramic moldings and borders and can put a hand-carved relief pattern on pavers.

Leopold Lambo
5905 N. Minnesota
Portland, OR 97217
(503) 289-3863

Wood, bronze, limestone, brass, and copper. Specializes in wood and bronze sculpture; free-standing and bas-relief.

John Rogers
3125 S.E. Van Water Avenue
Portland, OR 97222
(503) 653-5230

A ceramic sculptor who does slip cast architectural bas-reliefs in porcelain—suitable for exterior use in cold climates. He does porcelain lighting fixtures, moderate size "wall reliefs," and large-scale brick and porcelain modular relief sculptures. He is presently researching the possibility of using these sculpture/molding techniques to design form liners for concrete. His present works range in size from a foot or so across to 24 feet high. In addition to hand-pressing patterns on tiles, he does sandblasted and handpainted glazed patterns; also decorates commercial tiles. He creates custom designs for bas-reliefs and murals; he installs; and he can work up an architect's design from a rough sketch or pattern. He has collaborated with fiber artists on large sculptures.

LeRoy I. Setziol
Rte. 2, Box 192
Sheridan, OR 97378
(503) 843-3614

Works in marble, limestone, and all types of woods, (mostly hardwoods). Free-standing and bas-relief.

Nils Lou
Willamina, OR 97396
(503) 876-4984

Bas-relief sculpture in hot glass combined with ceramics, stainless steel, bronze, or corten steel. Preferred style: "abstract realism." Does install; has photos of work.

Edward V. Fraughton
10353 S. 1300 West
South Jordon, UT 84065
(801) 254-3303

Marble and bronze. Prefers to sculpt "representational works in classical American style." Does free-standing and bas-relief. Brochure $0.25.

Leogriff, hand-carved in granite using power tools. Sculptor: Harold C. Vogel, Fairfax, Virginia. The Asia Society, New York City, Edward Larrabee Barnes, Architect (1981).

Norman Warsinske
3823 94th N.E.
Bellevue, WA 98004
(206) 454-4727

"Modern, abstract, growth forms." Free-standing and bas-relief. Works in brass, bronze, steel, and brick; welding and casting.

Harold Balazs
Rte. 2, Box 208
Mead, WA 99021
(509) 466-3831

Welded and cast sculpture using steel, copper, brass, and bronze. Also works in such other materials as cement, wood, brick, and vitreous and porcelain enamel on iron or copper. Free-standing and bas-relief. "Tends towards nonobjective or highly abstract forms. Bold and linear." Does his own designs only.

Richard S. Beyer
122 Madrona Place E.
Seattle, WA 98112
(206) 325-3770

Granite, sandstone, cedar, oak, cast brass, bronze, aluminum, clay, and carved brick. Preferred media: granite or brick. Works in a realistic style. His sculptures "have significance for the average taxpayer, often humor, and sometimes a comment on common experiences in life."

Robert I. Russin
716 Ivinson
Laramie, WY 82070
(307) 745-3548

Marble, wood, brass, bronze, copper, bonded bronze, steel, corten steel, and onyx. Specializes in marble carving.

Key

See also sections on the materials in which you are interested for other artists or companies that will execute bas-relief and free-standing sculpture.

- **X** Service, technique, or material is available
- **+** See listing for further information
- ***** Sometimes offers this service

	Materials									
Northeast	**Wrought iron**	**Marble**	**Wood**	**Bronze**	**Cast stone or cement**	**Limestone**	**Brick**	**Other**	**Will interpret an architect's idea**	**Brochure or photos available**
Stanley Bleifeld Weston, CT		X		X	X			+	X	X
Richard Fisher Prospect Harbor, ME			+	+						X
Mico Kauman Tewksbury, MA		X		X	X	X		+	X	X
A. Monti Granite Quincy, MA	See listing under Stone									
George Ciocher Guttenberg, NJ	X	X	X	X	X			+	X	
Anthony Notaro Mendham, NJ		X	X	X	X	X		+	X	
Roland Roberge Princeton, NJ		X	X					+	X	
Michael Gressel Armonk, NY		X						+	X	
George Sell Brooklyn, NY	See listing under Glass									
Schwartz's Forge Deansboro, NY	See listing under Iron									
Alton S. Tobey Larchmont, NY	See listing under Murals									
Michael J. Colonna Middle Village, NY		X						+		X
Renata M. Schwebel New Rochelle, NY			X	X				+		+
Mitzi Cunliffe New York, NY		X		X	X	X		+	X	+
Domenico Facci New York, NY		X	X	X	X	X		+	X	
Richard Lichtenstein New York, NY	X							+	X	X
Ivan Olszewski New York, NY			X					+	X	X
The Sculpture Studio New York, NY								+	X	X
Ned Smyth New York, NY				X	X			+	X	+
George Gách Roslyn Heights, NY		X	X	X	X			+	X	

Key

See also sections on the materials in which you are interested for other artists or companies that will execute bas-relief and free-standing sculpture.

- **X** Service, technique, or material is available
- **+** See listing for further information
- ***** Sometimes offers this service

	Wrought iron	Marble	Wood	Bronze	Cast stone or cement	Limestone	Brick	Other	Will interpret an architect's idea	Brochure or photos available
Clemente Spampinato Sea Cliff, NY		X		X		X		+	X	X
Thomas G. Lomedico Tappan, NY		X	X	X				+	X	X
H. J. Schaller Valhalla, NY		X				X		+	X	X
Donald R. Miller Warwick, NY		X	X	X		X		+	X	X
Frudakis Gallery Philadelphia, PA		X		X					X	X
Maddalo Enterprises Philadelphia, PA								+		
Cristopher T. Ray Philadelphia, PA	X									X
Designers Forge Pittsburgh, PA								+	X	
Jozeph Stachura Pittsburgh, PA	X	X	X	X		X		+	X	X
Clifton A. Prokop Scranton, PA			X	X				+	X	X
Eric Parks Unionville, PA				X				+	X	X
Edward Fenno Hoffman III Wayne, PA		X		X		X		+	X	+
Giuliano Cecchinelli Barre, VT		X				X		+	X	
Frank C. Gaylord Barre, VT		X	X	X				+	X	X
South										
Julian H. Harris Atlanta, GA		X	X			X		+	X	
Thomas H. Williams Atlanta, GA			X	X					X	X
Barney Bright Louisville, KY				X				+	X	+
Anthony DiMarco New Orleans, LA		X	X		X	X		+	X	+
Ralph Ransome De Witt Baltimore, MD								+	X	+

Key

See also sections on the materials in which you are interested for other artists or companies that will execute bas-relief and free-standing sculpture.

- **X** Service, technique, or material is available
- **+** See listing for further information
- ***** Sometimes offers this service

	Wrought iron	Marble	Wood	Bronze	Cast stone or cement	Limestone	Brick	Other	Will interpret an architect's idea	Brochure or photos available
Giannetti Studios Brentwood, MD									X	X
Hal McWhinney Kensington, MD		X	X		X			+	X	X
Studio of Jack and Eva Grauer Memphis, TN					X			+		
Ted Guenther Rocky Gap, VA			X	X	X			X	X	+
Raymond Kaskey Washington, DC				X	X			X	X	+
Don Turano Washington, DC		X	X	X		X		X	X	
Harold C. Vogel Fairfax, VA			X			X		X	X	+
Skip Roberts Bethany, WV	X		X	X				+	X	+
Silvana Cenci Spencer, WV								+		X
Hopen Studios Sutton, WV		X	X	X	+	X		+	X	
Midwest										
Gast Monuments Chicago, IL				X				+	X	
Mara Smith Naperville, IL							X	+	X	X
Ferdinand Rebechini Park Ridge, IL		X	X	X				+	X	+
Richard Bauer Columbus, IN	X			X				+	X	
Warner Williams Culver, IN				X					X	X
Joseph N. DeLauro Canton, MI		X	X	X	X	X		+	X	
Raubar Granite Detroit, MI		X		X		X		X	X	
Eyrie Studios Lansing, MI				X	X			+	X	+
Marshall M. Fredericks Royal Oak, MI		X	X	X	X	X		+	X	

Key

See also sections on the materials in which you are interested for other artists or companies that will execute bas-relief and free-standing sculpture.

- **X** Service, technique, or material is available
- \+ See listing for further information
- * Sometimes offers this service

	Wrought iron	Marble	Wood	Bronze	Cast stone or cement	Limestone	Brick	Other	Will interpret an architect's idea	Brochure or photos available
Reno Studios St. Louis, MO				X	X	X			X	+
Herring Coe Beaumont, TX		X	X	X	X	X		+	X	+
Prof. Heri Bert Bartscht Dallas, TX	X	X	X	X	X	X		+	X	X
Larry M. Ludtke Houston, TX		X		X					X	X
Richard Herr Lake Geneva, WI			X	X	X			+	X	X
Al Blaukschien Milwaukee, WI								+	X	X
Rockies and Far West										
James Greenburg Hayward, CA				X	X			+	X	
Lyons & O'Haver La Mesa, CA								+	X	X
Fairbanks and Fairbanks Los Angeles, CA			X	X	X			+	X	X
Mary Fuller Petaluma, CA				X	X				X	X
Spero Anargyros San Francisco, CA		X	X	X	X	X		+	X	
Anthony Stellon San Francisco, CA		X	X	X	X			+	X	X
Franco Vianello San Lorenzo, CA		X	X	X				+		
Jacques Overhoff San Rafael, CA			X	X	X		X	+		X
Catherine Brant Sebastopol, CA								+		X
Enrique de la Vega Sherman Oaks, CA		X	X	X	X	X		+	X	X
John Edward Svenson Upland, CA		X	X	X	X			+	X	X
Hal Reed Woodland Hills, CA				X	X			+	X	X
Roy Erickson Denver, CO						X		+	X	X

Key

See also sections on the materials in which you are interested for other artists or companies that will execute bas-relief and free-standing sculpture.

- **X** Service, technique, or material is available
- \+ See listing for further information
- * Sometimes offers this service

	Wrought iron	Marble	Wood	Bronze	Cast stone or cement	Limestone	Brick	Other	Will interpret an architect's idea	Brochure or photos available
Ree Gorshow Denver, CO		X	X	X				+	X	+
Robert Tully Denver, CO			X						X	X
Ken Williams Pueblo, CO							X	+		X
Leopold Lambo Portland, OR			X	X		X		+	X	
John Rogers Portland, OR							X	+	X	X
LeRoy I. Setziol Sheridan, OR		X	X			X			X	
Nils Lou Willamina, OR				X				+	X	X
Edward V. Fraughton South Jordon, UT		X		X					X	+
Norman Warsinske Bellevue, WA				X			X	+	X	
Harold Belazs Mead, WA			X	X	X	X	X	+		
Richard S. Beyer Seattle, WA			X	X			X	+	X	X
Robert I. Russin Laramie, WY		X	X	X				+	X	X

SIGNS

Sign manufacturing companies are usually small and adaptable; they should be one of the designer's more valuable resources for producing exterior architectural ornament. We say this because many of the sign manufacturers we contacted were equipped to do much more than simple lettering of signs. A number had resident craftsmen who were able to:

Paint ornament in a variety of styles (on glass, wood, or tiles)
Carve (wood and stone bas-relief)
Cast (metals, plastics, and cement)
Silkscreen (on ceramic tiles)
Sandblast (wood, stone, and glass)
Acid-etch (glass and metals)

They were also set up for jigsawing wood patterns, laying mosaics, doing porcelain enamel, and, of course, custom neon.

Sign manufacturers are, by and large, accustomed to working with designers. Since their work is "custom," they are naturals for producing whatever creation the architect might come up with.

Neon deserves a special mention here. Although usually thought of only in terms of advertisement, neon can also be pure ornament. Its linearity makes it a powerful graphic device for accentuating a two-dimensional plane or defining a three-dimensional volume.

"Flamingo Hilton," Las Vegas. Heath and Co., A Fischbach Company, Los Angeles, CA. (Photo by C. Steven Short, courtesy of Heath and Co.)

Regional Listings

Northeast

Lassman Sign Co.
52 Old Iron Ore Road
Bloomfield, CT 06002
(203) 247-6522

Consultants to architects since 1938. All types of signs and letters—every description and style, many different materials. Lassman has an in-house artist for custom ornamental work; can work from rough sketch. Hand-painting on wood, tiles, and glass; wood and stone carving; casting of metals and plastics; silkscreening onto tiles; sandblasting stone; custom neon; wrought iron and porcelain enamel.

City Sign Inc.
1813 Park Street
Hartford, CT 06106
(203) 247-6522

"No sign too small or too large."

Solaray Sign Co.
67 Diamond Street
New Haven, CT 06515
(203) 562-5050

Fabricates metal, illuminated, plastic, and plywood signs; also casts bronze plaques.

Bangor Neon
1567 Hammond Street
Bangor, ME 04401
(207) 947-2766

A family business since 1948. Bangor Neon has compiled references and resource material on graphics and signs; a nationwide broker researches unusual requests and advises on availability or feasibility of components. Most work is custom; will subcontract sometimes when more sophisticated methods work to the advantage of the client. Identification signs, interior and exterior. Can do in-house sandblasting of stone and wood, plus jigsawing wood patterns; will subcontract carving, casting, silkscreening, and acid-etching. Estimates on standard items. Custom work requires detailed information.

Bailey Signs, Inc.
Box 761, Thomson Point
553 Commercial
Portland, ME 04104
(207) 774-2843

Plastics, neon, metal, and wood. Can sandblast and carve wood; ornamental hand-painting done on wood, tiles, and glass. Can cast metals and plastics; silkscreen on ceramic tiles; acid-etch glass and metals; jigsaw wood patterns; do wrought iron work. Bailey employs a complete staff of designers as well as service and construction crews.

Salem Sign Co., Inc.
230 Highland Avenue
Salem, MA 01970
(617) 744-1964

In-house artist. Custom neon; hand-painting on wood, tiles, and glass. In addition, can do bas-relief wood carving, sandblasting, custom graphics and signs. Custom wood turnings (length: 6 feet; diameter: 1 foot maximum size for balusters).

Barlo Signs
158 Greeley Street
Hudson, NH 03051
(603) 882-2638

Custom neon. In-house designer capable of working from sketch or producing own designs. Can do hand-painting on wood, tiles, and glass; silkscreening on tiles; sandblasting wood and glass; acid-etching of metals; casting metals, plastics, fiber glass, and cement; also jigsaw work.

Jutras Signs, Inc.
607 Mast Road
Manchester NH 03102
(603) 622-2344

"All custom made signs."

Franklin Neon Sign, Inc.
607 Hicksville Road
Bethpage, NY 11714
(516) 433-3710

An in-house artist can do hand-painted ornamental work from rough sketch or provide own designs. Painting can be done on wood, tiles, or glass, all suitable for exterior installation. Styles: figural, floral, abstract, and scrollwork. Custom neon, jigsawed wood patterns; porcelain enamel work; etching on glass and metals.

Boro Sign Service
399 Atlantic Avenue
Brooklyn, NY 11217
(212) 875-6400

Neon and plastic signs.

Silverescent Sign Co.
260 Bushwick Avenue
Brooklyn, NY 11206
(212) 386-5515

In addition to manufacturing custom neon, this company makes plexiglass, does metalwork (cutting, bending, and welding of stainless steel, aluminum, and bronze), and hand-painting. Can use experienced subcontractors for stone carving, silkscreening, metal casting, and sand blasting. Telephone estimates on small jobs only. Can create a design from the slightest hint of an idea.

The Solar Sign Company
Attn. Stephen Bernard, President
Natural Energy Sign Corporation
2311 Avenue I
Brooklyn, NY 11210
(212) 258-3465

This company distributes one of the few new ideas in signs since neon. The product is called the "solar sign" because, once installed, it needs no artificial energy source to activate it. The heart of the idea is a simple plastic disk called a

Hand carved and painted sign for "Watson's," by Mary Shelley, West Danby, NY. (Photo courtesy of Mary Shelley and America's Folk Heritage Gallery, New York, NY)

"flicker," available in twelve colors and two diameters (30mm and 20mm). Hundreds, even thousands, of these flickers are fixed to the company's prefabricated panels in such a way as to permit them to move freely in the wind. The flickers are highly reflective, and so produce a shimmering, sweeping effect that is to the eye what a wind chime is to the ear. The panels come in two sizes—to accommodate the different diameter disks—and any number of panels can be combined on a signboard or side of a building to create murals or signs of any size and shape.

While they seem to have been used only for advertising thus far, the flickers have an obvious application in architectural decoration—a band of these in a solid color running the width of a façade would be as decorative as neon, but less predictable because they respond to the slightest air movement rather than being programmed electronically.

The flickers are manufactured by Nippon Sheet Glass, Ltd. Their chief designer, Taketoshi Kato, has worked out admirably simple techniques for creating any effect, including relatively delicate gradations of tone achieved by arithmetic progressions. These gradations can be applied to any color change, over any length or number of panels. Combinations of different colors will yield neutral tones. Custom designs are transferred into "flicker" graphics by a system worked out by the designer. Colors are gold, silver, red, dark blue, light blue, dark green, light green, black, brown, yellow, purple, and pink.

Artistic Neon by Gasper
76–19 60th Lane
Glendale, NY 11385
(212) 821-1550

Specializes in neon art. In-house artist can do your ornamental work from a rough sketch. Also does floor lighting.

Greeley Sign
35 W. 36th Street
New York, NY 10018
(212) 736-8683

Hand-crafted, custom sign work, designs, and graphics.

Let There Be Neon
451 West Broadway
New York, NY 10012
(212) 473-8630, (212) 473-7370, (212) 473-7371

Specializes in designing and installing innovative neon graphics and designs. This is a group of twelve artists, designers, and craftsmen who work with neon. The group's gallery in New York City has displayed creative uses of neon since the early 1970s. Let There Be Neon is a design and consultation service for architects, interior designers, scenic artists, graphic artists, and other types of designers. Can design, fabricate, and install all manner of neon objects, large and small, in stores, office buildings, homes, theaters, etc. Architectural applications. In addition to neon, they can do ornamental hand-painting in figural, floral, and abstract styles. Rudi Stern's *Let There Be Neon* is available through this company; hardcover $18.95; softcover $8.95. When ordering, please add $3.00 shipping and handling (New York residents add 8 percent tax).

Supro-Neon Corp.
111 School Street
Yonkers, NY 10701
(914) 963-6466

Custom neon signs. Also, hand-painting on wood, tiles, and glass; bas-relief carving of wood; casting of plastics; silk-screening on ceramic tiles; sandblasting wood and glass; wrought iron; jigsawing wood patterns; and porcelain enamel work.

Mary Shelley
West Danby, NY 14896

See listing under Wood.

Dunn Signs
Attn. Joseph A. Dunn
11 S. 56th Street
Philadelphia, PA 19139
(215) 476-9463

Neon and plastic custom signs.

Maddalo Enterprises
Philadelphia, PA 19140

See listing under Sculpture.

Ste-Mel Signs, Inc.
Attn. Louis Cardonick, President
2730 N. 2nd Street
Philadelphia, PA 19133
(215) 634-5621

Manufactures and installs custom lighted signs.

F. S. Avenia Sign Co.
474 Woodward Road
North Providence, RI 02904
(401) 353-3300

Full range of signs and graphics: neon, plastic, metal, carved wood, hand lettering, ornamental iron.

Federal Neon Signs, Inc.
P.O. Box 502
135 Dean Street
Providence, RI 02903
(401) 421-9643

Fabrication of neon, plastic, metal, and wood signs. "All shapes and sizes."

Vermont Art Studio
Pittsford, VT 05763

See listing under Decals.

Catozzi Signs
103 Bellevue Avenue
Rutland, VT 05701
(802) 773-6676
(802) 773-3006

This one-man business does window and truck lettering; gold leafing; lettering in metal, plastic, and wood. Custom designs from sketch or photo. Also manufactures exterior and interior decals: polyester, vinyl, reflective film, and water-applied. Large orders may be possible.

South

Chamblee Sign Co.
3545 E. McCall Place
Doraville, GA 30340
(404) 451-6406
(404) 455-6405

Neon, lettered, and all other types of signs. In-house artists do painting (on wood, tiles, and glass), wood carving, silk-screening on ceramic tiles, sandblasting of stone and glass, acid-etching of glass, and jigsawing of wood patterns.

Bailey's Forge
Savannah, GA 31401

See listing under Iron.

A-1 Signs
3950 Metropolitan Street
New Orleans, LA 70126
(504) 947-8381

Any neon or electrical sign. Also works in porcelain, plastic, and metal.

"Barbary Coast," Las Vegas by Young Electric Sign Co., Salt Lake City, UT. (Photo courtesy of Young Electric Sign Co.)

Folks and Miller Sign Co., Inc.
312 E. Diamond Avenue
Gaithersburg, MD 20760
(301) 948-2680

Custom electric signs.

M. B. Signs, Inc.
P.O. Box 8705
Jackson, MS 39204
(No phone)

Electrical signs, cast and engraved plaques, metal and plastic letters, porcelain enamel, custom formed plastic, logos, etc.

Davis Neon Signs
P.O. Box 206
Heath Springs, SC 29058
(803) 273-8491

Neon, metal, "channelume" letters; also custom formed plastic logos.

Simmons Sign Co., Inc.
430 Front Street N.
Memphis, TN 38103
(901) 525-3279

Manufactures neon and plastic illuminated signs; will install within 300-mile radius.

Norvell Signs
5928 Nine Mile Road
Richmond, VA 23223
(804) 737-2189

Exterior hand-painting on wood and glass in any style.

Neon skyline for the Backstreet Restaurant, New Haven, CT. Designed by Mark Simon, Architect; Moore Grover Harper P.C., Architects and Planners. (Photo by Norman McGrath)

Staff designers can work from your sketch or from own designs; also, custom neon and jigsawed wood patterns.

Tyson Sign Corp.
P.O. Box 6098
1606 Magnolia Street
Richmond, VA 23222
(804) 329-7186

An in-house artist can do original ornamental work or your design from sketch. Hand-painting on wood, tiles, and glass; bas-relief wood carving and sandblasting; jigsaw work; custom neon; and porcelain enamel.

Midwest

Best Neon Sign Co.
6801 S. Bell Avenue
Chicago, IL 60636
(312) 434-3700

Neon signs.

Staley Signs, Inc.
P.O. Box 515
515 N. Park Avenue
Indianapolis, IN 46206
(317) 637-4567

Custom signs of all sizes in neon, fluorescent, plexiglass, sheet metal, and aluminum. Also electronic message signs; cast bronze and aluminum plaques.

Bonded Sign Service, Inc.
932 Cheyenne
Kansas City, KS 66105
(913) 371-1800

Custom neon designs from working drawings. In-house artist can do ornamental work including ornamental hand-painting on wood, tiles, and glass; silkscreening on ceramic tiles; and jigsawing of wood patterns.

Eureka Neon
10615 Cadieux Road
Detroit, MI 48244
(313) 886-6599

Custom signs of all types.

Hacker Sign Studio
4550 W. Boston Boulevard
Detroit, MI 48204
(313) 933-2200

Complete sign manufacturing and painting.

Mobil Neon Sign Co.
7129 W. Vernor
Detroit, MI 48209
(313) 842-3408

"Any form of neon architectural display."

Carved wood sign for carpenter's shop (34 by 17 by 2 inches). Robert C. Kinghorn, Excelsior, MN. (Photo courtesy of Robert C. Kinghorn)

Universal Sign Co.
Attn. Lee M. Palmateer, President
1033 Thomas Avenue
St. Paul, MN 55104
(612) 645-0223

Fabricates and installs neon, plastic, metal, and wood signs—lighted and unlighted.

Media Signs
615 Old Ballwin Road
Ballwin, MO 63011
(314) 527-4733

Internally illuminated signs, fluorescent or neon. Channeled letters with neon tubing.

Boyer Signs and Graphics
27101 Tungsten
Euclid, OH 44132
(216) 731-5100

All types of electrical and non-illuminated signs.

Cummings, Inc.
P.O. Box 11416
Columbus, OH 43211
(614) 294-3521

Illuminated identification displays. A large company with designers, planned maintenance programs, etc.

Wally Delvaux, Sr.
3533 Harley Road
Toledo, OH 43606
(419) 472-1334

Complete sign and lighting services, including handpainting, silkscreening, site signs, truck painting, maintenance, and energy surveys.

Southwest Neon Signs, Inc.
P.O. Box 20317
San Antonio, TX 78220
(512) 648-3221
(512) 443-9255 (Direct line from Austin)

Pylon signs, illuminated letters, cabinet signs. Also manufactures skylights and custom plastic panels.

Ad-Art Studios
Fort Worth, TX 76104

See listing under Decals.

Al Blaukschien
Milwaukee, WI 53202

See listing under Sculpture.

20th Century Signs
5723 W. Burleigh Street
Milwaukee, WI 53210
(414) 445-7723

Manufactures, installs, and services illuminated signs, including custom neon. Also makes plastic skylights.

Sign for White Hardware Co., Savannah, GA. Ivan Bailey, Bailey's Forge, Savannah, GA. (Photo courtesy of Ivan Bailey)

Rockies and Far West

Signs by Fred
709 W. International Airport Road
Anchorage, AK 99502
(907) 276-4222

Cloth banners, magnetic appliques, and other signs and graphics including sand-carved and hand-carved wood, painted wood and metal, gold leafing, plexiglass (lighted and unlighted), single and multiple silkscreen runs, painted wall murals, and lettering. Also manufactures exterior and interior decals: nylon, polyester, vinyl, prismatic, frosted, reflective film. Small and large decal orders. Sizes: minimum 1 by 1 inch; maximum size for one piece is 2 by 6 feet.

Bleier Sign and Graphics Co.
2030 W. Desert Cave Avenue, Suite B
Phoenix, AZ 85029
(602) 944-3117

Custom manufactured electrical signs and graphics systems. Serving Arizona, New Mexico, and southern California.

Royal Sign Co.
2631 N. 31st Street
Phoenix, AZ 85061
(602) 278-6286

Custon neon signs. Handpainting, wood carving, silkscreening, and sandblasting.

"Neon Frieze," by Jean-Pierre Heim and Rudi Stern, template by Chris Richartz; Let There Be Neon Workshop. Commissioned by Eleanore and Michael Kennedy for their New York City residence. (Photo by Abe Rezny)

Custom Neon
3804 Beverly Boulevard
Los Angeles, CA 90004
(213) 386-7945

All types of functional and decorative lighting in neon. A "large inventory" of stock designs that could be considered sculpture (flamingos, palm trees, a 6-foot tall cactus, etc.). Will also do custom pieces—words and designs. Large or small orders.

Heath and Company
Attn. Murray McCullagh, Art Director
3225 Lacy Street
Los Angeles, CA 90031
(213) 233-4141

Provides diverse services: electric signs and displays, dimensional architectural graphics, multiple-location signs, electronic signs, and exterior lighting. Call or write for other locations around the country. Has done spectacular mural/signs in Las Vegas.

Crystal Neon Signs
Attn. William McCrystal
8402 N. Magnolia
Santee, CA 92071
(714) 562-1700

Neon black light, neon decorations for home or business. Custom designs from working drawing only. Can combine neon with ceramics.

Architectural Signs
8200 East Pacific Place
Denver, CO 80231
(303) 696-6106

Anything from aluminum, brass, bronze, and wood including custom cut and cast logos and letters.

Gordon Neon Co.
2930 W. 9th Avenue
Denver, CO 80204
(303) 633-7763

Can design, engineer, fabricate, install, maintain, and lease neon and plastic signs.

Q. R. S. Neon Sign Laboratories
1681 Kapiolani Boulevard
Honolulu, HI 96814
(808) 941-3366

Specializes in neon.

Blaze Sign Co.
3500 S.W. Bard Avenue
Portland, OR 97201
(503) 226-6551

Custom neon signs.

Columbia Neon Co., Inc.
1820 E. Burnside
Portland, OR 97214
(503) 232-8153

Custom neon signs.

Young Electric Sign Co.
1148 South 300 West
Salt Lake City, UT 84125
(801) 486-1351

Ornamental hand-painting for exteriors; wood, tiles, and glass. Can also do custom neon; wrought iron; jigsawed wood patterns; wood bas-relief carving; sandblasted wood.

Independent Neon Corp.
3800 Woodland Park Avenue N.
Seattle, WA 98103
(206) 632-2500

"Each and every type of sign."

Meyer Sign Co., Inc.
512 1/2 Minor Avenue N.
Seattle, WA 98109
(206) 624-4243

Custom neon signs.

National Sign Co.
1255 Westlake Avenue N.
Seattle, WA 98109
(206) 282-0700

Neon and plastic business signs. Extruded aluminum sign cabinets in variety of colors.

Key

X Service, technique, or material is available
+ See listing for further information
* Sometimes offers this service

Northeast	Custom design from sketch	Brochure available	Telephone estimates	Neon	Other materials or techniques
Lassman Sign Bloomfield, CT	X	X	X	X	+
City Sign Hartford, CT	X		X	X	
Solaray Sign New Haven, CT	X		X	X	+
Bangor Neon Bangor, ME	X			X	+
Bailey Signs Portland, ME	X	X	X	X	+
Salem Sign Salem, MA	X		X	X	+
Baro Signs Hudson, NH	X	X		X	+
Jutras Signs Manchester, NH	X		*	X	
Franklin Neon Sign Bethpage, NY	X			X	+
Boro Sign Service Brooklyn, NY	X		X	X	
Silverescent Sign Brooklyn, NY	X		+	X	+
The Solar Sign Company Brooklyn, NY	X	X	X		+
Artistic Neon by Gasper Glendale, NY	X			X	
Greeley Sign New York, NY	X	X	X		+
Let There Be Neon New York, NY	X	X	X	X	+
Supro-Neon Yonkers, NY	X		X	X	+
Mary Shelley West Danby, NY	See listing under Wood				
Dunn Signs Philadelphia, PA	X		X	X	
Maddalo Enterprises Philadelphia, PA	See listing under Sculpture				
Ste-Mel Signs Philadelphia, PA	X		X	X	
F. S. Avenia Sign North Providence, RI	X		X	X	+
Federal Neon Signs Providence, RI	X		X	X	

Key

X Service, technique, or material is available
\+ See listing for further information
* Sometimes offers this service

	Custom design from sketch	Brochure available	Telephone estimates	Neon	Other materials or techniques
Vermont Art Studio Pittsfield, VT	See listing under Decals				
Catozzi Signs Rutland, VT	X		X		+
South					
Chamblee Sign Doraville, GA	X		X	X	+
Bailey's Forge Savannah, GA	See listing under Iron				
A-1 Signs New Orleans, LA	X		X	X	+
Folks and Miller Gaithersburg, MD	X		X	X	
M. B. Signs Jackson, MS	X		X	X	+
Davis Neon Signs Heath Springs, SC	X		X	X	
Simmons Sign Memphis, TN	X	X	X	X	
Norvell Signs Richmond, VA	X		X	X	+
Tyson Sign Richmond, VA	X		X	X	
Midwest					
Best Neon Sign Chicago, IL	X		X	X	
Staley Signs Indianapolis, IN	X		X	X	+
Bonded Sign Service Kansas City, KS	+		X	X	+
Eureka Neon Detroit, MI	X		*	X	
Hacker Sign Studio Detroit, MI	X		X	X	+
Mobil Neon Sign Detroit, MI	X		X	X	
Universal Sign St. Paul, MN	X		X	X	+
Media Signs Ballwin, MO	X		X	X	+
Boyer Signs and Graphics Euclid, OH	X		*	X	+

Key

- X Service, technique, or material is available
- \+ See listing for further information
- * Sometimes offers this service

	Custom design from sketch	Brochure available	Telephone estimates	Neon	Other materials or techniques
Cummings Columbus, OH	X	X	X	X	
Walley Delvaux, Sr. Toledo, OH	X		X	X	+
Southwest Neon Signs San Antonio, TX	X	X		X	
Ad-Art Studios Fort Worth, TX	See listing under Decals				
Al Blaukschien Milwaukee, WI	See listing under Sculpture				
20th Century Signs Milwaukee, WI	X		X	X	
Rockies and Far West					
Signs by Fred Anchorage, AK	X		X		+
Bleier Sign and Graphics Phoenix, AZ	X			X	
Royal Sign Phoenix, AZ	X		X	X	+
Custom Neon Los Angeles, CA	X	X	X	X	
Heath and Company Los Angeles, CA	X	X		X	
Crystal Neon Signs Santee, CA	+		X	X	
Architectural Signs Denver, CO	X	X	X		+
Gordon Neon Denver, CO	X	X		X	
Q. R. S. Neon Sign Honolulu, HI	X		*	X	
Blaze Sign Portland, OR	X	X		X	
Columbia Neon Portland, OR	X		X	X	
Young Electric Sign Salt Lake City, UT	X	X		X	+
Independent Neon Seattle, WA	X		X	X	+
Meyer Sign Seattle, WA	X		X	X	
National Sign Seattle, WA	X			X	

STONE

Cut stone as a building material is not so anachronistic as one might think: a building recently erected in New York City used a cut stone curtain wall that cost less per square foot—installed—than some glass curtain walls then being erected ($34 versus $35 per square foot, according to the architect). In addition to a possible initial savings, the thermal advantages of stone over conventional modern materials offer long-term energy savings through lower heating and cooling costs. Another factor that deserves mention is the way modern materials react in fire; experience with lightweight curtain walls led New York City's Fire Commissioner John T. O'Hagan to observe that this type of construction was not as safe as the earlier, masonry-cladding (see *High Rise: Fire and Life Safety*). In his estimation, lightweight curtain wall construction encourages the vertical spread of fires in modern buildings.

As with any decoration, machine-cut designs in stone are more economical than those done by hand. The least expensive type of ornamental stone cutting consists of straight repetitive cuts. One of the simpler forms of this is *rustication*—deep cuts that emphasize the (usually fake) joints. Examples of contemporary ornamental stone include the large, striated blocks made by gang sawing stone slabs; the final texture of these cuts depends on the type of abrasive used during the gang sawing. As with ridged concrete block, this simple kind of ornament yields a uniform texture. More individual forms of decoration can be achieved by using cuts traditionally employed in lettering to make ornamental patterns. These are the raised cut, V cut, large V cut, square cut, and sandblast.

Another possibility is *intaglio,* or incised carving (see photo of the sculpture of Mercury). This process is the opposite of

The Greek god Mercury, incised in limestone; Lee Lawrie, Sculptor, 1933. Rockefeller Center.

Bear gargoyle; limestone (18 by 10 by 10 inches). The donor for this gargoyle was from St. Louis and wanted Eero Saarinen's famous arch incorporated into the design. Pig gargoyle; limestone (28 by 14 by 13 inches). Frog gargoyle; clay model from which stone carvers worked (28 by 14 by 13 inches). The Washington Cathedral. Donald Miller, Warwick, NY. (Bear and pig gargoyle photos by H. Byron Chambers. Frog gargoyle photo courtesy of Donald Miller)

relief carving; the figure is recessed into rather than raised above the wall plane.

Most of the companies listed below can carve a variety of architectural elements, including balusters, railings, columns, capitals, moldings, gargoyles, and bas-relief sculpture. It is sometimes necessary for the designer to provide full-scale models or drawings for decorative stone carving.

The most common building stones are granite, limestone, and marble. Granite is the densest of the three. It is an igneous rock composed mainly of quartz and feldspar, and commonly occurs in tints of white, gray, yellow, green, and pink. Limestone is composed of carbonate of lime—the skeletons of billions of sea creatures deposited on ocean floors. In its pure state, limestone is white. When it combines with other chemicals, it often takes on different casts: yellowish or creamy (iron oxide or iron carbonate); bluish (iron sulfide, pyrites, or marcasite); gray or black (carbonaceous or bituminous substances); red (hematite); green (glauconite or chlorite).

Marble is also composed of carbonate of lime, but the term "marble" is restricted to crystalline and metamorphosed carbonates of lime (compacted under great pressure and heat) that are dense enough to take a polish. The "polish" is the result of light penetrating the surface slightly and being reflected by the facets of the internal crystalline structure. Some marbles are consistently colored throughout: white (the famous Pentelic marble of Pheidias), gray, black, and in rare cases, red. Others, sometimes called "veined" marbles, are variegated. This is often the result of stalagmites depositing carbonate of lime and other chemicals in concentric layers; these are then metamorphosed into marble. When these deposits are sliced through, the concentric layers of different minerals give the appearance of "veins." The colors, like the colors of limestone, are a function of the chemical deposited.

It should be kept in mind that stone can be imitated, either by cast stone or fiber glass-reinforced plastics that use stone powders as additives. See the introductions and listings under Cast Stone and Plastics.

Special Listings

The stone institutes listed below can be of help in detailing stone construction. They are particularly helpful if the decoration involves traditional forms—Gothic or Classical moldings, for example. They can provide architects with the technical knowledge necessary to make drawings from which stone cutters and carvers can work. Some will also recommend fabricators and carvers in your region.

Building Stone Institute
420 Lexington Avenue
New York, NY 10170
(212) 490-2530

BSI represents 300 producers, fabricators, and installers of natural building stone materials: granite, limestone, marble, slate, quartzite, etc. *Building Stone Magazine* goes out to most architectural firms; anyone can subscribe. Offers printed material, gives technical advice, and will recommend fabricators, suppliers, etc., in your area.

Granite Cutters International Association of America
Attn. Joseph Riciarelli, Director
18 Federal Avenue
Quincy, MA 02269
(617) 472-0209

Call or write for information regarding granite craftsmen who can do architectural work in your area. The association will also recommend cutters for elaborate ornamental work.

Indiana Limestone Institute of America, Inc.
Attn. William H. McDonald
400 Stone City Bank
Bedford, IN 47421
(812) 275-4426

Offers suggestions and technical information about the uses of limestone. Can recommend fabricators in your area. No charge for these services.

A 3-foot-high capital for the French Market Homestead, Savings & Loan Assoc., Metairie, LA. Quarried and carved from a 4-foot-square block of limestone by Bybee Stone Co., Bloomington, IN (1980). (Photo courtesy of Bybee Stone Co.)

Marble Institute of America
Attn. Robert Hund, Public Relations Executive
33505 State Street
Farmington, MI 48024
(313) 476-5558

The Marble Institute has printed material available about marble, offers technical advice, and can recommend fabricators. The only charge for printed material at present is for the *Marble Design Manual 1-R* ($12.50).

RESTORE
The Municipal Art Society
Attn. Jan C. K. Anderson, Director
30 Rockefeller Plaza
New York, NY 10020
(212) 586-4761

RESTORE is a training program for restoration skills in all types of masonry including stone, cast stone, brick, and terracotta. Call or write if you are interested in receiving training in these fields. Furthermore, because of RESTORE's experience in teaching, the staff may be able to help you locate skilled craftsmen in your area. At the time of this writing, RESTORE was offering a thirty-week course in restoration and preservation maintenance of masonry structures. We were also told that the society would be offering an intensive, one-week course in the near future. The shorter course should make it possible for those living outside the New York area to take advantage of the program. In the future, RESTORE expects to branch out into other materials, so keep abreast of the developments.

Regional Listings

Some of the stone carvers will travel to carve "in place." This is important in restorations and when blocks of stone in a new or old building have been left uncarved because funds were not available at the time of construction.

Limestone fountain (8 feet high; diameter at bottom, 10 feet). Quarried and carved by Bybee Stone Co., Bloomington, IN. (Photo courtesy of Bybee Stone Co.)

Northeast

A. Monti Granite Co., Inc.
266 Centre Street
Quincy, MA 02169
(617) 773-6940

Fabricator, carver, and sculptor; marble, limestone, brownstone, and granite. Can do cutting, carving, and rustication using incising and sandblasting techniques. Also does bas-relief and free-standing sculpture; moldings. Can give technical advice during design; works in any style. Can make a pattern from rough sketch or more specific information. Has showroom, as well as photos of work.

Anthony Notaro
Mendham, NJ 07945

See listing under Sculpture.

Roland Roberge
Princeton, NJ 08540

See listing under Sculpture.

Michael Gressel
Armonk, NY 10504

See listing under Sculpture.

Michael J. Colonna
Middle Village, NY 10113

See listing under Sculpture.

Domenico Facci
New York, NY 10011

See listing under Sculpture.

Limestone capitals. Quarried and carved by Bybee Stone Co., Bloomington, IN. (Photo courtesy of Bybee Stone Co.)

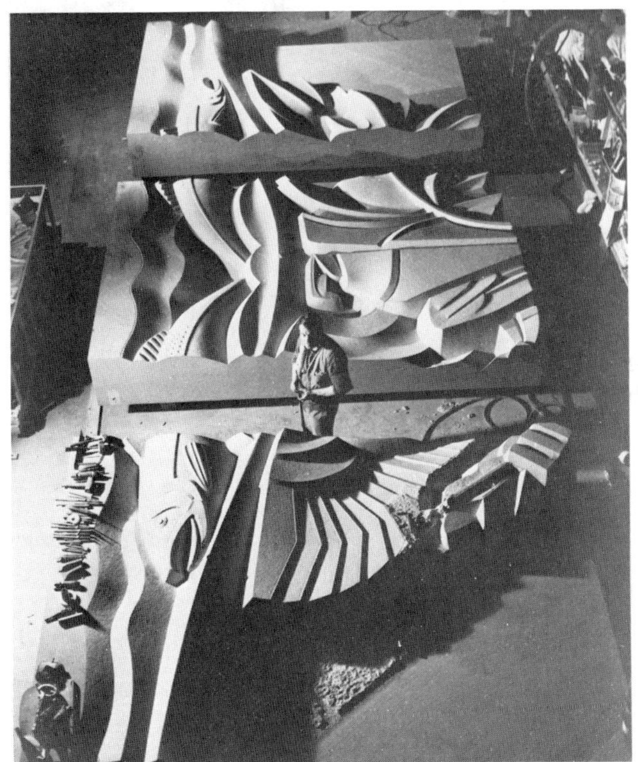

Granite panels (each approximately 12 by 18 feet), nine of which were used on the Libby Dam in Montana. Quarried and carved by Rock of Ages Corporation, Barre, VT. (Photo courtesy of Rock of Ages Corp.)

Miller-Druck Co., Inc.
Attn. Malcolm S. Cohen or Barbara E. Cohen
41 E. 42nd Street
New York, NY 10017
(212) 557-1980

Fabricator, importer, and installer working in limestone, granite, marble, sandstone, slate, quartzite, other natural stones, cast stone, and precast concrete. Can do all types of architectural decorations using techniques such as sandblasting, incising, and carving. Can help in the design process, provide designs, and can make patterns. Works in floral, figural, geometric, modern, or any other style. Gives technical advice and can recommend carvers who travel to carve "in place."

A. Ottavino Corp., Granite
80-60 Pitkin Avenue
Ozone Park, NY 11417
(212) 848-9404

Quarriers, fabricators, carvers, and designers; the company works in limestone, granite, marble, sandstone, bluestone, slate, etc. Can carve all types of architectural ornament, including rustication, capitals (all styles), bas-relief and free-standing sculpture, gargoyles, and moldings. Can help in the design process or provide designs. Floral, figural, geometric, modern, and other styles. Gives advice on all technical aspects of architectural stonework. Can recommend designers who travel to carve "in place."

This company originated in 1913 as a fabricator of architectural ornament, statuary, and monuments. Ottavino presently specializes in restoration (work on the Metropolitan Museum's Egyptian Temple of Dendur and the Soldiers and Sailors Monument, both in New York City). Restoration services consist of the furnishing and setting of stone; traditional stone cutting, carving, and tooling is combined with the most modern conservation research and structural techniques.

H. J. Schaller
Valhalla, NY 10595

See listing under Sculpture.

Donald R. Miller
Warwick, NY 10990

See listing under Sculpture.

Giuliano Cecchinelli
Barre, VT 05641

See listing under Sculpture.

Frank C. Gaylord
Barre, VT 05641

See listing under Sculpture.

Rock of Ages Corp.
Attn. John Corrigan, Vice President
Box 482
Barre, VT 05641
(802) 476-3115

This company quarries, fabricates, designs, and carves granite. Rock of Ages has a designer on staff for bas-relief and patterns (three-dimensional sculpture is subcontracted). Two hundred carvers doing cutting, sandblasting, incising, rustication, and bas-relief. Can carve all types of traditional and modern architectural ornament including capitals, moldings, gargoyles, bas-relief and free-standing sculpture, and arches. Can

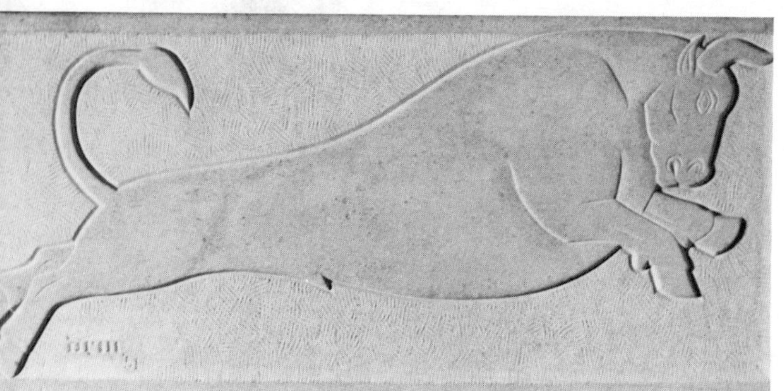

"Taurus," limestone (13 by 33 inches). Donald Miller, Warwick, NY. (Photo courtesy of Donald Miller)

help in design process; works in figural, geometric, and modern styles. Can give technical advice and make a pattern from rough sketch or more complete information. Will recommend stone carvers who will travel to carve "in place."

South

Alabama Limestone, Inc.
Route 3, Box 95
Russellville, AL 35653
(205) 332-3700

Quarriers and fabricators of a delicately veined, warm-toned limestone called "Shadow Vein." This stone is "remarkably sound, having virtually no cracks, mud seams, or other flaws"; it is possible to fabricate fairly large pieces—dimensions of 20 by 8 feet are not uncommon for single panels. Will give technical advice about detailing, etc., and can produce a wide variety of machined textures.

Julian H. Harris
Atlanta, GA 30313

See listing under Sculpture.

Cut Art Stone Co.
Savannah, GA 31405

See listing under Cast Stone.

North Carolina Granite Corporation
P.O. Box 151
Mt. Airy, NC 27030
(919) 786-5141

Quarrier and fabricator of granite; sandblasting. Custom designs from rough sketch or more detailed information. Samples of the company's stone are available.

Harold C. Vogel
Fairfax, VA 22030

See listing under Sculpture.

Bill Hopen
Sutton, WV 26601

See listing under Sculpture.

Granite and brick rustication, pool house, Llewellyn Park, NJ. Robert A. M. Stern, Architects, New York, NY (1981) (Photo of model by Bruce Wolf, courtesy of Robert A. M. Stern, Architects)

Midwest

Galloy & Van Etten, Inc.
11756 S. Halsted Street
Chicago, IL 60628
(312) 928-4800

A fabricator working with limestone and marble; does cutting and carving. Can produce rustication, all styles of capitals, statues, bas-reliefs, gargoyles, arches, and moldings. Can help in the design process and can provide designs. Patterns for stone cutting can be made from a rough sketch. Will recommend stone carvers who will travel to carve "in place."

Gast Monuments
Chicago, IL 60640

See listing under Sculpture.

Architectural Stone Sales, Inc.
P.O. Box 637
Bedford, IN 47421
(812) 279-2421

Fabricator of limestone. Cutting, incising, sandblasting; bas-relief and free-standing sculpture; rustication and carving of all styles of capitals, moldings, gargoyles, arches, etc. Can give some help during the design and can provide designs. Works in any style, gives technical advice, and can make patterns from rough sketch or more detailed information. Can recommend carvers who will travel to carve "in place." Can give delivery and cost estimates by telephone. Will send stone samples.

Harding and Cogswell Corp.
P.O. Box 714
Bedford, IN 47421
(812) 279-9744

Quarriers, fabricators, carvers, and designers of limestone. Cutting, incising, sandblasting, and carving; all styles of capitals, moldings, arches, gargoyles, bas-relief and free-standing sculpture. Can help in design process and can provide designs.

Before: supermarket, Manchester, CT. (Photo courtesy of Allan Greenberg)

After: Superior Court Building for the State of Connecticut, Manchester, CT. Rustication in limestone. Associated Architects: Allan Greenberg and Peter Kosinski. (Photo courtesy of Allan Greenberg)

Works in all styles. Can give technical advice and make patterns from sketch or more detailed information. Can recommend carvers who will carve "in place." Will estimate time of delivery.

Indiana Limestone Co., Inc.
405 N. I Street
Bedford, IN 47451
(812) 275-3341

Quarriers and fabricators of limestone; cutting, incising, rustication, and carving of all styles of capitals, moldings, arches, and gargoyles. Also bas-relief and free-standing sculpture. Works in any style. Does not help in design process or give technical advice. Can make patterns from rough sketch or more detailed information. Will estimate time of delivery.

Bybee Stone Co., Inc.
P.O. Box 968
Bloomington, IN 47402
(812) 875-2215

Quarriers, fabricators, and carvers of limestone. Cutting, incising, sandblasting, rustication, and carving; all styles of capitals, moldings, gargoyles, and arches. Will help in the design process and work in any style. Can also do turned stone columns, bases, balusters, and urns. Gives technical advice; can usually make patterns from a sketch—surely from more detailed information. Can recommend carvers who will carve "in place." Will estimate time of delivery.

Woolery Stone Co., Inc.
P.O. Box 40
Bloomington, IN 47402
(812) 332-3301

Quarriers, fabricators, and carvers of limestone. Cutting, incising, carving; all styles of capitals, moldings, gargoyles, arches, etc. Also can do bas-relief and free-standing sculpture. Can help in design process, providing shaded details of traditional and bas-relief ornament; work in all styles and give technical advice. Patterns made from sketch or more detailed information. Cost estimates only with explicit detail. Will estimate time of delivery.

Raubar Granite Co., Inc.
Detroit, MI 48209

See listing under Sculpture.

Marshall M. Fredericks Studio
Royal Oak, MI 48072

See listing under Sculpture.

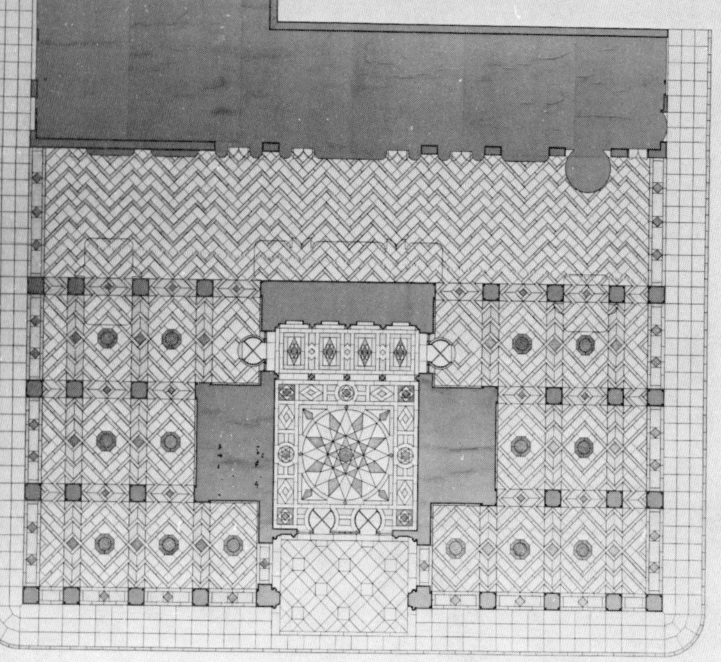

Granite paving pattern (ground floor level). A.T.& T. Headquarters, New York City. Johnson/Burgee Architects, Simmons Architects, Associates (1981). (Photo courtesy of Johnson/Burgee Architects)

Vetter Stone Company
P.O. Box 38
Kasota, MN 56050
(507) 345-4568

Quarriers and fabricators of limestone and dolomite—"our dolomite is also classified commercially as marble." Does cutting, carving, incising, sandblasting, rustication of capitals, statues, bas-reliefs, moldings, gargoyles, and arches. Can carve in any style, is willing to help in design process or to provide designs, will give technical advice, and can make patterns from rough sketch or more detailed information. Will recommend carvers who will travel to carve "in place." Estimates given "if information can be conveyed by phone."

Mankato Stone Center
Mankato, MN 56001
(507) 388-7135

Quarrier and fabricator of limestone and marble. Cutting, incising, sandblasting; can make bas-reliefs, and cut rustication and arches. Gives technical advice, and can make a pattern from a rough sketch.

The Johns-Carabelli Co.
Attn. Michael J. Johns
4202 Mayfield Road
Cleveland, OH 44121
(216) 382-8150

Fabricators, carvers, and sculptors of granite and marble. This company does cutting, incising, sandblasting, and carving of capitals (Doric, Ionic, and Corinthian), moldings (including egg and dart), gargoyles, and arches; also bas-relief and free-standing statues. Can help with the design, and works in all styles. Can give technical advice, make patterns from sketches or more detailed information, and will recommend carvers who will travel to carve "in place." Can estimate delivery time.

John Winterich and Associates
Solon, OH 44139

See listing under Murals.

Rockies and Far West

Spero Anargyros
San Francisco, CA 94115

See listing under Sculpture.

Roy Erickson
Denver, CO 80204

See listing under Sculpture.

Hawaii Marble & Granite Co., Ltd.
650 Kakoi Street
Honolulu, HI 96819
(808) 836-2695

Fabricator. Cutting, incising, sandblasting, and carving of ornamental motifs, all styles, in marble and granite. Also statues. Can give design advice and can possibly offer technical advice. Can make a pattern from rough sketch or more detailed information. Can recommend carvers who will travel to carve "in place." Gives delivery cost and estimates by telephone.

Le Roy I. Setziol
Sheridan, OR 97378

See listing under Sculpture.

Robert I. Russin
Laramie, WY 82070

See listing under Sculpture.

Key

See also Sculpture for artists who work in this material.

- **X** Service, technique, or material is available
- **+** See listing for further information
- ***** Sometimes offers this service

					Materials							
Northeast	**Quarrier**	**Fabricator**	**Carves architects' designs**	**Carves own designs**	**Limestone**	**Granite**	**Marble**	**Architectural ornament**	**Bas-relief**	**Statues**	**Brochure or photos available**	**Cost estimates by telephone**
A. Monti Granite Quincy, MA		X	X	X	X	X	X	+	X	X	+	X
Anthony Notaro Mendham, NJ	See listing under Sculpture											
Roland Roberge Princeton, NJ	See listing under Sculpture											
Michael Gressel Armonk, NY	See listing under Sculpture											
Michael J. Colonna Middle Village, NY	See listing under Sculpture											
Domenico Facci New York, NY	See listing under Sculpture											
Miller-Druck New York, NY		X			X	X	X	X	X		X	X
A. Ottavino, Granite Ozone Park, NY	X	X	X	X	X	X	X	X	X	X	X	X
H. J. Schaller Valhalla, NY	See listing under Sculpture											
Donald R. Miller Warwick, NY	See listing under Sculpture											
Giuliano Cecchinelli Barre, VT	See listing under Sculpture											
Franke C. Gaylord Barre, VT	See listing under Sculpture											
Rock of Ages Barre, VT	X	X	X	X		X		X	X	X	X	X
South												
Alabama Limestone Russellville, AL	X	X			X						X	
Julian H. Harris Atlanta, GA	See listing under Sculpture											
Cut Art Stone Savannah, GA	See listing under Cast Stone											
North Carolina Granite Mt. Airy, NC	X	X				X					+	
Harold C. Vogel Fairfax, VA	See listing under Sculpture											
Bill Hopen Sutton, WV	See listing under Sculpture											

Key

See also Sculpture for artists who work in this material.

X Service, technique, or material is available
+ See listing for further information
* Sometimes offers this service

Midwest	Quarrier	Fabricator	Carves architects' designs	Carves own designs	Limestone	Granite	Marble	Architectural ornament	Bas-relief	Statues	Brochure or photos available	Cost estimates by telephone
Galloy & Van Etten Chicago, IL		X			X		X	X	X	X	X	
Gast Monuments Chicago, IL	See listing under Sculpture											
Architectural Stone Sales Bedford, IN		X			X			X	X	X	X	X
Harding and Cogswell Bedford, IN	X	X	X	X	X			X	X	X	X	X
Indiana Limestone Bedford, IN	X	X			X			X	X	X		
Bybee Stone Bloomington, IN	X	X	X		X			X	X	X	X	X
Woolery Stone Bloomington, IN	X	X	X		X			X	X	X	X	+
Raubar Granite Detroit, MI	See listing under Sculpture											
Marshall M. Fredericks Royal Oak, MI	See listing under Sculpture											
Vetter Stone Company Kasota, MN	X	X			X		+	X	X	X	X	+
Mankato Stone Center Mankato, MN	X	X			X		X		X		X	X
Johns-Carabelli Cleveland, OH		X	X	X		X	X	X	X	X	X	X
John Winterich Solon, OH	See listing under Murals											
Rockies and Far West												
Spero Anargyros San Francisco, CA	See listing under Sculpture											
Roy Erickson Denver, CO	See listing under Sculpture											
Hawaii Marble & Granite Honolulu, HI		X				X	X			X	X	X
Le Roy I. Setziol Sheridan, OR	See listing under Sculpture											
Robert I. Russin Laramie, WY	See listing under Sculpture											

STUCCO AND PLASTER

Stucco

Stucco has an ancient lineage. The yellow sandstone columns of the Temple of Apollo at Bassae, built in the fifth century B.C., show remnants of white, lime stucco. Roman pomp, as you might expect, led to the perfection of modelled plaster that served rather more theatrical purposes than those to which the Greeks had put it. Some say the Romans spread the use of decorative plaster as far as India, bringing it with them when they arrived in A.D. 166. The Romans also invented an extremely hard stucco that could be polished to look like marble and that withstood long exposure to weather. Unfortunately, its secret died with the Empire.

The use of ornamental stucco in the West virtually ended with the rise of Christianity, because of that religion's ban on all church ornament with the exception of didactic paintings. For nearly a thousand years, stucco's main connection to decoration was as the foundation for frescoes. After a revival during the Renaissance, stucco remained a popular, and durable, ornamental material for centuries. In *Plastering, Plain and Decorative* (1897), William Miller mentions a house in Ipswich whose elaborate stucco ornament had survived the difficult English climate in excellent condition for over two hundred years.

Exterior plaster, whether lime or cement, is commonly called "stucco." The white, lime stucco mentioned above is seldom used nowadays; rock lime has been replaced by the easier to use—and safer to mix—Portland cement. It is called "Portland" cement because its color when set resembles a limestone quarried on the Isle of Portland, near England.

There are several traditional ornamental stucco finishes. Rough stucco can be scored to imitate various kinds of stonework. Rough cast (or pebble dash) is formed by throwing small pebbles at a wet second coat and then brushing it with a thin lime mortar. This is usually applied in panels that are separated by sections of another finish.

Sgraffito (from the Italian meaning "scratched") requires a more elaborate procedure. A base layer of Portland cement and sand is applied, then a layer or layers of colored plaster, followed by a coat of white plaster. A paper cartoon of the design is placed over the panel and the design is transferred by pricking through the paper with a small, sharp stylus. The top coat is then scratched away where necessary to reveal the color or colors beneath.

Stucco is the most common source of exterior plaster ornament. It can be modelled into endless varieties of forms and finishes, and can imitate all manner of stone, wood, metal, brick, etc. It can also be painted to give an even broader range of choices.

Plaster

Plastering is another ancient trade. All of the tools used by plasterers today were depicted on the walls of the pyramids. Egyptian plaster was made with burnt gypsum and was similar to our plaster of Paris.

When we began writing this book, we visited an ornamental plaster studio whose owner shrugged his shoulders and said, "I guess I was born in the wrong century." A year and a half later we visited him again, and he happily reported that business was booming and he was employing several apprentices.

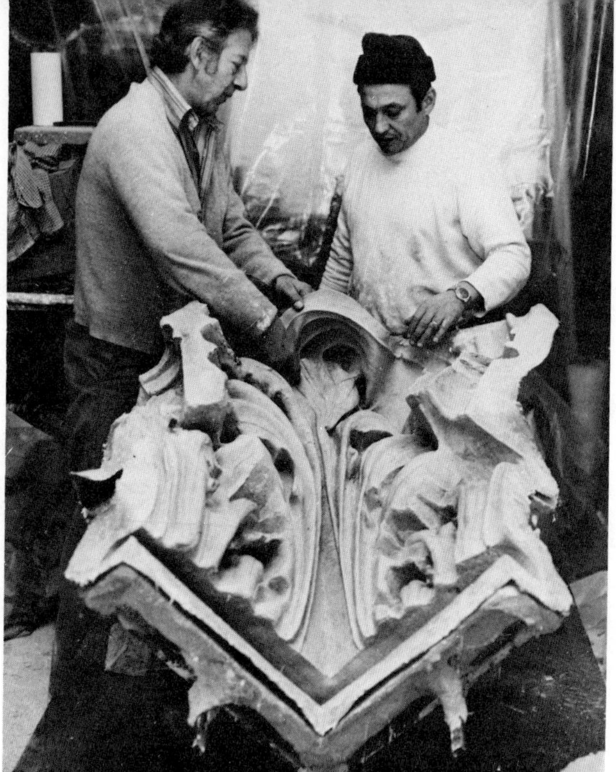

A latex mold of an element for the New York Stock Exchange being prepared for plaster casting. Gabe Petrella and assistant, Saldarini and Pucci, New York, NY.

Floral sculpture by Ray Kaskey, used as model for cast stone architectural element (see photo under Cast Stone). (Photo by Arnold Kramer, courtesy of Ray Kaskey)

Plaster is not generally recommended for exposed exterior use. However, some craftsmen told us that it is possible in restricted situations: the plaster must be "properly" treated and not directly exposed to the weather. The traditional method of sealing involves prolonged soaking in boiled linseed oil, followed by painting; the back must also be thoroughly caulked and moistureproofed before installing. For details about this and more modern methods of waterproofing, contact one of the plaster experts listed below. In general, however, it is easier to use a cement and sand mixture for exteriors.

Plaster models of intricate columns, capitals, or bas-reliefs are regularly used to make models for metal or fiber glass castings; they also serve as models for stone or wood carvers.

These splendid craftsmen have often had decades of experience, and their skills as ornamenters deserve to be taken advantage of by designers.

Special Listings

Chicago Plastering Institute
Attn. John Boland, President
5859 W. Fullerton Avenue
Chicago, IL 60639
(312) 237-6910

An organization formed by agreement between the unions and the employers for the purpose of promoting the trade of plastering (including stucco and cast stone). There are over twenty-five similar institutes around the country. They offer printed material and technical advice, and will recommend skilled plaster workers in their area. This Institute represents over 100 contractors in the greater Chicago area who will work anywhere in the region. There is no charge for any of the services.

International Institute for Lathing and Plastering
Attn. Clay Johnston, Executive Director
25332 Narbonne Avenue, Suite 170
Lomita, CA 90717
(213) 539-6080

Can provide names and addresses of lathing and plastering bureaus around the country. Local bureaus will be able to give you names of ornamental stucco and plastering contractors in your area.

Operative Plasterers & Cement Masons of the United States and Canada
1125 17th Street, N.W.
Washington, D.C. 20036
(202) 393-6569

This is the national headquarters for the 70,000-member union of plasterers, cement masons, casters, modelers, and shophands. They can give suggestions and technical advice on the use of their products, and will recommend skilled mechanics in your area. There is no charge for this service. The national headquarters has an on-the-job and classroom apprentice program. They can put you in contact with one of the forty or so lathe and plastering promotional bureaus around the United States. These bureaus have access to contractors, designers, materials dealers, and are familiar with building codes and other technical information.

Grays Ferry Community Center, Philadelphia, PA. Gable pattern in two colors of stucco. Friday Architects/Planners, Philadelphia, PA. (Photo courtesy of Friday Architects/Planners)

The stone pilaster capitals, bases and arch keystones were carved from plaster models made by Saldarini and Pucci, New York, NY. Addition to the Frick Collection, New York. Harry van Dyke, Architect (1976).

Regional Listings

Many of the studios listed below also work in fiber glass, cast stone, or other materials. Some will cast plaster elements in Fiberglas-reinforced plastic or cast stone, both of which are suitable for exterior use.

American Plasterers, Inc.
Attn. James McCarthy
280 Lawlor Street
New Britain, CT 06051
(203) 229-9895

Ornamental stucco contractor. Can duplicate various stone finishes, brick, and wood; can do sgraffito. Custom work from rough sketch, sample, photo, or drawing.

Northeast

Garden State Brickface Co.
843 St. George Avenue
Roselle, NJ 07203
(201) 925-0080
(212) 448-3636

A large ornamental stucco contractor doing work all over the United States. Employs 150 people, of whom approximately 40 percent are apprentices. All types of stucco work including sgraffito. Custom work from sketch or more detailed information.

G. Moffett
Attn. Gene Moffett
111 Berkeley Place
Brooklyn, NY 11217
(212) 638-4922

Ornamental stucco contractor. Can duplicate various stone finishes, brick, and wood; can do sgraffito. "Can do anything in cement." Custom work from rough sketch, sample, photo, or drawing.

Gargoyles, Inc.
38 E. 21st Street
New York, NY 10010
(212) 228-8887

Manufacturer; sells directly. A lively variety of stock items in "Hydrastone" (a plaster product of U.S. Gypsum) including gargoyles, grotesques (a grotesque is similar to a gargoyle but is not used as a roof drain), satyrs, and (for interiors) frames and sconces in wood or stone. Can fill small or large orders. Will do custom work in quantitites only. Can make a model to architectural specifications in plaster, and can then reproduce it in plaster. Recommends protected exterior use only of those pieces with "stone" or "metal" finishes.

Saldarini and Pucci
New York, NY 10012

See listing under Plastics.

Restoration of a townhouse façade in progress, Greenwich Village, New York City. Ornamental stucco contractor, G. Moffett, Brooklyn, NY.

Ornato Decors
Ridgewood, NY 11385

See listing under Plastics.

Frank Mangione
21 John Street
Saugerties, NY 12477
(914) 246-9863

Specializes in exterior and interior ornamental stucco and plaster work. Can duplicate any material in stucco; will duplicate any molding or interior architectural ornament in plaster. Custom work from sketch, sample, or more detailed information. Also works with fiber glass.

Felber Studios
Ardmore, PA 19003

See listing under Plastics.

Tayssir Sleiman
423 Horsham Rd.
Horsham, PA 19044
(215) 672-2607

This gentleman makes a variety of items in plaster including architectural sculpture, architectural scale models, models for plaster, stone and bronze casting, as well as period ceilings, domes, shells, and capitals. Specialty: designing and making Islamic ornamental plaster; Sleiman worked on the State Palace in Abu Dabi. Also has extensive experience in Western-style restorations; among other projects, Slieman did work on the Blue Room and the Jefferson Room of the White House. Will install and supervise any work in ornamental plaster. Will advise about waterproofing plaster for exterior use. Also works in cast stone.

South

Albert Lachin and Associates
New Orleans, LA 70119

See listing under Cast Stone.

Giannetti Studios
3806 38th Street
Brentwood, MD 20722
(301) 927-0033

Specializes in reproducing ornamental elements in epoxy "fiber glass" and plaster. Many samples of ornamental plaster in stock and can duplicate from small sample or rough sketch. Can give design, technical, and installation advice. Brochure $2.00 (refunded with purchase).

Midwest

C. G. Girolami and Co.
Chicago, IL 60651

See listing under Cast Stone.

Luczak Brothers, Inc.
4052 Elston Avenue
Chicago, IL 60618
(312) 478-3570

Exterior stucco contractor able to do custom designs in stucco from rough sketch or more detailed drawings. Can match a sample finish and do stucco versions of all types of finishes including wood, limestone, brick, etc. Can do sgraffito.

Sander & Co., Inc.
9530 James Avenue S.
Minneapolis, MN 55431
(612) 884-8128

Ornamental stucco contractor; can imitate stone, wood, and brick finishes in all colors. Prefers doing custom work from sample, but can work from sketch or photo.

Adams & Williamson Co., Inc.
7209 St. Charles Rock Road
St. Louis, MO 63133
(314) 862-9200

Exterior ornamental stucco contractor who can imitate limestone, stone, brick, and wood in stucco. Works in colors and does sgraffito. Can realize your design from rough sketch, photo, sample, or working drawing.

Brown Plastering Co.
5012 Calvert Street
Cincinnati, OH 45209
(513) 731-9200

Ornamental stucco contractor; can imitate stone, wood, and brick patterns; also does simulated carvings. A limited selection of colors available.

R. B. Brunemann & Sons, Inc.
11120 Kenwood Road
Cincinnati, OH 45242
(513) 793-3070

Ornamental stucco contractor; can imitate all types of materials including stone, wood, brick, as well as a variety of ornamental textures. Also does sgraffito.

Fischer and Jirouch Co.
4821 Superior Avenue
Cleveland, OH 44103
(216) 361-3840

Manufacturer; sells directly. Gives technical and installation advice. Custom work from sample. Plaster models made to architects' specifications from sample or working drawing. Items can be cast in either plaster or fiber glass. Large, small, and one-of-a-kind orders. Brochure (over 1,500 items) $25.00.

Jas. C. Oren
7275 Bridgewater Road
Dayton, OH 45424
(513) 233-7621

Ornamental stucco contractor; works in all colors and can imitate brick and stone. Custom work from measured drawing only. Also does sgraffito. Specializes in plaster casting and has done restoration work at Dayton's Arcade and the Victory Theater.

Hendrix, Heikkilä, and Terry, Inc.
Norman, OK 73069

See listing under Murals.

Maidt Plastering Co., Inc.
Attn. Robert L. Maidt
16 N.W. 42nd
Oklahoma City, OK 73118
(405) 528-1041

Exterior ornamental stucco contractor. Can imitate all types of limestone, stone, brick, and wood in stucco; also does sgraffito. Your design can be produced from sketch, photograph, sample, or working drawing.

Orlandini Studios, Ltd.
Decorative Plaster Supply Co.
633 W. Virginia
Milwaukee, WI 53204
(414) 272-3657

Founded in 1937, this company can give design, technical, and installation advice. All types of architectural items reproduced in plaster, cast stone, and metals. Can imitate terracotta in cast stone; provide molds for terracotta; can make models and molds for nonferrous metals. Specialty: designing and making models and molds for casting, and installing almost any plaster ornament. Can also duplicate existing work for restorations; a good selection of patterns for cornices, columns, capitals, etc., in stock. Models made in plaster, clay, wood, metal, styrofoam, and other materials to architects' specifications. He has also enlarged and fabricated sculpture.

Rockies and Far West

Leyva's J. P. Weaver Co.
Alhambra, CA 91803

See listing under Cast Stone.

Robert C. Scott
362 Front Street, Suite B
El Cajon, CA 92020
(714) 579-8499

Ornamental stucco contractor; can imitate brick patterns. Custom work from sample or working drawing only.

E. F. Brady Co./San Diego
P.O. Box 968
La Mesa, CA 92041
(714) 462-2600

Ornamental stucco contractor. Can imitate brick, stone, and wood; works in all colors.

Pierce & Rahn Enterprises
3705 Hancock Street
San Diego, CA 92110
(714) 298-6603

Ornamental stucco contractor. Can imitate all types of stone; works in all colors. Custom work from sketch or photo.

Portland Plastering Co.
4609 N.E. Ainsworth
Portland, OR 97218
(503) 285-0654

Exterior ornament stucco contractor; can imitate all types of limestone, stone, brick, and wood in stucco. Can do your design from rough sketch, photo, sample, or working drawing.

Key

See also Sculpture for artists who work in this material.

- **X** Service, technique, or material is available
- **+** See listing for further information
- ***** Sometimes offers this service

	Distributor	Manufac-turer	Stock items	Custom items from sketch	Makes models to specifications	Fiber glass	Cast stone	Brochure available	Ornamental stucco contractor
Northeast									
American Plasterers New Britain, CT		X	X	X				X	X
Garden State Brickface Roselle, NJ		X	X	X				X	X
G. Moffett Brooklyn, NY	X	X	X						X
Gargoyles, Inc. New York, NY		X	X	+	X			X	
Saldarini and Pucci New York, NY	See listing under Plastics								
Ornato Decors Ridgewood, NY	See listing under Plastics								
Frank Mangione Saugerties, NY		X		X		X		X	X
Felber Studies Ardmore, PA	See listing under Plastics								
Tayssir Sleiman Horsham, PA		X		X	X		X	X	
South									
Albert Lachin New Orleans, LA	See listing under Cast Stone								
Giannetti Studios Brentwood, MD		X	X	X	X			+	
Midwest									
C. G. Girolami Chicago, IL	See listing under Cast Stone								
Luczak Brothers Chicago, IL		X	X	X					X
Sander Minneapolis, MN		X		+					X
Adams & Williamson St. Louis, MO		X	X	X					X
Brown Plastering Cincinnati, OH		X		X					X
R. B. Brunemann & Sons Cincinnati, OH		X		X				X	X
Fischer and Jirouch Cleveland, OH		X	X	X	X	X		+	
Jas. C. Oren Dayton, OH		X		+					X

Key

See also Sculpture for artists who work in this material.

- **X** Service, technique, or material is available
- **+** See listing for further information
- ***** Sometimes offers this service

	Distributor	Manufac-turer	Stock items	Custom items from sketch	Makes models to specifications	Fiber glass	Cast stone	Brochure available	Ornamental stucco contractor
Hendrix, Heikkilä, and Terry Norman, OK	See listing under Murals								
Maidt Plastering Oklahoma City, OK		X	X	X					X
Orlandini Studios Milwaukee, WI		X	X	X	X		X		
Rockies and Far West									
Leyva's J. P. Weaver Alhambra, CA	See listing under Cast Stone								
Robert C. Scott El Cajon, CA		X		+				X	X
E. F. Brady La Mesa, CA		X		X					X
Pierce & Rahn San Diego, CA		X		X					X
Portland Plastering Portland, OR		X	X	X					X

WOOD

Creating ornament from wood is probably one of the more ancient means of architectural embellishment. Wood can be incised, carved, painted, burned, jigsawed, and turned, as well as built up into complex ornamental sections. Since wood decays easily, we have been deprived of virtually all of the earliest examples of wooden decoration. Due to the extreme dryness of the climate, however, a few Egyptian wood carvings (from about 4000 B.C.) have survived. But there are few examples of European decoration in wood from before the twelfth or thirteenth centuries.

Moldings

It would take a volume just to study basic molding shapes and their uses. Some have practical functions—drip moldings, for example, prevent rain from washing down the face of a wall—but most seem to have been devised for purely aesthetic ends, each designed to cast a particular shadow and to be seen from a certain angle.

Moldings are a powerful architectural tool because of their ability to establish scale—to enable you to estimate your own size relative to that of the building. When you see a molding that is located somewhat above grade, but below window sill height, the general expectation is that it is "around waist level." The reasons for this are obscure; perhaps it has something to do with people wearing belts around their waists, or the simple fact that moldings often are placed at waist height. Regardless of the cause, your expectation is often so strong that you unconsciously estimate your own size in comparison to that of the building based on the presumed, waist-height location of the molding.

When a molding's placement turns out to be different from what you expected, you can misjudge a building's size. Robert Venturi has often used molding placement to change our perception of a building. In one of his first houses (see photo), a molding that you would expect to find at waist level has been placed nearer to shoulder height. Because it is the strongest scale indicator you see when you approach, it is the one used to estimate the size of the house. As it is higher than you expect, the house seems smaller than it actually is. Only when a person enters the picture do you realize the building's true size.

Moldings can be made in virtually any material: brick, ceramics, stone, stucco, ornamental metals, lightweight polymers, other plastics, neon, and wood (either worked directly into the wood, or, in the case of smaller moldings, nailed or screwed in place). Because of the variety of materials in which moldings are made, you should also contact craftsmen and manufacturers in these other categories.

Turned Ornament

Wood turning is one of the clearer examples of how the art of decoration is often closely tied to technology. The word "lathe," meaning a machine to turn wood or metal, only entered the English language around 1600, and it is interesting to note that the furniture of that period shows extensive use of lathe-turned spindles. The fashion for exterior architectural decoration in turned wood probably peaked around the end of the nineteenth century, as a part of the explosion of late Victorian ornament that was tied to industrialization.

The molding on this early house by Robert Venturi appears to be at waist level. Going on that assumption, it seems to be a rather modest size house. However, with a life-size figure in the picture, we see that the molding is nearer chest height than waist height. We have been fooled; the house is larger than it first seemed. By Venturi & Rauch.

Balusters, faceplates, columns, finials, etc. Courtesy of Haas Wood and Ivory Works, San Francisco, CA. (Photo courtesy of Haas Wood and Ivory Works)

The subtleties of a beautifully balanced composition are created by the shape and proportion of the turnings, and by the spaces left between them. The same shape turnings are usually used in the same panel (A-A-A-A-A or B-B-B-B-B), but alternating shapes can also yield a rich visual texture (A-B-A-B-A-B-A). We found that the easiest way to design turnings was to cut them out of folded paper, the same way you would paper dolls. With a little practice, you can get two-dimensional, scale cutouts of several different designs within a few minutes.

Sawed Ornament

In addition to moldings and turnings, there are sawed ornaments. One of the more familiar of these, from our recent Victorian past, is the bargeboard—the piece used to protect the ends of roofing timbers at the gable end of a building. It is important to remember that sawed decoration performs on two levels: both the piece itself, and its shadow, ornament the building. The same is true of built-up ornaments, such as composite moldings and cornices with dentil courses and other elements that are emphasized by sunlight.

Nowadays, carved elements are usually confined to smaller areas: doors, overdoor panels, and bas-relief insets into walls. Carving can be done by hand, machine, or laser.

Shingles

Ornamentally cut shingles were particularly popular near the turn of the century, when they were often used to create complex patterns on façades and roofs. Today they can be purchased in nine stock decorative cuts (see **Dick Young's Puget Sound Shake Brokers,** below). The more traditional way to use ornamentally cut shingles is in one or more horizontal bands of the same cut. Bands of different cuts can also be used, and can be laid in vertical and diagonal patterns as well as horizontally. Decoratively cut shingles offer the possibility of extraordinary richness through relatively simple means.

Special Listings

Local Lumber Company
161 Bowers Hill Road
Oxford, CT 06483
(203) 888-6509

This company provides high quality seasoned native lumber most of which is purchased green and cut to their specifications. The kiln-dried lumber is first air-dried to a moisture content of between 15 and 18 percent, then kiln-dried to between 6 and 8 percent moisture content. Stock: white ash, butternut, aromatic cedar, black cherry, white elm, hickory, hard and soft maple, red oak, white oak, white pine, sassafras, tulip, and black walnut.

Red Cedar Shingle and Handsplit Shake Bureau
515 116th Avenue N.E.
Bellevue, WA 98004
(206) 453-1323

Offers technical advice and printed material on the use of their product. Publishes a newsletter; architects can send a letter requesting it.

Wood Molding and Millwork Producers, Inc.
Attn. Neal T. Heflin, Director of Marketing
P.O. Box 25278
Portland, OR 97225
(503) 292-9288

Will give suggestions for the use of the product, technical advice, recommendations of fabricators and suppliers, and information about how to avoid the most common pitfalls. Offers a variety of printed matter for a nominal charge; these include "WM Series Moulding Patterns Catalog" and a series of three pamphlets on quality standards. Also offers audio-visual programs. Membership consists of sixty producing mills.

Regional Listings

The craftsmen and companies listed below can produce moldings, wood turnings, fretwork, and wood carvings. The list of architectural elements that they can supply includes everything made of wood—columns, balusters, railings, bas-relief panels, doors, windows, stairs, faceplates, finials, drops, crockets, gargoyles, ornamentally cut shingles, moldings, and other elements.

While many of the smaller shops have no brochure, most can supply photos of their work.

Lathe work, Haas Wood and Ivory Works. (Photo by Donna Morrison, courtesy of Haas Wood and Ivory Works)

Northeast

Barrie Faulkner
Fine Woodworking
"Oakleigh" RR 1
Gadshill, Ontario N0K 1J0
Canada
(519) 656-2873

A highly skilled wood carver who can do restoration work, panels, moldings, and gargoyles. Specializes in Gothic and Jacobean millwork and manufacturers custom shapes only; can work from sketch. Does custom turnings, jigsaw ornament, and incision and bas-relief hand carving. He has done extremely fine woodworking and joinery and quite a lot of gingerbread work on houses and cupolas. Also does turnings and inlay work (interior only). Small orders. Brochure of interior work only at this time.

Maurer and Shepard, Joiners
122 Naubuc Avenue
Glastonbury, CT 06033
(203) 633-2383

Authentic, hand-produced, eighteenth-century millwork with planed interior and exterior surfaces and mortise and tenon joints held with square pegs: doors, entryways, fluted columns, rosettes, swan's neck pediments, etc. Will sometimes do turnings: finials and drops. Can also do restoration work.

Elliot Fishbein
2 Spear Avenue
Eastport, ME 04631
(207) 853-4750

Carves panels and moldings. Specializes in gold leaf application to ornament and signs; also turnings, restoration, antiques reproductions. Gives advice on warping. Large and small orders. Works in glass and metals as well.

Bailey Signs, Inc.
Portland, ME 04104

See listing under Signs.

Detail, Winooski Block, Winooski, VT, restored by Moose Creek Restorations, Burlington, VT. (Photo courtesy of Moose Creek Restorations)

John Leeke, Woodworker
RR 1 Box 244
Sanford, ME 04073
(207) 324-9597

Custom millwork and turnings including large, hollow columns. Can work from rough sketch or more detailed drawing. Specializes in hand and machine work on projects (including restoration) requiring particular attention to detail: "carvings, hand-planed weather boards, fancy doorway, and window treatments." Traditional and modern designs.

Anderson-McQuaid Co.
170 Fawcett Street
Cambridge, MA 02138
(617) 876-3250

Specializes in architectural lumber and millwork. Also has site furniture and planters.

Albany Street Woodshop
533 Albany Street
Boston, MA 02118
(617) 338-8011

Finials, drops, columns, and balusters. Can give design advice. Also does millwork and carving. Custom turnings (only dowels are automatic turnings); small orders. No maximum size for turnings.

Downes Millwork Co.
60 Bradston
Boston, MA 02118
(617) 445-7208

Specialty: custom milling of hardwoods and moldings. Also turnings: stock and custom.

J. J. Browne Co.
828 Washington Street
Hanover, MA 02339
(617) 826-2930

Wood and copper sheet cupolas; custom and readymade designs. Will install on all structures.

Medford Woodworks Corp.
200 Boston Avenue
Medford, MA 02155
(617) 395-4955

Specializes in architectural woodworking; stock and custom items.

Cape Cod Cupola Co.
78 State Road
North Dartmouth, MA 02747
(617) 994-2119

Manufactures cupolas; works in wood and sheet copper. Does not install.

Amherst Woodworking and Supply, Inc.
Box 575, Hubbard Avenue
Northampton, MA 01060
(413) 584-3003

Specialty: raised paneling and architectural millwork.

Salem Sign Co.
Salem, MA 01970

See listing under Signs.

Detail Millwork Co.
118 Bacon
Waltham, MA 02154
(617) 893-2241

Specializes in doors and windows.

David Hull Masury
RFD 1, Robert Gould Road
Contoocook, NH 03229
(603) 746-3049

Specializes in custom, one-of-a-kind design and woodwork, exterior and interior, including millwork and hand carv-

Stock columns and balusters. E. A. Nord Co., Everett, WA. (Photo courtesy of E. A. Nord Co.)

ing. Also does custom doors and furniture for residence and business. Contemporary design drawing from many styles—Art Nouveau, Oriental, Egyptian, etc. Will do custom work from rough sketch, photo, or more detailed drawing.

Keller Products, Inc.
41 Union
Manchester, NH 03103
(603) 627-7887

Laminated extrusions and engineered molded plywoods. Standard and custom shapes.

N-J Woodturning Corp.
181 Lincoln Avenue
Fairlawn, NJ 07410
(201) 427-6650

Custom hand turnings; small and one-of-a-kind orders. Finials, drops, columns, and balusters. Maximum sizes 10 feet by 20 inches. Can give design advice.

Dr. Edison Shows, Inc.
Attn. Toby Grace, Master Joiner
Minnisink Hill House
Mill Road
Matawan, NJ 07747
(201) 566-0157

Will undertake almost any type of ornamental project, providing it is not on too large a scale. While the company makes a limited amount of custom moldings and turnings on original, nineteenth-century machinery upon request (clients must call at the office to select and pick up the finished moldings), Edison's main business is "the design and creation of exotic and unusual architectural ornament." Designs and builds gazebos, clock towers with mechanical figures, shop fronts, coffered ceilings, etc. Works in wood, fiber glass, and other plastics. Specialty: "fantasy elements" of the Victorian period.

Bendix Moldings
235 Pegasus Avenue
Northvale, NJ 07647
(201) 767-8888

Carved wood ornaments and moldings. Many carved and embossed moldings, mostly smaller scale, in a variety of patterns. Catalog $2.00.

Stanley D. Saperstein
Master Wood Carver and Joiner
103 Corrine Drive
Pennington, NJ 08534
(609) 737-9364

Carves panels, murals, moldings, and furniture. Expert in wood drying. Specializes in period furniture and does restoration work. Can also do turning. Brochure $0.50.

Bailey Architectural Millwork, Inc.
125 Slack Avenue
Trenton, NJ 08648
(609) 392-5137

Custom turnings; finials, drops, and balusters (small orders). Maximum size: 9 feet long; 8 inches in diameter. Also does millwork and wood carving.

A selection of stock elements from Cumberland Woodcraft Co., Carlisle, PA. (Photo courtesy of Cumberland Woodcraft Co.)

Door and embellishments: carved garlands and moldings. The Wood Shop, Boyne City, MI. (Photo courtesy of The Wood Shop)

American Wood Column Corp.
913 Grand Street
Brooklyn, NY 11211
(212) 782-3163
(212) 782-3164

Readymade and custom turnings; will make columns from any kind of wood. No maximum length or diameter stated. Columns manufactured in any diameter or height, full or half-round (various styles including roped or twisted); square or flat pilasters. Handcrafted or automatic turnings of balusters, spindles, or posts from sketch or measured drawing. Column capitals from 2 to 25 inches in round, flat, square, or as per detailed drawing. Capitals are made in staff, wood and composition, or carved wood to specifications. Capitals used for exterior are warranted to withstand all weather conditions. Can give design advice. Small, large, and one-of-a-kind orders (American has a maximum size order). Also does millwork and carving.

Dimension Lumber and Milling Corporation
517 Stagg Street
Brooklyn, NY 11237
(212) 497-1680

Standard and custom hardwood moldings.

Old World Molding
115 Allen Boulevard
Farmingdale, NY 11735
(516) 293-1789

Specialty: embossed wood moldings—mainly small scale—and custom finishing. Custom shapes from measured drawing only. Brochure $1.00.

Michael's Fine Colonial Products
1284 Townline Road
Hauppauge, NY 11787
(516) 979-9473

Custom turnings, readymade newel posts, balusters, finials, columns, capitals, and bases. Specialty: replacement of unusually shaped sashes (Gothic, triangle, segment, quarter, half and full circle) and shutters. Also does architectural millwork. Large, small (minimum order), and one-of-a-kind orders. Brochure with SASE.

Merit Molding, Ltd.
95-35 150th Street
Jamaica, NY 11435
(212) 423-2200

Embossed wood moldings.

Paul Tankel
1748 Hydesville Road
Newark, NY 14513
(315) 331-1989

Specializes in bas-relief panels. He uses different thicknesses of wood joined together to make three-dimensional pieces emphasizing wood grain. Also makes custom furniture, cabinetry, and stairs for interior. Can work from sketch, sample, or finished drawing. Can give advice about installation. Brochure $1.00.

Spaso Gajic, G.M.S.
503 E. 72nd Street
New York, NY 10021
(212) 734-2581

Does hand and machine carving of panels, murals, moldings, columns, and other façade elements. Can work from sketch or more detailed information. Does own installation; takes small or large orders. Specializes in interior decorative work, but has done exterior work as well.

Ivan Olszewski
New York, NY 10012

See listing under Sculpture.

Restoration Workshop
Attn. Alan Keiser, Director
635 S. Broadway
Tarrytown, NY 10591
(914) 631-6696

The workshop performs preservation and restoration work for nonprofit National Trust member organizations, private owners of National Historical Landmarks who are members of the National Trust, and private owners of National Register properties who are members of the National Trust, where the services are essential for emergency restoration work or as a means of demonstrating new developments or techniques in architectural preservation. Work involves mainly carpentry and millwork, but also includes masonry, painting, roofing, and sheet metal work. Call or write for more information.

Mary Shelley
Box 94
West Danby, NY 14896
(607) 564-3527

Hand incision carving; can do panels, murals, signs, etc. Specializes in folk art carvings. Will send photos of work on request.

Cumberland Woodcraft Co.
2500 Walnut Bottom Road
Carlisle, PA 17013
(717) 243-0063

A large selection of exterior moldings including corbels, brackets, spandrels, balustrades, and rails. Cumberland has a special line of Victorian millwork made from kiln-dried oak or poplar with other hardwoods available on special order. Will manufacture custom reproductions from hardwood on request. Brochure (many color illustrations) $3.00.

A. F. Schwerd Manufacturing Co.
3215 McClure Avenue
Pittsburgh, PA 15212
(412) 766-6322

Specializes in readymade colonial wood columns. Will also do custom columns from sketch or more detailed drawing.

Wynnewood Woodworks
317 Aubrey Road
Wynnewood, PA 19096
(215) 642-8934

Specializes in wood carving and turning. Custom carving only. Custom and stock turnings. All custom work from sketch or more detailed information. Also will do custom jigsaw or gingerbread ornament.

Moose Creek Restoration, Ltd.
12–22 North Street
Burlington, VT 05401
(802) 862-6765

Specializes in architectural reproductions, repairs, and moldings. Can recommend a skilled wood carver.

Sawn grape ornaments on clock tower, Vintage Faire Mall, Modesto, CA. John Ward, Artisan Woodworkers, Sonoma, CA. (Photo courtesy of Artisan Woodworkers)

Woodshop, Inc.
Box 412
Johnson, VT 05656
(802) 635-7326

Custom millwork only. Primarily a custom cabinet shop, but has done exterior trim and decorative hand carving of panels and moldings. Can work from sketch; gives installation advice.

The Millworks, Inc.
403 Barre Street
Montpelier, VT 05602
(802) 223-6210

This company does cornice and porch details, numerous base molds, etc. Can also custom jigsaw gingerbread ornament. Approximately 500 separate cutter heads on hand for all conceivable styles of moldings—interior and exterior. Also does custom turnings from sketch or more detailed drawing.

Norman Vandal
Housewright & Cabinetmaker
P.O. Box 67
Roxbury, VT 05669
(802) 485-8380

A craftsman who is a restoration consultant and cabinetmaker. He specializes in historically accurate eighteenth-century, Federal, and Greek Revival woodwork. Prefers to do his own designs in these styles but can produce anything in wood from sketch or more detailed drawing. Brochure $1.00.

Sparky Potter
P.O. Box 283
Waitsfield, VT 05673
(802) 496-2318

Hand carves murals, signs, doors, etc. Does incision, bas-relief, and burning. Specializes in taking a motif and carrying it through signs, doors, murals, etc.—interior and exterior. Uses woodburning tools in painted work to achieve a pen-and-ink effect. Can give technical advice about warpage, etc. Also designs and fabricates leaded glass windows.

Vermont Cabinetworks
FEA Building 8
Winooski, VT 05404
(802) 655-2645

Incision and bas-relief carving by hand and machine: panels, murals, and moldings. Will do own decorative designs or can work from sketch, sample, or measured drawing. Specialty: custom millwork and cabinets. Has stock turnings—will do custom turnings; finials, drops, columns, and balusters. Small and large orders. Can give design advice. Does millwork and carving as well.

South

Marsh Industries
P.O. Box 3687
Birmingham, AL 35211
(205) 328-1300

Manufacturer of custom architectural millwork.

Laser Works
629 17th Avenue
Bradenton, FL 33505
(813) 748-4727

Does incision carving with laser beam. It is precise and can reproduce virtually any image, even with fine detail. Can carve acrylics as well as wood.

Wight Millworks
1695 E. 11th Avenue
Hialeah, FL 33010
(305) 691-5362

Specializes in custom doors, moveable plantation shutters, circular stairs, and fixtures. Will do custom turnings.

Rich's Cabinets and Wood Working
Attn. Richard M. Ott
1524 Four Winds Boulevard
Kissimmee, FL 32741
(305) 846-7147
(305) 847-7290

Manufacturer and distributor of custom and readymade cupolas (American Cupola Co.) in wood, fiber glass and copper sheet. (Shop address: **10 East Keen St., Kissimmee, FL 32741.**) Brochure available.

Authentic eighteenth-century joinery. Norman Vandal, Roxbury, VT. (Photo courtesy of Norman Vandal)

A fully equipped woodshop with good source for all types of woods. Builds custom wood products: doors, jambs, signs, large and small wood brackets, and hardwood moldings.

Atlantic Millworks
3550 N.W. 58th Street
Miami, FL 33142
(305) 633-3277

Specializes in custom architectural millwork. Can also laminate wood to wood and plastic to wood.

Rich Woodturning
98 N.W. 29th Street
Miami, FL 33127
(305) 573-9142

Finials, drops, columns, and balusters. Maximum size: 20 feet by 54 inches. Can offer design advice. Also does millwork and carving. Small and large orders.

Wingate Millworks
3074 S.W. 37th Court
Miami, FL 33146
(305) 445-8636

Sections of wooden cresting being sand-painted to resemble stone for the restoration of Lyndhurst, Tarrytown, NY. Restoration Workshop, National Trust for Historic Preservation, Tarrytown, NY (Photo courtesy of Restoration Workshop)

Specializes in custom moldings, doors, stairs, windows, and louvers.

Evariste A. Faucher
300 Hunt Road
Athens, GA 30606
(404) 548-6834

Hand- and machinemade custom ornamental joinery, windows, moldings, etc. On request will manufacture stone building blocks from fieldstone. "If you cannot buy it from someone else—come see me."

Legacy Pine Limited
P.O. Box 52614
Atlanta, GA 30355
(404) 233-0067

This company specializes in architectural elements, interior and exterior, made from hand selected, kiln-dried, retrieved and remilled Virgin Longleaf Heart Pine. This is virgin-growth pine, some of it originally cut centuries ago, that has been recovered from old buildings. In addition to standard and custom elements—including cornice brackets, spindles, moldings, and fireplaces—Legacy does standard and custom turnings.

Xylo
P.O. Box 8062
2000 Louisville Road
Savannah, GA 31412
(912) 233-1263

Standard and custom wood moldings from measured drawing or sample only. Also makes glued items.

Woodcrafters Workshop
Attn. Mike Borgmeier
15116 Old Taylorsville Road
Fisherville, KY 40023
(502) 267-0709

Finials, columns, drops, and balusters. Maximum size: 8 feet by 12 inches. Can offer design advice. Also does millwork and carving. Custom turnings; small and large orders.

Audubon Millwork and Supply Co.
1301 S. Claiborne Avenue
New Orleans, LA 70125
(504) 581-2569

Stock and custom millwork plus specialty items.

Gulf Enterprises, Inc.
P.O. Box 13984
New Orleans, LA 70185
(504) 822-0785

Distributors of Nord wood products: doors, columns, spindles, etc.

Lafitte Sash and Door Co.
1228 S. Dupre
New Orleans, LA 70125
(504) 822-4010

Custom and stock architectural millwork.

Heartwood
P.O. Box 1375
Thaibodaux, LA 70301
(504) 445-3255

Manufacturer of standard and custom moldings and turnings. Can work from sketch or more detailed information. Specialty: cornice brackets, spindles, moldings, mantels, etc.

Walbrook Mill and Lumber Co.
2636 W. North Avenue
Baltimore, MD 21216
(301) 462-2200

Specializes in custom millwork and turnings.

Mahany Associates, Inc.
5806 Johnson Avenue
Bethesda, MD 20034
(301) 530-2405

Finials, drops, columns, and balusters. Maximum size: 8 by 2 feet. Custom turnings; large, small, and one-of-a-kind orders.

Gregory Manufacturing Co., Inc.
P.O. Box 1303
110 Capers Avenue
Jackson, MS 39205
(601) 355-1594

Stock custom and stock machine turnings; large orders only. Maximum size: 4 by 2 inches.

Joyner-Black, Inc.
P.O. Box 31812
691 E. Bay Street
Charleston, SC 29407
(803) 577-0730

Specializes in custom millwork: circle head, special cornices, doors, etc. Also stock items and turnings. Any type of architectural design.

Custom House Molding Manufacturing Co.
P.O. Box 4372
5117 D Baldwin Road
Columbia, SC 29240
(803) 754-3642

Specializes in stock and special moldings; also standard and custom turnings.

Driwood Molding Co.
Attn. R. E. Gelzer
P.O. Box 1729
Florence, SC 29503
(803) 669-0761

Large manufacturer of embossed wood moldings designed so they can be combined into cornices and other larger elements. Also does turnings. Brochure free; catalog $6.00 (for two)—credited against orders.

Robert T. Wrisley
417 Childers Street
Pulaski, TN 38478
(615) 363-7765

Custom hand carving of various architectural elements including scrolls, brackets, capitals, and doors. Has done carving for restoration buildings as well as manufacturing 8-foot columns and curved staircases in wood. Also does hand turnings of finials, drops, and balusters (maximum size: 35 by 10 inches). Can work from rough sketch, photo, or detailed information. Small orders, although he will consider large orders.

Period Productions, Ltd.
1823 W. Main Street
Richmond, VA 23220
(804) 353-5976

Specializes in curved work: circular and elliptical staircases, bow and fan windows—natural finish. Will do custom turnings from sketch.

Frederick Wilbur
Route 1, Box 106
Shipman, VA 22971
(804) 263-4827

Hand carving of panels, murals, moldings, pediments, finials, crockets, and signs. Specializes in ecclesiastical and heraldic carving; has active wood-routed sign business.

Midwest

Northwest Mill and Supply Co.
130 S. Lincoln Avenue
Carpentersville, IL 60110
(312) 428-3122
(312) 428-3125
(312) 428-3144

Specializes in architectural woodwork. Turnings: stock and custom.

Berman Sales
1728 S. Michigan
Chicago, IL 60616
(312) 427-6500

and

230 Fifth Avenue
New York, NY 10001
(212) 725-0942

Custom turnings from measured drawing: finials, columns, and balusters. Maximum diameter: 8 inches. Can give design advice. Large orders only.

Victorian restoration, 943 S. Van Ness Street, San Francisco. All woodwork and painting by San Francisco Renaissance. (Photo courtesy of San Francisco Renaissance)

George Pagels Co.
2534 S. Western Avenue
Chicago, IL 60608
(312) 847-7086

Custom turnings; large, small, and one-of-a-kind orders. Finials, drops, and balusters. Estimates given "reluctantly." Maximum size: 20 by 2 feet. Minimum order $50.00. Does mill work also.

Rinn-Scott Lumber Co.
2759 S. Kedzie Avenue
Chicago, IL 60623
(312) 247-4080

Distributor of embossed, prefinished moldings. Can have custom shapes done.

H.P.M., Inc.
1580 Old Skokie Road
Highland Park, IL 60035
(312) 831-2770

Distributor of standard and custom architectural woodwork.

White Pine Cupolas
297 E. North Avenue
Villa Park, IL 60181
(312) 834-1769

Manufacturer of readymade and custom cupolas; sells directly. Will install. Materials: wood, aluminum, sheet copper.

R. K. Degroot, Cabinetmaker
126 E. Hawthorne Boulevard
Wheaton, IL 60187
(312) 665-2685

Does hand carving of panels and moldings. Specialty: custom cabinetmaking. Will work to architect's sketch, sample, or measured drawing. In addition, Degroot does turning, lamination, steam bending, veneering, scrollwork, and oil gilding. Accepts small orders.

William J. Schnute
The Oak Leaves Studio
RR 6, The Woods, #12
Iowa City, IA 52240
(319) 351-0014

Custom hand carving (incision and bas-relief) for interior and exterior installation; panels, murals, and free-standing pieces. Can do own designs or is willing to work from an architect's sketch, photo, sample, or working drawing. Gives advice about exterior installations. Brochure $0.50.

The Wood Shop
111 East Street
Boyne City, MI 49712
(616) 582-9835

Specializes in custom wood carving, wood signs, and graphics.

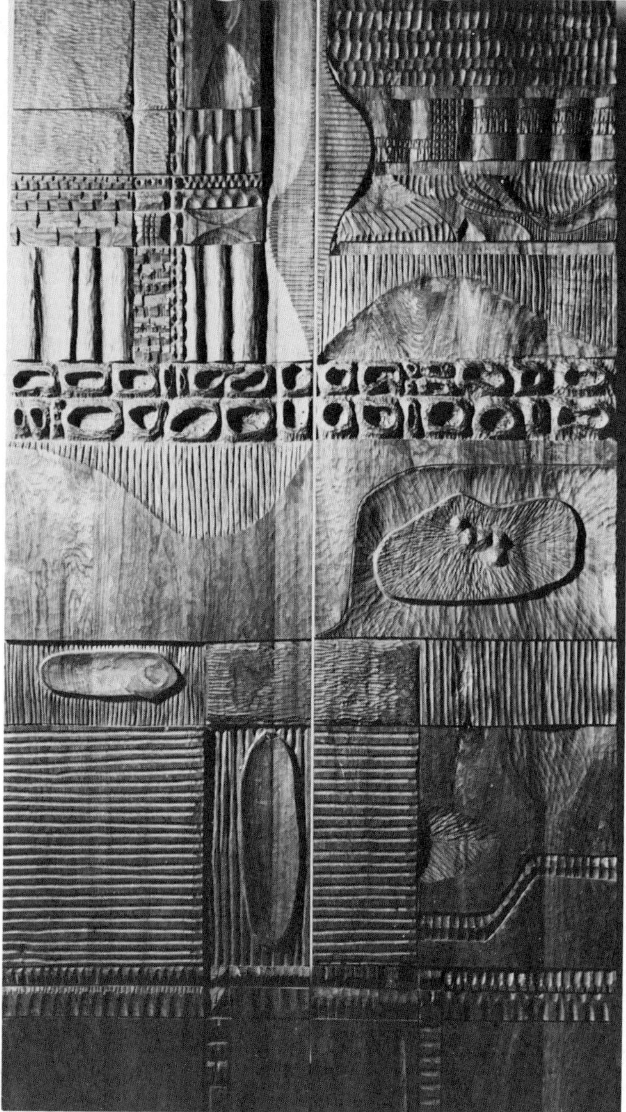

Hand-carved wood doors (approximately 5 by 9 feet). Thomas H. Williams, Atlanta, GA. (Photo courtesy of Thomas H. Williams)

Rasmussen & Son Woodworking Co.
9430 Livernois
Detroit, MI 48204
(313) 933-1155

Finials, drops, columns, balusters; hand turnings. Maximum size: length, 97 inches, diameter 18 inches. Can give design advice. Custom turnings; large, small, or one-of-a-kind orders. Does mill work also.

M. A. Kirk
Creative Designs, Inc.
821 E. Kalamazoo
Lansing, MI 48912
(517) 487-6965

All types of architectural millwork, including turning and built-up pieces such as dentil courses. Also does incision and bas-relief carving. Custom designs only; can work from rough sketch or more detailed information. Specializes in restoration and reproduction work. Has access to subcontractors for ironwork and other metal ornament; marble and other stonework, etc. Large and small orders.

O. & W. Millwork
37385 Little Mack
Mount Clemens, MI 48043
(313) 465-5141

Manufacturer of custom and stock architectural millwork.

J. B. O'Meara Co.
Box 1111
901 E. Cliff Road
Burnsville, MN 55337
(612) 890-8604

Readymade turned columns and balusters. Maximum size: 20 feet by 20 inches. Distributors of Nord wood products. Large and small orders.

Robert C. Kinghorn
22785 Murray Street
Excelsior, MN 55331
(612) 474-9588

Does hand and machine carving (incision and bas-relief) of exterior panels, signs, and murals. Also jigsaw work, weather vanes, lettering, and traditional lamp posts and fences. Can do decorative designs in any style involving wood. Will work from architect's sketch, measured drawing, or sample. He also cuts and inlays such metals as brass. Large and small orders.

Nelson Johnson Wood Products
4326 Lyndale Avenue N.
Minneapolis, MN 55412
(612) 529-2771 (day)
(612) 529-2978 (night)

Does custom woodworking of all kinds including turning and carving. Maximum size: 10 feet by 16 inches. Turnings of finials, drops, columns, balusters. Also does millwork—single run items only. Minimum and maximum orders. Brochure only for stock distributed turnings. Estimates can be made on turnings which have no details. Custom turnings; large and small orders.

Johnson Wood Products
5900 Main Street N.E.
Minneapolis, MN 55432
(612) 571-8180

Specializes in custom commercial woodwork. Maintains an inventory of hardwoods; estimators, draftsmen, and project managers in the plant. Also handles brass railings, fittings, and fixtures.

Shaw Lumber
217 Como Avenue
St. Paul, MN 55103
(612) 488-2525

Custom millwork only. Large stock of hardwoods.

North elevation of Izenour House. Cedar shingles and trim, including nautical motif. Designed by Steven Izenour; Venturi, Rauch & Scott-Brown, Architects. (Drawing courtesy of Steven Izenour; Venturi, Rauch & Scott-Brown, Architects)

Ray Donaldson
Wood Graphics
Box 85
Taylors Falls, MN 55084
(612) 465-7122

Does any kind of wood carving; prefers contemporary style and will do very large carvings, free-standing or bas-relief. Is willing to interpret an architect's idea.

The Top Shop
801 E. 31st Street
Kansas City, MO
(816) 561-8199

Custom finials, drops, and balusters; hand turnings. Maximum size: 34 by 8 inches. Small orders.

Crescent Planing Mill Co.
3227 N. Ninth Street
St. Louis, MO 63147
(314) 231-4118

Only custom millwork. Has been manufacturing architectural woodwork since 1890. Sells to general contractors. Also does custom turnings.

Brown Woodworks
1003 Avenue A
Kerney, NE 68847
(308) 234-9616

Gingerbread, brackets, and gable adornments. Carving, custom millwork, and turnings (can do wood faceplate turnings up to 48 inches in diameter, spindles, etc.). Architectural restoration.

Kay Dee Company of Omaha
2101 Cuming Street
Omaha, NE 68102
(402) 341-0820

Restoration work, all types of moldings, oval windows, church and residential furniture. "Anything made of wood."

Manfred Millwork, Inc.
1221 Nicholas Street
Omaha, NE 68102
(402) 341-0777

Manufacturer, sells directly. Specialty: architectural millwork and casework. Stock shapes; custom shapes from sketch or working drawing.

Taft Wood Products Co.
6520 Carnegie Avenue
Cleveland, OH 44103
(216) 881-8937

Turnings: finials, balusters, and columns. One-of-a-kind, small, and large orders. Also does custom millwork.

Doddington Millwork Inc.
35 Derrer Road
Columbus, OH 43204
(614) 274-1188

Standard and custom woodwork. Prefers measured drawings for custom work. Also does custom turnings from measured drawings.

Smith Dodson Lumber Co.
200 Colton Road
Columbus, OH 43207
(614) 491-5221

Standard and custom moldings—preferably from measured drawings or sample; also cabinets, siding, etc.

Webb Manufacturing, Inc.
P.O. Box 707
Conneaut, OH 44030
(216) 593-1151

Fabricator; product sold through distributors as Stephenson Cupolas. Readymade designs in redwood. Also has readymade round, oval, and fan windows with beveled glass and hand-cast aluminum weather vanes.

John W. Winterich and Assocs.
Solon, OH 44139

See listing under Murals.

Hendrix, Heikkilä, and Terry, Inc.
Norman, OK 73069

See listing under Murals.

Custom Kraft Woodshop
324 S.E. 69th
Oklahoma City, OK 73149
(405) 632-2786

Hand and machine, custom and readymade turnings: finials, columns, and balusters. Can give design advice. Small and large orders.

B. & E. Wood Manufacturing of Tulsa
7441 E. 46th Place
Tulsa, OK 74145
(918) 681-0749

Specializes in all sizes of stock lathe work; custom designs from working drawings. "Porch columns our specialty." Sells directly or through distributors.

Architectural Restorations, Inc.
Attn. Doug Strange
311 Colorado
Austin, TX 78701
(512) 472-8390

Specializes in entryways, doors, and wood sash windows. Also does standard and custom turnings from measured drawing. Provides assistance in all areas of woodworking.

Castleberry Mill
2507 E. 11th Street
Dallas, TX 75203
(214) 946-7511

Manufacturers of custom architectural millwork.

J. P. Jackson and Son
Architectural Millwork
1909 Renner
Fort Worth, TX 76104
(817) 536-3333

Manufactures a full line of architectural millwork; stock and custom. Also custom turnings.

McMurray Wholesale Turnpost Co.
Attn. Keith McMurray
Rte. 13, Box 94
Ft. Worth, TX 76119
(817) 478-0094
(817) 478-6555

Columns, newels, balusters, capitals, spindles, and brackets. Maximum size: 13 feet by 6 inches. Readymade only; small orders.

W. Hugh Vance
1111 Sealy
Galveston, TX 77550
(713) 765-2949
(713) 765-5842

Finials, balusters (may have access to larger lathe for columns). Maximum size: 36 by 8 inches. Prefers doing custom work from sample. Custom turnings; large, small, and one-of-a-kind orders.

Paul Stein
1 Buell Court
Houston, TX 77006
(713) 529-1891
(713) 524-3265

Hand and machine carving of panels and murals—specializes in doors. Does incision carving plus laminated, built-up forms and details.

Allen and Allen Co.
P.O. Box 5140
1621 N. Comal
San Antonio, TX 78284
(512) 733-9191

Specializes in hardwood moldings and paneling. Stocks readymade turnings including finials and twisted moldings; also carved and embossed moldings. A complete stock of imported and domestic hardwoods and mill facilities for manufacture of hardwood moldings, trim, and solid paneling. Also specializes in "exquisite" decorative hardware from around the world. (Plaster ornaments for interior as well.) Several large catalogs.

A. Pullen
203 S. Frio Street
San Antonio, TX 78207
(512) 223-6521

Custom turnings: finials, drops, columns, and balusters. Can give design advice. Also does millwork and carving. Small and large orders.

Vintage Wood Works
Attn. Gregory Tatsch
Main Street
Quinlan, TX 75474
(214) 356-3667

Specializes in Victorian gingerbread and fretwork—standard and custom designs. Brochure $1.00.

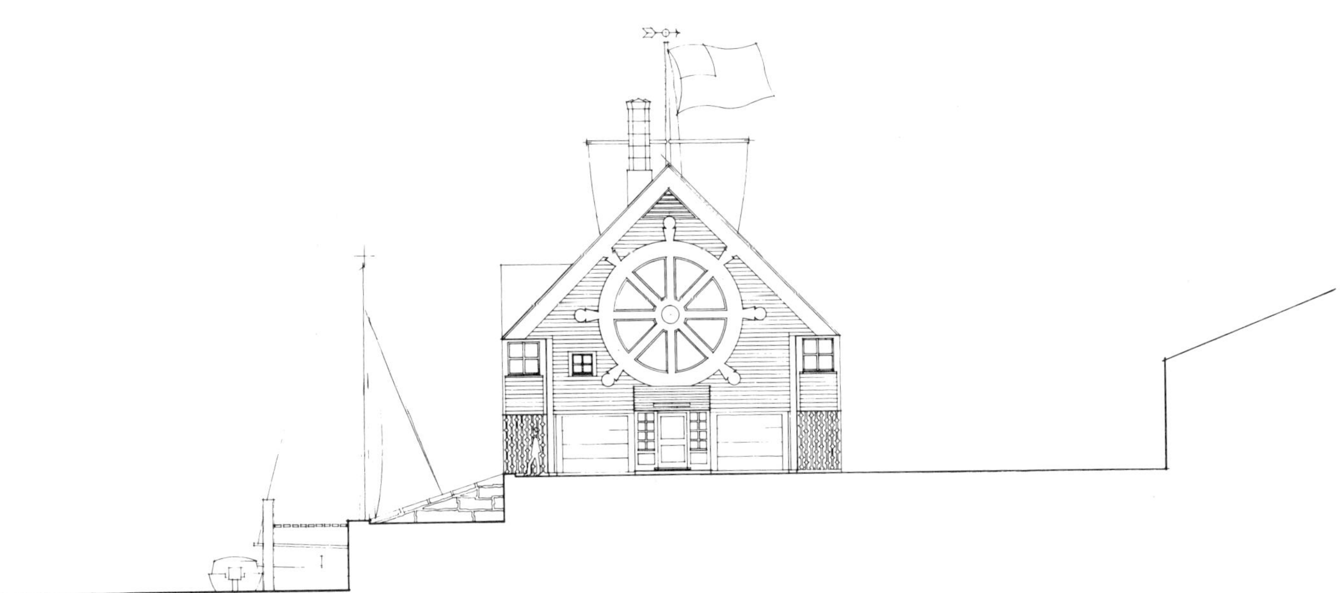

House based on Mt. Vernon, project. Trim, including rustication, in wood. Venturi, Rauch & Scott-Brown, Architects. (Drawing courtesy of Venturi, Rauch & Scott-Brown, Architects)

Traditional ornamentally cut shingles, from the late 19th or early 20th century, West Springfield, MA.

A. B. Manufacturing Co.
1168 N. 50th Place
Milwaukee, WI 53208
(414) 258-1308

Custom turnings: maximum size: 23 feet by 20 inches. Produces finials, drops, columns, and balusters. Does millwork and carving as well. Small and large orders.

Rockies and Far West

Bel-Air Door Co.
304 S. Date Avenue
Alhambra, CA 91803
(213) 283-3731

Manufactures and distributes entry doors; primarily stock designs; some custom work from working drawing only.

Quality Frame and Door
12120 E. Park
Cerritos, CA 90701
(213) 926-3337

Manufacturer of standard and custom architectural millwork for commercial and high-rise buildings.

Round Valley Woodwrights
Attn. Marc Breséе
76500 Short Creek Road
Covelo, CA 95428
(707) 983-6337

A custom woodworking shop. Can work from photo, rough sketch, or "even a vague idea." Makes all types of architectural elements including doors, windows, cabinets, chests, lighting, tables, etc. Pieces generally built of locally milled hardwoods.

Crowe's Woodturning
1136 Industrial Avenue
Escondido, CA 92025
(714) 741-2069

Finials, drops, columns, balusters. Maximum size: 9 1/2 feet by 16 inches. Can give design advice. Does some architectural millwork as well. Custom and readymade turnings; large, small, and one-of-a-kind orders.

North Pacific Joinery
76 W. Fourth Street
Eureka, CA 95501
(707) 443-5788

Specializes in sashes, doors, moldings, and turnings. Standard moldings and turnings. Will also do custom work, including jigsaw ornament. Brochure $1.00.

Coast Planing Mill
2170 E. 14th Street
Los Angeles, CA 90021
(714) 622-1181

Specializes in custom planing of customer's lumber.

Hallelujah Wood Products
39500 Comptche Road
Mendocino, CA 95460
(707) 937-0076

Specializes in sawn and molded work—brackets, moldings, etc. Has standard shapes and can make custom designs from rough sketch or more detailed information. Can also design and install exteriors on old and new buildings, using stock components where possible. Brochure $1.00.

Bartley's Mill
Attn. Steve Bartley
8515 San Leandro
Oakland, CA 94621
(415) 569-5533

Specializes in reproductions of moldings and turnings.

John Munch
Adelaida Star Route
Paso Robles, CA 93446
(805) 239-0190

Victorian millwork reproductions are his specialty. Also

does custom turnings. He is a licensed general contractor in California.

F. S. Buckley Door Co., Inc.
1698 Evans Avenue
San Francisco, CA 94124
(415) 282-2277

Manufacturers and distributors of stock millwork, doors, and wood sash windows.

Haas Wood & Ivory Works, Inc.
64 Clementina Street
San Francisco, CA 94105
(415) 421-8273

This firm, in business since 1887, turns wood only. Custom hand turnings for new construction as well as restorations. Typical items include newels, brackets, crestings, scrolls, dormers, handrails, moldings, columns, caps and hoods, drops, and balusters. "Virtually any type of Victorian ornamentation imaginable." Maximum size: 20 by 2 feet; faceplates can be up to 84 inches in diameter. Also has a custom cabinet shop, building all types of hand-constructed and finished pieces for private and commercial clients. Large, small, and one-of-a-kind orders.

Timothy Howe
838 Hyde Street, Suite 11
San Francisco, CA
(415) 885-2520

Machine carving of lettering, logos, and "some decoration." Small and large orders. Brochure $1.00.

Lowpensky Moulding
1030 Quesada Avenue
San Francisco, CA 94124
(415) 822-7422

Manufactures custom millwork from measured drawings only. Specializes in Victorian restoration.

San Francisco Renaissance
Attn. John Jacobson
2501 Bryant Street
San Francisco, CA 94110
(415) 826-0447

This company provides a variety of services in the following categories. *Decorative painting:* stencilling, gilding, woodgraining; stencils and patterns prepared. *Plastering:* fully cast ceilings, run moldings, and enriched moldings; units made at site or delivered and installed. Cast pieces include capitals and gargoyles. Also does carved plasterwork. Makes patterns to be cast in such other materials as concrete, metals, and plastics. *Millwork:* short runs of shaped pieces including patterns for casting, Corinthian abacuses, fitted trim. *Wood turning:* short runs of typical finials, fancy porch columns, newels, plus rough cuts for carving. *Sculpture:* grotesque faces, curious panel motifs, rosettes, etc. Will make replacement parts for cast iron façades, cresting, and special hardware. Will supervise casting by others. In addition, will do "site deciphering"—an analysis to suggest likely past appearance of a building; its

"Wheat," handcarved wood (height, approx. 6 feet). William J. Schnute, the Oak Leaves Studio, Iowa City, IA (Photo courtesy of William J. Schnute)

Exuberant, jig sawed and turned wood ornaments from the turn of the century. Oak Bluffs, Martha's Vineyard, MA.

color, details, etc.—for those who would like to restore. The company has consultants for color, wood turning, carving, façade design, and period façade restoration. California contractor's license.

San Francisco Victoriana
2245 Palou Avenue
San Francisco, CA 94124
(415) 648-0313

Manufacturer and distributor of Victorian style custom and stock architectural millwork. One hundred and fifty molding profiles (circa 1850 to 1915), door and window trims, fancy cedar shingles, crowns, beds, panel moldings, fancy fretwork, and wood grilles. Custom designs from working drawing only. Also does stock and custom turnings. Plaster and wood duplication services from model. Cast iron stairs; brass and bronze hardware. Elaborate brochure. Catalog (architectural moldings) $5.00.

Developers' Finish Supply
1565 La Mirada Drive
San Marcos, CA 92069
(714) 744-3754

Specializes in stock and custom (from measured drawing) residential and commercial sashes and doors. Also does custom turnings.

Hector Bezanis
Wood Turning & Carving
25 W. Gutierrez Street
Santa Barbara, CA 93101
(805) 965-9876

Readymade and custom hand turnings from rough sketch or more detailed information. Maximum length: 20 feet, any diameter; small or large orders. Also does stair railings, fluted columns, doorway rosettes. Specializes in wood carving, interior and exterior—exact duplications from photos and samples—and light milling and bandsaw work. Most work is done in either clear fir, redwood, or oak.

John Ward
Artisan Woodworkers
21415 Broadway
Sonoma, CA 95476
(707) 938-4796

Will do all types of ornamental woodwork including monumental details ("fabricated and built up"), furniture, cabinets, etc. "We are a group of custom woodworkers and commercial artists who work with many kinds of projects. We design, coordinate, and build railings, posts, trim, friezes, screens, lighting fixtures, cabinetry, etc. Our specialty is quality craft and versatility. We will consider anything and we accept only what we can do." Does not do custom millwork, but can arrange it in conjunction with a job. Custom turnings: finials, drops, and columns; maximum size: 12 feet x 12 inches. Has access to wood carvers and will act as coordinator.

Abaroot Manufacturing Co.
1853 W. Torrance Boulevard
Torrance, CA 90501
(213) 320-8172
(213) 320-8173

Readymade and custom turnings, hand and machine: finials, drops, columns, and balusters. Maximum size: 20 by 2 feet. Small and large orders.

Roger's Woodturning
1404 S. Santa Fe
Vista, CA 92083
(714) 724-4070

Readymade and custom turnings: finials, drops, columns, and balusters. Maximum diameter: 18 inches. Also does millwork and wood carving. Small and large orders.

Criterion Woodwork, Inc.
2200 Seventh Street
Denver, CO 80211
(303) 455-4058

Custom woodwork.

Robert Tully
Denver, CO 80204

See listing under Sculpture.

J. M. L. Company
Attn. Jim Littlehorn
3940 S. Jason
Englewood, CO 80110
(303) 781-1874

Hand and machine turnings, readymade and custom: columns, drops, finials, and balusters. Maximum size: 12 by 1 1/2 feet. Also does millwork. Small and large orders.

First Impressions
Fort Collins, CO 80502

See listing under Ornamental Metals.

Silverton Victorian Mill Works
Attn. George Crane
Box 523, Dept. HAO
Silverton, CO 81433
(303) 387-5716

This company has an instructive catalog that includes forty working drawings showing detailing for exterior and interior situations involving moldings. Specialty: stock moldings and blocks for interior and exterior trim. The catalog costs $3.50, and shows virtually every type of wood molding—each with several variations.

American Lumber Co.
8503 N. Denver Avenue
Portland, OR 97217
(503) 289-5517

Distributor and manufacturer of finished woodwork.

Blair's Woodworking Co.
8930 N.E. Killingsworth Street
Portland, OR 97220
(503) 252-2425
(503) 252-2426

Specializes in detailed millwork: sashes, doors, fixtures. No production items.

L. Samuel Fort
5316 S.W. Westwood View
Portland, OR 97201
(503) 244-8763

Does hand carving of panels and murals. Specializes in carved doors. Can do own design or work from architect's sketch, etc. Gives installation advice; large and small orders.

Specialty Woodworking Co., Inc.
1434 N.W. 22nd Avenue
Portland, OR 97210
(503) 224-5465

Produces a full line of custom architectural millwork and cabinetry.

Turncraft
White City, OR 97501
(503) 826-2911

Readymade turnings from 8 feet by 6 inches to 20 feet by 20 inches. Offers fluted columns, porch posts, lamp posts, spindles, newel posts, and rails. Small and large orders.

Rosander Woodturning
1001 Hillview Drive
Salt Lake City, UT 84117
(801) 266-1639

Custom hand turnings: finials, drops, columns, and balusters. Maximum size: 14 feet by 12 inches. Small and large orders.

Old and Elegant Distributors
Bellevue, WA 98004

See listing under Metals.

Sheppard Millwork
21020 70th Avenue W.
Edmonds, WA 98020
(206) 771-4645

Manufacturer of standard and custom millwork and turnings. Specializes in doors, windows, and masts.

E. A. Nord Co.
P.O. Box 1187
Everett, WA 98206
(206) 259-9292

Manufacturer of stock turnings: spindles, drops, columns, and balusters. Specializes in doors, spindles, and wood columns. Also has carved panel doors—some with glass inserts. Small and large orders. Sells through distributors only; call or write for the distributor in your area.

Kaymar Wood Products
4603 35th Street S.W.
Seattle, WA 98116
(206) 932-3584

Custom turned finials, columns, and balusters. Maximum size: 6 feet by 12 inches. Also does millwork. Small orders.

Millwork Supply Co.
2225 First Avenue S.
Seattle, WA 98134
(206) 622-1450

Large selection of stock moldings. Stock and custom sashes, doors, and frames.

Triad Creative Woodturning
29 Dravus
Seattle, WA 98109
(206) 284-9104

Finials, drops, columns, and balusters. Maximum size: 36 by 8 inches. Can give design advice. Custom turnings; small and large orders.

Dick Young's Puget Sound Shake Brokers
12301 218th Place S.E., Suite 711
Snohomish, WA 98290
(206) 568-6642

Fancy-butt red cedar shingles in at least nine different ornamental cuts plus square. Will give you information about how to estimate the number of shingles you will need and how to install standard and fancy-cuts.

Key

See also Sculpture for artists who work in this material.

- X Service, technique, or material is available
- + See listing for further information
- * Sometimes offers this service

Northeast	Carving	Millwork	Turning	Stock items	Custom items from sketch, etc.	Custom items from working drawing	Will design	Works by hand	Works by machine	Brochure or photos available	Uses other techniques	Distributor	Manufacturer	Miscellaneous
Barrie Faulkner Ontario, Canada	X	X	X		X	X	X	X		X	+		X	
Maurer and Shepard Glastonbury, CT	X	X	*		X	X	X	X		X			X	
Elliot Fishbein Eastport, ME	X				X	X	X	X					X	
Bailey Signs Portland, ME	See listing under Signs													
John Leeke Sanford, ME	X	X	X		X	X	X	X	X				X	
Anderson-McQuaid Cambridge, MA		X		X	X	X			X	X	+		X	
Albany Street Woodshop Boston, MA	X	X	X			X	X	X	X				X	
Downes Millwork Boston, MA		X	X	X	X	X			X				X	
J. J. Browne Hanover, MA		+		X	X	X							X	
Medford Woodworks Medford, MA		X		X	X	X			X				X	
Cape Cod Cupola North Dartmouth, MA				X					X	X	*		X	
Amherst Woodworking Northampton, MA		X		X	X	X			X				X	
Salem Sign Salem, MA	See listing under Signs													
Detail Millwork Waltham, MA		X		X	X	X	X		X				X	
David Hull Masury Contoocook, NH	X	X			X	X	X	X		X			X	
Keller Products Manchester, NH		X		X	X	X			X	X	+		X	
N-J Woodturning Fairlawn, NJ			X		X	X		X					X	
Dr. Edison Shows Matawan, NJ		X	X		X	X		X	X	X			X	
Bendix Moldings Northvale, NJ		X		X		X				+		X		
Stanley D. Saperstein Pennington, NJ	X				X	X	X	X		+	+		X	

WOOD

Key

See also Sculpture for artists who work in this material.

X Service, technique, or material is available

\+ See listing for further information

* Sometimes offers this service

	Carving	Millwork	Turning	Stock items	Custom items from sketch, etc.	Custom items from working drawing	Will design	Works by hand	Works by machine	Brochure or photos available	Uses other techniques	Distributor	Manufacture	Miscellaneous
Bailey Millwork Trenton, NJ		X	X		X	X		X					X	
American Wood Column Brooklyn, NY		X	+	X	X	X	X	X	X	X			X	+
Dimension Lumber Brooklyn, NY		X		X	X	X	X		X			X	X	
Old World Molding Farmingdale, NY		+		X		X			X				X	
Michael's Fine Products Hauppauge, NY		X	X	X	X	X		X	X	+		X	X	
Merit Molding Jamaica, NY		X			X	X			X				X	
Paul Tankel Newark, NY					X	X	X	X	X	+	+		X	
Spaso Gajic New York, NY	X	X			X	X		X	X	X			X	
Ivan Olszewski New York, NY	See listing under Sculpture													
Restoration Workshop Tarrytown, NY	X	X	X		X	X		X	X	X	+		X	
Mary Shelley West Danby, NY	X				X	X	X	X		X			X	
Cumberland Woodcraft Carlisle, PA		X		X	X	X				+			X	
A. F. Schwerd Manufacturing Pittsburgh, PA			+		X	X			X	X			X	
Wynnewood Woodworks Wynnewood, PA		X	X	+	X				X				X	
Moose Creek Restoration Burlington, VT	X	X			X	X	X		X	X			X	
Woodshop Johnson, VT	X	X	X		X	X	X	X					X	
The Millworks Montpelier, VT		X		X	X	X			X				X	
Norman Vandal Roxbury, VT		X		X	X	X	X	X	X	+			X	
Sparky Potter Waitsfield, VT	X				X	X	X	X		X			X	
Vermont Cabinetworks Winooski, VT	X	X	X	X	X	X	X	X	X				X	

Key

See also Sculpture for artists who work in this material.

X Service, technique, or material is available
\+ See listing for further information
* Sometimes offers this service

South

	Carving	Millwork	Turning	Stock items	Custom items from sketch, etc.	Custom items from working drawing	Will design	Works by hand	Works by machine	Brochure or photos available	Uses other techniques	Distributor	Manufacture	Miscellaneous
Marsh Industries Birmingham, AL		X			X	X							X	
Laser Works Bradenton, FL	X				X	X	X		X	X	+		X	
Wight Millworks Hialeah, FL		X	X		X	X			X				X	
Rich's Wood Working Kissimmee, FL		X		X	X	X	X		X	X	+		X	+
Atlantic Millworks Miami, FL		X		X	X	X			X	X			X	
Rich Woodturning Miami, FL		+	X	X	X	X		X	X	X			X	
Wingate Millworks Miami, FL		X		X	X	X			X	X			X	
Evariste A. Faucher Athens, GA		X	X		X	X		X		X			X	
Legacy Pine Limited Atlanta, GA		X	X	X		X			X	X			X	
Xylo Savannah, GA		X		X		X			X	X			X	
Woodcrafters Workshop Fisherville, KY	X	X	X			X	X	X				X		
Audubon Millwork New Orleans, LA		X		X	X	X			X			X	X	
Gulf Enterprises New Orleans, LA		X	+	X						X		X		
Lafitte Sash and Door New Orleans, LA		X		X	X	X			X				X	
Heartwood, Inc. Thibodaux, LA		X	X	X	X	X	X		X	X			X	
Walbrook Mill and Lumber Baltimore, MD		X	X	X	X	X			X				X	
Mahany Associates Bethesda, MD			X			X	X	X					X	
Gregory Manufacturing Jackson, MS			X		X	X			X				X	
Joyner-Black Charleston, SC		X	X	X	X	X			X			X		

Key

See also Sculpture for artists who work in this material.

- **X** Service, technique, or material is available
- **+** See listing for further information
- ***** Sometimes offers this service

	Millwork	Turning	Stock items	Custom items from sketch, etc.	Custom items from working drawing	Will design	Works by hand	Works by machine	Brochure or photos available	Uses other techniques	Distributor	Manufacture	Miscellaneous
Custom House Molding Columbia, SC		X										X	X
Driwood Molding Florence, SC		X	X	X	X	X			X	+			X
Robert T. Wrisley Pulaski, TN	X		X		X		X	X		X			X
Period Products Richmond, VA		X	X	X		X			X				X
Frederick Wilbur Shipman, VA	X				X	X	X	X		X			X
Midwest													
Northwest Mill Carpentersville, IL		X	X	X	X	X			X	X		X	X
Berman Sales Chicago, IL			X			X			X				X
George Pagels Chicago, IL		X	X			X							X
Rinn-Scott Lumber Chicago, IL		X		X	X	X			X			X	X
H.P.M. Highland Park, IL		X		X	X	X			X			X	X
White Pine Cupolas Villa Park, Il		+		X	X	X				X			X
R. K. Degroot Wheaton, IL	X		X		X	X		X			+		X
William J. Schnute Iowa City, IA	X				X	X	X	X		X			X
The Wood Shop Boyne City, MI	X				X	X		X					X
Rasmussen & Son Detroit, MI		X	X			X	X	X					X
M. A. Kirk Lansing, MI	X	X	X		X	X	X	X	X	X	+		X
O. & W. Millwork Mt. Clemens, MI		X		X	X	X			X				X
J. B. O'Meara Burnsville, MN			X	X								X	X
Robert C. Kinghorn Excelsior, MN	X				X	X	X	X	X	X	+		X

Key

See also Sculpture for artists who work in this material.

- X Service, technique, or material is available
- \+ See listing for further information
- * Sometimes offers this service

	Carving	Millwork	Turning	Stock items	Custom items from sketch, etc.	Custom items from working drawing	Will design	Works by hand	Works by machine	Brochure or photos available	Uses other techniques	Distributor	Manufacture	Miscellaneous
Nelson Johnson Wood Minneapolis, MN	X	+	X	X		X			X			X	X	
Johnson Wood Products Minneapolis, MN		X		X		X			X	X			X	
Shaw Lumber St. Paul, MN		X		X	X	X			X	X		X		
Ray Donaldson Taylors Falls, MN	X					X	X	X		X			X	
The Top Shop Kansas City, MO			X		X	X		X					X	
Crescent Planning Mill St. Louis, MO		X	X		X	X			X				X	
Brown Woodworks Kearny, NE	X	X	X		X	X	X	X	X				X	
Kay Dee Company of Omaha Omaha, NE		X		X	X	X	X		X	X		X	X	
Manfred Millwork Omaha, NE		X		X	X	X			X				X	
Taft Wood Products Cleveland, OH		X	X		X	X		X	X				X	
Doddington Millwork Columbus, OH		X	X	X		X			X			X	X	
Smith Dodson Lumber Columbus, OH		X		X	*	X			X			X	X	
Webb Manufacturing Conneaut, OH		+		X						X			X	
John W. Winterich Solon, OH	See listing under Murals													
Hendrix, Heikkilä, and Terry Norman, OK	See listing under Murals													
Custom Kraft Woodshop Oklahoma City, OK			X	X	X	X		X	X	X			X	
B. & E. Wood Tulsa, OK			+	X	X	X		X	X	X			X	
Architectural Restorations Austin, TX		X	+	X	X	X	X	X	X	X			X	
Castleberry Mill Dallas, TX		X			X	X			X				X	
J. P. Jackson and Son Fort Worth, TX		X	X	X	X	X			X				X	

WOOD

Key

See also Sculpture for artists who work in this material.

X Service, technique, or material is available

\+ See listing for further information

* Sometimes offers this service

	Carving	Millwork	Turning	Stock items	Custom items from sketch, etc.	Custom items from working drawing	Will design	Works by hand	Works by machine	Brochure or photos available	Uses other techniques	Distributor	Manufacture	Miscellaneous
McMurray Turnpost Fort Worth, TX			X	X				X		X			X	
W. Hugh Vance Galveston, TX		X	X		X			X		X			X	
Paul Stein Houston, TX	X				X	X	X	X	X	X			X	
Allen and Allen San Antonio, TX		X	X	X		X			X	X		X	X	
A. Pullen San Antonio, TX	X		X		X	X		X					X	
Vintage Wood Works Quinlan, TX		X		X	X	X				+			X	
A. B. Manufacturing Milwaukee, WI	X	X	X		X	X		X	X				X	
Rockies and Far West														
Bel-Air Door Alhambra, CA		X		X		*			X	X			X	
Quality Frame and Door Cerritas, CA		X		X	X	X			X	X			X	
Round Valley Woodwrights Covelo, CA	X	X	X		X	X	X	X	X	X			X	
Crowe's Woodturning Escondido, CA		X	X	X	X		X	X	X	X			X	
North Pacific Joinery Eureka, CA		X	X	X	X	X			X	+			X	
Coast Planing Mill Los Angeles, CA		X			X	X			X				X	
Hallelujah Wood Mendocino, CA		X		X	X	X							X	
Bartley's Mill Oakland, CA		X	X		X	X			X				X	
John Munch Paso Robles, CA		X	X		X	X		X	X				X	
F. S. Buckley Door San Francisco, CA		X		X					X			X	X	
Haas Wood & Ivory San Francisco, CA		X	X		X	X		X		X			X	
Timothy Howe San Francisco, CA	X				X	X	X		X	+			X	

Key

See also Sculpture for artists who work in this material.

X Service, technique, or material is available
\+ See listing for further information
* Sometimes offers this service

	Carving	Millwork	Turning	Stock items	Custom items from sketch, etc.	Custom items from working drawing	Will design	Works by hand	Works by machine	Brochure or photos available	Uses other techniques	Distributor	Manufacture	Miscellaneous
Lowpensky Moulding San Francisco, CA		X				X			X				X	
Renaissance San Francisco, CA	X	X	X		X		X	X	X	X	X		X	
Victoriana San Francisco, CA		X	X	X		X		X	X	+		X	X	
Developers' Supply San Marcos, CA		X	X	X		X			X			X	X	
Hector Bezanis Santa Barbara, CA	X		X	X	X	X	X	X		X			X	
John Ward Sonoma, CA	+	X	X		X	X	X	X		X			X	
Abaroot Manufacturing Torrance, CA			X	X	X			X	X				X	
Roger's Woodturning Vista, CA		X	X	X	X	X		X	X	X			X	
Criterion Woodwork Denver, CO		X			X	X			X				X	
Robert Tully Denver, CO	See listing under Sculpture													
J. M. L. Company Englewood, CO			X	X	X	X		X	X				X	
First Impressions Fort Collins, CO	See listing under Metals													
Silverton, Victorian Silverton, CO		X		X	X					+			X	
American Lumber Portland, OR		X		X	X	X			X	X		X	X	
Blair's Woodworking Portland, OR		X		X	X	X			X			X	X	
L. Samuel Fort Portland, OR	X				X	X	X	X		X				
Specialty Woodworking Portland, OR		X				+							X	
Turncraft White City, OR			X	X					X	X			X	
Rosander Woodturning Salt Lake City, UT			X		X	X		X					X	
Old and Elegant Bellevue, WA	See listing under Metals													

Key

See also Sculpture for artists who work in this material.

X Service, technique, or material is available
\+ See listing for further information
* Sometimes offers this service

	Carving	Millwork	Turning	Stock items	Custom items from sketch, etc.	Custom items from working drawing	Will design	Works by hand	Works by machine	Brochure or photos available	Uses other techniques	Distributor	Manufacture	Miscellaneous
Sheppard Millwork Edmonds, WA		X	X	X	X	X			X				X	
E. A. Nord Everett, WA		X	X	X					X	X			X	
Kaymar Wood Products Seattle, WA			X		X	X		X					X	
Millwork Supply Seattle, WA		X		X	X	X			X	X		X	X	
Triad Woodturning Seattle, WA			X		X			X					X	
Puget Sound Shake Snohomish, WA				+									X	
Jacques Overhoff San Rafael, CA			X	X	X		X	+		X				

INDEX

See Matrix for index entries marked "†." Parentheses following "†" indicate matrix category. Bold figures indicate illustrations.